RUN
RUN
RUN

The Lives of Abbie Hoffman

RUN RUN RUN

JACK HOFFMAN
and
DANIEL SIMON

A Jeremy P. Tarcher / Putnam Book
published by
G. P. Putnam's Sons
New York

Most Tarcher/Putnam books are available at special quantity discounts for bulk purchases for sales promotions, premiums, fund-raising, and educational needs. Special books or book excerpts also can be created to fit specific needs.

For details, write or telephone Special Markets, The Putnam Publishing Group, 200 Madison Avenue, New York, NY 10016; (212) 951-8891.

A Jeremy P. Tarcher/Putnam Book
Published by G. P. Putnam's Sons
Publishers Since 1838
200 Madison Avenue
New York, NY 10016

First Trade Paperback Edition 1996

Excerpts of "Howl" and "America" from Allen Ginsberg's *Collected Poems 1947–1980*, copyright © 1988, used by permission of HarperCollins Publishers.

Excerpt of "In Goya's Greatest Scenes We Seem to See" from Lawrence Ferlinghetti's *A Coney Island of the Mind*, copyright © 1958 by Lawrence Ferlinghetti, used by permission of New Directions Publishing Corp.

Library of Congress Cataloging-in-Publication Data
Hoffman, Jack, date.
Run Run Run: the lives of Abbie Hoffman / Jack Hoffman, Daniel Simon.
p. cm.
Includes bibliographical references (p.) and index.
ISBN 0-87477-811-5
1. Hoffman, Abbie.   2. Radicals—United States—Biography.
3. Radicalism—United States.   I. Simon, Daniel, date.
HN90.R3H577   1994   94-12576 CIP
303.48′4—dc20
[B]

Design by Rhea Braunstein
Cover design by Lee Fukui
Cover photo © by William Coupon

Printed in the United States of America
1   3   5 ' 7   9   10   8   6   4   2

This book is printed on acid-free paper.♾

To Dad and Abbie
I know you're out there somewhere fishing
and Abbs is about to rock the boat

Revolution is not something fixed in ideology, nor is it something fashioned to a particular decade. It is a perpetual process embedded in the human spirit.

—Abbie
Soon to Be a Major Motion Picture

Run run run
Fast as you can
Can't catch me
I'm the gingerbread man

—nursery rhyme

CONTENTS

PREFACE
BY JACK HOFFMAN

Abbie Hoffman was famous and infamous for three of the five decades we shared our lives. As his kid brother, my life was intertwined with his from beginning to end. The friendship and love we shared was, in many ways, quite typical; like many older brothers, Abbie made his mark on me, molded me and bullied me; and like many younger brothers, I could not refuse him anything.

Abbie's notoriety put an intense strain on his family: our parents, our sister Phyllis and her family, my wife Joan and our children. We were harassed by the FBI; saw some of our dearest friends turn their backs on us; and many longtime business relationships were destroyed. Because of Abbie, we were led to make sacrifices that were part of his life but not of ours. For his part, Abbie once said that he could never have survived without his family—a family that loved, cried, laughed, protected, and stood by one another through good times and bad.

When Abbie took his life a part of me died. For many weeks following his suicide, I was besieged by all the publicity and media attention surrounding his death. Just as I was beginning to experience my own sense of personal grief, I received a call from publisher and writer Dan Simon who asked if I could lend a hand to complete an anthology of Abbie's most popular writings and speeches. I knew that I owed it to Abbie's memory to cooperate in any way I could and felt that it would contribute to a book I had planned to write on my own. During our discussions, Dan and I began to see that we had formed a collaborative team that might keep Abbie's legacy alive, so we started working together on *Run Run Run*. I envisioned a different approach from that of a historical biography, in which I intended to offer information about Abbie's personal life that was previously unknown to the public, the media, and academicians—information that only a brother could share.

In order to collect all the facts and connect with the subject matter, I realized that I would have to delve into my own life and that of my family. That meant opening some painful memories but reliving the joyous times as well. Ultimately, the book became a focal point for me, marking the beginning of my own catharsis toward resolving my relationship with both Abbie's life and his untimely death. In the writing I found a way to put some of my life back together again.

The book began as a 1,000-piece puzzle. I first began by interviewing and conversing with many friends new and old, relatives, former lovers, ex-wives, lawyers, doctors, bookies, agents, government employees, former police, and FBI Special Agents. I heard the same Abbie stories so many times that I began to realize only my recollections could finally tie all the years together, but even after I finished, I felt that some pieces of the story were still missing.

For most of the factual information, I retrieved court documents and government archives; and I collected thousands of articles from libraries and existing data banks. Ironically, the best source on time reference was approximately 15,000 pages of FBI files. My research told me that they destroyed another 30,000 to 40,000 pages. Included in all of this was a thousand pages of New York City Police files gathered by their Bureau of Special Service Intelligence. Who knows what I might have found had I continued researching the other seven federal intelligence agencies and many local police units in America. When we could, we used Abbie's own words from personal letters, videos, books, and articles he had written and interviews given.

Abbie taught me that survival depends a lot on the family. It is from our family, he always said, that we learn so many of our most important values. Like my family, this book has unique strengths as well as weaknesses. I have no regrets and make no apologies.

On Monday, June 24, 1991, Jack and I drove down to Washington, D.C., in a small, square, late-model Plymouth (his mother's) that looked so much like an unmarked government car it wasn't funny. We were on our way to spend two days at the FBI central office to pore over 15,000 pages of Abbie's FBI files—among the fifty fattest files the FBI has—that were being made available to us under the Freedom of Information Act. Other grave national security risks on J. Edgar Hoover's list besides Abbie had been Robert Kennedy, Dr. Martin Luther King, Jr., novelist Nelson Algren, film stars Lucille Ball, Marilyn Monroe, Jean Seberg. Comparatively few real criminals ever made the list. As we drive, I consider the interesting threat these individuals presented alongside the danger to our national well-being once posed by Hoover himself.

The book Jack and I are writing about Abbie has had a difficult winter and spring. We snarled ourselves in the early years, crucially important because of what they tell us about Abbie, yet hard to render in their fullness since they describe a time that has left few traces. By now when Jack and I talk about his brother, as we enter our second full year of such talks, there are echoes, antecedents, and overtones, background rumbles and short tempers. At our worst moments, we are like two grave diggers on a very cold day. The ground is rock hard, our hands are shaking and hurting, we only want to be done; we no longer give a thought to the dead. At our best moments, we connect with each other and commune with Abbie's spirit.

This time, as we labor along the highway just over the speed limit, we begin to talk about Abbie's death and what led up to it. It is the thousandth time we have freshly assaulted the wall of misunderstanding surrounding the suicide. Sometimes, as now, at the moments we seem closest to understanding Abbie, we feel most alienated from the world around us, and vice versa. Thinking about Abbie is a way of sharing his solitude.

We talk about why there wasn't a note. I say, the suicide was a final act, an end; I think it is important to allow Abbie that. The act was not meant to be understood. It is not meant to be interpreted. It is the complete darkness behind a closed door, not a passageway through which you see a far-off light. It is utterly clear to me as I say it, concluding with: If Abbie had been able to write a note on April 12, 1989, then on that day he would not have been able to kill himself. That he was unable even to write a few words to explain why he was putting an end to his life *is* why he killed himself. To picture Abbie lucid enough to write a note is still not to accept what happened.

Jack agrees with me—or is polite enough not so say otherwise—and appears appreciative of the insight we have arrived at. We sit in the car for a few minutes in silence, cruising along at sixty down Interstate 295 in our unmarked Plymouth, contemplating the hugeness of the sky.

When Jack and I start talking again, it is about the fame factor, what he likes to call the celebrity virus. I'm not an ideologue, but in our discussions a theory has surfaced. It has attached itself to so many of the facts I've learned about Abbie, like frost-burn or a yellowing at the edges of things: While so much of Abbie's life and work was a triumph of consciousness, of right thinking, of light, there was also, like a gradually increasing darkness, a force out of control. It was, quite simply, his need to be famous, and it was a completely unconscious, naturally occurring, but nonetheless disturbing and, in Abbie's case, debilitating element. At key moments in his life, when he needed to make the right decision he made the wrong one. And on each occasion he was blinded by the Klieg lights when he did so. On each occasion he let the needs of his public persona drown out those of the private individual. This isn't to say that he let something false overcome something real: Abbie was as real a public figure as they come, with deep convictions and needs, including the need to be famous. But in Abbie's case, the public and the private were not clearly distinguished, and several consequences, including the fatal one, can be linked to this blurring in his life, this failure to separate.

Of course, what Abbie deeply wanted wasn't fame but fame's better brother—the recognition and respect he had earned over and over in his lifetime fighting for freedom for us all. But respect and recognition were never within his grasp the way they should have been. Jack and I keep talking in the last light of the day. Our theory fades, resurfaces, fades again. Every answer leads to another question.

We miss the turn somehow, and find ourselves heading for Baltimore. We backtrack, find the right turn. Eventually, this book is completed and delivered to our publisher. Our years-long conversation continues.

ACKNOWLEDGMENTS (HOFFMAN)

This brother's story could never have begun and continued on without the help, encouragement, and love of the many who are a part of this book.

Dan Simon, the alchemist, who helped turn scattered memories into hard copy. A special thanks to Jonathan Silvers, who gave me the encouragement to continue when things looked like they would end; Andrea Fine, who began this collaboration; Nancy Love, the relentless agent who introduced me to Jeremy Tarcher; Jeremy, who has the patience of a saint and the wisdom of Solomon; Robin Cantor-Cooke, for her editing; Daniel Malvin, for his "drudgery"; the other staff members at Jeremy Tarcher and Putnam who have worked to help this book on its journey.

Interviews with Marion Perlman Chafetz, Esther Bean, Bella Cohen, Milt Frem, Rabbi Fogelman and Rabbi Klein, Dorothy Cotton, Marty Kenner, Don Hodes, Manny Schrieber, Jonah Raskin, Yvette Leventhal, Father Bernie Gilgun, Dan Dick, Carole Ramer, Dr. Braverman, Lynda Plante, Bill Stankey, Dr. Oscar Janiger, Richard Spiro, Bobby Sasso, Art Nascarello, Dr. Lawrence Epstein, Dan Ellsberg, Paul "Sharky" Cotton, Haskell "Buddy" Morin and Cody.

Research from Lisa Jedrziynski, Worcester State Hospital; Research Department at McLean's Hospital; Goddard Library at Clark University; The Brandeis Alumni Office; Judy Atkinson, The National Archives, Waltham, MA; Nancy Gaudette, Worcester Public Library; Geo Cummings, Boston Library; Brian Stacey, Larry Goldberg Esq., Mark Shepard, New York Department of Corrections; The Framingham Public Library; The Library Staff at CNN; Jeri G for AOL work; Annie Steinfeld at *Playboy;* Boston TV Channels WBZ, WGBH, WHDH; Wendy Chmielewski at Swarthmore College Peace

Library; Faigi Rosenthal at the *New York Daily News*; Amy Zuckerman, Devon Yates, and Monica Freeman at the FBI FOIPA section; Maryjo Pelletier for her Bible stories.

Mike Pinto, Sally Baxter, Joe and Richie Aboody, who kept me well fed; Dr. Bill Long, Rick Goldman, and Art DeLoto kept me healthy; Dan's parents, Jo and Morris Simon, and Joe and Roberta Bressman, for the use of their homes; Ray Biolodeau, who believed in my perseverance; Morton Glazer, who kept me out and in legal trouble; Milton Schwartz, who kept the books together; Carole Abbott, friend and associate, who was always there when I needed her help; Carol Dixon and all our brothers and sisters in Ireland, who are fighting for peace and freedom; Eli, Bucky, Sammy, and Joe, who gave Abbie and me the best line and were wrong on Buffalo; Linda Meservi and Donna Lavalley, who got me there on time; Lois and Beau, my canine traveling companions; Roger Aransky, who watched the store; Andy Toorock, for the catches.

Evie Barkin and MDDA of Boston; The National Manic Depressive Support Group in Chicago—*For information call 1-800-826-3632.*

All my friends in Worcester, Framingham, and coast-to-coast who have supported the project; Michael Shapiro and Ellen Sklarz for their coaching; Kinky Friedman for the supportive calls.

Aunt Sarah and Uncle Schmule, for family background; Betty Dyer, Aunt Rose, Sarah Schanberg; Richie Lenett, who is more than a friend; my Mom and Phyllis who had to relive painful memories; my children, Jaime and Justin, for their understanding; my wife, Joan, for her support and love, and who shared with me the heartache and joy of this book.

ACKNOWLEDGMENTS (SIMON)

Thanks to Jack Hoffman, for repeatedly leading me to water on the very many dry, hot days during the five years of our collaboration; and to my partner, John Oakes (who tells me I don't express gratitude often enough), for being another self—true to the spirit of our ongoing endeavor. Thanks to John Schultz, for his knowledge and insight into what really happened in Chicago; to Joan Hoffman, for her hospitality, kindness, and suspension of disbelief; to Ralph Meronit, for sharing with me part of his COINTELPRO library; to Al Zuckerman, for directing me to S. N. Behrman; to Steve Jesse Rose, for his postcards; to Neil Ortenberg, for lending me his copy of Abbie's autobiography—which is now mine; and to Bill Hurst, for sending me the Krassner book, which I will return. Thanks to Nancy Love, who led us to Jeremy, and to Jeremy Tarcher, our editor and publisher—patient before all else—and to his outstanding associates, especially Robin Cantor-Cooke, Lisa Chadwick, Dan Malvin, and Robert Welsch. Thanks to John Hayes, David Lida, Gene Fellner, and to my brothers Mark, Adam, and Jason Simon, for odd words of encouragement and unwavering support. Special thanks to Johanna Lawrenson, Christine Kelly, Mort Leavy, Martin Garbus, Murray Kempton, Barbara Walters, Allen Ginsberg, and Bob Rosenthal. To Roz and Howard Zinn, thanks for always saying the right thing at the right time. Thanks to my parents, Jo and Morris Simon, who never claim to know the future and thus continue to welcome surprises of all kinds; to my grandmother, Esther Rubin, who has the best sense of humor of anyone I know; and to my wife, Adriana, for our love that has blossomed during the writing of this book.

1936–1948

I never felt I rejected any of my past. Ever.

—ABBIE

TO REALLY BEGIN to understand my brother Abbie, you've got to try to picture Aunt Rose, our mother's sister, a diagnosed schizophrenic who has not been able to look after her own basic needs for most of her life. If Rose is crazy, Abbie was crazy like a fox; they had nothing in common on that score. But something happened to Rose that led her to spend the rest of her days without a purpose, lost in the futility of her life. And in Abbie, the same sense of futility became the source for his extraordinary optimism. Yet his deep optimism, that he carried with him from the cradle to the grave, held the same tragic seed as her despair. His vision for revolutionary change, for a better world to come, came naturally to him. No different from Rose, our parents, or me, Abbie too was caught. Every family has its madness.

What had happened to Rose was the sudden death of her older brother, our uncle Abe, one June afternoon in 1935. Abe, aged twenty-four or twenty-five, took a ride with a friend into downtown Boston to get the diamond engagement ring he had chosen for his fiancée. The car was a convertible and the weather must have been fine because they had the top down. They took Route 117 out of Clinton to Route 2, one of the frost-ruined paved roads that carried produce from rural Massachusetts to the shops of Boston. A truck passing on their left caused Abe's friend to swerve abruptly, throwing Abe from the car, killing him instantly.

Uncle Abe's death, coming some seventeen months before his

namesake, my brother Abbie—conceived in sadness and mourning—was born, would be part of Abbie's inheritance. And when I was born, three years after Abbie, it also became part of mine.

Abe was of medium height, and had curly black hair. Before he died, he ran a restaurant the family owned and was rumored to run a bookmaking operation on the side. Family lore describes him as a risk-taker, a willing child of destiny, and a charmer. The accident came just eight months after my parents' marriage in October 1934. It served up a deep well of bitterness and guilt as a kind of belated wedding gift to the couple. These are things I surmise. What is factual is that it brought on the tragedy of Rose's life.

Of course Abbie and I came to know Aunt Rose only later, when her explosive laughter was all that was left of what had been her personality. As the youngest of four children, she spent her childhood as the family jewel. She became the family stand-out as well, first as New England Spelling Bee champion and then, in 1933, as the first Jew admitted to prestigious Pembroke College. Although large and not pretty, she was well-liked, quick of mind, complex, curious, and trusting.

Rose played basketball on an all-girls team and took the sport very seriously. She went to lectures, including one in 1934 by Rabbi Israel Goldman on Hitlerism—nearly five years before the war. She was impressionable and read voraciously everything she could get her hands on, from Matthew Arnold's poetry to pulp novels. A popular Hollywood magazine once had such an effect on her that she wrote in her diary: "after reading 'Screen Romances,' decided to always smile."

Her brothers and sister—our mother—acted very protectively toward her. In a family without favorites, something special was always reserved for Rose. She was coddled not just by her mother but by everyone. Naturally shy, she began to test her limits. She transferred from Pembroke to the Middlesex Medical School in Waltham on the outskirts of Boston, moved into her own apartment with a girlfriend and, against her parents' wishes, began to date a gentile.

The accident that killed her brother occurred after she had completed her first year at Middlesex, and in December, back at school,

Rose was still feeling unaccountably responsible. Abe had been her favorite brother, the one with whom she shared secrets at a time when, as I've learned while reading the diary she kept, she was experiencing a painful process of sexual awakening. She wrote of feeling jealous of Abe's fiancée, and perhaps felt the accident was somehow connected to her antipathy toward her brother's marriage. In December 1935, Rose had a complete mental collapse.

After various consultations and mild treatments that did not help, the family admitted her to McLean's mental hospital, where, after several months, the initial diagnosis of manic depression was revised to schizophrenia. After nearly a year, when the money ran out—the cost at McLean's was an exorbitant $150 a week—my grandparents, Ida and Jacob, were forced to transfer her to Worcester State Hospital, where, along with hundreds of ice baths, she received no fewer than 150 electroshock treatments over the next fifteen months.

A decade later, she was still at Worcester State and in deteriorating health. The hospital urged that neurosurgery would improve her quality of life. The family went along. A frontal lobotomy was performed in 1946, when Rose was in her early thirties.

Rose didn't become a vegetable. She is not able to look after herself, but somehow she has kept her sense of humor. I sometimes think that she is the happiest member of the family, even though she has spent the last sixty years in institutions. Abbie used to say—and to this day I can't say for sure whether he was serious or kidding— that with a little therapy she could get out more, be more active and productive. But she has always been considered part of the family. That was Ma's doing.

As the eldest, Ma always felt she had to look after the younger children. With her brother's death and her sister's nervous breakdown, now it was Ma's turn to feel overwhelmed by guilt, as if nothing had caused the tragedies as much as her own recent bid for personal happiness. The sequence of events was almost too much for her to bear—her marriage, a brother dead, her only sister insane, both these latter occurrences serving as fresh reminders of the death of her mother's firstborn many years before. Suddenly her newfound independence and her happiness hardly seemed to matter. Her confusion was temporary, but the guilt was something that would be passed along to each of her three children, Abbie, Phyllis, and me.

Like Abe's death, the agony of Rose's madness preoccupied our parents and the other adults in the family while Abbie, Phyllis, and I were growing up. We never tried to make sense of Rose; to us she was wondrously strange and unfathomable, not frightening. In our teens, Abbie and I used to let our friends call her Crazy Rose. And Rose did go mad sometimes, although who's to say how much that was the result of her illness and how much it was caused by the barbarous medical care she received? But whether she was at the institution where she resided, or with us at home on Ruth Street for a Sunday afternoon meal, we were taught never to be ashamed of Rose—although I remember waiting in the hospital corridor outside her room while Ma visited and the terror that came over me in waves whenever the other crazy patients passed by.

Describing the end of the life of Simón Bolívar, García Márquez remarks: *The revolutionary ploughs the ocean.* The words convey our universal sense of futility—I think of Rose. But they also describe that futility transformed into its very opposite: someone able to express his vision so fully that he can beat the odds, harness the moon, plough the ocean. It captures my brother as I knew him at certain moments, when the splendor of his nature showed through the riffs and contradictions.

If the fathomless sadness of our Aunt Rose in 1935 is one of the keys to understanding my brother, another is the meeting of our parents three years before. For some reason, picturing Ma and Dad meeting one night at the bowling alley comes easily to me. I picture it from her side. As I've seen him in photographs, Dad had a wide, confident, complex smile. He was large and strong. At twenty-five, he was in his prime, while Ma, two years older, might have felt a little over the hill. Probably she heard his laughter across the room before she saw him. He must have appeared suave but also intelligent, tolerant, and serious. His white shirt was clean and starched, his face cleanshaven. He had a good job at his uncle Kanef's drugstore. And he lived in—by comparison with Clinton, where she lived—the sprawling and dynamic city of Worcester. Dad must have seemed like a wish come true that night to Ma. And he was the best bowler in the place.

And from his side? They say Ma was sexy. Probably he saw her more as a likely date than as a future wife. I imagine him *pleased* with her rather than knocked out, and pleased with himself for finding her. Easy pickings. Not yet love.

In his autobiography, Abbie imagines it happened this way:

"My mother fell in love with [my father] because he wore a clean white shirt every Friday night. Since my father never spoke of intimate things, I have no idea why he married Mama. It could have been for her looks, for her superb penmanship, or for love. Perhaps nobody knows why their parents married. The reasons hidden in the back of the bureau drawer along with the prophylactics."[1]

Two years later, in October 1934, they were married. That was fifty-five years before my brother's death by suicide, forty years before Dad's fatal heart attack, and forty-five years before the business I had built into the success Dad had always dreamed of came crashing down around my head. These events, along with the divorces and car accidents, the births, marriages, and remarriages, flowed one from the other as naturally as the New England seasons. But on that day life seemed a whole lot simpler: Florence Shanberg and John Hoffman, aged twenty-nine and twenty-seven respectively, were ready for their piece of happiness.

Dad had already begun evening pharmacy classes, traveling by train from Worcester to Boston at the end of each work day. Before long he hoped to become a pharmacist and make much more money. Then he would open his own drugstore. Buy a house. Have a large family. A car. Two cars, one a showpiece Packard or Cadillac. A prominent seat up front at temple. Well-dressed children. Standing in the community. A regular supply of the best Cuban cigars. All the trappings of a man who has achieved something. People listening to his opinions. The respect of his peers. This was the view from 1934. Success meant status and respectability, and seemed close enough for him to be able to reach out and touch it. Then had come the catastrophes of Abe and Rose, changing everything. Nineteen thirty-five had been the year of their misery. By its end, their future seemed to have been stolen from them.

In late November 1936, everything changed again. When, on the thirtieth day of the month, Ma gave birth to her first son, it was like a miracle. The young marrieds, whose home had already been marred by premature death and madness, were surprised by the sudden good fortune of my brother's birth as by a shattering infusion of light. He was their reprieve from the bitterness that had entered their lives. On the back of a baby photo, Dad wrote, "Hell Unleashed."

Abbie was a sickly child, sickness coming mainly in the form of asthma attacks. From the very first, he combined the frailty of his health with a lovable and outgoing temperament: He was a ham. But hell in the form of a noisy, sickly, love-hungry, adorable baby boy was just the kind of trouble that our parents desperately needed. And he must have felt from the first just how welcome he was. He must have intuited that the noise he made and the attention he demanded were received by Dad and Ma as nothing less than the signs of a great blessing.

An ancient Hebrew aphorism goes, "Where life is, death is not; where death is, life is not." And as at the close of the evening prayer, Abbie arrived with the angel Michael at his right hand, Gabriel on his left, Uriel before him, and Raphael above him. In the commotion, *Malakh-hamoves,* the Angel of Death, vanished. My brother came as a consoling messenger who chased death from the house, and for the rest of their lives, our parents would look to him in expectation of more great good news.

Three years later, on September 13, 1939, I came along. The story goes that after giving birth, Ma got a call in her hospital room from the baby-sitter, who said that Abbie seemed sick. Ma left in such a hurry she forgot to sign my name into the hospital records. My birth came as an echo of Abbie's. Quieter, but also sweet. If the lesson of humility was one that Abbie never learned, I learned from day one—as does any younger sibling—the particular kind of courage it takes to enter life preceded by the word "little," as in "my little brother Jack."

My arrival, like Abbie's, was heralded by two stunning losses.

The year before, my father's brother, Jacob, died from injuries sustained in a freak car accident. The story that has been passed along to me through the grapevine of hushed voices among my living relatives is that his car was broadsided by a car driven by an off-duty policeman, who had had a few too many. And that shortly after the accident, while Uncle Jacob was still fighting for his life, the Hoffmans received a visit from several of Worcester's finest, threatening retaliation if anyone testified against their drunk-driving fellow officer. The officers brought with them the chill of a dark, horribly ancient and familiar world waiting just around the corner from our American Dream. Joining memories of pogroms, of Cossacks, this small act of intimidation would have lent credence to our grandparents' sense that this new world was not so very different from the old one.

The other death that preceded my birth was that of Ma's father, also named Jacob, for whom I was named. When Jacob went, it was in the practice of his craft—wrecking. One of the acetylene tanks he used on heavy jobs, to prepare the steel beams for cutting, fell on his leg. By the time he got to the hospital, he was beyond saving; whether death came by pulmonary embolism, shock, or some combination of the two, I don't know. In the 1940s, when my uncle Sam, back from the war, began to take an interest in reviving the family wrecking business, my grandmother Ida absolutely forbade it, insisting on a safer profession for the family's surviving male, the last chance of continuing the family name into the next generation.

When Abbott Howard Hoffman—Abbie—was born that November in 1936, he was not only our parents' first-born son, he was also the first first-generation child of the greater Hoffman-Shanberg clan, the first Hoffman who might grow up to be a doctor. Furrowing the history of our family doesn't give me quick solutions to the riddle of Abbie's nature or my own, but it does provide me with clues.

On our mother's side, our great-grandfather Saul Shanberg arrived at Castle Garden in Lower Manhattan—the disembarkation station in the years before Ellis Island—in July of 1881 or 1882. He was thirty-one or thirty-two years old and he came alone. Like the millions before him and since, he was one of the have-nots of Europe looking here for better odds. His wife and their two young sons had been temporarily left behind in Rzeszow, a city in Galicia, then a part of the Austro-Hungarian empire. The life that he found here was physically arduous—anti-Semitism was prevalent, work was hard to find—not yet a new world at all. But he found comfort in the ghetto-like Jewish community of the bustling Lower East Side. As a recent arrival, you stayed among your own people and kept a low profile, a stance of apartness already familiar from the *shtetls* of Europe. The name of the game wasn't success, but survival. Saul stayed in New York City at first, living on Willet Street with a friend from the old country and working in the junk trade. After a year, he sent for his wife and children. One son, our grandfather Jacob, then nine years old, was sent to him, but his wife refused to make the voyage or to allow the other child to go. When her refusal proved unbending, Saul set about obtaining a divorce through the rabbinical authorities. Very quickly afterward, he married the sister of his best friend—in time to have five children before the end of the decade. His new wife, Betsy, was twenty years his junior.

Sometime in 1896 or 1898, Saul heard that in the Massachusetts mill town of Clinton a dam was being constructed to provide water for the city of Boston. Thinking he might do well peddling to the hundreds of workers that were congregating there, he decided to go and have a look, taking with him his new wife Betsy, and their five children, several of whom were still infants. His eldest son, Jacob, was already grown, and stayed behind. After two days on the dusty, unpaved roads, they got as far as Worcester. Worcester already had a sizable Jewish community, and Saul liked it enough to spend several months there trying to sell his wares. But eventually they set off again, traveling the last sixteen miles to Clinton, his original destination. As the new century began, he sent for Jacob to follow from New York.

In Clinton, Saul plied his trade, buying and selling junk off his horse-drawn cart with Jacob sitting beside him. In 1902, Jacob, in his prime at the age of twenty-eight, married our grandmother Ida.

Born in 1881 in Pskov, a very European cultural center in western Russia, Ida was the daughter of a rich brewer whose beer and schnapps were famous. Ida was accustomed to fine things. She read a lot and could quote all the great Russian novelists. In the old country, she had lived in a large house on an estate filled with servants. She was intelligent and cultured. For so many others life in the new world meant reaching for the golden ring; for Ida it was a kind of downfall. Ida spoke German fluently, and in all her census papers she identified herself as Russian-German, perhaps to indicate that she thought of herself as an upper-class Jew.

Decades later Ma showed me what she said was Ida's will. It ran on for thirty pages, telling in material terms her precise feelings for friend and foe. There were few friends. To my father—her son-in-law—she left exactly five cents, explaining this was repayment for one occasion when he had kept her waiting for five minutes at the Meola Dairy Stand. My own memory has her once forcing me to sit outside on a wooden chair for three hours after I refused to eat my breakfast. I still have the chair, and my ass still hurts when I look at it.

Ida was the only one of my relatives that I didn't like—except for her wonderful *tsimmes,* a side dish of sweetened fruit and vegetables, usually carrots, sweet potatoes, and prunes. Only recently, with a heart heavy for having misunderstood her for so long while she lived, have I come to see her more clearly. She never quite learned how to accept the *softness* of the new world, was never quite able to see herself in it. And so she was forever building walls and being misunderstood. For her, the new world was an unbroken nightmare. She was not cruel, I see now, so much as stern, bitter, and disappointed.

With grim determination, Ida produced five children for Jacob. Their firstborn died in infancy of spinal meningitis. Their second child, born on November 17, 1905, was Florence, our mother. Ma was followed by Abe, then another son, our uncle Schmule (Sam), and last, a daughter, our aunt Rose.

At the time of his marriage to Ida, my grandfather Jacob was a handsome and a generous man. He had started out in the family trade as a junk peddler: pots and pans, old clothes, old horses, and horse carts. As his family grew around him, he transformed the business into the thriving Shanberg Wrecking Company, which demolished buildings and sold off the remaining scrap metal and other materials.

Wrecking can be a highly profitable business, but it is extremely dangerous. You have to have it in your blood. There is the joy of the architect, the joy of the artist, and the joy of the builder—men who create. Then there is the passion of the wrecker, who levels. They say that Jacob was a wrecking genius.

Abbie and I share Jacob. I was named after him. Abbie inherited his appreciation of the possibilities that open up when you tear something down. Since his death occurred around the time of our births, we grew up with the sense that our lives were in some sense a continuation, a gift from the dead as well as the living.

In 1916, sometime after the birth of the third child, a fire razed their apartment, and Jacob purchased the home of Clinton's sheriff, a man named John McGhee. Built to be the Clinton jail and sheriff's quarters, the modest yellow clapboard building at 817 Main Street might have seemed to the neighbors a strange place to raise a family. But the square structure had its own charm and gave the impression of an awkward trustworthiness. Today it is an historic landmark. Of course Jacob had wanted it primarily for the steel used to construct the jail cells in the basement, a wrecker's dream, which he sold off to help defray the cost of the house.

As the eldest, Ma had to set an example. She was an excellent student and a star gymnast. For pocket money, she did secretarial work at one of the local textile mills. After finishing high school, she commuted to the Bryant Stratton school in Boston, completing the two-year program with an associate degree in business. And then, still living at home and looking after her younger brothers and sister, she began working as a secretary, joined in the social activities of the small Jewish community of Clinton, and waited. She was shy, did not consider herself pretty, and Ida would not let her date gentiles—which didn't make for an active social life in Christian Clinton.

On our father's side, our grandparents were Russian Jews named Morris and Anna Shapoznikoff who bought the name Hoffman from a dead neighbor in the old country. All my surviving relatives have heard me ask why the name was changed; each one has a different story, but I still don't feel that I know the answer. Morris, Anna, and Dad passed through Ellis Island on November 15, 1908, twenty-five or so years after our mother's grandfather arrived at Castle Garden. Family lore has it that Dad, aged one or so, had pneumonia when they arrived, so our grandmother covered his mouth with rags, hoping to suppress the infant's racking cough.

The procedure at Ellis Island at that time was to mark the backs of the seriously ill with an "X" and send them back across the ocean on the same ship that had brought them. Had the immigration authorities noticed how sick Dad was, the family would have been refused entry. And Dad would not have survived the trip back to Europe.

After a short stay in New York, they moved on to Fall River, Massachusetts, then to Malden, and finally settled in Worcester, an industrial town where an able-bodied man could count on plenty of work and where Jews looked out for one another.

Zayde (Grandfather) Morris Hoffman (né Shapoznikoff) was a fruit and vegetable peddler, buying produce from the farms of Grafton and selling it near the downtown market of Worcester. He spent most of the time traveling between the two places, on the same wagon on which the family had made the trip from New York. The most discouraging part for him was that his horses never lasted very long, since the trips were difficult and frequent, and he could afford only the cheapest horses—they went for five dollars. My zayde used to say there was nothing so sad as watching a horse die. Eventually he was able to open his own grocery store on Providence Street, and then the "Spa" on Main Street I remember as a child—across the street from the Pearlman Funeral Home—where we could bring our friends for a "tonic," a Moxie, or a vanilla coke straight from the fountain—or a "college ice," what is now called an ice cream sundae. Zayde smoked three packs of Chesterfields every day and walked with a noticeable limp. He said he got that from a fall on a banana peel in the old country. And I remember him on his deathbed breathing pure oxygen from two tanks at his bedside and asking for just another cigarette, just another puff.

Bubbe (Grandmother) Anna was the perfect bubbe: ebullient, warm, wonderful. She used to baby-sit for us on weekends to allow our parents to go off to Boston or New York on trips. Once Abbie and I decided the basement needed redecorating and poured red paint all over it. When Ma and Dad returned, Bubbe Anna said the paint "fell." And on *Shabbes,* whenever Dad complained that we weren't dressed up enough, Anna would say, "It's not important what they wear. The only important thing is that we're all here."

In the recipes bubbe taught us, and which we still use, the unit of measure for spices isn't tablespoons or teaspoons but "handfuls" and "pinches." Of all our relatives, we loved and trusted Anna the most, so much so that once when hamburgers she cooked for us tasted strange, we ate every bit without a trace of doubt in our faces. Years later we learned that laundry soap had accidentally fallen into the mixing bowl when she was making the patties.

I sometimes have tried to imagine our grandparents during the last century and early in this century—as young Jews and as poor working people. But it seems so many worlds away. To picture them—crabby Ida as a laughing, marriageable *shayner maidele*—a pretty girl—old Jacob as a young ragman, his hat tilted back, his body muscular; Morris's steps loose, his voice free of the cough—tires me out, and seems impossible. The world has changed too much. The closest I can come to that experience is on occasion to notice a tic or habit of my own, or remember one of Abbie's, that suddenly makes sense as an artifact from the world of our fathers. Perhaps the identification with people in trouble, or the way Abbie always ate as fast as possible, as if that were going to be the only way to get his share, as if there weren't enough food to go around. And also, perhaps, our always taking for granted that there would be physical suffering in our lives, as if our lives and our grandparents' were in some uncanny way interchangeable.

A dozen times Dad took and failed the Pharmacy Board exam. It seems so many tries to have tried and failed. I feel not shamed but proud of the earnestness of my father's exertions. After his hopes of becoming a pharmacist were dashed, and until the day he died, he never once spoke to us of what had happened. Dad had no words to describe it. Eventually, Kanef died, leaving the store to his son Leonard and excluding Dad altogether, and it was Leonard who told me only recently what had happened.

The hurt Dad felt was so much larger than the small rage he could muster. He wanted nothing to do with failure and longed to identify himself in terms of affluence and success. But even after he eventually earned some amount of success, somehow the sweetness was sucked out of it. All that remained was a bitter taste.

Long after Worcester Medical Supply—Dad's medical and drug

supply company—became a solid component of the city's business community, I remember how the very mention of the Massachusetts Board of Pharmacy rankled him, and the contempt he felt for the pharmacists of Worcester. "Frig you!" I would hear him hiss under his breath as he rang up the purchase if a pharmacist came into Worcester Medical. He believed, perhaps rightly, that they had conspired against him, refused to let him pass the exam because he was a Jew. And his natural response to that feeling of victimization was outrage, followed by resignation. Dad had an inner store of perseverance he was able to call on. He could reach inward and find he had the strength to absorb adversity. But what he was never able to do was fight back. And I believe that just as Aunt Rose's illness could call forth in Abbie and me the desire to be healers, Dad's peculiar helplessness made us want to be fighters.

Ma's approach to the subject of the failed pharmacy exam was a little different. If I ever tried to raise it with her, out came the familiar gesture of the hand: a short, sliding, flat-handed motion, moving from the heart outward. Age-old, it wasn't a gesture of despair but rather a claim to deeper understanding. It said: Speech too has its limits, not everything can be talked about, sometimes things just happen. Abbie used to say, "Jews survive on ambiguous gestures."

On March 16, 1941, our sister, Phyllis, was born, a daughter to complete the family's joy at a time when things all around were looking up. A thousand dollars saved over the years by Ma's part-time bookkeeping job enabled Dad to put a down payment on a nicer house on Ruth Street, a few blocks from where we were living at the time.

In 1944, when I was four or five, I remember sitting with Abbie on the floor, gathering the nuts and bolts that Dad was dropping as he built the shelves in the basement of his new business (made possible by a $5,000 loan from Ma's parents), while in the background the radio blared out, blow by blow, the landing of the ships at Normandy. And how proud we were of our uncle Sam who had enlisted. And our slight embarrassment over Dad's being too old to go.

A year later, I remember sitting again with Abbie in that basement, disassembling U.S. Army first-aid kits, which Dad and his friend Al Tessier had gotten cheap. We got a penny for each kit we took apart. Dad could then sell the individual items—a dressing compound and an envelope of sulphur—on his sales routes. Tessier would go on to make his fortune off of royalties on a gauze pad manufacturing machine he invented. Years later, I remember a Johnson & Johnson salesman in his Palm Beach three-piece suit sitting in Dad's Worcester office, telling him he would have to drop Al Tessier's merchandise as a prerequisite before picking up the J & J line. And how proud I was that Dad refused.

At heart, Dad's business depended on having friends. And the measure of his true success in Worcester was that he seemed to know more people than any other Jew in Worcester who wasn't a rabbi. His friends called Worcester Medical Supply the "Pill Palace." If you knew "Johnnie" personally, you could go over and get your vitamins wholesale. Back then, doctors also dispensed medications, and they too would get the wholesale rate from Dad. Practically everybody in Worcester wanted to be on John Hoffman's good side. But only friends got the free samples.

Once, Dad sent Tessier a personal check and forgot to sign his name. When Al called, Dad told Al to just sign it. But instead, Al came over to the store, bringing the unsigned check with him. Dad exploded in anger and hurt pride. He felt slighted that Al would not sign Dad's name. I imagine that what offended him was the implication that, out of respect for the impersonal and conventional proprieties represented by his signature on a check, Al would disregard the spirit of their friendship.

A man of his generation, Dad loved to tell jokes that were bawdy but not dirty, and he never once said the word "fuck." Nor, in all the years that I knew him, did he ever say the words "I love you." Perhaps his way of showing love was teaching you to do something well, but to us it only sounded like criticism. "You'll never get anywhere," he'd say, "if you don't read at least one book a week." Yet he himself read books only in the condensed versions available from *Reader's Digest*. His source of news was *The Boston Record,* a tabloid that featured murders, Walter Winchell and, in the '50s, a gaggle of right-wing columnists taking pot shots at alleged Communists.

He'd pick up the *Record* every weekday evening from Worcester's number one newsboy, Homer, at the corner of Main Street and Chandler. Grown men hung around that corner and everyone knew Dad. The most important part of the paper was the page that carried the racing track numbers. The right numbers paid off against the two bits you had placed with the local bookmaker the day before. Just like everyone else, Dad always checked his luck before turning to the day's news.

His existence consisted almost entirely of work, softened only by the life of the temple and active membership in civic organizations like the Probus and Rotary clubs. He carried in his mind an idea of something sweet called success, which in his dreams could take away the bitterness. We, his family, were a part of his life, an essential part, perhaps even his reason for living. But in no way did we seem able to ease his suffering. And at no time did he feel that his success was so secure that he could rest. He always saw the shadow of the wolf out of the corner of his eye.

On Sundays, he'd head over to Water Street. He'd pick up bagels from Lederman's and lox from Whitman's, where he always found time to argue with old man Whitman for shaving the salmon too thin. Then, if business had been good that week, he might head over to see the Weintraub brothers and order up a few very lean corned beef sandwiches, sour pickles, and hear the day's *kibbitz*. On the way home, he'd pick up *The New York Times* from the Broadway. But the *Times* was for his family to read. He himself only glanced at the paper, which must have been inscrutable to him, except for the Wholesale Offerings section, which he read slowly and with care, looking for the deal that would make him rich.

Abbie, Phyllis, and I always had the latest toys. When we were old enough, Dad took us on trips to New York, where we saw the hottest Broadway shows, paid for by one of the drug companies as a reward for meeting quotas. We lacked for nothing. But we did not know at the time that these outings were expressions of love. So we felt a hollowness, even a coldness, from our parents.

In his autobiography, Abbie compares Dad to Willy Loman in *Death of a Salesman:* "A middleman, who carried home each night the great anxiety [that his suppliers would decide to] 'go direct' . . . rendering him instantly expendable." At the time Abbie wrote those words, Miller's tragedy was his favorite play.

Ida, Ma's mother, had decided that she didn't like Dad as soon as he was introduced to her and held to that opinion for the rest of her life. To anyone who'd listen she'd complain that he didn't have *yeches,* the Yiddish word for class, good upbringing, culture. On the other hand, the Hoffman family would complain that Ma was no *balebosteh,* Yiddish for a good homemaker, and would wonder aloud what Dad saw in her.

Dad used to tell his brother that Ma was a good lover. She may have been. But that he would say so tells me more about the world of loneliness that must have separated them than it does about her lovemaking. I remember Ma as quiet, perhaps cowed a little by Dad. She loved us and felt deeply protective of us. But she also felt a kind of discomfort, or perhaps the better word would be resentment. Whether we somehow made her unhappy, or her attitude toward us was only the outward reflection of an inner sorrow, I don't know. But her words always exhibited a tangle of contradictions. Thus she would say to me, "I love you as much as I love Abbie." But that wasn't what I wanted to hear. "As much as" was relative, and sounded evasive to my ears. What I wanted was a straight declaration.

Ma didn't keep order in the house. Beds stayed unmade, dishes piled up in the sink. Ma made dynamite blintzes; otherwise, Dad, Abbie, Phyllis, and I did most of the cooking. But Ma made the house a warm, friendly place to be. And maybe that was more important than keeping it neat.

She used to type our papers for school and talked with us about our ideas as she did. She had a strong social conscience, and it came out in her opinions. She loved the garden we kept at the back of the house. She loved animals, and looked kindly on the ones I was always bringing home—the snakes from the woods nearby, the squirrel monkey I sneaked onto the plane back from Florida one year. When a friend sent me a baby alligator, I kept it in the bathtub, and Ma agreed to let us take sponge baths so as not to disturb it. So in a way,

Ma taught us something about respect for life, for life in all its forms, for the spirit of life—something that didn't exclude people but didn't have them at its center either.

Phyllis remembers, when she was seven or eight, that Ma was reading *Anna Karenina*. Did she see herself as an unfortunate woman, as her mother Ida did, not unlike Tolstoy's Anna? When Abbie, Phyllis, and I were grown up with kids of our own, Phyllis remembers Ma turning to her and saying, "I wish I had been as good a mother as you are."

You often felt that deep inside her somewhere there was something that wasn't right, some way in which she felt at odds with the world around her. I like to think Ma was—not strange or eccentric— but *preoccupied*.

It was not unusual for her to drive the car into downtown Worcester on some errand and then return by bus, simply leaving the car wherever she had parked it. Phyllis might say these were small actions of protest and that she wasn't happy with her lot. Yet on Shabbes, in the flickering somber light of the white candles, Ma was the one who set the tone and made sure that *time was taken*. And I think Ma was happy enough, at peace, as the center of our family, not permitting herself to reflect too much about the reasons behind things.

During our childhood much of her time was taken up by Abbie's constant demands. He expected her devotion and he got it. As the first-born son, he could do no wrong. But Abbie too must have hungered after the words of endearment that were not forthcoming.

Our parents lived in the new world, but they were of the old one. They knew how to work, how to learn, and how to improve themselves. They knew the Jewish tradition and believed in America. But we, nurtured by the emotionalism of radio, and later of Hollywood, were already several times removed from the world of our parents.

I don't think they were even aware that our world existed, filled as it was, even as early as the mid-'50s, with rhythm and blues and expectations of happinesses that had nothing to do with material success.

Sometimes we put a glass to the wall to hear them make love.

There was a lot of noise—at first I thought they must be fighting. In my mind, there would never be any link between what I heard those nights and what I later learned, partly from Abbie, about making love.

What I would learn of *joy* was not something I can imagine them having known. Perhaps I am wrong; perhaps I underestimate them. I hope so. But I don't think so. While Abbie, our kid sister Phyllis, and I were growing up, somehow it was understood that some amount of happiness was to be *our* birthright, the reward for all *they* had been through.

As early as I can remember, Abbie used to eject me from our shared bed every night with a hard kick. I would climb back in, heavy with the understanding that, as the defeated party, I would now have to accept a smaller area of the mattress.

One day Dad came home with two surplus hospital beds he'd gotten cheap—complete with the then-new Trandelenberg feature, which raised and lowered the upper part. From then on we each had separate beds, which could be made to rise like sea creatures for purposes of war and defense. But we continued to share the room.

Until I was fifteen and he went off to Brandeis, Abbie was stuck with me. I think it suited him to have someone on hand who could serve both as apprentice and audience; I don't remember feeling in the way much. Abbie was my whole world. Whatever the game, we played by Abbie's rules.

Abbie wasn't mean-spirited, and he wasn't completely fair-minded either. But I think he always felt he could do something with me, that I was worth bothering with, that I might reward any efforts he made toward setting me on the right track.

There is a friendship between brothers. It's colder hearted than the love of a parent, but it's also a lot more direct, and simpler. And something else: You can always make your mark on a brother, you can mold him. He cannot refuse you. The power of a brother over a brother is great and cannot be set aside. It's almost impossible for an older brother to resist being a bully. And Abbie was no exception. But to make up for his occasional cruelty and more frequent bruising physicality, he was also filled with largesse toward me, his younger brother, and toward our sister Phyllis, often surprising us with gifts or saying things to make us laugh.

In his autobiography, Abbie describes how I always seemed to be right in harm's way whenever he was wielding a hammer or a golf club.

> *Jack's my younger brother. Not an easy thing. If we were building a tree hut and the hammer fell, Jack's head was always somewhere beneath, waiting. If I was swinging a golf club driving golf balls into yonder neighbors' windows, for some reason Jack always managed to straighten the tee at the right moment to get a whack.*[2]

My memory differs from his. Where he was willing to summarize our relationship, willing almost to reduce it to comic-strip proportions, I remember it as complex and changing. I suppose that difference in perspective is typical between a younger and an older brother.

Memory erases pain, and sometimes early pain is transformed into something we later cherish. Once when Abbie was about eight and Phyllis three, Abbie hoisted her on to his shoulders to pilfer some candy from Uncle Schmule's ration kit hidden in a high cabinet in the kitchen. Afterward, Abbie unintentionally pushed our little sister into a radiator, cutting her head open. Years later, when a cosmetic surgeon suggested removing the scar, Phyllis, by then a lovely, mature young woman, refused, because the scar helped her remember her brother.

One day while Abbie and I were wrestling, Abbie kneed me in the nuts. The combination of pain and the sense of betrayal I felt left me bawling. After something terrible like that, Abbie would lead me back upstairs to our bedroom, our private domain, and spend an hour teaching me to play chess. Not out of pity, but perhaps with an instinctive knowledge that the moment of defeat was among the ripest moments for instruction. In chess he taught me that you've got to think seven moves ahead. When you're playing a guy who's thinking only three moves ahead, you're going to beat the shit out of him. Until

I was about twelve, we played frequently, sometimes daily. Eventually, I improved by his instruction to the point where I could give him a game. Then he changed the rules to ten seconds a move. One day I beat him at ten-second chess, and he never played against me again.

Later I learned what it meant to play by Abbie's rules. We were playing mini-football tackle in the living room. As soon as he hiked the ball to me, I called for a quick kick—not something you usually did in living-room ball—and immediately kicked the ball into Abbie's teeth. With blood filling his mouth, Abbie had the good sportsmanship to giggle and then laugh out loud. He didn't mind being beaten. He loved a street fight, win or lose. Once every decade or so for the rest of his life, on occasions when we were together, Abbie would bare the chipped tooth, smile, and remind me of the day.

I wouldn't know how to explain the intensity of the occasional flashes of violence, except to say that at such moments the rage we felt was as real as the love was at other times. We weren't timid or repressed about expressing anger. It came, then passed and was forgotten.

One of the reasons you couldn't hate Abbie for long was that, although he was strong for his size, and fearless, he had remained a sickly child. Later in life he tried to hide his frailty. His need to overcompensate may have added to the urgency with which he liked to jump into the middle of things; Abbie could never sit on the sidelines and wasn't afraid to get hurt. But those of us who knew him well weren't usually fooled. I think I worried about him most when he wasn't complaining about anything, because I knew that often meant he was hurting bad.

Often, Abbie's asthma attacks were horribly frightening. "I'm having an attack," he'd say, becoming pale, his breathing coming in fits. Abbie said it was like having two tons weighing on his chest, or like being in a vise. Whenever the attacks came, they brought our world to a sudden standstill. If we were on vacation, as far away as Maine, we simply came home to Worcester. Eventually, we got used to traveling with an emergency oxygen supply. Even so, Abbie usually ended up spending a couple days in the hospital two or three times a year, with a big tank of oxygen by his bedside.

* * *

In the earliest photos of Abbie and me, he is looking at the camera and I am looking at him. He is laughing, his teeth visible right up to the molars; I am smiling up at him, my mouth lightly closed.

Parts of that model would crumble. There are photos of us in later years with both of us looking into the lens and neither of us smiling; more significantly, I eventually grew to a height several inches taller than Abbie, which was perhaps the only thing for which he never forgave me. But part of that first image of the pair of us would endure like a rock. Even today, with my brother absent, he is my phantom self, and I almost constantly feel twitches of pain or pleasure that are rightly his. Unthinkingly, my mouth lightly closes and I am reassured by the feeling that he is there, beside me or in another state, but there, grinning; and each time the shock is repeated when I remember that he is gone.

From the way he put it in his book, "Jack's my younger brother. Not an easy thing . . ." you'd almost think that by the mid-'70s when, as a fugitive, he wrote those words, my brother felt guilty about what I had to put up with as his younger brother. Maybe he did . . . Even as a kid, Abbie never let us down if he could help it, and our expectations of him—mine, Phyllis's, and our parents'—were always of greater things to come.

Chapter Two

1945–1955

I'm not the hustler I pretend to be. I've lost my share. There was just too much that couldn't be won by hustling. Despite a common opinion, I'm only half a hustler. Half a martyr, half a hustler.

—ABBIE

WHILE ABBIE AND I were growing up, the ragtag splendor of Worcester lay before us with a beauty all its own. It was a small but thriving city of industry, proud of the billows of smoke pouring out of the smokestacks of Wyman & Gordon, which made airplane forgings, the Norton Grinding Company, which made grinding wheels, the giant American Steel and Wire Company, the Knowles Loom Works, and the United States Envelope Company—huge manufacturers supplying a world market at their height in the '40s and '50s.

Built on seven hills like ancient Rome, the city had a spread-out quality that is unusual for the Northeast. You felt that it was still a question of land in Worcester, and not of the vertical space of other cities. Civic and commercial buildings were larger than houses, but not by much. The gorgeous train station looked to us like a cathedral that made Worcester the center of the world.

Today all but one of the great factories are closed, and the train station is boarded up. And if you ask a Worcester native where he's from, he'll usually say Boston. That's how much things have changed.

As kids, our pride in America was painted in the bright colors of a local history we only half understood. Yet we realized what it meant for certain events, some hundreds of years past, still to be important. Concord Bridge, where the first shots of the American Revolution had been fired, was only a half-hour's drive away. The Patriot publisher of *The Massachusetts Spy*, Isaiah Thomas, had come to

Worcester to escape Tories in Boston and continued printing his paper here. In the 1850s, the first International Peace Society was founded in Worcester. At the turn of the century, the anarchists Emma Goldman and Alexander Berkman ran an ice cream parlor here right before Berkman took the train to Pittsburgh, where he attempted to assassinate Henry Clay Frick. In 1909, Sigmund Freud gave his only lecture in America at Clark University in Worcester. In the 1920s, Robert Goddard tested rockets and developed rocket technology here that the Germans used later for their V2s. In 1926, Margaret Sanger gave what may have been the first speech on birth control, also at Clark. And Judge Webster Thayer, who presided over the Sacco and Vanzetti trial, lived here on Salisbury Street, where his home was bombed by anarchists. M-14 and M-16 rifles used to come from the Huntington-Richardson munitions factory a few blocks from where we grew up. The birth control pill was invented here too. In his speeches, sometimes, Abbie used to say, "The two greatest things to come out of Worcester were the pill and me, and some folks here wish the pill came first."

The city's most distinctive architectural feature is the Worcester three-decker house. The large, hard-cornered boxlike structures aren't exactly pretty. But they are homey in the best sense—built from the inside out with a real sense of the needs of families. They are homes that meet the sky low to the ground and embody one of the fairest low-income housing deals ever agreed to. Originally designed to keep workers close to the factories, they are the most decent way I know to fit three families into one house. They are large, spacious, and practical, a middle-class solution that might have worked well in other cities.

Nowhere in Worcester does it feel like you are in a bedroom community of Boston, although the state capital is only forty miles east on the Massachusetts Turnpike. To Boston, Worcester is an unwanted relative, unmannered and arrogant. And many of Worcester's best and brightest children agree. They leave at the first chance and don't look back. Even with wave after wave of new immigrants arriving, the Worcester population has dropped by almost half since postwar days—to around what it was in the 1930s.

The people who stay have a good toughness about them. Among

them are some of the people who seem to miss Abbie most. In the minds of many of his Worcester friends, Abbie was a sign of hope. Out of the anonymity of Worcester, he went on to be famous. Is it their own anonymity, I sometimes wonder, that frightens them the most, and was that what Abbie released them from? Not only was he from Worcester, he was proud of it. Since his death, sometimes, I see a searching look in their eyes. They do not compare me to him. But it is as if, being Abbie's brother, I am what is left of him. And perhaps something more. I am a part of him that has survived. In the end, I'm still Abbie's manager here. Seeing me helps them remember him. Binding contract.

Growing up in Worcester, Abbie and I had to sort out the Judeo-Christian world into its component parts. At the predominantly Irish-Catholic public grammar schools we attended, they wanted us to act like good Christians. The teachers were often spinsters who cracked our knuckles with wooden rulers, and who sometimes had our entire class practice silence for periods as long as an hour. At Christmas time, we silently mouthed the words to "little Lord Jesus, asleep in the hay," which our classmates sang with all their hearts.

As we passed the Church of the Blessed Sacrament on the bus home from Saturday afternoon movies, we took off our caps and crossed ourselves just like the other kids, without irony, but also without any understanding of what the gesture meant, or why we were doing it. Phyllis remembers one of the boys from the neighborhood accusing her of having killed God, sending her home sobbing to Ma. And I'll never forget the day Billy Mitchell, my best friend until I was ten, punched me in the nose for killing Jesus. After being punched once, you might say you were only half-Jewish.

Starting in grammar school, we went to *yeshiva* after regular school, four days a week and Saturday. The rigor of it could be tough on an eight- or nine-year-old. When your gentile friends were out on the street playing, you were studying the Talmud with ten or so other Jewish boys under the comfortless fluorescent lights of the *shul* parlor.

Rabbi Fogelman, short, stocky, bearded, humorless, and arrogant, was a disciplinarian. The way he bore down on us between the rows of desks, we thought he hated us. And I can't remember anything I learned from him. The experience of Fogelman's yeshiva was followed by Mr. Plich's Conservative shul, which struck me as no less authoritarian. Then came the more progressive Reform temple, where the services were shorter and the songs were livelier. *"Ein Keiloheinu"*—the Jewish equivalent of the Baptist "Free at Last"—suddenly had a beat. The teachers were more open at Reform temple as well. We actually had classroom *discussions,* my first experience of a class, religious or otherwise, as the site of an open exchange of ideas. And most important, at the Reform temple boys and girls were mixed in together.

We learned how to dance, and, when left to our own devices, how to kiss and play spin the bottle. We also learned that Judaism was not just a religion but also a way of life, one that embraced open thinking.

Cantor Adler, who prepared boys for their bar mitzvahs, let us ask questions. Then he would get us used to looking for our own answers to our questions. And once we'd spoken, however timidly, he would throw his hands up in the air and say, "Well! Whatever you think!"

Then there was Mrs. Williams's class, where we talked about the history of the Jews. The recently concluded second world war was discussed, and the Holocaust, although we didn't call it that. The term we used was "the camps." History, and by that I mean the horror of history, was something we never talked about anywhere else, not at school, at home or with the boys. That class was meant to teach us more than what had happened: It was designed to impress on us that somehow we were connected to what had happened. And we were meant to understand that because of what had happened we, as Jews, were different from other people. We carried in us a more weighty burden of responsibility. You could say history was taught to us as the underpinning of our guilt. History, the way Mrs. Williams taught it, made us believe we had a place reserved for us in eternity. Whatever the horrors, there was, as a counterbalance, a thin thread of underlying optimism, reminding us that since we as a people had survived, the downturns of history were in some sense transitory, a part of a larger picture. That, more or less, was the philosophy.

As young as we were, we came to experience at temple release from a certain weight of guilt or despair that was thick in the air but never actually articulated at home. At temple you could talk about the bottomless things, the things you carried with you which made you brood and for which you thought there were no words.

In 1936 and 1939, when Abbie and I were born, worldwide anti-Semitism made our parents and the Jewish-American community around them timid and fearful. Hitler was representative, not exceptional, in many of his opinions. Before, during, and even directly after the second world war, Hitler's attitude toward the Jews was not one of the things about him that rankled other world leaders. At no time during the war, for example, were any of the trains to any of the internment camps disrupted by Allied bombardment. As an anti-Semite, Hitler was a leader of government in step with his times.

There were daily discussions and arguments about war and peace in Europe whenever a newspaper found its way into the house. The shadow of anti-Semitism was omnipresent. And yet our early years were cloaked in safety. By comparison with the Jews of Europe and around the world, American Jews like our parents felt that they had received a special blessing by being American: Where others were perishing, they would have to bear the particular responsibility of having survived. And I believe that sense of safety, so excessive by comparison with the worldwide suffering of the Jews at that time, tended to drown out the timidity and the fear.

And there was another, even more powerful influence: By the time of the second world war, the *Jewish* experience had already become the *Jewish-American* experience, a complex, layered phenomenon. Already by the end of the war, the passion which Abbie and I embraced most proudly, aged ten and seven respectively, was patriotism. We used to arrive hours early for the parade on the Fourth of July or Veterans Day—then called Armistice Day. And not we alone, but as many as 100,000 or 150,000—in Worcester, a city of only a quarter of a million! The crowd lining the thoroughfare would be fifteen deep on either side, and not a dissenter among us. Not a breath of irony anywhere. Not a pacifist for miles.

Abbie and I would hold in our chests as the procession advanced before us: the broad-bellied civilian leadership of Worcester first, putting on a stately front. The drummers behind them began their flams, followed by the amphibious "ducks," and then the lumbering brown tanks, preceded by a rumbling sound like gathering thunder that shook the buildings up and down the street. Then the smartly dressed troops, every soldier a hero in our eyes, and last the cops—Worcester's finest in their elegant blue uniforms. There were no war-mongering generals, only peace-loving ones. Men like Omar Bradley and George Marshall were admired for the Berlin Airlift and their plans for the reconstruction of Europe. They were thoughtful, reasonable fellows, leaders among men, American paragons.

Later, when Ethel and Julius Rosenberg were accused of giving the secrets of the nuclear bomb to the Russians, they were accused not only of treason but, implicitly, of failure to assimilate. Their names were never mentioned in our house, not during the trial, or even later at the time of their execution in 1953. Today the thought that world peace might have depended on a balance of nuclear power between the two countries, the thought that the Rosenbergs might have been right, doesn't seem so unthinkable. But at that time it was. We were Americans and Jews, in that order. Americans first.

Being American meant we were large in our hearts and we always won. It meant that what was good for us was also good for the world. It meant that even those we beat to a pulp would be better off afterwards, since they would then benefit from our superior democratic institutions. However large one's imagination might be, the breadth and vastness of the land could match it. As children we took these notions in with every breath and heartbeat, and never doubted them. On every street in Worcester there were flags flying in front of most of the houses. Nothing made you so proud as seeing those flags waving. Jewish, Irish, Italian, Polish, Greek, Swedish, French, Armenian—you knew there were names people might call you to put you down, based on where you came from, dirty names, but you knew you were also American, and there was nothing wrong with that.[1]

The post-war years were among the happiest of our lives. Between 1946 and 1950, America was having an irresistible love affair with itself and we felt a part of it. These were Abbie's preteen years, when "freedom" meant the ability to explore Worcester, with me tagging along behind. Ma was happy. The world was about as young as it was going to get.

In the years after World War II, The March of Dimes was leading the fight to find a cure for polio. It wasn't uncommon to know someone who had been stricken with the awful disease, or who had a family member who was. So a lot of children did what we did, which was to raise money for the March of Dimes. Abbie came up with the idea of doing a variety show modeled after the "Ted Mack Amateur Hour," a popular radio program. We built a stage in our basement with wood and orange crates, solicited "acts" from the kids in the neighborhood, and rehearsed for weeks. On the afternoon of the performance, the few kids from the neighborhood who weren't performing as well as some of the parents paid a dime each to catch the show. Abbie served as emcee, starting with a pitch about the battle against polio. I did my impersonation of Al Jolson. Phyllis danced.

Some of the things American didn't mean yet: the utter destruction of the various American-Indian nations, heedlessly wiped out by violence, disease and deceit; the violence which destroyed the great American workers' movements of the late nineteenth and early twentieth centuries; the ignominy of slavery, which created much of the wealth of the nation in the eighteenth and nineteenth centuries; and other incontrovertible facts. These other particularly American legacies would have been unimaginable to us. Literally unimaginable. They were not taught in the schools or discussed in the press. No one seemed to find anything disquieting in the myth that Columbus had "discovered a new world" already inhabited by more than a million Native Americans. Such was the velocity of the general rush to the center of American culture that people acted almost as if nothing else existed, not really. So that years later, when through music and television, cracks of light began to fall on us, their effect would be truly explosive and enduring.

The first presidential election I can remember was in 1948, when I was nine. In our family we liked Dewey, the Republican, over the incumbent Truman. A Dr. George Gallup polled voters up to two weeks prior to the election, then stopped. He felt that responsible people, the bulk of voters, would have made up their minds by then, and he posted a sweep for Dewey. Truman was reelected. Although the exploitation of the fickle electorate would have to wait another decade and a half, it was with the election of 1948 that the fickle electorate was born. From then on Gallup would know to poll up until the last minute.

Television imagery began to rivet us in the early '50s—I remember Senator Estes Kefauver from Tennessee, who headed up the Senate Subcommittee on Crime. In my brain he will always be coupled with his arch-enemy Frank Costello, boss of the New York crime family. Their faces were spliced side by side on the nightly news like the two were prom King and Queen. But the real influence to which we opened up our hearts and minds during the late '40s and '50s was the movies, which filled our Saturdays now, replacing yeshiva.

Walking down to June Street on Saturday mornings, Abbie and I would take the number 5 Speedway bus—which had superseded the nickel trolley—all the way to downtown Worcester. Getting off at City Hall, we would make our way over the Commons to the Capitol Theater for a comedy or an adventure. Then back across the Commons at noon for lunch at the Woolworth's counter: a hot dog and Coke followed by their home-made waffle with three-flavored ice cream—all for twenty-five cents. After lunch, we would walk back over to the movies.

In those days each theater was associated with one of the major studios. You went to the Warner for an RKO thriller, to the Loews for an MGM musical, and to the Capitol for a Paramount adventure. If you wanted a Republic cowboy picture, you headed for the Plymouth. The Plymouth was special to us. Once a month, for an extra fifty cents, you could see a live show: the Great Blackstone, a magician, or Tex Ritter, who came on stage riding a huge, sixteen-hand horse surrounded by Indians on foot. Abbie and I were usually the only ones cheering the horseless Indians and booing Tex.

All the theaters were magnificent, with huge crystal chandeliers which dimmed. Then the trumpet call which heralded the Movietone newsreel, narrated by Ed Herlihy, whose voice was much better than the nasal tones of Walter Winchell on the radio at home.

We saw a lot of Western talking pictures, starring Randolph Scott, Roy Rogers, Hopalong Cassidy, Gene Autry, or Gary Cooper. In 1947, we saw *Unconquered,* in which a drenched Paulette Goddard—in her white satin blouse through which her nipples pressed gently—is swept away by the raging river and into Cooper's arms. That night, I had my first nocturnal fantasy. I can still see her reaching for the tree limb, and then valiantly hanging on. She was the female star I can remember best from those early days. Much later, we learned that Paulette Goddard was Jewish and had married Erich Maria Remarque (after an earlier marriage to Charlie Chaplin, who would become one of our favorites later on), the author of one of my all-time favorite books, *All Quiet on the Western Front.* When she died in Switzerland a few years ago, a long way from her roots in Brooklyn, I wept for all she had meant to me.

In the late '40s, Dad's business started to flourish. You could always measure success in those days by the automobiles people drove. Dad wouldn't get his first Cadillac for many years, but already in the late '40s he'd go every year to the Ford dealership across the street from his office for a new station wagon for Worcester Medical deliveries. The dealership was secretly owned by a Jew, Eugene Ribakoff, since Ford wouldn't allow Jews to own dealerships, with another guy named Malboeuf who acted as the front man. But Dad always made sure he dealt directly with Gene. He believed you always did business with your own kind. And it never would have occurred to him not to buy a Ford because of the company's anti-Semitism.

Also in the late '40s, Abbie's horizons began expanding beyond the family and the temple. He was bored by the separatism, the self-ghettoization, of Jewish-American life at home and at temple. By the time he reached his early teens. Abbie was "going down the line" to hang out on the corner of June and Chandler Streets with the *shtarker goyim* (gentile toughs). He learned to shoot craps and play in alleyways. He smoked cigarettes, rolled his Lucky Strikes into his tee shirt sleeve, and taught himself to play pool and bowl until he was good enough at both to earn money hustling at the rec hall in downtown Worcester. The living-room mantelpiece started to fill up with trophies Abbie had won in bowling, Ping-Pong, Duncan yo-yo tournaments and, later, tennis. Abbie loved the trophies. They were his earliest attempt to define himself, create himself. From the age of thirteen until he went off to college, the culture that he steeped himself in was street culture. He wanted to see himself in terms of an American experience, one that resembled the world he watched on the big screens downtown. And the craft he studied to perfection was the street hustle.

Not only was Abbie a pretty good gin rummy player, he knew how to deal from the bottom of the deck in poker. And he was a pretty good shoplifter. He carried a knife and wasn't shy about using it. Abbie wanted his new friends to think of him as one of them, and made sure of it by acting differently from the other Jewish kids.

I missed Abbie's companionship and resented the attention he got. When I felt lonely, I would hide away in the basement and sometimes no one would notice. They were too busy dealing with the *vildah-chayah*—the wild and crazy one. I remember squeezing myself under a long work table with a lit candle and my eyes pressed shut, pretending I really had run away to a distant city. After what seemed like hours, I heard Ma and Dad asking where I was. But whatever I did, I wasn't able to elicit the drama that Abbie seemed to evoke without even trying. I thought I was less loved, expendable. Somehow it seemed to me that the qualities I had weren't as important as the qualities Abbie had. The bleakness I felt was indescribable. And at such moments I hated him.

But then, with an uncanny instinct, Abbie would seem to know just what I was feeling, and he'd turn on the charm, inviting me to a movie or a high school football game. All of a sudden you realized that you didn't hate him after all, actually you loved him a lot. He had that ability to make you miss him. The terrible thing was that Abbie never seemed to depend on you in the same way as you depended on him, and that always gave him the advantage.

Summers were always the measure of our family joy and prosperity. In the late '40s, we'd spend a few weeks each summer at the largely Jewish resort of Old Orchard Beach in Maine, closing up the house and piling trunk after trunk onto the train for the day-long journey in the heat. The heart of Old Orchard Beach was its huge, mile-long pier, cluttered with the tourist attractions of the day, sort of a New Englander's Coney Island. Something for all ages. I loved the magical horses of the carousel and the freshly cut potatoes sizzling in the Frialators at the French fry stand, and the big bands—including the Count Basie Orchestra, Benny Goodman, and the Dorsey Brothers' and Harry James's bands—that played in the Casino. I've never been able to find anywhere else a fullness in the air like the smells of the fresh fruit mixing in the salt air as we walked down the main street toward the pier. And, thrilling to us at the time, fireworks were legal then in the state of Maine. Abbie and I could, and did, blast off rockets from the beach.

One year when money was tight, Ma shipped Abbie and me off to people she knew who lived on a farm in the town of Hudson outside of Worcester. There my brother and I worked hard, rising at dawn, milking cows, gathering eggs from the hen coop, tilling the ground, and planting the late crop. I suppose Ma's plan was to get a break for herself, get some fresh air into us, and teach us about work, all at the same time. That year I resented my role as my brother's "companion," as if I were little more than a sidelight to Abbie's limelight, even in Ma's eyes.

Starting in 1951, summers became really earthshaking for us. Cape Cod, the most desirable Massachusetts sun spot, wasn't open to Jews. Whether they refused to serve you or were suddenly completely booked when you arrived, hotels and restaurants always made the point clearly. But that year we began vacationing in Onset, a town right on the Cape Cod Canal just north of Cape Cod. And it is because of Onset that, even now, the last days of June are filled for me with a powerful feeling of imminent happiness.

With Truman in the presidency, and Dad's business showing a small profit, we began renting our own house for the whole summer season in Onset—just the four of us, Ma, Phyllis, Abbie and me, with Dad driving his new Buick down for weekends only, since he couldn't leave the business for extended periods.

The water was warmer in Onset Bay than up in Maine, and calmer too, so we sometimes spent whole days on the beach. Abbie and I liked to take a bottle of catsup from the house, and go clamming for quahogs, splitting them open as we found them and eating them on the spot. We couldn't bring them home because they weren't kosher. *Trayf,* Ma would say. She swam a mile a day, from one end of the beach to the other, with Abbie and me running along the beach keeping pace with her. Or she would teach us to swim, the four of us splashing around together. Phyllis remembers Onset as where she first came to know, and like, how she looked in a swimsuit.

Abbie and I sometimes hired ourselves out on Johnny Lopez's "White Lady," starting at five A.M., with the lady shining from her polished brass fittings to her white prow and sails. Olive-skinned, short, with a Latin-lover's mustache, Johnny always wore the same matching khaki shirt and pants, his personal uniform. Johnny's claim to fame was a cousin or nephew who was a Brooklyn Dodgers pitcher. But Johnny was formidable in his own right, weather-beaten and as terse and sweet as a young hero out of Hemingway—the guy that loves the girl but whose manliness somehow can't accommodate love.

Abbie and I baited and untangled the lines for Johnny's tourists and helped them gaff their fish into the boat and off the hooks. When they disembarked, they would tip us, less if they hadn't caught anything, more if they had. And we would repeat the apocryphal story Johnny had taught us about the German sub that had come up the canal and torpedoed the sunken boat at the end of the canal that we passed on every trip.

Once a week Abbie took me to the movies at Onset's only movie theater. The one I remember best was *Mighty Joe Young,* and for one scene in particular. About halfway through the movie, after Joe, the great ape, has been taken from his island—where he was treated as a god—and brought back to New York in a steel-barred cage to suffer the humiliation of serving as a mighty prop in a night club act, the film approaches its emotional climax. We see Joe rise from beneath the stage, holding Terri Moore seated at a piano playing "Beautiful Dreamer." I had already fallen in love with Terri Moore, but this is the scene in which you realize how much you love her because, of course, you see how she has made even Mighty Joe vulnerable and gentle—and Mighty Joe is the one with whom you identified. You loved Mighty Joe too, but only in the way you loved yourself, that is, with pity, not passion. Abbie and I were both crying our heads off. Afterward, Abbie tried to play the tough guy, saying, "It's only a monkey." I didn't believe him for a second. When we heard later that Howard Hughes had shacked up with Moore and then gotten her to give up her acting career, we felt he had stolen her from us. So sincere was our resentment of Hughes that when he died decades later, we didn't mourn him at all.

Onset had a penny arcade where the local Cape Verdians gathered, with a jukebox and a penny machine that pounded out cards of your favorite hero—Roy Rogers, Gene Autry, Hopalong Cassidy. Or Claudette Colbert and Paulette Goddard. You could shoot down a Japanese Zero or a German Messerschmitt. Or you could play a poker machine for five cents. It was here that we first heard Fats Domino.

And on Tuesday nights, I would pull out my trumpet and play "Oh My Papa" at amateur night at the bandshell in the park. Never anything else. I knew the song, made famous by Eddie Fisher, by heart, so I didn't need music. Every week I played "Oh My Papa" and I never won. My sister Phyllis suggested I learn another tune. But I was adamant.

Friday evenings Dad would arrive, bringing fresh corn and the gladioli he always brought and which Ma hated. She would accept them graciously, then turn to us and say that they belonged in a funeral home. Saturday nights he might take us to wrestling matches at the Onset Casino. Or, if he'd heard of a restaurant on the Cape, we would pile into the Buick Roadmaster and make the drive across the Sagamore Bridge. Most of the time, the restaurant would let us eat, even though they recognized that we were a Jewish family. The rest of the time we'd double back to Tiny Tim's Pizza in Buzzard's Bay, just the other side of the Canal from where we started out, where it was a safe bet they'd let us eat. Once, in Hyannis, we walked into a nearly deserted restaurant to be told all the tables were reserved. When Dad said that seemed unlikely, the man blocking our way said simply, without anger or passion, but perhaps with a slight edge to his voice, "We don't serve people of your persuasion." Like he was describing a law of nature or something: No hard feelings, that's just the way it is.

The Onset Hotel, where Abbie and I played the pinball machines, was a run-down, small establishment without a pool, without a golf course, without horses. But it was only a block away from the ocean. It had a great patio and on this great patio it had a great shuffleboard. On the screened-in porch sat the local big shots—the *alter kockers,* or A.K.s, as we called them—with their fat cigars. They lorded over the view of the still, empty, and quiet green commons and the bay.

At the back of the hotel, the main attraction was the jukebox, the hottest juke box around, featuring Vaughn Monroe's "Ghost Riders in the Sky," along with tunes by Al Alberts and the Four Aces, and Teresa Brewer. Put another nickel in the nickelodeon and you could close your eyes and imagine dancing with your darling while Patti Page crooned the "Tennessee Waltz."

In Onset, Abbie became my best friend. He found it in his heart to treat me as an equal, somebody he could teach and somebody he could trust. Our sister Phyllis remembers Onset as a place of "incredible freedom." How much of this was due to the fact that Dad was only an occasional presence? If you ask Phyllis, the answer is a lot. If you asked Florence, our mother, perhaps the answer would have been a lot. For Abbie and me, though, the freedom had more to do with our ages—in the summer of 1952 he was fifteen and I was twelve—and the sun, the sea, and the great brashness and optimism all around us.

Somewhere around Abbie's sixteenth birthday, he made friends with two of his classmates at Classical High School back in Worcester. And this time, the friendship grew into a real bond. Both Paul Cotton and Haskell Morin were Jews, and both, like Abbie, were exploring the world around them, looking for adventure. Paul was a large, quiet kid who played left end on the high school football team and whose family were Conservative Jews. Haskell, "Hack," was smaller than Abbie and shy. The two boys quickly took Abbie as their leader, and together they called themselves the Motley Three, or the Ruth Street Stomping Society. They were in search of big blasts. "Skin me, man, in the name of the almighty A"—for radio disc jockey Alan Freed—was their greeting. Paul and Hack followed Abbie because of his daring and boundless energy. Leadership went right to Abbie's head. He became the wild man of Classical High. He even started getting into fights, although not because he sought them out; he had gained a reputation for toughness and people liked to put it to the test.

With his friends, Abbie stole cars for joyrides, usually returning them after they were done. They'd play chicken on what we used to call the "Speedway," Mill Street in Worcester. The posted speed limit on the speedway was thirty-five miles per hour, but the challenge there was to drive it at seventy-five to ninety. Then they started to play a variation of the game that involved trying to see how long the driver could go at speeds of twenty-five or thirty miles per hour without touching the steering wheel. Once when Abbie was showing me the game in Dad's station wagon, I chickened out first by opening the door and rolling out minutes before Abbie let the car go off the road and right into Coes Pond.

Halloween got to be his favorite night of the year, the official occasion when Abbie and his friends would go out to raise hell, cutting clotheslines and slitting convertible tops around the neighborhood with their switchblades. But they quickly extended the occasion to include the nights before and after Halloween as well, and before long Halloween became a state of mind that encompassed just about every night of the year.

Abbie also started bringing girls up to his room to have sex around this time, while Ma and Dad were downstairs watching t.v., with Hack posting guard at the top of the stairs. And one day Abbie decided that since he was the local expert on jerking off, it was his civic responsibility to educate the neighborhood kids on the art of masturbation. He gathered four or five teenagers in our basement and placed a gallon jug on the floor, challenging them to fill the jug with jiz, and guessing how long it would take. Nobody thought this was anything out of the ordinary. Abbie used to go into the bathroom, lock the door, and jerk off into a shot glass that he kept in the medicine cabinet for that purpose. Then he would dutifully transfer the semen into the gallon jug. He used to time his efforts and said he could come in fourteen seconds flat. Years later I asked Hack if Abbie used any props, like underwear or pictures. Hack's response was that Abbie had a photographic memory, which was true. I'd never thought of that.

When Abbie was sixteen he met Herbie Gamberg, someone with whom he could let his guard down. Gamberg was an all-around regular guy, a jock, but also took his brain seriously, and it was the combination that Abbie admired. About five years older than Abbie, Herbie attended a nearby college called Brandeis, and after a hard weekend game of softball or basketball, he'd fill Abbie's head with the ideas of people like Nietzsche, Freud, and Camus. Abbie was impressed. And Gamberg, like Abbie, was a little guy and a Jew, so Abbie would have seen more than a little of himself in Gamberg's words. I think Herbie Gamberg was the first person Abbie emulated, and I think that what Abbie emulated in Herbie was the synthesis Herbie seemed to represent of physical strength and intellectual sensitivity. Abbie hadn't seen that before.

Throughout his high school years, Abbie's sex life kept increasing. Nobody was getting laid more than Abbie. The girls just adored him. Abbie looked at sex as an experience of life that was more than sexual. What Abbie did he did spontaneously. Once, Abbie told his friend Haskell, he picked up a hitchhiker about his age one night on his drive back from a visit to his girlfriend Suzie in Everett. The hitchhiker and Abbie pulled over and jerked each other off for the hell of it. As far as I know, that was his only gay flirtation.

Throughout his youth, Abbie was moving in two directions at once. Part of him was assimilating, getting tougher, bringing his persona of the all-American hustler toward seamless perfection. The other part, wholly unassimilated, tender and fragile, was retreating ever further inward. But it was this second part, hardly visible, that was the stronger, more determined side of his personality. Abbie used to say he was never more than half a martyr. That was true. But it was this half, increasingly in later life, that would lead actions and trigger his responses.

Others around Abbie, including me, were growing taller than him. At 5'7", he'd stopped growing. And he suffered from his asthma, which meant that the specter of emergency oxygen treatments was a constant companion. As a Jew he felt he was accepted by many of his non-Jewish friends only up to a point. Of course, these limitations only made Abbie more daring, more adventurous, more gregarious.

And so the tender part of his nature became an alienated part of Abbie's personality.

On June 9, 1953, in the late afternoon, Abbie was at home talking on the phone to Suzie during a raging storm. The operator interrupted the call to say that the Worcester Chief of Police was trying to reach Dad. Since Dad was out of town on business, Abbie took the call. The police chief told him that the storm had created a health emergency and that medical supplies were urgently needed. Even through he was only sixteen, Abbie figured that the responsibility fell on him as the oldest son. Following the police chief's instructions, Abbie drove the family station wagon into downtown Worcester to open up the store. He was met there by a Red Cross representative. Abbie began supplying intravenous solutions and other first aid supplies for the Red Cross emergency stations. He also called New York suppliers to arrange for an orderly flow of resupply shipments. Meanwhile, outside it had grown pitch dark. Fist-size hailstones were falling at high velocity and there were wind gusts blowing well over a hundred miles per hour. In the middle of it, Abbie started driving the station wagon through the most ravaged areas of North Worcester dispensing supplies. He saw huge areas flattened by the storm: "Trees smashed into houses. Rooftops torn off. . . . It was a war zone. We lugged plasma into tents, climbing over dead bodies and people screaming. I worked the entire night."[2] The next day, Abbie returned to help with the horrific job of searching through the rubble. The Worcester Tornado turned out to be one of the worst storms in the country's history, with thousands injured and over a hundred people killed.

In his telling, Abbie always emphasized the excitement of moments like these—the speeding through downtown Worcester on his way to reach the injured, for example—as if all he was interested in was the action. But what I remember is something else altogether. Abbie needed to help people. Doing so was the only way to express something deep inside himself that he didn't like to let people see, not even me. Underneath his wild persona, he felt a connection to human suffering powerful enough for him to feel the need to hide it much of the time. Maybe it had to do with some very needy part of himself, or something in him that was so pure that he was a little embarrassed about it, afraid you'd laugh at him if you knew how much he cared.

I don't want to make my brother sound like a hero. He wasn't the type to throw himself on a grenade. But I want people to see the side of him that he came to hide so well, because it's the best lens through which to understand the strength of his convictions later on.

In the spring of 1953, Abbie argued with a biology teacher and found himself expelled from Classical High. The following fall, Ma and Dad enrolled him in Worcester Academy, a private prep school. The money didn't matter to them, as long as Abbie was happy.

The family began to watch television more. We watched John Cameron Swayze, the original anchor, on NBC, which was, with its stars Howdy Doody and Milton Berle, the station to watch. Eisenhower seemed to have things well in hand but was always playing golf. We might have wondered, who was running the country? In 1954–55, the McCarthy trials were televised. It wasn't a matter of "politics" to us. The point was McCarthy seemed scary—you naturally identified with his victims, and when he questioned them, not allowing them to speak, not respecting them, accusing them of the worst kind of betrayal of their country, you almost felt like you were being accused yourself. Of course we didn't understand what was going on, didn't really know what McCarthy meant by the word "Communist," or whether those he accused were innocent or guilty. By their very helplessness and confusion, we found ourselves questioning our own patriotism. It was the first crack in the dam, the beginning of the end of the America we had until then believed was eternal. But one still didn't question authority. Abbie thought he was going to be a doctor. I planned to be a veterinarian. We both believed that the world was immutable and that all you had to do was to find your place in it.

Chapter Three

1955–1961

What a man can be, he must be.

—ABRAHAM MASLOW

PICTURE ABBIE IN the spring of 1955: bright, good-looking, clean-cut, adventurous, and college bound. A sharp dresser—in his pegged pants, suede shoes, and black leather jacket with the knife cut in it—his hair greased back in a "duck's ass," he had danced his way into more teenage hearts than any other Worcesterite I knew or knew of. His act was so smooth that he kept his tweed jacket and tie in his school locker, changed clothes twice a day, and never wore his uniform outside the school walls. He didn't think twice about the daily costume changes, any more than he did about singing "Onward Christian Soldiers" every morning at assembly.

Abbie drove a black, '49 Ford two-door, paid for by working summers making deliveries for Dad. The car radio was tuned most of the time to Alan Freed's WINS 1010 out of New York—rock and roll groups like The Drifters, Ruth Brown, Ivory Joe Turner, the immortal Fats Domino, Sam the Man Taylor, Red Prysock, The Clovers, The Cadillacs. He spent Saturdays at the race track: early spring at Lincoln Downs, then moving with the horses to Suffolk Downs, on to Rockingham in late summer, and then back to Suffolk. Abbie didn't bet large, I guess, but to me it was large: $10 bets with an occasional $50 bet when the spirit moved him. He still shot pool down at the Recreation Bowling Alley—we called it "Recs"—and hustled gin games up on Newton Hill. Saturday nights were reserved for his girl Suzie from Everett, and by then they were doing it in the backseat or at her house when her parents were away. Sex, gambling, and rock and roll occupied him almost entirely.

Around the house none of us paid much attention to how hard Abbie was working to be cool. In the Hoffman family there wasn't yet any sign of a culture gap or a generation gap. In fact, we all got along just fine. Abbie, Dad, and I spent a lot of time together—at the Y, where Abbie won the pool championship, at Holy Cross football and basketball games, and on trips to New York. Abbie and I both lived within the spread of Big John's understanding. We were tough, strong, and outgoing. Our values were no different from his.

Abbie applied to three colleges that spring: Columbia, Tufts, and Brandeis. For Columbia and Tufts, he had a medical career in mind, yielding to Dad's prodding. Ma wanted him to be a psychiatrist, so that he might help with her lobotomized sister Rose. But Tufts and Columbia turned him down—strong test scores, but mixed grades, and weak recommendations. That left only Brandeis. Herbie Gamberg went there and so did Sid Goldfader, another one of our boyhood heroes, an all-city Jewish all-star—basketball, football, and baseball—so we knew it wasn't a sissy school. But Dad was suspicious of the place from the start.

Brandeis had been formed in 1948 by a group of prominent Jewish professionals that included Albert Einstein. Their aim was to create a university that would serve the Jewish community and also be open to people of all faiths. The group purchased failing Middlesex College, renamed it after the late U.S. Supreme Court Justice Louis D. Brandeis, and set up shop. Launched with just 14 faculty members and 107 freshmen, Brandeis's faculty in the early years would include composer Leonard Bernstein and the (non-Jewish) historian Henry Steele Commager, anthropologists Alfred Kroeber and Paul Radin, and cultural historians Irving Howe and Ludwig Lewissohn. Eleanor Roosevelt taught international affairs. By the fall of 1951 there were six hundred students. In the spring of 1952, the first class graduated, although the school was not yet accredited. And in 1955, the year Abbie arrived, Brandeis established formal departments according to traditional disciplines, after experimenting with a more open system.

The newness of Brandeis was still palpable when Abbie arrived, and still contagious. This was a school with a mission, one that thrived on its uniqueness despite the inhospitable intellectual climate that pervaded the country. Miraculously, Joe McCarthy had not gone after any part of Brandeis for fear of being labeled anti-Semitic, and so it continued as an oasis where many of the best and most controversial minds of the era found refuge.

At Brandeis the world began to open up to Abbie, and it never closed again. He read Dostoyevsky, Camus, Freud, Tolstoy, Rilke. His teachers were among some of the most exciting thinkers of the period. They included Marxist philosopher Herbert Marcuse, Frank Manuel, Max Lerner, Paul Radin, Philip Rieff, Kurt Goldstein, and, most importantly, psychologist Abraham Maslow. It is almost incredible that Abbie had the good fortune to find among his professors several of those whose ideas would seed the '60s counterculture. Nowhere else in the world could Abbie have stumbled upon such an awesome anti-establishment. Brandeis had defined itself as a subversive institution, and that colored everything he read and heard there. The post-war America of the '40s and '50s, which until then had seemed unchangeable, began to look like only one among many possibilities.

Abbie had been open to change all his life, but at Brandeis he was able to experience firsthand and way in advance the ferment that a decade later would explode all over the nation. Of course, he didn't experience his professors as radical extremists in science, psychiatry, and sociology. This was college, as far as he knew, no different from other colleges across the country. He received the new ideas he was hearing not as radical notions but as normal teachings. Many of these ideas became the basis of his personal philosophy.

In his sophomore year at Brandeis, Abbie broke off with Suzie. He met Sheila Karklin, a beatnik painter who danced, wore mostly black, and came from a Conservative Jewish family. Sheila was a year behind Abbie and a good student studying psychology. She was tiny, around five feet one inch or so, and she had beautiful emerald green eyes, like a delicate Elizabeth Taylor to Abbie's Montgomery Clift in *A Place in the Sun*. That year, along with his wrestling and other macho sports, Abbie took a modern dance class and went bohemian with Sheila as his guide. Not one to do anything halfway, he even began wearing a beret. Together, Abbie and Sheila went to folk concerts and listened to Pete Seeger records. Within a few months Abbie was head over heels in love.

He brought Sheila home to meet Ma, Dad, Phyllis, and me, and told us that evening that this was the girl he was going to marry. Abbie and Sheila were very affectionate with each other, and they seemed to share political ideas and dreams. She led and he followed—you could see how much he respected her. The only thing out of place was how different their styles were. Sheila was serious, quiet, even somber, and Abbie was exuberant and arrogant. And the funniest part was the quieter she got, the louder he seemed to get. So even early on there was that tragic flaw between them, and if you squinted you could catch a glimmer of how they might "enable" each other in the wrong way. But there didn't seem to be any doubt that they loved each other.

Partly under Sheila's influence, Abbie began to take an interest in psychology. He took a class with Abe Maslow, and that may have been the single most important decision of his life. Maslow was asking hard questions in 1956. What is self-fulfillment really about? What values make for a worthwhile life? To whom can we look for models of "self-actualizing" men and women? Even unanswered, those questions presented a forceful threat to the materialism of the '50s world. But Maslow was also suggesting answers that were as profound as the questions.

Maslow taught that sexual openness was to be encouraged in the form of honest self-disclosure, and at an earlier teaching position at Brooklyn College had even asked his students to keep sexual autobiographies. He believed that masturbation was good and healthy, and advocated early education of children in sexual matters. Maslow also advocated and experimented with communal living, inviting a variety of family members to live in his home with chores and responsibilities for the household and children assigned to each.

In both his writings and in talks, Maslow emphasized that true fulfillment in life comes from satisfying our higher needs, particularly what he called our need for self-actualization. His idea was that self-actualization, self-fulfillment, was a part of human nature, common to all of us, and that those who actually find this self-fulfillment are not superior, just normal, although rare. Rare because in most people human nature is thwarted by events in their lives, usually in childhood. "There seems no *intrinsic* reason why everyone shouldn't be this way [self-actualizing]," he said; "I think of the self-actualizing man not as an ordinary man with something added, but rather as the ordinary man with nothing taken away."[1] "What a man *can* be, he *must* be," he wrote.[2]

To Abbie, Maslow represented the perfect bridge between his own past and future. Raised in Brooklyn, Maslow, like Abbie, had grown up Jewish, and like Abbie had shown a distaste for religion early on, substituting for it a serious interest in socialism. Maslow belonged to Dad's generation, and had been barred from the college of his choice by anti-Semitism. But by temperament Maslow belonged to the new age that was dawning on the horizon. When he had been urged to change his given name from Abraham to something less obviously Jewish—at one point his own wife had threatened to divorce him if he would not do so—he had refused, considering the very idea ridiculous. Unlike our parents, or their parents, Maslow represented a welcome and fruitful break with tradition, one that could be taken by Abbie as a model of intellectual freedom, ambition, and personal happiness. Maslow came from the world of our fathers yet had an utterly contemporary mind—by dint of both its audacity and empathy.

Under Maslow's influence, Abbie chose psychology as the profession he would pursue upon graduation. Abbie also became one of a relatively large number of students who turned to Maslow and his wife for advice on personal matters, visiting them in the evenings at their residence on campus. Abbie began to see America through Maslow's eyes, and through other visionaries Maslow assigned in his classes, including Aldous Huxley, Erik Erikson, D. T. Suzuki.

In his autobiography, Abbie wrote:

Most of all, I loved Abe Maslow. I took every class he gave and spent long evenings with him and his family. There was something about his humanistic psychology (considered radical at the time) that I found exhilarating amidst the general pessimism of Western thought. [He] laid a solid foundation for launching the optimism of the sixties. Existential,

*altruistic, and up-beat, his teachings became my personal
code.*[3]

Then there was Herbert Marcuse. If Maslow was inventing a
form of psychology to suit the new America, Marcuse, his colleague
at Brandeis, was reinventing Marx. Ten or fifteen years later, every
Leftist on every college campus in America would be reading Marcuse's *One Dimensional Man, Eros and Civilization,* and *Reason and
Revolution.* But Abbie's connection to Marcuse was less profound
and less personal than what he felt for Maslow. Mostly, Abbie considered Marcuse a kind of "corrective" to Maslow, completing the
psychologist's thought and modifying it theoretically.

While his thinking matured under the guidance of Maslow, Marcuse, and other professors, Abbie had developed a great entrepreneurial hustle to make money on the side. He'd worked out a deal
with a submarine sandwich shop in nearby Waltham, and every night
Abbie would drive into town and pick up dozens of deli sandwiches
which he would then sell for sixty cents apiece in the Brandeis dorms.
Abbie and other students he hired crying out "sand-wich-es" became
one of the most familiar and welcome sounds on campus, as doors
flew open and students gathered for evening study breaks.

With Abbie gone, I felt some amount of pressure to fill his blue
suede shoes around the old neighborhood. I got myself thrown out of
Classical High and enrolled at Worcester Academy, just as Abbie had
done three years earlier. I found an old drum set at the Salvation
Army and bought it for twenty-five dollars, thinking that drummers
made the most noise and got the most girls. I didn't really miss my
brother. Mostly I enjoyed being the center of attention for a change.
Dad and I got closer, Ma took more interest in my schoolwork. I
enjoyed my classes. My girlfriend and I were having sex in the back of
the Pontiac convertible that my uncle Schmule had helped me buy a
week after my sixteenth birthday.

Then, after a few months, the novelty of my new freedom began
to grow old, and the hole Abbie had left in my life seemed to expand.
The new, bohemian, intellectual stuff he talked about on visits home

didn't make any sense to me at all. During this period of enormous growth for Abbie, each new idea he learned was a new source of estrangement to me. And, sensing that I didn't understand his new interests any better than our parents did, Abbie kept his distance from his kid brother.

In the summer of 1958, after Abbie's junior year at Brandeis, he decided to embark alone on a European tour—London, Paris, Barcelona, Madrid. He ran with the bulls in Pamplona and would claim ever after that he'd been gored and had the scar to prove it. In Paris, he stumbled upon his first political demonstration. It was the summer when, with France losing the French-Algerian War, the government had collapsed and de Gaulle had been summoned from retirement to put the pieces back together. Just hours after getting off the plane from London, Abbie saw a mass of French students marching along the Champs Elysées singing, and joined them without a second thought. The next thing he knew, the world around him was a churning mass of soft bodies and swinging clubs:

> *this wave of club-swinging gendarmes swooped down on us, trapping students beneath their capes and pounding them to the ground. The whole area came alive with swarming, shoving students. I got clubbed to the ground, staggered up and ran, following racing bodies. . . . It was my first political demonstration. My first beating by police. To this day I have no idea what the marching and clubbing was about. . . . Paris spotted the troublemaker in me even before I did.*[4]

Abbie in the Paris of 1958 turned out to be like Candide in the Eldorado of gold and emeralds. His encounter didn't yet make sense to him, but he gloried in it anyway out of his pure love of experience.

Back at Brandeis for his senior year, Abbie didn't miss a single political or psychological heavyweight who came to visit. He heard lectures by Erik Erikson, the world-famous figure in the field of psychoanalysis and human development; political activist Dorothy Day, the founding editor of the *Catholic Worker,* who talked about the soup lines outside her Bowery mission; and Martin Luther King, Jr., speaking on the recent successful bus boycott in Montgomery, Alabama; among many others. But Abbie was still the political *ingénue* whose primary interests, other than the usual Saturday night escapades, were still perfectly conventional: He was chairman of the campus Film Society, president of the Psychology Club and, captain of the Tennis Team. Bud Collins, who was the tennis coach that year, describes Abbie on the court as an "ultraconservative," who stayed at the baseline but rarely missed a shot and always won. That year the team was unbeaten, probably the only time Brandeis has fielded a winning team in any sport.

Meanwhile, I was a University of Illinois freshman, with plans to become a business major. But lost among the more than 35,000 students, I spent the fall reeling from the sudden change of environment, recognizing for the first time how my family and friends had shielded me all my life, and how unprepared I felt without them.

On January 1, 1959, as Abbie prepared for his last semester at Brandeis, Fidel Castro entered Havana, placing a Communist regime within eighty miles of the U.S. Castro's ascendance signaled, if not an end to '50s isolationism, then at least a very large crack in its surface. And in March or April, Abbie drove to Harvard Stadium in Cambridge to hear the young Castro speak to his North American comrades.. Abbie remembered Fidel as "young and flashing in his green army fatigues. Tall and bearded, at thirty he could have been one of our younger professors, and here he was International Champ of Liberty; Guerrilla Fighter Extraordinaire. A real hero."[5] Abbie had heard that Castro liked to have U.S. newspapers flown in daily, and when they arrived he "quickly turned to the baseball scores and then threw the [rest of the] paper into the trash barrel."[6] Abbie loved that. The appeal to Abbie of a revolutionary hero with a passion for sports (and women and good cigars) was enormous. Why not live the macho myth and the ideals of justice and revolution at the same time? Castro's successful revolution was living proof that you could *challenge the power structure, give it your all, and win.* As the '60s approached, Castro was Abbie's money-back guarantee that the system was beatable.

* * *

Sometime in March 1959 I was sitting in my dorm room at the University of Illinois listening to Dave Brubeck when my roommate, an agriculture student, came in smelling of cow shit. He looked at me and asked me what kind of music I was listening to. He asked earnestly, and I have nothing against cow dung on a guy's boots, but something inside me snapped and I decided right then that I was going home without waiting for the semester to end—without waiting for the week to end. The University of Illinois wasn't a bad place, but it was a mistake for me to be there, too far from my brother and my parents. It was too large, and too dominated by ROTC and fraternities. The truth was I was as unhappy as I could be. And besides, Dad was sick; his business was suffering. I could be of use if I went home; I wasn't being of use to anybody if I didn't.

Abbie tried to persuade me on the phone to switch to Berkeley, where he was hoping to do an advanced degree in psychology after he graduated. He said I'd like the weather. But nothing could tempt me more than the thought of going home right then. I rented a U-Haul, packed my drum set, pulled my '54 green Ford convertible around to the front of the dorm and said goodbye to the cow shit in time to get a partial refund on Dad's tuition payment. Two days after reaching Ruth Street, I was back at work in the family business, and looking up old friends.

I had become friendly with a neighbor of my friend Richie Lenett named Yvette Leventhal. She and her husband Teddy lived just a few blocks away from us and they were both therapists, he a psychologist, she a psychiatric social worker. Both had been trained at the famed Menninger Institute at the University of Kansas. The Leventhals were the only head shrinkers I knew personally and they were a couple of true-blue originals. They became my unofficial therapists.

Lost in the '50s like all the rest of us, Yvette had no trouble expressing herself. Born and raised a nice Jewish girl from Ocean Parkway in Brooklyn, she never tried to cover her origins. We'd see her walking down Pleasant Street in Worcester wearing her gold leotard and tights, gold lamé slippers, with her big hair, white plastic sunglasses, globs of makeup, and two mini poodles by her side, and I loved her for that craziness. It was nice to see a grown-up act like that.

And then she was so smart underneath, with all her Freudianisms and her Behavioralisms.

On one of Abbie's frequent weekend visits home from Brandeis, I took him over to meet Yvette and they hit it off. Yvette soon became one of Abbie's most trusted advisors too. Soon, to Dad's horror— Dad liked to keep family business private—Abbie was quoting Yvette in family squabbles.

In September 1959, Abbie joined the graduate program in psychology at the University of California at Berkeley. His academic interests tended toward the offbeat: hypnosis, extrasensory perception, even witchcraft, which had been the subject of his senior dissertation. Almost immediately he realized that his real education was going to happen outside of school. Berkeley was first among the centers of discontent in America. Once again, Abbie just happened to be there.

Across the bay in North Beach, he started dropping in on the poetry readings that were already raging against official American culture—by Allen Ginsberg, Lawrence Ferlinghetti, Gregory Corso, Kenneth Rexroth, et al. In Abbie's autobiography, he remembers poets "shouting angry poems." It was the year of Ginsberg's "Howl": "I saw the best minds of my generation destroyed by madness, starving hysterical naked,/dragging themselves through the negro streets at dawn looking for an angry fix . . ."; and "America": "America I've given you all and now I'm nothing. . . ."

These poems, railing against "freeways fifty lanes wide/on a concrete continent/spaced with bland billboards/illustrating imbecile illusions of happiness,"[7] were filled not only with anger but also with alternative ways of seeing. Every one of them suggested implicitly that one didn't automatically have to be a part of the America they described with so much love mixed with so much scorn. Abbie was curious, and delighted by the energy of the readings but still about five years away from being able to apply any of what he was hearing to his own life. For now he still had both feet in the straight world. His main fascination was still sports, and when a school chum tried to tell him about the covert activities of a government organization called the CIA, Abbie exclaimed, "The CIA, what the hell is that?"[8]

In November, he formed a travel club, hiring a charter plane to ferry all the East Coast natives at "Cal" home for the holidays at a discount rate. He called it the BO-RAH Travel Club, an amalgam of bohemians and college rah-rahs. And he actually managed to make the thing work, getting a free ride home in the process. It would be the last Christmas Abbie would have nothing better to do than come home. Almost the day the 1950s ended, the world around him started changing very fast.

January and February 1960 saw the first stirrings of student activism making waves across the upper South. In February 1960, students at all-black Southern colleges were organizing sit-ins at lunch counters, providing a nonviolent model and a training ground for many of the black activists who would lead the civil rights movement during the next few years, and the mostly white student activists who would come after. It all began at a Woolworth's lunch counter in the town of Greensboro, North Carolina. Many from this first wave of black student activists would come to organize the Student Nonviolent Coordinating Committee (SNCC). Their goal was desegregation. Their history-making civil rights successes would grow into a large part of Act One of the two-act play that was the '60s. And Abbie still wasn't even thinking about becoming a part of it.

In the spring of 1960, during his second semester at Berkeley, Abbie was feeling lonely. He wrote to Ma and Dad to tell them how much he loved Sheila and missed her; he asked them to help pay for airfare for Sheila to come visit during the spring break in late March. To Dad the thought of Abbie in Berkeley, California, studying psychology and driving around in his yellow Volkswagen convertible was already a nightmare. Adding Sheila to the picture was more bohemianism than Dad could bear. But Ma took charge this time and sent Abbie the money anyway. Sheila arrived and they spent a wonderful week camping in some of the most picturesque countryside within driving distance of the Bay Area. The trip began with redwood forests and the hills of Sausalito and ended in a cabin by the sea in Big Sur, where Abbie and Sheila made love for the first time.

After Sheila left at the end of March, Abbie began to connect more with the political atmosphere of Berkeley; he began to feel for the first time that things concerned him personally. It wasn't a conscious choice. The ferment around him had finally reached him. His first political action came soon after.

Caryl Chessman had been convicted of rape and sentenced to die in the gas chamber in 1948 on the basis of circumstantial evidence. Chessman had managed to obtain repeated stays of execution and had even written several books in prison. He had convinced many people that he was innocent, and regardless of guilt or innocence had become the human face of the anti-capital punishment movement.

For twelve years, support for Chessman had grown steadily. His current execution date was May 1, 1960. As the date approached, petitions circulated across the country and silent vigils were organized at U.S. embassies all over the world. In California, there was a last-minute flurry of newspaper editorials and radio announcements pleading for Chessman's life to be spared.

On the night of April 30, Abbie joined a few hundred silent witnesses, including the actors Shirley MacLaine and Marlon Brando, who stood and waited in the light rain outside the walls of the San Quentin Federal Penitentiary in nearby San Rafael. Coffee and doughnuts were served to the demonstrators by prison staff. The warden himself addressed the protesters and announced that he was personally opposed to capital punishment. California Governor Pat Brown issued a statement from the governor's mansion that he too was against capital punishment—but that the laws of the state must be obeyed.

The next morning, May 1, it was still raining when the warden reappeared and announced to the crowd that Caryl Chessman had succumbed peacefully at 10:10 A.M.—according to the laws of the state of California. "Around me people were in tears," Abbie would write. "Someone moaned, 'No! No!' as if he had been wounded. No one shouted. No one threw a rock."[9]

On the way back to Berkeley, one of the people sharing a ride in the same car as Abbie asked, "How does that work? In a democracy, I mean. No one wants to see him die and the state kills him?!"

Less than two weeks later, Abbie witnessed firsthand another shattering local event. On the afternoon of May 13, 1960, House Un-American Activities Committee (HUAC) field hearings being held in San Francisco turned violent. One of the subpoenaed witnesses was a Berkeley professor; another was a sophomore who had allegedly been active in Leftist causes. Indignant at what seemed to be clear violations of political freedom, busloads of Berkeley students, including Abbie, were among those who came to protest.

No violence had been intended, but after the students were denied entrance to the crowded hearing room, they tried to push their way in and a policeman was knocked down. Suddenly all the police in the vicinity were wielding billy clubs and hoses. By the end of the half-hour battle, twelve people had been injured and fifty-two demonstrators had been arrested. If the Chessman vigil had been Abbie's first protest, the HUAC hearings gave Abbie an idea of some of the responses protests could elicit other than coffee and doughnuts.

Around the middle of May, Sheila called Abbie at school to say the rabbit had died: She was pregnant. For a few weeks, Abbie was on the phone almost daily to Yvette to help him decide between abortion and marriage. He told Yvette he thought Sheila was beautiful, exciting, and intelligent. He said he would not live with any other woman. He said Sheila was the one. But at the same time he was obviously scared. Yvette sensed his predicament and tried to persuade him against the marriage. But he wouldn't listen, he couldn't listen.

To Sheila, he was full of certainties: "I'll be there in a week. We can get married," he told her. Sheila hadn't planned on that. But neither did she want an abortion.

Abbie came home in his yellow Volkswagen special, moved back into our parents' house on Ruth Street, and began to make preparations for his wedding. With help from Dick Lazarus, one of his Berkeley professors, Abbie landed a job at Worcester State Hospital that started right away. That year the state of Massachusetts had more federally funded psychologist positions than it had applicants. So the state loosened its academic requirements and allowed some candidates who had not finished their studies to be licensed. Dad was unimpressed. He considered psychology voodoo science. But to Ma, Abbie's new job was the next best thing to having the doctor-son she'd dreamed of, and she was happy. And Abbie himself felt that he was at the beginning of a brilliant career. His first assignment, which lasted through the summer and into the fall, was to interview some of the forty couples gathered by the local Lutheran church for a study on "Normalcy in the Community."

So Abbie was a psychologist, about to be married, well on his way up the ladder of success, just like we had all expected he would be by now. Abbie didn't consider himself to be choosing a lifestyle. Like a lot of people, he did not see any alternative to the one lifestyle that was grabbing him by the balls. He wasn't choosing to conform. He didn't think about it in those terms. It would never have occurred to him that there might be a conflict between his personality and his current aspirations. Getting a job and getting married were things you did. There wasn't really any alternative, wasn't any other place you could go, in 1960.

Almost from the hour of his return, Abbie and Dad fought. The skirmishes centered on the insurance on the Volkswagen. Abbie had it registered in California, where auto insurance was not compulsory. Dad insisted that he register it in Massachusetts and get insurance as required by state law. But Abbie didn't see it that way. He wasn't planning on getting into any accidents, so why waste the money on insurance? Dad was apoplectic. To Dad, Abbie's forthcoming wedding was a mistake, his job was unimportant, and being uninsured was the icing on the cake.

The wedding, in Warwick, Rhode Island, on July 10, was a traditional affair. Abbie wore white—a showy rented tux—and a black bow tie. His Brandeis roommate Manny Schreiber was his best man. There was a lot of back slapping and an enormous buffet built around a mountain of oleomargarine carved in the shape of a swan. Dad got drunk on the punch and cursed Brandeis to anyone who would listen. Uncle Al, Dad's brother, walked around with his right sleeve rolled up, swinging his forearm up and down, and saying loudly, "The kid's got a schlong the size of an elephant."

Abbie and Sheila got lost on their way to their honeymoon and ended up in a half-deserted hotel. While Sheila vomited in the bathroom, Abbie read a book titled *Love without Fear* and listened to his own terror-stricken interior monologue: "She doesn't close the bathroom door. What am I doing here? We're strangers. No we're not. She's my wife. Shouldn't she close the door? What should I do when it's my turn to go?"[10]

A few weeks after the wedding, Abbie was driving down Shrewsbury Street one afternoon when he rammed another car at a traffic light. He was arrested for being uninsured. From the police station, he had to call Dad at the office and ask him to put up a substantial bond for the damage done to the other car. It was Abbie's first arrest, and perhaps his last concession to Dad while Dad was alive, the last time he would say, "Dad, you were right."

Abbie and Sheila rented one floor of a two-family house on Trowbridge Road in Worcester, in a neighborhood of young married professionals in the shadow of Worcester Tech, and began their young married life with all the usual appurtenances and the conviction that nothing at all was wrong. Abbie went to work every morning wearing a thin tie and sports jacket, and with his hair neatly cropped. He looked like a psychologist, with just a tasteful touch of bohemia—basketball sneakers instead of dress shoes. And he looked forward happily to performing his own personal experiment on the subject of normalcy. Sheila stayed home, painting her paintings, large, colorful abstractions, and playing the part of Abbie's young, pretty, and interesting young wife. And that summer she started the Trowbridge Candle Company, making candles in their kitchen to bring in extra money.

From almost the first day, with Sheila now visibly pregnant, the marriage was fouled by daily disagreements. Abbie had entered the marriage with the best of intentions. He genuinely wanted and expected his marriage to work. But husband and wife were both extremely stubborn. Years later, Abbie would write, "I didn't know how to be married. As it turned out, she didn't know how to be married either. She would say she did. And I would say she didn't. Silence. 'I do.' 'You don't.' 'I do.' "[11]

Both Sheila and Abbie were serious about their political activities. But other than that, they had little in common. And in many ways, Sheila's dissatisfaction with their marriage may have been more forceful than Abbie's, since he at least was living a full life outside the home, whereas her outside life had abruptly terminated when her pregnancy and marriage had begun.

At a few minutes before midnight on December 31, 1960, as the apple began its descent in Times Square, their first child, Andrew, was born, raising the stakes further on Abbie and Sheila's life together. Sheila continued to paint, now having their infant son to look after as well.

In the two years Abbie stayed at Worcester State, he made a life for himself—replacing the wrecked Volks with a used Volvo because it seemed just the thing for a young psychologist, and trying to enjoy going home in the evenings to Sheila and Andrew. He went bowling a couple of nights a week with his old friends from high school. At work, the staff found him likeable and loved the stories he told them of the exploits of his reckless youth. His exuberance was infectious: Whether the subject was sex, sports, or patient care, he made things exciting.

Abbie had organized a softball game for the patients a couple of times a week. He pitched at these games, and marveled at the patients' ability to enjoy the fun without paying any attention to the rules. His centerfielder was a heavily medicated schizophrenic who always dropped the ball. Abbie called him Jethro, after the Boston Braves' centerfielder, Sam Jethro. A batter would hit the ball and then run straight to third, or the pitcher's mound, where Abbie would give him a big hug before walking him to first. Abbie sometimes called me in the evening to give me the play-by-play on the day's game. We laughed at the patients, but for Abbie, laughing at them was a way of relating to them, not a way of shutting them out. He laughed at me and at himself in the same way.

And the more intractable his problems at home became, the more he poured his boundless energy into his work and outside activities. At Worcester State, Abbie felt that he was helping people whom others tended to scorn, and that satisfied some very deep need in him. But it reached the point where each hour of fulfillment on the job seemed to be matched by one of trouble at home.

Abbie and I used to have lunch at a Greek social club near Worcester Medical, where I was working with Dad. Abbie would

double-park out back and honk twice. I'd drop whatever I was doing
and rush out to meet him in thirty seconds flat, by which time Abbie
was already talking with the bookmakers who hung around the parking lot, waiting for the limousine to take them to the Suffolk, Rockingham, Lincoln, or Narragansett horseracing tracks. We'd head off
on foot to "the club," as we called it, to stuff ourselves on stuffed
cabbage, potatoes, moussaka, and baklava.

Over lunch, Abbie talked and I listened. He usually had a lot
more answers than questions. And he wanted me to know everything
that was happening to him. He'd describe how he administered Ror-
schach tests on patients prior to their being started on medication.
He'd tell me about the most recent softball game. And he talked
about the fierce rivalry between the psychiatrists who vaunted the
healing power of drugs, and the psychologists who wanted to rely
more on testing and therapy. Abbie sided with the psychologists, of
course, and used all his hustling experience to delay having his patients put on drugs.

Usually by the end of our lunches at "the club," Abbie finally got
around to what he most wanted to talk about: his problems at home.
He would tell me that he wasn't getting enough sex, that Sheila was
rejecting him sexually. And I got the impression that Abbie's sexual
energy may have frightened her. I was having trouble with my girlfriend, a Boston University student from New York named Bobbi, so
Abbie and I commiserated and got to laugh together at our various
romantic trials.

In a way my life echoed Abbie's. Sharing an apartment in Boston,
commuting back to Worcester Medical to work part-time selling am-
phetamines to doctors for five dollars a thousand (which they then
sold to their patients for ten dollars a hundred), and attending business classes in the evening, I felt that my career was back on track. But
my inner life was a shambles. Bobbi, a tall liberal arts student with a
quick wit, was the first girl I had ever fallen in love with. I was drowning in new emotions, feeling intensely unhappy, and had no idea who
I was.

Sitting around his living room one evening, with Sheila painting
in the next room, Abbie got me talking and analyzed me with his
latest, mostly Freudian, theories. His professional opinion was that

my problem went deeper than my difficulties with my girlfriend. Abbie knew I talked informally with Teddy and Yvette about my problems, but he decided I needed something "more intense," and suggested I see a therapist he knew at Worcester State. With no other options, I went along. What Abbie hadn't told me was that the doctor's work involved studying responses to LSD in humans, mostly schizophrenics. Without knowing what I was getting into, I became a paid volunteer.

The next thing I remember I was sitting in the waiting room watching a parade of fellow volunteers pass by, all institutionalized patients at Worcester State, many of them obviously under heavy sedation. It was like a scene from *Night of the Living Dead*. I wondered, How crazy am I?

The good doctor greeted me at his office door, showed me to a chair, and spoke not another word for the next hour as I talked on and on about Bobbi, my brother, and our parents. At the end of the session, he offered me what turned out to be a low-dosage LSD sample in a cup, which I dutifully ingested.

Immediately I was ushered into a room with a couch, mood music coming through a loudspeaker, and a wall made of dark glass through which, I assume, they monitored me. After a few minutes, the drug hit me. Mostly, the effect was perceptual: straight lines curved, objects warped, colors took on a magical phosphorescence. The gravitational pull seemed to ease, leaving me with the impression that I was floating. Subtly, the hallucinations suggested a whole other reality, and made me feel that the everyday reality we normally accept as concrete, objective fact was actually just one perceptual twist among an infinite number of possibilities. That was what boggled the mind, like I had walked into a fourth dimension.

As I was leaving the hospital afterward, I saw Abbie out on the grounds, leading a group of patients in a game of softball. I started to move toward them, to join the game. Then I had a horrible intuition, like a daydream, in which I saw myself on the field playing softball the way Abbie had described the patients playing, completely without rules, without purpose, hitting the ball in any direction, running in any direction. Suddenly nauseous, I found a seat on a bench, then left the hospital without saying a word to my brother.

I participated in the low-dosage LSD experiment twice, and each time the experience was mildly mind-stretching. But I was in no condition to enjoy what I felt while on the drug. There was not yet any context, as there would be in the late '60s, of openness, of exploration into alternative realities. Not in the culture and not in our minds. I felt totally unprepared for the experience I'd had, and it left me shaken. I blamed Abbie for bad advice carelessly given and promised myself I wouldn't turn to him again anytime soon. My confusion and unhappiness only increased in the next few weeks. Then came the serious accident that you could say was my final SOS.

When you need help, the people who care about you notice and want to help, but mostly they don't know how; they just can't touch the part of you that's hurting. And, in a way, that's what hurts the most, the feeling that your pain is a world all its own that no one can enter. I was sitting with my friend Richie Lenett on the porch of another friend's house one afternoon in August 1960, when Richie suggested that I lighten up a little on Bobbi and try to date other people. He wanted to call an old girlfriend of mine who was a friend of his and set us up. I told him to forget it. But he wasn't listening. He got up, went into the adjoining kitchen, and started to make the call. Before I even knew what I was doing, I stood up and lunged through the plate glass door that separated us to stop him. There was blood everywhere. My right arm, hanging heavily like a wet rag, was nearly severed. The last thing I remembered was the look of helplessness on Richie's face as he stood there, still holding the phone. Then I passed out and when I came around I was in the hospital emergency room. Today my right arm is still partly paralyzed and held together with plastic. It is like a shy acquaintance I can't get rid of, who goes wherever I go.

While in the hospital after injuring my arm, I was treated with Percodan, a powerful narcotic painkiller. In August 1961, about a year after the injury, I was still taking Percodan for the pain. A year of Percodan three or four times a day can add up to a pretty serious addiction. Abbie knew exactly what was going on. He was sensitive enough not to nag me about it but he was watching closely. And at some point he decided on his own that my ongoing depression had a lot to do with the Percodan.

Almost as if it were a little game he was teaching me, Abbie showed me all he knew about self-hypnosis, something he'd been playing around with since high school. He insisted that I could learn to live with the pain without the pills through hypnosis. I went along. Over a period of weeks, Abbie hypnotized me a dozen times. And the funny thing was, it worked. He got me off the Percodan. And that's how it was sometimes with Abbie: When you came to him with high expectations, he'd sometimes let you down, almost like he needed to be free of them; then the minute you gave up on him, he'd surprise you; he'd show up just when you needed him, with a smile on his face, solid as a rock.

At Worcester State, Abbie became particularly close to one of the staff psychologists, Eli Strum, a three-hundred-pound, blond-haired, blue-eyed bon vivant. Eli liked Abbie's stories and Abbie liked Eli's openmindedness. They both favored talk therapy and were critical of the staff doctors who relied too heavily on medication. But the main enthusiasm they shared was an interest in film.

Abbie had always wanted to be on *The $64,000 Question,* and if he'd ever gotten on, the subject he would have chosen first was movies. His bookshelves were filled with books on film; he dreamed that someday he'd be a director. But it was Eli who introduced the art films of the European directors to Abbie. Bergman became Abbie's favorite for a while, then Fellini. Abbie was easily drawn to these self-aware and unembarrassed artists who seemed able to speak with authority on the meaning of life, and the hunger in the soul. In Fellini and Chaplin, Abbie saw great artists who were able to be serious and funny at the same time, something unthinkable of his college idols like Camus.

In September 1961, Abbie talked a Lebanese friend of our father's, a used car salesman named Duddy Massad, into letting Abbie open an art cinema house in an empty movie theater building he owned. Abbie convinced him that art films were going to be the wave of the future. And Duddy, who probably hadn't ever seen an art film, went along. The Park Arts became Abbie's newest passion. He selected the films and wrote the program notes. For music, Abbie brought over his own phonograph and record collection. He used to work at the theater from 5:30 P.M. until midnight, going there directly from Worcester State. The wife of the projectionist used to bring him meatball and sausage sandwiches out of pity.

Within weeks it became clear that the Park Arts wasn't going to be a profitable venture. And I remember Duddy trying to pressure Abbie into having a popcorn stand on the premises so that he might at least have a chance to recoup some of his lost investment. And Abbie refused, saying that people had to be able to think while they watched these films and that people eating popcorn in the theater would make too much noise.

My favorite memory of the Park Arts Theatre was that about a month after it opened Abbie was playing a documentary about the Newport Jazz festival, and from the projection room he noticed me dancing in the aisles to the blues singer Big Mae Bell. Seeing how much I enjoyed the show, Abbie scheduled a repeat performance for the following Saturday night at midnight, and let me invite all my friends to come free.

At the Park Arts, Abbie was searching for a new way to be himself, testing a new persona as if he didn't have a moment to lose. Listen to him being interviewed by the *Worcester Telegram* in an article that appeared in October 1961, soon after the Park Arts opened, sounding off with all the unblemished intellectual enthusiasm of a young Truffaut:

> *In a way I may be idealistic, but I believe there's entertainment in a thought-provoking adult theme. . . . To me, a Hollywood production which is geared to the emotions of a mass audience and which inevitably ends happily is obscene. Such a production is obscene because it isn't real . . .*[12]

Abbie was looking for new ideas and a new way of being in the world. In a way, in his job and marriage he was living out the kind of happy ending he now found despicable in Hollywood movies. And his alienation from the "obscene" Hollywood values of the day was also an expression of the nausea his own life inspired in him:

*Looking back, I could scarcely say I was in love with Sheila
or she with me. . . . We respected each other as worthy opponents in some eternal struggle of the sexes.*[13]

I don't think he ever came to understand his marriage to Sheila,
because I don't think he ever acknowledged, even to himself, how
confused and unready he was. I don't doubt that he had loved her.
Abbie didn't fight harder to save his marriage only because he didn't
know how. A truly conventional marriage would have been impossible for Abbie. And an unconventional marriage wasn't yet something
any of us could have considered or even imagined.

If Abbie had been able to make his relationship with his wife
work, then his idyll would have been complete, and he might have
remained in Worcester, his father's son—and his son's father—to the
end. Instead, his contentious marriage became the catalyst with
which to probe his own deep inner dissatisfaction and push beyond
his nice little life. In the end, Abbie would forgo the stability and
fulfillment of work he valued, and the satisfaction he might have
found in fatherhood, in order to get away from Sheila, establishing
what would become a pattern in his life. Abbie always had reasons
for leaving, good reasons usually, perhaps never quite admitting to
himself that his guiding light, the north star he followed faithfully,
was his own need for change, what he called "action," what others
have called his egotism. Whatever the reason, by 1962, after a couple
of years in which Abbie had built a life around his faith in psychother-
apy, marriage, and foreign films, he found them to be false gods and
moved on to other things.

Chapter Four

~~~

1962–1966

The things that I learned in the early sixties [as a local activist in Worcester] were lessons that I carried with me throughout my career . . . how the ball of wax is put together, and more importantly, how to take it apart: how power structures control people and how they divide people, how the gaps are between the mythology of what is said and reality as it exists; the hidden oppression and the hidden resistance to oppression.

—ABBIE

IN EARLY 1962, Abbie participated in a signature drive to put Stuart Hughes, a dovish Harvard professor who was also co-chairman of the Committee for a Sane Nuclear Policy (SANE), on the ballot as a peace candidate in the Democratic primary for senator. It was the first time Abbie had taken his passionate, obsessive, manic energy and applied it to a political cause, "bouncing," he would write, "from art to politics."

Having recently left his Worcester State job, Abbie had enough free time to lead the drive in central and western Massachusetts. He organized teams of volunteers to man tables and knock on doors throughout the region. The blitz worked. Largely due to Abbie's efforts, the campaign obtained nearly 150,000 signatures and Hughes got on the ballot. Now, partly inspired by the growing civil rights movement, the Hughes organization, and Abbie in particular, used every organizing technique they could learn or invent, from sit-down afternoon teas, bake sales and car washes, to press conferences and head-to-head negotiations with union leaders, government officials, and city desk editors. By October, polls showed Hughes favored by up to 20 percent of the electorate. Not enough to win but enough to establish an important state-wide power base for future elections.

Just as the Hughes campaign was gaining momentum, the Cuban Missile Crisis came along, and Hughes went on record attacking President Kennedy for his brinksmanship. To do that in Massachusetts was like attacking the pope in Rome, and in a matter of days the support that had been building for Hughes evaporated, and he eventually lost the race badly.

Despite the discouraging conclusion, it had been an exhilarating few months for Abbie. He had participated in a significant way in a powerful grassroots campaign that had introduced him to Worcester's close-knit community of civil rights activists. In particular, he had met Father Bernie Gilgun, a fiery and impassioned orator, who with other Catholic activists had just opened the Phoenix, a local store front meeting place, and D'Army Bailey, an angry black Clark University student who had been thrown out of the University of Louisiana for civil rights activities.

But Abbie still didn't know what he wanted to do with his life. Alarmingly, shortly after the November election, sick at heart on account of his marriage not working out, he packed two suitcases and left for New York City, leaving his wife and son with hardly a word of explanation. He got a job at the new Baronet Theater on Third Avenue near Fifty-Ninth Street and found an apartment across town on West Seventy-Sixth Street in Manhattan. Within a few weeks he was calling to tell me, not how his job was going, but that the best place in New York City to find a piece of ass was Bloomingdale's department store.

I had been drafted into the army in the summer of 1961, during the Berlin Wall Crisis, and then managed through a friend of Dad's in the National Guard to get preenlisted into the Guard, where I would be a medic in the 121st Battalion. My training consisted of weekly meetings in Worcester, weekend duty once a month, plus two weeks in the summer, until February 1962 when, after the longest bus ride of my life, I arrived for basic training at Fort Dix in New Jersey, followed by O.J.T. (on-the-job training) at Walson Army Hospital, which was attached to Fort Dix. That was when I first began to hear about a "police action," soon upgraded to an "incursion," in Southeast Asia. They told us that "there was a possibility that in thirty days we'd ship off to Saigon." The idea wasn't necessarily unappealing. I'd always wanted to be a doctor or veterinarian and here I was learning emergency surgery, suturing, patient care. I was single and the Far East sounded attractive.

Then, one by one at first, and then in a trickle, black plastic body bags started arriving out of the side doors of cargo planes returning from Southeast Asia. There weren't many, but I remember seeing them, staring at them, wondering what they meant, and not coming up with any answers at all. The hard heaviness of those body bags, unyielding of meaning, was my introduction to the Vietnam War, somewhat different from Abbie's a few years later. It wouldn't have occurred to me to try to put a stop to the body bags coming out of those planes, any more than a few years later it wouldn't have occurred to Abbie not to try and stop them. We were traveling different roads, although we didn't know it yet.

After basic training ended, I was still returning to active duty for one weekend a month as part of my National Guard duty. Abbie had recently been promoted to manage the Baronet's soon-to-be-opened twin theater, the Coronet, right next door. Sometimes, before returning to Worcester, I'd go into New York and visit Abbie, and together we would go down to the Village to see Lenny Bruce or Odetta, the two artists he admired the most at the time. Abbie was making the best of things and trying to enjoy himself, but, although he didn't want to admit it, he felt alone and confused without Sheila and Andrew. Living in his cramped studio apartment, without friends, the contrast between his present existence and the full life he'd left behind in Worcester was unbearable to him.

In the early spring of 1963, Abbie was blamed for problems that had occurred during the grand opening of the Coronet, and he quit. Without a job he began to realize how much he missed Sheila and their life together and kept calling her to tell her so. He wanted to come home and make a new start. Our whole family became embroiled in the discussion, with Dad against his returning to Sheila, whom he didn't like, and Ma in favor of his going back to her, because she was afraid of what might happen to him alone in New York City. In February or March, Sheila visited Abbie in New York, then it was Abbie's turn to visit her. And in the middle of the chaos, Abbie and Sheila decided to make another go of their marriage. Abbie returned home to Worcester. Soon afterward, Sheila discovered she was pregnant again. Abbie got a job as a regional salesman for Westwood Pharmaceuticals.

This was the year when Timothy Leary got himself tossed out of Harvard for meddling with the minds of undergraduates and took his experiments to a millionaire heir's mansion in upstate New York, where psilocybin was replaced with the stronger LSD. But Abbie still hadn't heard of Tim Leary, or the words "Tune in, turn on, drop out." He needed something else in his life, but didn't know what. Sheila decided that what Abbie needed was a cause he could believe in, and that his finding one would help save their marriage.

The Westwood job, with its good salary, free time, and company car, made intense political activity possible; after six months or so, Abbie found he could keep up appearances working at the job no more than ten hours a week. And Sheila constantly encouraged him in his political attachments, partly because she saw their shared political activism as the only hope for their marriage. They bought a house in Worcester. Their second child, Ilya, also called Amy, was born on November 11, 1963. This was the time of Abbie's real beginning, the time when he chose the path that he would pursue, without straying, for the rest of his life. But it wasn't his family life that made it so. Increasingly, life for Abbie began and ended with his work in the civil rights movement. In his autobiography, he would refer to 1963–1965 as "filled with the cry of a movement at its purest moment."[1]

The assassination of JFK on November 22, 1963, colored that moment with the taint of tragedy, since, despite everything, young people in America felt a sense of kinship with the president. As Abbie wrote of that day, "Kennedy heated our passion for change, and when he was killed that chilly day in November, we mourned. Kennedy often lied to our generation, but nevertheless he made us believe we could change the course of history. Inspiration can come from strange and unusual places."[2]

Together with Father Gilgun and D'Army Bailey, Abbie organized a takeover from within of the placid local National Association for the Advancement of Colored People (NAACP) chapter by recruiting large numbers of new members and setting up a Direct Action Committee to bypass the established leadership. The combination of Abbie's energy, Bailey's righteous anger, and Bernie Gilgun's passionate speeches mobilized people in Worcester in a way that nothing else could have. "An Irish priest, a Jewish salesman, and a hungry black law student," Abbie would write: "We were the perfect American Trinity."[3]

Meetings that had attracted two dozen people now attracted hundreds. Within months, the three had transformed the local NAACP into one of the most militant chapters in the country and had started up a local Congress on Racial Equality (CORE) chapter as well. There were voter registration drives. Discrimination suits were filed against landlords. Stores were picketed. Daycare centers were established. At the Worcester Student Association, which Bailey started up, students were assigned the task of researching the minority hiring practices of local companies. Then the consortium of organizations organized protest marches and boycotts against companies with unfair practices.

I remember one day at Worcester Medical Supply when Dad got a call from the Wyman-Gordon defense plant, one of Worcester's largest employers and an important account of ours. After picket lines had failed to elicit a more equitable hiring policy, the demonstrators had switched to civil disobedience, lying down before the front gates, preventing the trucks from entering the plant. Abbie was among the first to lie down in front of the trucks. Someone had recognized him and called Dad.

As Dad listened to the report of his son's actions, his face turned bright red and then deathly pale. He could only understand what Abbie was doing as an attack on himself personally, an attempt to embarrass him. In his autobiography, Abbie remembers Dad coming to the demonstration and describes the confrontation in a humorous light: " 'Okay! Okay!' says my father. 'So it's what you believe in. But do you have to get your shirt so dirty?' "[4] But, in reality, Dad could neither understand nor forgive Abbie for what Dad saw as the shame his eldest son was bringing on the family.

In February 1964, Abbie began publishing *The Drum*, which served the local activist community by listing movement activities, analyzing pending civil rights legislation, reprinting the texts of freedom songs, and promoting fund-raising events. And as "program director" for Gilgun's Phoenix, Abbie organized Friday night discussion programs, inviting people like Father Robert Drinan, the dissident Jesuit priest from Boston College who was later elected to Congress; Howard Zinn, the radical historian from Boston University; and Dorothy Day, the editor of the *Catholic Worker* whom Abbie had once heard speak at Brandeis.

Often Abbie and Sheila hosted dinners for visiting activists at their home. And there were movement slogans painted on signs on their front lawn. Abbie and Sheila both led Friday night Phoenix discussions, his on Maslow's self-actualizing philosophy, hers on sexism in Henry Miller's writings during a panel on Betty Friedan's *The Feminine Mystique*. To illustrate her point, Sheila read aloud a steamy section from Miller.

In early 1964, Abbie was enlisted as a worker for the Student Nonviolent Coordinating Committee (SNCC). And although Abbie went south only briefly for Freedom Summer that year, he mobilized support groups in the Worcester area to raise funds. And in August he traveled to Atlantic City to support the Mississippi Freedom Democratic Party which was attempting to loosen the stranglehold of the one-party South at the 1964 Democratic National Convention. And after Prospect House was founded in Worcester, modeled after the Freedom Houses in Mississippi, Abbie became heavily involved in its ongoing programs.

In the spring of 1965, the Voting Rights Act was passed by Congress, officially institutionalizing civil rights as what '60s historian Todd Gitlin would later call "an apple-pie issue."[5] But this nod from the Johnson establishment came too late to mean as much to the activists whose accomplishments it encoded into law as it would have had it come earlier. Immediately, Abbie organized a sit-in at the Worcester FBI offices protesting nonenforcement of the new law.

Abbie was making plans to spend the summer doing civil rights work down South, while Sheila stayed home with the kids. In a letter to Father Gilgun, Abbie tried to describe the spirit that moved him. The portrait he painted of himself was telling. He was first and foremost, he said, "a guy who loves action"—and who hated the status quo. As to why he was headed down to Mississippi, the reasons Abbie gave Gilgun weren't just political; they were personal. He needed the Movement, he said. He wanted to be with people who were deeply committed to change.

Abbie left Boston for Jackson, Mississippi, at the beginning of July. On July 2, FBI agents filed their first report on Abbie's activities. The report included mention of an authorized phone tap on Abbie's home.[6]

Abbie arrived in McComb, Mississippi, and Americus, Georgia, at a time when the solid front of the civil rights movement was beginning to break apart. In McComb, Abbie taught U.S. history, arithmetic, and reading at a freedom school. On an almost daily basis, he participated in marches, got arrested, made bail, and marched again. When he returned north, he brought with him not only a wealth of new organizing experience but also a newfound humility based on a recognition of the distance that can exist between the organizers and the people they are trying to organize. This was something Abbie hadn't felt in Worcester, where the people he was organizing, and even the people he was organizing against, felt almost as close as family members. But in the South, he entered a more complex historical reality.

One day while he was teaching in McComb, the casket of a local black soldier killed in Vietnam was brought into the school, and Abbie was shocked to find that none of the black students were willing to talk about it: "It was difficult for a middle-class white to understand their resignation in the face of death. That was the moment I most felt the separation between myself and those I wanted to organize. It was an emotional chasm no amount of good feelings could overcome."[7]

In the fall of 1965, Abbie and Sheila participated in Worcester's earliest peace demonstrations. And as the anti-war movement gained force, it called forth a much more widespread and hateful countermovement than anything Abbie had experienced previously. After all, opposing the government during a war has always been the least popular thing anyone can do in America. Protesters were called traitors and Communists. Organizers received threats. A bomb was left on a porch. Protesters were thrown to the ground and beaten while police looked on. Suddenly it looked to Abbie as if the challenge up North might be an even harder battle to win than the fight against racism in the South.

Around the same time Abbie was broadening his political activities to include the early actions of the anti-war movement, he was also beginning to experiment with drugs. It was already more than a year since Ken Kesey's Merry Pranksters had set out on their journey around the country seeking enlightenment or drug-induced madness in a beat-up bus they called "FURTHER." But it was still a few years before a whole generation would begin to seek alternative realities through drugs. Abbie first tried LSD with his friend and former roommate Manny Schreiber. Manny, now an army psychologist, had access to the drug because the army was conducting secret experiments with LSD as a possible weapon of war. Pretty soon Abbie and his Worcester artist friend Marty Carey were doing acid and smoking grass whenever they could get hold of it—still not very often in 1965 and early 1966.

I'm looking at a photo of Abbie taken on January 21, 1966. He's standing up at a local political meeting in Worcester, wearing the SNCC "uniform"—white shirt, thin, dark tie loose at the collar, and cotton suit with narrow lapels. But his hair is still combed up high over his forehead like he'd walked right off the set of *West Side Story,* a vestige of his high school days, and there is as much mischief as earnestness in his eyes. I believe that by then he'd set his course in life, knew how important a choice he'd made, but perhaps still didn't understand what the lasting ramifications would be.

In the spring of 1966, Westwood Pharmaceuticals gave Abbie a gentle push in the right direction when they finally realized how little Abbie had been doing for them and fired him. The company car he now had to return carried "SNCC" vanity plates Abbie had purchased on his expense account. Meanwhile Abbie and Sheila's marriage had deteriorated to the point where they had begun talking divorce.

In August 1966 I married Joan Bressman, whom I'd first met three years earlier. All I'd seen in Joan at first was a typical Emerson College coed. But then her parents happened to drive up in their rickety Nash Rambler—not exactly an ostentatious display of materialistic values. I started talking to Joan and immediately got a taste of her caustic sense of humor. We went on a few dates, and before I knew it I was in love. Dad loved Joan from the very first time he met her. After the fiasco of Abbie's first marriage, Dad took to "my Joanie" as he called her, as if she were the first rose of summer, someone to give him hope of grandchildren continuing the family traditions.

We got married in a weekend-long affair at the Malverne Jewish Center (respectable, but not religious) near her parents' home on Long Island. On Saturday, the day before the wedding, Abbie arrived passing out joints to all my friends. For most of them, it was their first time. On Sunday, in his black tux, with closely cropped hair, Abbie still looked like a man with success on his mind, but it was just an illusion. He was happy for me but not necessarily proud of what I was doing—marrying the nice Jewish girl from Long Island, running the family business, etc. And although he had a good time that weekend, his life was already moving elsewhere. To anyone who asked, Abbie would say his marriage to Sheila was over. He was going forward with the divorce, not yet clear about what he would do next. Sheila came alone to the wedding ceremony and left soon after. I don't remember seeing Abbie and her together at all. Without its having been planned that way, my wedding was a kind of celebration for Abbie as well, his farewell to the life he'd known.

A few weeks later, Abbie again filled two suitcases with his belongings and gave his bowling balls and television set to his friend Paul Cotton. He moved Sheila and their two kids into an apartment on Massachusetts Avenue in Cambridge. The house they had bought together was sold.

Sheila had been the catalyst, the transformational force, for change in Abbie's life. During the years that he pursued her, married her, and tried to make their life together work, she had represented all his best impulses. It was while he was with her that Abbie committed himself to the highest principles. He was now a radically different person from when he'd first left Worcester, and most of that metamorphosis had happened in the fertile angst of his relationship with Sheila. He had found his calling, thanks in large part to her. But despite Sheila's influence, and despite their passionate lovemaking, they had never been happy. Their marriage had failed. Abbie was moving on.

For Sheila's move to Cambridge Abbie borrowed friend and fellow activist Dan Dick's Volkswagen van, and Dan went along to give a hand. On the hour-long ride, Abbie talked almost non-stop about how hard it had been to keep the marriage together, and how hard it was now to have to leave it behind. But writing about the move later, the image Abbie liked to use is revealing: He said he felt like "a kid shortstop being called up to the majors."[8]

One subject that never came up during the drive to Cambridge was Lenny Bruce's recent death from a morphine overdose, on August 3. I think the death of the artist he most identified with may have felt to Abbie like a brush with his own mortality, and impressed upon him the urgency of getting on with what he had to do.

Abbie's divorce from Sheila wasn't officially granted until November 4, 1966, and not finalized until May 1, 1967, less than seven stormy years after it began. But by late September 1966, just weeks after leaving, Abbie had already put his old life behind him. This time there was no talk about missing Sheila. That chapter in his life was officially closed, this time for good.

Years later, Abbie would look back on his Worcester experience with pride and satisfaction: "The things that I learned in the early sixties in the social movements were lessons that I carried with me throughout my career . . . how the ball of wax is put together, and more importantly, how to take it apart: how power structures control people and how they divide people, how the gaps are between the mythology of what is said and reality as it exists; the hidden oppression and the hidden resistance to oppression."[9]

He was off to find the '60s, and now, finally, the new youth culture he was looking for was out there and ready for him. The irony was that Abbie, who will always be associated in our minds with that youth culture, was turning thirty now and a good ten years older than most of the people who would share it with him, and ten years politically more experienced. By the time the youth of America began to awaken to the anti-war movement and the counterculture that went with it, Abbie had had a long running start.

Now the Revolution begins.

—FIDEL CASTRO

ABBIE ARRIVED ON New York's Lower East Side convinced that America desperately needed to be more free. The sexual revolution, the drugs, the music, and even new clothing styles and long hair represented chinks in the walls of the power structure, and thus were the building blocks of a new nation. If all the fun, all the excitement, all the good sex could be on our side, we could not lose the battle for the hearts and minds of the people—and that, after all, was what he was fighting for. Abbie wasn't a hippie and he wasn't even a typical Lower East Sider. He was still, compared to his new crowd, a pretty straight-looking SNCC staffer, a politico, who believed you could solve problems through discussion and hard work. But his openness to experience pushed him right into the middle of what was happening anyway.

He opened Liberty House in the West Village as a continuation of a project he had begun in Worcester, selling handicrafts from the Poor People's Corporation of Mississippi as a way to raise consciousness in the North and generate cash to send back down South to support worker-owned enterprises. He lived with a roommate on Avenue C and Eleventh Street in a $49-a-month railroad apartment and called himself a Marxist.

That fall Joan and I were just getting to know one another as husband and wife, and we often visited her parents on Long Island. Abbie always made sure he was on our itinerary, calling us before we left home, then calling Joan's parents to see if we'd arrived. He wanted to show me the changes going on in and around him.

On our way to dinner in Manhattan, Joan and I would show up at Abbie's apartment in our dining-out-in-New-York smartest clothes, and walk in to hear strange music, smell a mixture of dope and incense, and then see Abbie, his roommate Harvey, and a few other people sprawled around the apartment. Abbie might be zonked out on acid. And almost before we had a chance to sit down, and without actually saying hello, he would launch into what sounded like a speech—"the new cultural revolution is coming," etc.

It looked to me like Abbie was just having fun. I didn't take it any further than that; when I tried, I felt confused. I was working to make a success out of a business and a marriage. Abbie had left his marriage and job behind him. I wasn't angry at him. But for the moment, Abbie's world and mine seemed to have nothing in common. Abbie was still a part of my life, but not in a way that could make sense to me. I felt as if together we were mourning the passing of a loved one. Not him or me exactly. . . . Our past, I suppose, suddenly seemed closed to us, and I couldn't do anything about it.

In 1966 the civil rights movement that Abbie loved was rapidly changing. Its core was becoming more militant as the Black Power movement gained momentum, while middle-class whites were turning to the anti-war effort on one hand, and a freer lifestyle on the other. Abbie saw both the increased political will and the new culture as equally important to what he increasingly saw as a second American Revolution in the making.

That winter at a National SNCC conference all white members were purged from the organization. Abbie was outraged and decided to go public in a long essay that was published by the *Village Voice*, on December 15, 1966. Despite racism, Abbie argued, most of the nation's poor were still white, and as activists it was still important to frame the struggle along class lines, not race lines.

The previous summer Abbie and SNCC leader Stokely Carmichael had been beaten up by police at the Newport Folk Festival. More recently they had shared a panel on Johnson's War in Asia, at which Stokely had thrown his arms around Abbie and announced to

everyone present, "Abbie's in SNCC, he's white and he's beautiful."
Abbie considered Stokely to be a friend, but he also thought Stokely
was wrong to throw aside SNCC's original biracial philosophy and
didn't mind saying so in a public forum. In the *Village Voice* piece, he
wrote:

> One thing that has always been present in the Movement
> has been the attitude that if you feel something is wrong you
> say so regardless of the consequences. . . .
> I feel recent SNCC decisions have hurt the chances of
> seeking the radical kinds of changes in this system which
> most of the New Left seeks. It has turned its back on the
> concept of class struggle, negated the moral battle of good
> vs. evil, and instead substituted a racism that even Malcolm
> X in his last few months had turned his back on. . . .
> I am interested in fundamental changes in American
> society, in building a system on love, trust, brotherhood,
> and all the other beautiful things we sang about. Trust is a
> sharing thing and as long as Stokely says he doesn't trust
> any white people I personally can't trust him. It doesn't
> matter how beautiful he thinks I am.

Abbie was roundly attacked from some quarters within the Movement for having with those words exposed divisions within the Left
for all to see, and along racial lines. In other circles he found high
praise, and that week his article was the talk of the town on the liberal
cocktail party circuit. Playing on his newfound notoriety, Abbie
penned a longer, and in many ways stronger article that appeared the
following week, in the December 22 issue of the *Voice*:

> There is nothing in the system out there that demonstrates
> that love is a force that can win. Our American system tells
> a black man that if he wants something, he has to riot to get
> it. He has to kill. He has to kill white people. It says it over
> and over again. There are those of us, however, who listen
> to a different drummer, who listen to our own system. That

is, we look inward and do as the spirit says do. I learned that very clearly when all the major news media descended upon me for the "inside dope on SNCC." I told them all the same thing: "[President] Johnson is a bastard. This is a family quarrel and you're not members of the family."

Abbie's vision was growing into a highly idiosyncratic, global, and somewhat playful vision of an ongoing class war waged by people of all kinds, with beautiful ideas, emotions, and desires against a fixed and lifeless, materialistic, war-mongering, prudish, and morally bankrupt status quo. It was a wonderful vision because it was so deeply optimistic, taking for granted that, at heart, most people were on the same side, the side of life, which meant the side of equality, justice, and peace.

Not long after the *Voice* articles appeared, Abbie and Stokely were both in Washington, D.C., visiting the home of SNCC leader George Brown. Stokely ribbed Abbie about the *Voice* pieces, and Abbie countered by joking about an ad executive who was trying to get Stokely to pose in a print ad campaign for a new line of clothing with the caption "Black Is Beautiful." "Only in America," Abbie and Stokely agreed.

In the spring of 1967, Abbie acceded to Stokely's request that he turn over Liberty House to black management, get out of the civil rights movement, and concentrate on ending the war in Vietnam.

As Abbie began to get the feel of his new neighborhood, he sometimes played pool at the local pool hall with local police officers. And he was friendly enough to the local precinct captain, a guy named Fink, for Fink, in Abbie's words, to start "constantly worrying about me."[1] At the other end of the spectrum, he looked on local drug dealers as benign and sometimes prominent members of the underground community—so much so that at least once he used money from a bail fund to bail one out of jail.[2] And though he never identified with the hippies—once calling them "fags" on national television, and always considering "dropping out" as "copping out"—Abbie tried to get runaway hippies, who were gravitating in increasing numbers to the Lower East Side, involved in local political issues. No one was excluded from Abbie's vision of a new America; he just expected that everyone could change a lot.

And Abbie was reading voraciously. Some of Marshall McLuhan's insights corresponded so neatly with his own that he began, with McLuhan, to see communication as having the same paramount importance in the contemporary world as labor had had in the industrial world. If Marx's means of production corresponded today to information, then, Abbie reasoned, "a modern revolutionary group headed for the television station, *not* for the factory."[3] And following that idea to its logical conclusion, Abbie decided that the entertainment factor could not be ignored by any serious politico. "If we were the TV generation, wasn't there a way of speaking that evoked visual images, rather than spewing forth dead words in rhythmic, religious procession that bounced off dulled eardrums and dissipated into empty space?"[4]

Part of the answer to his question came to Abbie from San Francisco, where the San Francisco Mime Troupe and others in the Haight Ashbury community were beginning to develop a whole new approach to societal problems. Calling themselves "Diggers" after an eighteenth-century English uprising, they used theater and spectacle to envision revolution as a celebration, thereby inviting participation, and effacing the contradiction between serious political action and great fun. To protest the local government's sluggishness when dealing with the rising rat population in the Haight, they descended on City Hall, playing penny whistles and dressed in pied piper costumes. In 1967, they opened a soup kitchen in Golden Gate Park with food donated from local restaurants, but also added their own music and dance to turn the soup lines into a social gathering. And they promoted the idea of a free, moneyless society by organizing a distribution network for free clothes and free housing.

It didn't take long for Abbie to search out and meet some Diggers visiting New York, and to start putting his own mark on the Digger-like activities he organized with a New York twist. That spring, together with Jim Fouratt, Marty, and Susan Carey and others, Abbie opened a Free Store on the Lower East Side in which all items—mostly used clothes—were free. Local media began to dote on Abbie, and after an appearance on *The David Susskind Show*, the *New York*

Post dubbed him its favorite "happy," meaning a hippie who didn't drag his feet. More and more involved in the street life of the Lower East Side neighborhood in which he lived, Abbie came up with a string of ideas for events that would help bring the power in the community to the people who actually lived there. These included blocking St. Mark's Place to traffic, setting up a music-filled pedestrian mall there instead (until the police broke up the party), and symbolic tree plantings.

On one occasion he came up with the idea of bringing clothes to Macy's department store and giving them away there to shoppers. When most shoppers refused to accept the free clothes, Abbie reveled in what he viewed as the complete success of the action: It had demonstrated to the shoppers their own misery and contrasted it with the generousness of the Digger way of life, thus serving as a lesson on the difficulty of change and an invitation to change as well.

One Saturday night, a group of around twenty local black kids from the neighborhood were arrested for smoking pot. As soon as he heard the news, Abbie pulled on his cowboy boots, grabbed three or four people who were hanging around, including our sister Phyllis who was in New York that year teaching at City College, and went down to the precinct house to lobby for their release.

First Abbie lay down in front of the station-house door, preventing people from leaving or entering. When Captain Fink arrived and complained to Abbie that he shouldn't be making a fuss since the arrested youths weren't hippies, Abbie responded, "What do you mean, 'hippie'? I'm a nigger and I was smoking pot with them. Arrest me or let them go." That got Abbie detained but not arrested. So Abbie threatened to burn down the precinct house. Fink still wouldn't arrest him, walking out of the detaining room instead. Abbie followed Fink into the main lobby, shouting, "Am I under arrest or not?" Still no response from the police captain.

In the middle of the lobby was a shining glass trophy case lined with trophies and medals. Abbie took one look at it, raised his boot, and kicked it to pieces.

"You're under arrest," Fink screamed at him.

"It's about fuckin' time," Abbie yelled back.

He'd gotten what he wanted, which was to show the kids he was on their side and outwit the divide-and-conquer law-and-order mentality of the police. And that earned him another night in The Tombs, sleeping the untroubled sleep of the just.

In early 1967, Abbie met Anita Kushner, a bright, young Jewish graduate fellow in English at Columbia, who had switched into a master's program in psychology at Yeshiva University, then worked for the local ACLU chapter, and was now a volunteer at Liberty House. Abbie walked in and swept her off her feet. Within a few weeks they were madly in love and renting an apartment together right on St. Mark's Place. Abbie admired Anita because she had all it took to be successful in the materialistic status quo world, and loved her for wanting to give all that up for a spot in his world. She was straight when he met her, had never tried pot or acid or participated in a demonstration. He gave her a crash course. Before long she was earning money stringing beads and accompanying Abbie to every event and demonstration.

Here's how he describes their meeting:

> *About a year and a half ago, while I was working at Liberty House, a girl came in to volunteer. We got to talking about civil rights, the South and so on. She asked me about drugs. I asked if she had ever taken LSD. When she responded that she hadn't, I threw her a white capsule. She juggled it the way you would a lighted firecracker. That night we made love and we've been doing it ever since. . . . I fell in love with her when she told me she didn't want to do anything. She is a true drop-out, a drop-out that could have made it, and made it big in the other world.[5]*

Smart, lovely, and capable, Anita was as new to the fresh world of drugs, sex, and politics as Abbie had been to bohemia ten years earlier when he met Sheila. Only this time, Abbie was the teacher. With Anita, there was love and sex in abundance, instead of arguments and battles. So in love was Abbie, in fact, that a year later when he tried to describe his feeling for Anita in *Revolution for the Hell of It,* this was the only part of the book he felt dissatisfied with. And in a footnote he explained, "Love is the one thing easiest to do and most difficult to talk about."[6]

Periodically, Abbie wrote back to the counterculture Worcester paper *Punch* to update his old friends on what he was doing. In April 1967, Abbie published two poems in *Punch* describing his New York home. What hits me now as I read them again is how comfortable Abbie already felt in his new environment—as if the glove finally fit, perfectly.

The first poem describes the poverty and degradation of the Lower East Side, and then strikes a heroic pose: "When there is so much to do / To change the way the wheels spin / So far to go before we win." The second poem, "Venceremos"—We shall overcome—ends in a powerful image of martyrdom in the battle between good and evil: "But now the Pentagon Power plans to see/just how many pins can fit in an angel's head, How many pins before he's dead."

At the same time that his credo expressed almost blind optimism, he began to encase himself in a contradictory personal vision of ultimate sacrifice, seeing himself as that martyred angel of the revolution, killed in the struggle and glorified in death. It was a destiny that he could accept—entering history as the Che Guevara of the second American Revolution.

Together with Jim Fouratt, Abbie organized a "Flower Brigade" to subversively participate in a "Support Our Boys in Vietnam" march organized by the Veterans of Foreign Wars for April 29, 1967. As Abbie expected, the less than twenty anti-war marchers were badly beaten up. Abbie marked the occasion a victory after the media, alerted by Abbie the day before, featured harmless hippies being beaten up by the war-mongers. And in the next issue of *WIN*, a national Movement weekly, Abbie could quip: "We were poorly equipped with flowers from uptown florists. Already there is talk of growing our own. . . . The cry of 'Flower Power' echoes through the land. We shall not wilt."[7]

On Easter Sunday, Abbie, Fouratt, and other East Coast Diggers gathered together thousands of participants in Central Park's Sheep Meadow for a Be-In, inspired again by the Haight Ashbury group, which in January had organized the first Be-In in Golden Gate Park. What was notable at the East Coast Be-In was that unlike its West Coast predecessor, it had no definable center—it wasn't based around a concert by name bands or readings by counterculture celebrities. Instead, people of all stripes simply gathered in the Sheep Meadow and were-in, getting high and getting to know one another. In a letter to *Punch* describing the Be-In for the June 1 issue, under the heading, "Hallucinations from the Real World," Abbie ecstasized:

Spring is here and things are popping. . . . On Easter Sunday there was a huge BE-IN in Central Park. There were probably 30,000 people that WAS-IN. . . . Everybody high on something: balloons, acid, bananas, kids, sky, flowers, dancing, kissing. I had a ball—totally zonked. . . . Leaving the park, I strolled down Fifth Avenue singing "In your Easter Bonnet. . . ." A line of cops [outside of St. Patrick's Cathedral] wiggling their index fingers, [saying] "You can't go in with that uniform" (flowers, gold paint, Easter bunny). Why not officer, you can go in with yours. . . .

I've tried LSD six times in the past three years. Feel it is worthwhile—but no illusions. It's what you do in between trips that counts and life is still a greater high than acid. If you're looking for an easy way out or a solution for life, you're not going to find it in any sugar cube. That's just mainstream American bullshit. "Things go better with coke." Things go better with things. I don't want to fall into the preacher bag. I urge everybody to try anything they feel like trying. The only thing I'm against, I guess, is people getting high on napalming villages. But life is more real than LSD. . . . [While I was co-hosting an all-night radio show] a guy called up and said, "Hell, I know how to get high on grapefruits. You just cut 'em in half and eat 'em." That's where it's at.

It was the year of America's cultural upheaval and the beginning of the Summer of Love. Around the corner from Abbie and Anita's pad, Bill Graham's Fillmore East was introducing the East Coast to Jimi Hendrix, Janis Joplin, Jim Morrison, The Grateful Dead, and The Band, among others. The Psychedelicatessen, the country's first head shop east of Haight Ashbury, was over on Tenth Street and Avenue A, next door to the Button Shop, where for a few dollars owner Randy Wicker would make you hundreds or thousands of buttons for your favorite cause. Paul Krassner's *The Realist* and the *East Village Other* were local counterculture institutions, as were Ellen Stewart's La Mama and The Living Theater, with street theater an essential element. There were free clinics, and free lawyers, and a commune called Food, which passed out free food in Tompkins Square Park.

For a while, Abbie and Jim Fouratt got themselves on the city payroll, serving as liaisons between Mayor John Lindsay's City Hall and the East Village. In that capacity, Abbie wrote a pamphlet he called "Fuck the System"—a guide to things that were free or could be stolen without getting caught—which would become the seed for his masterwork *Steal This Book*. But the two were fired after a few months.

On June 8, Abbie and Anita were married by their friend Linn House in a flower child wedding in Central Park behind the Metropolitan Museum. The ceremony was covered in the national press and started a trend of outside weddings in New York parks that year. Three weeks later, on July 2, they went before a rabbi on the Upper East Side and repeated the ceremony, with Abbie even stepping on the glass, as tradition demanded.

Increasingly enthusiastic about dreaming up actions that exposed contradictions in the conventional world, Abbie devoted more and more energy to what would come to be called—cynically, he always felt—his antics. The point, as he saw it, was reaching people, and if actions could be conceived in a way that would attract media attention, that meant you reached more people. It was as simple as that. Abbie cringed at accusations that he liked to grandstand for the media for personal rather than political reasons. To Abbie, his grand jests were grassroots organizing on a larger scale, pure and revolutionary acts, no less serious for being fun.

* * *

Before each action—sometimes the night before, sometimes a week before—Abbie would call the Worcester Medical office to tell us what he was going to do. He and I would talk, and then, almost shyly, Abbie would ask if Dad was there, and, feeling that this was the real point of the call, I'd say something like, "Yeah, he's right here; why don't you say hello." Dad would get on the phone, then he'd be quiet, listening, and I knew that Abbie was talking a mile a minute, telling Dad about the next day's action, trying to show him what a great thing it was going to be. And then I'd hear Dad say, through his clenched teeth, "You must be right, Abbie, and the whole world is wrong."

This was the year of our greatest difficulty at the business, with urban renewal programs forcing us to leave the premises we'd occupied for the last fifteen years and our best customers starting to buy directly from the pharmaceutical companies, cutting us out. And it was the year of Dad's first heart attack. With all that going on, Abbie's "achievements" were salt in Dad's wounds. And Abbie knew how hard things were for us. Maybe in his own mind that's partly why he made those calls, to try and cheer us up, let us know that at least one Hoffman family member was doing things we could all be proud of. But Dad didn't look at it that way.

In the third week of August came the first of a string of actions that would attract national media attention. Abbie placed a call to the New York Stock Exchange and asked for information about the public tour, using his favorite pseudonym, George Metesky (under which he'd written "Fuck the System"). Then, on August 24, he pulled together $300 and changed it into $1 bills, gathered together a dozen or so friends dressed in extreme hippie attire, and let sympathetic members of the press know that there was going to be something interesting happening down at the Stock Exchange. When the crowd of tourists, agitators, and journalists reached the gallery that overlooked the Stock Exchange floor, Abbie's group tossed out dollar bills by the handful. "Stock brokers scrambled over the floor like worried mice, scurrying after the money. Greed had burst through the business-as-usual facade."[8]

Almost immediately, guards pressed the troublemakers out of the Stock Exchange into the street. No law had been broken. No one had been hurt. Nothing had been stolen or damaged. And yet something extraordinary had happened, unlike anything in the country's history before or since: The logic, or illogic, of Wall Street and thus of Capitalist America, had been exposed, ridiculed, and weakened, elegantly, almost scientifically, and through a performance. Abbie didn't see a distinction between making art and doing politics.

Outside the Stock Exchange, Abbie, Jerry Rubin, whom Abbie had only just met, and other jesters, burned remaining dollar bills for the television network cameras, which had not been allowed onto the Stock Exchange gallery. And since the cameras hadn't been allowed onto the gallery itself, the Stock Exchange gag immediately leapt into the realm of myth, with different networks offering different versions: One channel reported that the money had been in $100 denominations, another that it had been worthless Monopoly money. A visiting Missourian was quoted as saying he'd joined in since he'd been throwing away money in New York for several days and found Abbie's way to be quicker and more fun. Abbie would henceforth refer to August 24 as the day "the stock market crashed" in the minds of America's youth, and the day he declared an "image war" against "the system."

In the last days of summer, Abbie and a friend visited Boston and Worcester—which Abbie had left only twelve months earlier—and made a side trip to the Revolutionary War monument at Concord Bridge early one morning, as if he were seeking some connection to that more distant past to replace the assumptions about America that he'd been discarding one after another with increasing fervor during the past winter and spring:

> *I stood on [Concord] bridge at 6 a.m. with a follower of Transcendental Meditation and described the [Revolutionary War] battle, joining myself with imaginary musket to the ragged guerrillas that shot from those peaceful hills in Concord on that April morning. The previous day we had stood in Harvard Square passing out free poems hurling*

*curses at the Pentagon gone mad and were attacked by
drunk marines as Harvard fairy professors stood in a circle
of Adlai Stevenson-nothingness and watched and appealed
to His Majesty's protectors of law and order, who finally
did something. They took down our names and told us to
get our asses out of Cambridge. I came away from sitting on
the Concord Bridge . . . knowing that some day I might just
have to shoot a few of His Majesty's gendarmes . . . forget-
ting those nights of practicing how to protect my head and
nuts in pacifist utero position and believing in the Second
American Revolution.[9]*

The next major protest was to be a week-long series of demonstrations in Washington to take place in October, organized by the
amalgam of anti-war organizations known as the Mobe, and announced on the day after Abbie and his friends threw money from the
Stock Exchange gallery. Jerry Rubin was project director for the October protests, which were to combine acts of civil disobedience with
a series of rallies and marches, including one right to the steps of the
Pentagon. Abbie suggested a new variation on the idea of marching
on the Pentagon. He offered to gather a group of people who would
encircle the Pentagon and perform an exorcism ceremony to rid it of
evil. Rubin loved the idea enough to include Abbie in the press conference announcing the October protests.

When it came Abbie's turn to speak at a press conference announcing the Washington demonstrations, he spontaneously extended his idea even further, announcing that during the exorcism the
Pentagon would rise one hundred feet in the air, and Jerry backed him
up all the way. As October approached, Abbie came up with a number of publicity-grabbing variations on the levitation theme. He visited Washington with his friend Marty Carey and attempted to
measure the Pentagon in order to estimate how many people would
be necessary to encircle it. He got himself quoted in the press requesting a permit for the levitation, and talked of negotiating a compromise with the generals whereby he would agree to raise the building
only ten feet in order to obtain the permit.

In response to threats by the Washington, D.C., police that they would use Mace on the demonstrators, Abbie held a press conference in which he introduced a chemical love compound he called Lace, spraying it on four couples sitting on a couch as a demonstration and then allowing journalists to take notes while the couples uncontrollably tore off their clothes and made love. The more he opposed the materialistic world with an alternative that included fantasy, imagination, and fun, the more his tactics seemed to be working.

On Saturday, October 21, 1967, Abbie, dressed in an American-Indian outfit under an Uncle Sam hat, and Anita, wearing a Sergeant Pepper outfit, dropped acid and participated in the successful levitation of the Pentagon—sometimes Abbie would say the actual levitation happened at dawn on Sunday. That isn't how the history books report it, but it's what Abbie would claim for the rest of his life. Most other people who were there happened to be looking the other way when the building actually rose ten feet in the air. The Fugs, who were chanting in the back of a truck as part of the exorcism, were prevented from getting closer to the building than a second parking lot. And soldiers and M.P.s prevented most of the exorcists from getting near enough to the building to encircle it.

After the exorcism, Abbie and Anita joined the core group of demonstrators sitting in on the Pentagon steps, where most would remain for the next twenty-four hours, until Sunday night. During that period, people came and brought the demonstrators food, there was singing and chanting, and during the night participants rested their heads on the shoulders of whoever happened to be sitting next to them. At first, on late Saturday night, there had been beatings at the hands of the generally much older U.S. marshals. But facing the demonstrators on the Pentagon steps were soldiers from the 82nd Airborne division, who had been flown in to protect the Pentagon, most of whom were kids about the same age as the majority of demonstrators. A camaraderie began to develop, with protesters singing to the soldiers to join them, and individual protesters explaining the reasons for demonstrating against the war to individual soldiers. And before it was over, many felt that the sorcery Abbie had half-jokingly attempted during the exorcism had been made very real and evident on the Pentagon steps.

*   *   *

On November 14, Abbie was arrested outside the Hilton Hotel in Manhattan protesting the arrival of Johnson's Secretary of State, Dean Rusk—in a melee complete with plastic bags of cow's blood flying through the air, tape recordings of battle sounds, war paint, fire alarms, and skirmishes between water-pistol-wielding demonstrators and tuxedoed bureaucrats.[10] And afterward Abbie decided he would come home to be with the family for Thanksgiving and his birthday. It would be an opportunity to introduce our parents to Anita, and to tell them what he'd been doing. Abbie felt he was achieving things in New York, making his mark, and doing good work. He didn't think of himself as a troublemaker or a rebel so much as a hard-working patriot. And he was becoming famous. He hoped Dad might understand some part of the whole, and that he might have something good to say to his eldest son. Dad had had his first heart attack in 1967, and Abbie wanted his visit, even if it were only a brief one, to help make Dad feel better.

Joan, Phyllis, and I went to pick up Abbie and Anita at the airport. When he got off the plane, we felt immediately that he was a celebrity. People all around him were staring; everyone seemed to recognize him. At least that was how it seemed to me, still the admiring younger brother. But what struck me more than his apparent celebrity was that he had tucked all his masses of hair under a dark blue woolen stevedore's hat. I think it may have been the first time I'd ever seen him hide a part of himself—or rather, the first time I'd ever seen him *show* that he was hiding something, since the hat bulged with hair.

When we got back to the house everything was in the usual disarray, just like old times. The table wasn't set, and Ma wasn't dressed. Uncle Schmule (Sam) and Gen, his wife, arrived soon after us, bringing Aunt Rose with them from the nursing home where she lived. Bubbe Anna brought the turkey, the tsimmis, and the soup. Uncle Lou and Aunt Sarah appeared, accompanied by their children, our cousins, Paul, Mark, and Jill. Ma had made the apple pie and baked the potatoes. Abbie and Anita had brought a couple bottles of good wine, not kosher, from New York. And Abbie kept his hat on, partly to avoid having to fend off comments about his hair, and perhaps partly as a sign that he had one foot out the door, and wasn't above getting right up and leaving if things got too uncomfortable with Dad. I couldn't stop looking at the hat, trying to figure out what he meant by it. Then it dawned on me that maybe, just maybe, he had covered his head, almost instinctively, as a sign of respect, as if Dad's house were a temple, as if to say to Dad, "We may believe different things, but we can still respect each other."

Our parents hadn't seen Abbie since my wedding over a year earlier—not having been invited to Abbie and Anita's Central Park and Upper East Side ceremonies. And they were strangely quiet at first, as if in the presence of a stranger. Of course, they would never raise the subject directly of not having been invited to their own son's wedding. And they were determined to be welcoming on this the occasion of first meeting their daughter-in-law. But there was a coolness in the air nonetheless. It had been a long time since we had all been together.

We all sat down at the long dining room table in the center of which was a wicker cornucopia centerpiece that had taken Dad the better part of three days of hard work to make. It held a beautiful arrangement of gourds, Indian corn, and some flowers. On Thanksgiving, Dad displayed talents we never knew he had the other 364 days of the year. And part of the sense of grace all of us have always associated with Thanksgiving has to do with memories of sitting at the table before the meal was served and taking in Dad's cornucopia each and every year.

Before long, everybody was talking at the same time, and then Abbie took control, talking about himself, talking away about his recent exploits, about Anita and their marriage, and most recently the levitation of the Pentagon, without any semblance of humility, as if being listened to was his natural-born right, or as if once he got started, he couldn't stop.

"Well, Abbie, it didn't rise," I suggested, teasing him a little in response to something he'd said about the Pentagon action.

"Naw, you weren't watching the right network," Abbie countered, teasing me right back.

Ma was listening and humming approvingly at whatever Abbie said, taking him at his word, ready to rise to his defense. Abbie continued unabated through the soup and the salad. As he talked, Abbie kept his eyes moving around the table, looking at everyone but Dad. Meanwhile, Dad was heading back and forth to and from the kitchen, seeing to the turkey, and not really wanting to have to look at Abbie either. Rose was talking to herself. Now and then she would address Abbie with a short phrase, following her own idiosyncratic rules of etiquette, usually when she wanted someone to pass her more food: "Abbie, you look good," or "Abbie, so that's your wife," and then, "Please pass the soup."

Since Sheila and Abbie's kids spent Thanksgiving elsewhere, there were no grandchildren present, and that meant Abbie, Phyllis, and I were the stand-in grandchildren for another year. Joan and Bubbe traded recipes. The television stayed on the whole time in the other room tuned to the football game. Eventually we got into talking about the war in Vietnam. To our surprise, Uncle Schmule, the W.W.II veteran, said he questioned our country's reasons for being in Vietnam. It wasn't quite a full-blown anti-war statement Schmule was making, but it was a step in that direction—in our direction— and we noticed. Dad kept a grim silence, knowing he was outnumbered. But as he listened he got more and more indignant. Still, without saying a word, he stood up, raised both hands over his head, and then snapped his hands forward toward us, before walking back into the kitchen to check on his turkey. "You don't know what you're talking about," was what he wanted to say, using instead the quintessential gesture of powerlessness all Jewish men use when they feel they're outnumbered and possibly wrong.

We all knew not to ask Dad about how business was, because business was bad, and we didn't want to get him *kvetching*. And as the meal wore on, Abbie and I both wanted to see how our bets on the Thanksgiving Day games were doing. Some of our old friends came over after the meal. And Abbie produced a joint that we passed around the table, after all the relatives except Bubbe had retired to the television or left. Bubbe sat with us for a while as we got stoned, not understanding what we were doing or saying, but enjoying our company anyway.

The next day, Joan and I, on our way to New York to visit with Joan's parents, gave Abbie and Anita a ride home. I was driving and Abbie was telling jokes, Jewish jokes. Abbie, Joan, and I were laughing our heads off. Anita was quiet, deferring to Abbie and not quite sure about Joan and me. Joan remembers that this was the first time she found Abbie relaxed enough to like him. We felt good about the Thanksgiving with the family and felt that all was well somehow. I was happy that Joan was liking my brother; at odd moments—and that drive from Worcester to New York was one of them—he still felt like a part of me.

Abbie was already a Yippie!, although the word didn't come into being until the very end of 1967, born in discussions aimed at getting people to go to Chicago for the forthcoming 1968 National Democratic Convention. It grew from the ashes of Paul Krassner's LSD hangover, when Paul noticed something that was, like most post-hallucinatory-voyage revelations, perfectly obvious once you thought about it sober: "When you make the peace sign of the V, the extension of your arm makes it a Y." Five stoned-out friends were packed together into Abbie and Anita's tiny living room, including Abbie and Anita, Krassner, Jerry Rubin, and Jerry's girlfriend Nancy Kurshan. Building on Krassner's "Y," someone else suggested Youth International Party. Y.I.P. YIP. Someone else said that hippies are dead. Paul cried out "Yippie!"[11]

Two weeks later every underground paper was carrying a Yippie! story. The next month "The Yippies are coming" appeared in *Newsweek*. A full-blown myth was born. Abbie was ecstatic: "Can we change an H to a Y? Can myths involve people to the extent that they will make the journey to far-off Chicago? Can magic media succeed where organizing has failed? Y not?"[12]

Abbie said being a Yippie! meant you were "A flower child who's been busted. A stoned-out warrior of the Aquarian Age."[13] The splendid anarchy of the word allowed it to have as many definitions as there were attempts to define it, and all of them could be true. Abbie used to tell me that Yippies were Jewish Hippies.

Chapter Six

1968

Abbie Hoffman was an inspiration. But he was not a leader. And I don't know anybody who would suggest that he was [except for] Newsweek, Time, and Richard Nixon.

—PBS *TALK SHOW HOST*

NINETEEN SIXTY-EIGHT may have been the most eventful, the most changeful year in American history—and not only for the quickening pace of the anti-war movement and the galvanizing effect of the presidential elections, although I think these things, like the acrid smell of fire in the air, lent a sense of drama to a wide range of events, large and small. The year had begun with a laugh (Rowan and Martin's *Laugh-In* hit the tube on January 22), saw the unexpected success of the McDonald's "Big Mac" hamburger which was "invented" that year, and ended with a nationally televised trip around the moon. It was a year of great leaps between large distances. And the trip to the moon was symbolic of, but not more extreme than, the distances that stretched that year between millions of mothers and daughters, fathers and sons, and brothers.

No longer was the anti-war movement perceived as a marginal trend. Martin Luther King, Jr., had begun speaking out against the war, connecting what he recognized to be its immorality to the struggle of the civil rights movement. Suddenly hundreds of thousands of people were actively involved in anti-war protests of one kind or another, a majority of the American people said they opposed the war, and Vietnam veterans against the war, whose sense of disillusionment and betrayal were based on first-hand experience of the war's horror, gave to the movement a new grounding and a driving force. Anti-war activism became a sort of gold standard of right and wrong. It was dividing families, and it was changing America.

Our family didn't fight about the war in the ways that many families did. No one was drafted and killed, and there were no screaming arguments, but the war came home to us in other ways. Abbie was arrested over and over in 1968, more often than during any other year of his life. Dad used to complain that UPI and AP were more likely than he was to know where in hell Abbie was: "Now we have to read the papers to see which jail he's in," he'd say bitterly. I felt like the bouncing ball going back and forth between Abbie and Dad, bound by my feelings of loyalty to them both.

Abbie and I were both active against the war. But Abbie took it a step further. To him, American middle-class values amounted to the same hateful point of view that had gotten the country into Vietnam in the first place. At the same time, part of him seemed still to appreciate and enjoy my conventional success. "Well, you got the business," he would say with a laugh. I think he liked to think we were a team, that between us we had *all* the angles covered.

But there was no real closeness between us. Just as the year before our parents had experienced Abbie as a stranger in their home when he visited for Thanksgiving, now I experienced that strangeness.

The funny thing was, Abbie loved what was going on; he loved 1968. He saw the walls of post-war '50s America finally crumbling and he thrilled to the excitement of it. To him it didn't just mean the destruction of something, it also meant new beginnings, the opportunity to get things right for once—revolution in all its glory. That's what he thought was happening in 1968. In his autobiography, Abbie would call it "The Year That Was,"[1] and by that I think he meant that it was a year that had everything, everything that could be desired.

On Friday, March 22, the night of the spring equinox, the Yippies! held a "Yip-in" in Grand Central Terminal, at midnight, designed as a foretaste of the Festival of Life planned for Chicago. Participants had been asked to bring "Flowers, Beads, Music, Radios, Pillows,

Eats, Love and Peace." Afterward, there was going to be a sunrise celebration in Central Park's Sheep Meadow to "Yip Up the Sun."

Thousands showed up at Grand Central, expecting a peaceful party reminiscent of the 1967 Be-In in Central Park. No one anticipated violence. But when they found Forty-Second Street cordoned off and hundreds of police milling about, people weren't put off by the threat of violence, either. This was very different from encounters with the police that had taken place before.

As the "Yip-In" got going, one Yippie! climbed the information kiosk and pulled the hands off the clock. Suddenly, cops advanced in droves, using the enclosed space of the cathedral-like main hall to flush out and corner their prey, beating people left and right. Several party-goers were thrown by police through plate glass. Abbie was beaten unconscious and had a vertebra smashed, and he would refer afterward to "The Grand Central Massacre" as having been more frightening than anything that would happen in Chicago. Many others were badly hurt by marauding police units. But the party-goers also exhibited a new defiance in Grand Central that night. Instead of getting away as quickly as they could, large numbers of Yippies! and Lower East Siders kept coming back to face the cops, and hours after the police had started breaking up the "Yip-In," it was still going on.

Abbie went from Grand Central to Bellevue Hospital, where he was bandaged and released. Then he went straight to WBAI radio, where he sat in on his friend Bob Fass's late night show to put a Yippie! spin on what had happened, claiming the bloodshed signified a new political activism and a new determination to end the war—which interpretation would be picked up the next day in *The New York Times*'s front-page description.

Out of the field of Democratic presidential candidates that had gone into the February New Hampshire primary, one had survived, the candidate of hope and peace, Minnesota Senator Eugene McCarthy, who had come in right on the heels of the incumbent Lyndon Johnson. McCarthy seemed to be the candidate to galvanize the youth vote and the anti-war vote. Then, in March, Bobby Kennedy joined the race. And on March 31, Lyndon Johnson announced that he would not seek reelection. Suddenly, peace candidates were everywhere.

But Abbie wasn't interested in the election. However left-leaning a Democratic candidate might be, he was part of the establishment, Abbie felt, and the establishment wasn't where change was going to come from. Instead, Abbie concentrated his energies on the forthcoming Festival of Life, which he hoped was going to steal the thunder from that summer's Democratic National Convention. Together with Jerry Rubin, Abe Peck, editor of the Chicago-based alternative newspaper, *The Seed,* and other Yippie! organizers, Abbie was busy applying for the proper permits for the Chicago festival and getting people energized.

Then on April 4, in Memphis, Martin Luther King, Jr., was gunned down, and that day everything changed. Everyone even peripherally associated with the civil rights movement took the hurt very personally. It was as if an attempt had been made to kill not just a man but a movement as well. There was rioting and police violence in 126 cities, mostly in black ghettos, resulting in 21,000 arrests, hundreds of injuries and 46 deaths. On Chicago's South Side, Mayor Daley showed his iron fist. In Washington, federal troops guarded the White House and a machine gun post was installed on the roof of the Capitol. Suddenly a lot of people who had been standing on the sidelines began to take sides.

Tom Hayden would say that the spring of 1968 signified the "decapitation" of liberalism, referring to the despair that so many people, black and white, felt after King's death, and the journey it sent them on toward new types of approaches to the problems we were all trying to solve. To Abbie, King's murder made the counterculture alternative, represented by the Yippies! and the Festival of Life, seem all the more important, and he stepped up his organizing efforts.

In New York, emboldened by the uprisings in the inner cities, the Columbia University campus was heating up around a combination of events, some related to the War in Vietnam, and others concerning local issues. The university president, Grayson Kirk, had gone on record as saying that Columbia was not a military contractor, and then it was revealed that he had lied, and in fact Columbia was a major weapons research contractor, part of a secret consortium of universities doing military work for the government. At the same time, Columbia was getting ready to build a new gym in the Morningside Heights area of Harlem, one that would destroy housing and a large part of the park and yet be off-limits to community residents. A group of students, led by Mark Rudd, decided to shake up the campus, and invited Abbie and other organizers from downtown to lend them some experienced help.

Help came, and the demonstrations succeeded, partly due to the discovery of a network of underground tunnels beneath the campus, which allowed the protesting students to maintain a siege. But before it was over, the university administration, working closely with New York police, chose a tough approach, aimed particularly at those they considered "outside agitators." Abbie and a number of his friends, including Gus Reichbach (now a New York State judge), Marty Kenner (his old buddy from U.C. Berkeley), and writer Jonah Raskin, were arrested on April 30 on charges of criminal trespass.[2] Abbie was badly beaten up by police at Columbia, and other demonstrators were beaten as well in full view of the crowd. The Columbia University actions that April and May were another critical stop on the road to the Chicago Democratic Convention, revealing a nation increasingly at war with itself, in which there were no ivory towers, no neutral observers.

These were the days when Yippie! was still in its infancy and needed all the nurturing Abbie and his cohorts could give it. And that's where Abbie's energy was going. It became an obsession with him, as all his projects did. Yippie! became the expression for Abbie of his joy, disillusionment, theatricality, McLuhanisms, Mailerisms, and Maslowisms. And the more Yippie! grew into something he felt could be a force for change, the more he saw the opening up of the electoral system to more progressive ideas as a threat to Yippie!. He saw McCarthy as a threat, and he feared Bobby Kennedy most of all.

Bobby had jumped in with a crusader's vehemence, opposing Humphrey, the Democratic Party's machine candidate. He was adamantly against the war and really seemed intent on listening to people's grievances. Bobby singlehandedly raised the flag of liberalism off the bloody battlefield and was the *only* candidate who looked like he could lead us to victory. But Abbie believed that Kennedy would be unable to bring about the revolutionary change that was necessary to end the war by working through the system.

Throughout April and May, Bobby Kennedy just seemed to get better and better—more committed to civil rights, more the people's candidate—and his popularity soared. And as Bobby's popularity grew each day, Abbie sensed the prospects for Yippie! sink:

> *Yippie stock went down quicker than the money we had dumped on the Stock Exchange floor. Every night we would turn on the TV set and there was the young knight with long hair [Bobby K.], holding out his hand (a gesture he learned from the Pope): "Give me your hand—it is a long road ahead."*
>
> *When young longhairs told you how they'd heard that Bobby turned on [smoked grass], you knew Yippie! was really in trouble.*
>
> *Yippie! grew irrelevant.*
>
> *National action seemed meaningless. . . . by the end of May we had decided to disband Yippie! and cancel the Chicago festival[3]*

Then, on June 5, in Los Angeles, Bobby was shot to death. Like all the rest of us, Abbie "shuddered at the recognition of our collective frailty,"[4] but politically he didn't miss a beat:

> *The statement [to disband Yippie!] was all ready when up stepped Sirhan Sirhan, and in ten seconds he made it a whole new ball game.*
>
> *We postponed calling off Chicago and tried to make some sense out of what the hell had just happened. . . .*
>
> *The United States political system was proving more insane than Yippie!.*
>
> *Reality and unreality had in six months switched sides.*
>
> *The calls began pouring into our office. They wanted to know only one thing: "When do we leave for Chicago?"*

As the summer drew on, more and more of Abbie's time was spent planning for the Festival of Life in Chicago, and with each passing week the plans seemed to grow larger, as events and the general mood of the country seemed almost to necessitate some kind of confrontation. The story Abbie liked to tell was that after his bags were packed, the last thing he did before leaving for Chicago was to call Ma in Florida.

"Chicago? What are you going there for?" she asked him.

"To wreck the Democratic Party, Ma," Abbie answered.

"Well, dress warm, it's a windy city," Ma replied.

In the spring of 1968, Ma and Dad had extended their annual stay in Florida. I had moved the offices of Worcester Medical into a building on Chandler Street we purchased with the help of a 3 percent loan from the Small Business Administration. Business in 1968 was booming, after I'd gotten us out of pill sales and expanded into new areas. I even owned a race horse. But psychologically and emotionally, I was at a low point. Joan was threatening divorce because of all the time I spent at the Scarborough race track. And the unhappier she seemed to be, the more time I spent at the track, just to avoid having to deal with our problems. We went bi-monthly to a marriage counselor, which hardly seemed to help.

Dad was largely ignoring the medical advice he'd gotten from his doctor following his first heart attack, and was well on his way to his second. Abbie called frequently, not really to see how I was doing but for me to pass along word of his exploits to our parents, to Phyllis, and to his old friends in Worcester. Not exactly home-town boy makes good, but home-town boy makes bad, which was even better.

Dad liked to say that he was staying in Florida because of Abbie's notoriety: "My son's driven me from my home." But really, Dad loved Florida. Miami Beach was like his second religion. Cruising his four-door dark brown Lincoln sedan down Ocean Drive meant something. So did the white shoes he wore and the game of golf he played every morning. Of course there was a catch. For Dad, retirement came on the heels of the collapse of the pill end of our business. So rather than being just a status symbol, time spent in Miami Beach became for Dad a kind of heroic act of defiance against what he saw as his failure in life. It hurt him to know that his pill palace had gone down, that his old enemies the pharmacists had beaten him in the end. Before leaving for Florida, he had watched as a wrecking crane reduced to a heap the building that had housed Worcester Medical Supply all those years.

Near their apartment in Florida, Ma and Dad were surprised one day by two FBI agents, who jumped out of the bushes and started snapping pictures. I don't think J. Edgar Hoover needed the photos. It was harassment, pure and simple, but in its own way highly sophisticated, because unlike Abbie, we—and especially John and Florence Hoffman—didn't know how to respond to this kind of attack. Did Ma and Dad somehow share responsibility with Abbie for whatever it was he had done? That was the implication. Dad had worked all his life for a place among the *alter kockers,* the big shots sitting in their deck chairs down in Miami, only to find that he himself was the father of their worst nightmare. At the spa, on the beach, Dad would hear comments about Abbie: "He's going to ruin it for the rest of us." "He's an embarrassment to the Jewish faith." He would just shake his head, basically in agreement with their criticisms, but unwilling ever to give up his son.

That summer, Phyllis was in Mexico, where she had a job as a guide at the Summer Olympics and where she would meet Hilario, her future husband. Dad and Ma stayed in Florida, spending most of their time inside where it was air-conditioned. Joan and I took our first trip to Europe that July, before starting our family (Justin, our first son, would be born exactly one year later). On our return, I mentioned to Abbie that some friends of mine were going to the Festival of Life and I was thinking of going, too. Chicago was a kind of hometown to me since my stint at the University of Illinois. Abbie warned me against coming. He expected large-scale violence, he said. He almost ordered me not to go. I wasn't looking for trouble, and when Joan also expressed concerns about the trip, I cancelled my plans and put Chicago out of my mind.

On the night of August 7, the Yippies! met with Deputy Mayor Stahl, and on August 8 submitted yet another of many applications for the Festival of Life to take place in Lincoln Park. Yet another application for which they would receive no reply. And on Friday, August 23, began the week which, for the rest of his life, Abbie would refer to not as a point in time but as the place where he entered the history and mythology of the nation: Chicago. What I have of the events of that week are the stories, like snapshots, which Abbie relayed to me at different times over the years. They don't always describe the main events, since Abbie's role was to participate in something free-flowing and chaotic. But they do give a sense of just how improvisatory, and at the same time how responsive and intense, Abbie's involvement that week was.

The only killing that occurred at the Chicago demonstrations took place on Thursday, August 22, several days before the convention opened. A Native American named Dean Johnson was shot dead by two police officers. Abbie was stunned when he heard the news, fearing that this might be the first of many murders by Chicago police. Mayor Daley's tough stance had already succeeded in scaring off most protesters from coming. Things were ludicrously unbalanced: some twenty-five thousand uniformed police officers, undercover agents, national guardsmen, and army reserve units faced off against a few thousand demonstrators. The protesters were determined to play it light and easy, but the forces of law and order had been pumped up by so much misinformation about the plans of the agitators—some of it put out by the Yippes! themselves—that the situation was out of hand before it began. Members of the police actually thought that their drinking water was going to be laced with LSD, and that Yippies! posing as taxi drivers were planning to kidnap convention delegates. Everything that the Yippies! said as a joke was turned into a threat within Chicago's law enforcement community. Abbie, perhaps alone among the activist leaders, saw the communication potential of the situation that had evolved. The more the protesters were outnumbered, the better it would look on television. And the more it became clear that far fewer people were going to show up than the festival organizers had hoped, the more Abbie insisted the festival go forward according to plan.

The next day, Abbie led a group of fifty or sixty protesters in workshops on self-defense and first aid in Lincoln Park. The group was surrounded by two hundred to two hundred and fifty police, both in and out of uniform, taking pictures and monitoring the group. And late that afternoon, police nailed signs all around the park announcing an eleven P.M. curfew. The Yippie! candidate for president, a large pig named Pigasus, was "arrested," together with Jerry Rubin, and the singer Phil Ochs.

On Saturday morning, August 24, Abbie turned around and faced the two undercover cops tailing him and demanded that they take him to see Police Chief Lynskey, who was in charge of the Lincoln Park area. When they found Lynskey, he told Abbie that under no circumstances was the Festival of Life going to be permitted, and furthermore, that if anyone broke a single city ordinance the police would clear the whole park, and that if Abbie in particular did anything wrong, Lynskey planned to arrest him personally. Lynskey suggested to Abbie, "Why don't you try to kick me in the shins right now?" Abbie responded that he didn't want to do that just then since NBC wasn't around. This prompted Chief Lynskey to praise Abbie for being honest, at least.

Later in the day Abbie helped organize a hash cookie production line. By mid-afternoon there were two thousand people in the park singing, smoking grass, eating hash brownies and enjoying the lazy weather. At a planning meeting, Abbie argued in favor of disobeying the curfew and trying to sleep in the park. He was outvoted by more moderate Yippies including Ed Sanders, Paul Krassner, and Allen Ginsberg. And at curfew, the remaining demonstrators left the park for the streets, only to be chased and clubbed anyway by waiting police.

On Sunday, the official inauguration of the Festival of Life, there were so many police and journalists in Lincoln Park that the festival didn't have a chance. Instead, there were skirmishes between jeering protesters and cops who yelled back at them. Abbie, dealing directly with Chief Lynskey now, managed to get him to allow the demonstrators to plug into the electricity at the refreshment stand for the rock concert part of the Festival. But then Lynskey was nowhere to be found and, at around 6:30 in the evening, with no warning and four and a half hours before being in the park would have become illegal under the curfew, a phalanx of two hundred police poured into the park and began bashing heads and making arrests. Abbie learned what had happened from Stew Albert, who had been clubbed and was bleeding profusely from the head and face as he relayed the information to Abbie. As Abbie would describe it in *Revolution for the Hell of It:* "The first blood I saw in Chicago was the blood of Stu Albert, Jerry's closest friend. . . . I embraced Stu, crying and swearing—sharing his blood."[5] Abbie grabbed a microphone and said to the people who had gathered around that the police had busted up the Festival of Life, that it was over. Then, sobbing, he introduced Albert, saying, "Here is one of my brothers from Berkeley; his blood is all our blood." At first the television crews had been prepared to turn the smallest Yippie! incidents into a national debate on decency and respect for authority. But now they had a better story to present to the nation: police brutality against the peaceful and unarmed children of America. The footage that aired on the nightly news shocked and frightened people everywhere.

Late that night, around 2 A.M., Abbie called Deputy Mayor David Stahl at home. By Abbie's account, when Stahl answered the phone, Abbie said, "Hi, Dave. How's it going? Your police got to be the dumbest and the most brutal in the country."

At 6 A.M. Monday morning, Abbie joined a friend to pray in church. Later he went to police headquarters to check on Rennie Davis and Wolfe Lowenthal, who had been arrested for deflating a squad car's tires. That night, after most of the demonstrators left Lincoln Park at curfew, about a thousand stayed, and at around 11:30 Abbie and Anita returned to the park to join them. Shortly afterward, a wedge formation of police attacked, clubbing people left and right, with tear gas canisters exploding everywhere. And again there were cameras to record what was happening.

At 6:00 A.M. Tuesday morning, Abbie hitched a ride with the cops who were tailing him and asked to be taken to the beach front section of Lincoln Park where there was going to be a sunrise service. Arriving at the beach, he found Allen Ginsberg and about 150 or 200 people, some of them with bandages on their heads and blood showing through, sitting in the lotus position, chanting and meditating. As he recounted it a year and a half later at the Chicago Conspiracy trial, Abbie joined the group and after a while stood up and spoke:

What is going on here is very beautiful, but it won't be on the evening news tonight. The American mass media is a glutton for violence, and only shots of what is happening in the streets of Chicago will be on the news. America can't be changed by people sitting and praying, and this is an unfortunate reality that we have to face. We are a community that has to learn how to survive. We have seen what has happened the last few nights in Lincoln Park. We have seen the destruction of the Festival.

I will never again tell people to sit quietly and pray for change.

Of course, I can't recall Abbie ever telling anyone to sit quietly and pray for change in all the years I knew him. But inside, I think he did respect that point of view. The question of nonviolence was one he was always wrestling with internally. And I know that the sight of Allen Ginsberg in Chicago had moved him enormously. He had seen the poet chanting O-o-m-m-m-m, playing the part of Yippie! religious leader, Ghandi-like, right in the middle of the worst police violence. He admired and respected Ginsberg for his courage in Chicago but still had to find his own way.

Later Tuesday morning, Abbie showed up at a Mobe press conference, carrying the branch of a tree and pissed off at the Mobe for advocating nonviolence. As he would say again and again over the years, Abbie believed arguments pitting violence against nonviolence presented a false dichotomy: "I burst in with karate jacket, helmet, and heavy club made from the branch of a tree. I announce to the press that we are arming the Yippies! and whatever the pigs dish into the park, we'll dish out. I keep slamming the club against my other palm."[6] Then he had a koan-like conversation with a reporter, one that crystallized, if not the spiritual synthesis of violence and nonviolence Abbie was seeking, at least the imaginative power of such a synthesis:

REPORTER: *Are you armed?*
ME: *I'm always armed.*
REPORTER: *Is that your weapon?*

ME: *This (holding club in the air and smiling), this is part of a tree. It symbolizes my love for nature.*[7]

Abbie could reconcile himself to violence as a tactic. He could admire those who practiced revolutionary violence, but he was never able to join them. And yet the determined brutality of the police smashing heads night after night, as large numbers of them stormed into Lincoln Park and gave chase through the streets, challenged Abbie to the point where he was no longer comfortable with his own nonviolence either.

And that was why the words he had uttered in Ginsberg's presence at the sunrise service on Tuesday morning were so emotionally charged. They show him casting off a pacifist point of view which, although he had never publicly endorsed it, had attracted him and one which, were it not for the violence he'd seen in the previous seventy-six hours, he had hoped to be free to embrace when he felt ready. But now, because of the violence in Chicago, Abbie seemed to feel distinctly less free to do so. As he would tell author John Schultz twenty years later just days before his death, "It wasn't in my head to pick up rocks and throw them [before Chicago]. In later years it was in my head—after Chicago. Chicago made us more militant."[8]

All his life, Abbie flirted with violence, liked to talk about it, admired the Black Panthers and the Weather Underground for arming themselves, even kept a gun in his apartment in New York at one point. But the truth was he was never comfortable with the prospect of shooting back. At heart, he may have felt closer to the pacifism of Ginsberg or *Liberation* editor and Mobe spokesperson Dave Dellinger. Abbie thrived on making things, dreaming up the Festival of Life, writing books, organizing demonstrations. But he felt caught between violence he couldn't really handle and his own sense of the insufficiency of nonviolence in such violent times.

On Tuesday afternoon, there were workshops throughout the park. At around 2:00 or 2:30 P.M., Abbie addressed a gathering of over a hundred people, saying, "America . . . is bent on devouring its children." In a speech later on that day, he made one of his more famous pronouncements: "The system is falling apart," he said, "and we're here to give it a push."

Tuesday evening, Abbie joined Phil Ochs, Ed Sanders, Jean Genet, William Burroughs, Dick Gregory and Dave Dellinger before a crowd of some six thousand at the Chicago Coliseum. When Abbie's turn to speak came, he told the crowd, "When you march to the amphitheater tomorrow, you should keep in mind a quote from a two-thousand-year-old Yippie with long hair named Jesus, who said that when you march into the dens of the wolves you should be as harmless as doves and as cunning as snakes."

Wednesday morning, Abbie rose very early, as he usually did. Forewarned by his police tails that he was going to be arrested that morning, and not wanting the event to become a media feeding frenzy, he took a black Magic Marker and wrote the word "Fuck" on his forehead, reasoning that it would keep newspaper editors from putting his picture in the paper. The word also summed up his attitude toward the deteriorating situation in Chicago. He then dressed in his cowboy boots, brown corduroy pants, and a work shirt, and pulled a gray felt ranger cowboy hat down over his eyes. At around 6:00 A.M., Abbie, Anita, Paul Krassner, and a friend of Paul's named Beverly Baskinger went out to eat breakfast, accompanied by the two police officers tailing Abbie and two others who were tailing Paul.

At the restaurant, the two cops came in and said that they had orders to arrest him for something he had under his hat. Abbie asked them if they had checked it out with Commander Braasch, a ploy that had worked the day before when Abbie had used it to get rid of a group of cops that were bashing heads in Lincoln Park. The cops left the restaurant but returned a short while later, joined by four or five patrol cars that surrounded the restaurant. The cops again asked Abbie to lift up his hat, and when he complied, they pounced on him, threw him to the floor, handcuffed him, and arrested him.

Wednesday night was the climax of convention week, with the nomination of the Democratic candidate, Hubert Humphrey, on the convention floor, and the Michigan Avenue–Balbo Drive free-for-all between police and demonstrators out in the streets. Once again, the nightly news featured footage of Chicago police spilling the blood of America's youth. Abbie spent the night in jail.

After he was released on Thursday, August 29, Abbie led an antiwar march from Grant Park along Michigan Avenue in the direction of the amphitheater. The convention was in progress within, and there was no way the authorities were going to allow the demonstrators to reach it. Tempers were ragged on both sides after the police violence the night before. At Sixteenth Street, the march was blocked by the fixed bayonets of the National Guard, backed up by an armored personnel carrier, on top of which, in full view, had been installed a large machine gun. Meanwhile, two blocks back was a line of Chicago police preventing the marchers from returning the way they had come. In between, on either side, there was a solid wall of buildings. The thousands of demonstrators were trapped. As John Schultz has pointed out, if Abbie had wanted a *Plaza de las Tres Culturas* (where, in October 1968, the Mexican army would shoot over five hundred students), if Abbie had wanted more violence in the streets of Chicago, as would be argued by the prosecution in the Chicago Conspiracy trial, this would have been the perfect opportunity to accomplish that goal. Instead, Abbie helped arrange an orderly retreat past the row of police behind them.

The night before, as I watched the convention coverage on t.v. with my friend Harry, the images of the police beating up the demonstrators in front of the Hilton seared my brain. My thoughts went to Abbie. The whole nation was shocked by what they saw. No one on the outside had expected it. I don't know how much the fear I felt was different from what Americans all over were feeling. Almost immediately, the phone started ringing, as it had each night that week. Phyllis from Mexico, Ma and Dad, along with local journalists. They all wanted to know if I'd heard from Abbie, but I hadn't, since Abbie was in jail, although I didn't know it at the time.

On Thursday night, around 1:00 or 2:00 A.M., out on bail, he called, sounding exhausted and exhilarated, and told me to tell everyone he was safe. "We're winning the war, Jack," he told me.

In 1989, days before his death, Abbie would say, "We expected many, many more people in Chicago than came" and "We expected there would be killing in Chicago."[9] The Festival of Life had been planned as the ultimate showdown. Seeing the Yippies! as revolutionary warriors, Abbie had looked to the third week in August 1968 as a good time to die, and went to battle like the Indian fighters we used to emulate as kids. To Abbie, winning in Chicago would have meant bringing down the Democratic Party and the U.S. government with it. And that didn't happen.

The nomination of Hubert Humphrey may have represented a defeat for the Yippies!. All the bashed heads hadn't had even the slightest impact on the decision-making of the Democratic party bosses. Hubert Humphrey's position on the war was hardly different from the dethroned President Johnson's. Not until October did Humphrey seem to grow more enlightened in his position on the war, and his standing in the polls began to increase, but it was too late to beat Nixon. By then many of us had already decided on a protest vote for Dick Gregory. Many others just didn't want to vote at all, disillusioned by the available choices.

I could argue that the election of Richard Nixon represented a victory for the Yippies!. But only in theory. After Nixon's election in November, the Yippies! lost their momentum, and it wouldn't be until his second term in office that Nixon would finally end the war.

By the time of Chicago, Abbie had learned how to put on a show in such a way that the television networks would present it exactly as he wanted. He wanted to see the war in Vietnam end, and he thought that wreaking havoc on prime time was going to ensure that end more decisively than getting the better candidate in office would. Through television he wielded enormous influence and was able to exercise a surprising amount of control over how the television cameras presented him. Again and again, during the Chicago demonstrations, Abbie had been able to show the nation the inhumanity of the government's police next to the humanity of the protesters. Almost no other public figure at this time both understood the power of television and was able to effectively use it to communicate with so many people. Abbie's legacy was that he knew how to present his ideas as images. Frank Stanton, head of CBS news, has said that Abbie understood television better than the networks themselves did at the time, that he was in fact ahead of the networks. Abbie knew that you had to make the news, not just talk about it.

In the weeks after Chicago, back in New York, Abbie worked furiously to finish writing his first book.[10] His publisher, The Dial

Press, had promised to have *Revolution for the Hell of It* out by the end of the year if he finished it on time. So in a span of just two weeks, if you believe my brother, he gathered together all his notes and wrote a fresh manuscript, longhand. It would come to 230 printed pages, and even if it took him a day or two more than two weeks, it was a phenomenal achievement. Of all his books, *Revolution* best expresses the historical moment in which it was written, mixing metaphysics with mania and capturing the exuberance that was always the Yippies!' greatest asset.

Revolution ranges from biblical reinterpretation (Abbie has Abraham "exhausted with joy [in an] orgasm of consciousness" after sparing Isaac), to recitations of the more recent glories of Fidel Castro and Ho Chi Minh, to McLuhanesque insights into contemporary American middle class values (" 'God is dead,' they cry, 'and we did it for the kids.' ") Much of it is in journal form, flashbacks on Abbie's actions in 1967 and 1968; all of it is hallucinatory. Some of it is a Yippie! how-to organizing manual ("Never explain what you are doing. . . . Always create art and destroy property. . . . Never forget that ours is the battle against a machine, not against people. If, however, people behave like machines, treat them as such"), and some of it is Abbie ego-tripping on what it's like to be Abbie ("At eleven I could deal off the bottom of the deck in poker; by thirteen I didn't have to, I was so good"). I think my favorite phrase from the book is "The ground you are standing on is a liberated zone, defend it." Curiously, he chose to publish the book under a pseudonym—sort of. On the cover was a Richard Avedon photo of Abbie in mid-leap, holding a toy rifle and with the word "Free" written on his forehead (changed from "Fuck" to please some editor or other). "Free" was also listed as the book's author. There was even a biography of "Free," using all the facts of Abbie's life. Abbie Hoffman was mentioned at the end of the bio as one of Free's aliases.

One of the most beautiful passages from *Revolution for the Hell of It* describes preparations for the 1967 Be-In in Central Park. And although it was written not more than a year after the events it describes, already there is in the writing an almost elegiac tone, as if the spring and summer of 1967 were a golden era long past:

Today I asked Joel [a runaway] . . . to go and buy three flowers: one chrysanthemum, one daffodil, and one daisy— and he did and returned with the change. We had a technological problem. Which flowers would be best suited to throw out of an airplane into the YIP-Out [the Be-In]? . . . So up the twelve flights of stairs I trudged, three flowers in hand, exhausted, puffing, out of breath. . . .

There were two men on the roof. Two old men, one in his late forties, the other about sixty-five. Old Italian men with old ways and old hats feeding pigeons, hundreds of them. It was their thing. "You can't come up here" one started screaming. . . . We did not speak the same language, and one old man ran into a little wooden shed on the roof and came out with a butcher knife, and the younger one restrained me as I stood with three flowers raised over my head ready to attack, and after we had all shouted I went down the stairs and there was Joel staring upward, and I said, "Joel, we'll try it from across the street." I climbed six flights to the roof of the Electric Circus, signaled to Joel, and threw the flowers down. First the chrysanthemum, then the daffodil, and finally the white daisy. Klunch, klunch, klunch. Each hit the sidewalk intact. I ran down the stairs and Joel, puffing, met me halfway and said, "A kid stole the chrysanthemum and somebody stepped on the daffodil." He was clutching a white daisy in both hands. He was smiling. The Scientific Method leads to joy. Daisies would make it to the YIP-Out.[11]

You can feel Abbie's exhilaration in every word, as if he were free-falling from a plane, joyously, and without a parachute. The two old Italians who chase him from their roof are described with affection and understanding. Abbie was often generous toward opponents and always liked to have hecklers at his speeches. I think Abbie's fantasy was that he really had no enemies, that underneath we were all on the same side, that the goal, for everyone, was nothing less than totality—utter freedom in an accommodating universe.

I was going to turn twenty-nine in September, and I wanted to make sure I spent my birthday with Abbie. Joan and I drove down to New York and when we arrived at his apartment on Thirteenth Street, Abbie took us up to the roof of the building and pulled out a wad of fresh airline tickets, probably supplied by some Yippie sympathizer who worked for an airline. Then he asked us, "If you could go anywhere in the world, where would you want to go?" I looked at Joan and in unison we both said, "China." Abbie flipped through the stack until he found a pair from Kennedy to Hong Kong, stamped and ready to go, and held them out to us. With that diabolical twinkle in his eye, he seemed to be saying that he had the power to make *our* fantasy reality. We laughed, shook our heads, and wouldn't touch the tickets. But we marveled, a little shocked, as we considered the possibilities. And Abbie got a kick out of seeing us stretch our imaginations.

On a Sunday night in September 1968, Roy Rogers and Dale Evans had appeared on *The Ed Sullivan Show*. Dale wore a shirt that looked like it was made from a U.S. flag. A few days afterward, Abbie called me, elated: He'd bought a flag shirt from the same store where Dale had gotten hers, he said, and he was going to wear it to the House Un-American Activities Committee (HUAC) hearing. The hearing had been called to investigate the Chicago demonstrations, and Abbie had been subpoenaed to appear before the Senate subcommittee in early October. And ever since receiving the "invitation," he'd been racking his brains to come up with the right thing to wear. To him, HUAC itself was the sum of all that was un-American, with its anti-Communist hysteria and its culture of finger-pointing and hate. He'd seen the hearings in action in Berkeley around the time of his earliest political awakening, and in the early '60s had toured Western Massachusetts with a film on those HUAC hearings, explaining to often unsympathetic audiences just how un-American they were. Now Abbie was as excited as a young debutante on her way to the ball—the hearing—with the cherished invitation, the subpoena, and the knowledge that no one else's dress would outshine his.

On October 2, the first day of the HUAC hearings, things went off without a hitch. Jerry Rubin brandished a toy M-16 rifle, while several Yippies dressed as witches moaned in the aisles, and for the most part the people conducting the hearings ignored the agitators. Abbie's carefully choreographed plan, set for the second day, was to paint a life-size, full-color Vietcong or Cuban flag directly onto the skin of his back underneath the flag shirt, in case some zealous cop tore the shirt off him.

On October 3, Abbie made his way to the HUAC subcommittee hearings wearing the flag shirt with two political buttons pinned to it: "Wallace for President, Stand Up for America," and "Vote Pig Yippie! in '68." He was arrested as he entered the building and charged with desecrating the American flag, under a law passed that summer. The law made it a federal crime to cast "contempt" upon the flag, carrying maximum penalties of one year in prison and a $1,000 fine. Abbie was also charged with resisting arrest.

He pleaded not guilty, told the judge that he was owed $14.95 for the ripped shirt, and was jailed overnight. Anita had jumped on the back of the cop arresting Abbie and was charged with felonious assault on a police officer (the charges against her were later dropped). Since no one ever tried to arrest Dale Evans for the same offense, Abbie's argument that the disturbance was caused by the police, not him, wasn't unreasonable.

Jerry Rubin, shirtless and wearing a Vietcong flag bandanna, made it to the second day of the hearings and spent the day sitting in the audience. He listened impassively as Cook County state's attorney undercover investigator Robert Pierson—who had infiltrated the Yippies! at the Chicago demonstrations as a friendly motorcycle gang member and personal bodyguard to Abbie and Jerry—testified that the Yippies! and other groups were intent on "overthrowing the United States Government by force." Pierson claimed that there had been plans to execute Chicago policemen and to bomb a ball-playing field in Lincoln Park. He even quoted Jerry, from memory, as having said, "We should kill all the candidates for president." Through it all, Jerry, smirched with red paint and carrying a toy M-16 rifle close to his chest, listened quietly. As the hearings progressed, paid spies like Pierson testified while, one after another, the legitimate Movement leaders refused to take the stand, and HUAC failed to unearth a Communist plot associated with the Chicago Democratic Convention protests.[12]

On October 9, 1968, a front-page article appeared in the *Worcester Telegram* based on an interview with me conducted the day before. What was unique about this article was that it was about me. Abbie was the pretext, but the subject was his brother's story.

The copy that I'm looking at is off microfilm from the local library, a pockmarked negative I obtained only recently. On that day, events kept me reeling, and I couldn't hold on to a copy of the newspaper for longer than a few minutes before one person or another asked to see it and it was gone. But even in the ghastly electric-white photograph that accompanies this microfiche, my clean-cut jacket, tie, and fresh trim are apparent. I remember that I had gone out and bought the jacket and tie and sat through the haircut a few days before—not to fool the interviewer but to make sure he understood that Abbie's brother was respectable, which was the truth. I knew that my respectability would give more weight to my words. The article, under the heading "An Idealist Brother Defends Abbie's Position," began:

> *"There are all these stories appearing in the paper, and none of them actually tell you what Abbie Hoffman is trying to do," said Jack Hoffman, vice president of Worcester Medical Supply Co. Inc. . . . [Abbie is] trying to prove that this isn't a free society. He's trying to show that a person can't dress the way he wants, say what he wants, or do what he wants without somebody like the police or HUAC persecuting him. . . . Abbie is trying to show that a man can't be himself in this society; that the freedoms guaranteed to you and me in the Bill of Rights no longer exist. . . . Abbie knows we will eventually return to being a free society. . . . However, before we can get there, Abbie believes, we have to rebel completely against the hypocrisy of our present society. That's what my brother is doing.*

The newspaper had accurately printed what I had said to the journalist. It didn't show me explaining Abbie away, or defending him exactly, but standing by him, doing exactly what any brother would do, I thought. The reporter might have asked me whether I agreed with my brother. If he had, he would have gotten a very different sounding article. I would have said that I had many of the same criticisms of my brother that most people had. But he never asked me that, so what he got was a brother's empathy, understanding, and loyalty. I continued:

> *All Abbie is saying is, "If a kid wants to wear his hair long— let him. If he wants to wear African clothes to school—let him. Let him do whatever he wants, short of hurting someone else." He's no more a Communist than the president of the United States. . . . He hopes that maybe freedom can be achieved by making an issue out of it. . . . So he gets investigated by HUAC. For running down the street with a pig, he's suspected of being un-American. . . . Why don't they investigate something really un-American, like the Mafia, or themselves?*

I walked into my office on the morning of October 9, 1968, looking forward to a great day. Regardless of what one thought or felt about Abbie, everyone would admire a man standing beside his brother. It occurred to me that there had been something *priestly* in the way I had handled the situation: I had sought to mediate peacefully between warring camps. And besides, I was only talking about freedom and democracy, basic American beliefs; whichever side people found themselves on, these were things on which everyone could agree, so I thought. Already, as soon as I arrived that morning, my secretary had told me how handsome I looked in the front-page photo that accompanied the article. I felt ready and deserving. Jack would bask in the limelight for a change. And I thought I had performed my role honorably.

The calls started coming in almost right away. But they weren't what I had expected. I picked up the receiver to hear expressions of hate from people whom I had known all my life and considered friends. They would begin with: "How dare you say those things?"

"What did I say?" I asked.

"You know, the garbage you put out about your brother, how could you defend him?"

"But he's my brother," I tried a few times. No one was interested.

Then there were the threats: "You won't get home to your family tonight," and others. Somehow, the most painful calls that day were those that were strictly business. I don't know why, but there's something particularly hurtful about being attacked by someone who doesn't even really know you. "We do not want to do business with your kind of people." There were two or three of those calls that day. The purchasing agent from one of our most important accounts, Memorial Hospital in Worcester, let me know that "If I buy from you I have to worry about LSD getting into the aspirin." With those words—which left me speechless—he ended our relationship, despite the fact that for as long as I could remember I had called on that account once a week like clockwork, order or no order. It was only business, but it was personal as hell. And although it happened a week or so later, I still remember and associate with October 9 the nursing home owner in Westfield—someone with whom I had already done significant business—who said, "You're Abbie Hoffman's brother?" and then tore up a $25,000 contract right in front of my eyes, right after his secretary had congratulated me on what I'd said in the newspaper. Many people stopped doing business with us because they despised Abbie, and yet I cannot recall a single individual or company that ever *started* doing business with us because they supported what Abbie was doing.

A woman sent me a note, which I have never forgotten. Her halting and awkward use of English made it clear that she was from the old country; and behind her anger you could taste her fear. Of course, what particularly pissed her off was having to share our religion and our last name. She said she had read my interview and because of it could not even address me as "Dear Sir." She added that she was ashamed of Jewish radicals, who "spoil it for good people." Her letter ended with the words, "God Bless America."

Of course, within the small circle of our closest friends, the article didn't cause the slightest stir; they already knew everything the article said, and most important, they knew Abbie firsthand. The deep misunderstanding, and the hate that grew from it, lay with people who didn't really know us, and especially those who saw my brother only in the papers and on t.v.

By four o'clock that day, several people in the Worcester Medical Supply office had gone home early out of fear. I was scared to leave the building. I was in a state of shock. If someone had told me this was going to happen, I would not have believed it. The things I learned that day came to me completely out of the blue.

After the Chicago 1968 Democratic Convention, and throughout the few remaining months of the year, the country was made well aware of certain aspects of the conflict. The youth culture, the revolution culture, the generation gap would all be adequately, if not excessively, described in the media. But there wasn't a whole lot of attention being paid to the reaction all this rebellion was producing. Most people who were in the Movement, or peripherally involved like I was, had no idea of the level of fear and hate they were prompting in mainstream society. And you wouldn't find out about that by reading the feature articles in *Time* and *Life,* or from a twenty-second segment on the evening news.

The conflict described in the media was between extremist elements on the Left and the police—as we had seen in the streets of Chicago—and portrayed the vast majority of Americans looking on silently, as more or less objective witnesses. But that wasn't it at all. The battlefield wasn't the streets of Washington and Chicago, or even the jungles of Vietnam; it was the hearts and minds of normal Americans. Leaders like Abbie were fighting for the support of America's youth. America's parents had little choice but to stand helplessly on the sidelines as everything they had fought so hard for, everything they believed in, was trashed by him and other leaders of the youth culture. I don't think many of them understood or cared much about the First Amendment to the Constitution. Many of them were not raised here, or—if educated here—had been raised, like us, in homes where the air was still heavy with the values of the old world. The First Amendment was truly a foreign idea to them. What they understood and believed in was freedom, but not Abbie's kind of freedom. What many of America's parents believed in was the more universally understood freedom that came as a reward for hard work: freedom to buy, freedom to own (and which, ironically, was as much in tune with the intentions of the founding fathers as was Abbie's vision).

But Abbie was attacking all that; he preached anti-materialism as the siren-song that would help him entice the children of America away from their parents' old world. In the old El Morocco, Abbie's favorite restaurant high up on one of the hills of Worcester, Joe Aboody, the Christian-Lebanese proprietor and our lifelong trusted friend, kept an autographed photograph of Abbie hanging prominently on the wall. An angry patron ripped it from the wall and smashed it. The fifty tables in the quaint restaurant were occupied at the time, and not one person objected to that act of desecration. We tended not to think about occurrences like that. How could we? They didn't seem real to us.

I can't say that October 9 radicalized me. It didn't. I'm not a revolutionary. But it left me more informed about what it meant to be Abbie Hoffman's brother. Among other things, to be the brother, sister, or parent of someone so publicly loved and hated as Abbie promises a high degree of isolation. Since you don't believe the same things he does, you can't quite be part of his community. But since you are undeniably his brother, it is difficult to join any other group. You find yourself in the middle, often unaccompanied. To be accused, even hated, for things you didn't do or beliefs you don't hold is a desert of a place to find yourself. Yet that is exactly where all the members of Abbie's family found ourselves in 1968. We were awakened to things, like how what others say about you can hurt, and how easy it is to be frightened.

I say to myself over and over: No, 1968 was not a very good year, not a good year at all. I remember 1968 as a year of sadness, when heroes died and many people let themselves be overcome with hate, and when my brother became so deeply immersed in his new life that for much of the year I lost track of him altogether. I hardly knew him, yet I felt tied to the things he did almost as if I had done them. The funny thing about the fall of 1968, despite all the trouble, was how proud I felt of Abbie, proud of all the trouble he was causing, proud of how important he had become. And I was one among hundreds of thousands of young people who felt that way.

In the fall of 1968, Abbie contracted hepatitis and found himself in Albert Einstein Hospital in a wheelchair. After a day or two, a young resident named Lawrence Epstein visited him. Dr. Epstein had a depressed and dying leukemia patient, he told Abbie, who had pictures of Abbie on the walls of his room. Epstein asked Abbie if he would come and visit him. Abbie jumped at the chance, saying how he was trained as a psychologist and was good at it. The patient turned out to be a school teacher in his early twenties, and every day Abbie would wheel himself down the hall and lock himself in with the young school teacher. During the ten days Abbie visited him, the patient emerged from his depression and began to laugh and be more talkative. His parents, who were visiting him every day, noticed the difference and asked Dr. Epstein if he had put their son on some new miracle cure. He told them, no, but that he was seeing a new therapist. The school teacher died about six months later, and the young resident never forgot how Abbie had been able to lift the young man's spirit.[13]

And then, along with my renewed identification with Abbie, came doubts. If it was just revolution for the hell of it, was it worth it? Now that we know that people were really watching and listening, did Abbie really know what he was doing out there? Was he a leader after all? Was he—indirectly and unintentionally, but nonetheless—hurting people?

It was important for me to be able to ask these questions. Still, in the end it wasn't so difficult to answer them. The threat that Abbie posed to the American way of life was largely a distorted shadow thrown by a national imagination run amok. In reality, Abbie fought for people power as propounded in the U.S. Constitution, and nothing more.

And people who hated Abbie—the majority of them—were fighting equally hard on behalf of authority, injustice, and the rights of privilege. If the youth of America, led by people like my brother, were calling the older generation liars, they were not altogether wrong. Did anyone believe Vietnam was a just war in 1968? Yes, of course. But many people on both sides believed it wasn't; for every young person who believed that it was wrong and unacceptable, there was an older person who thought that it might be wrong but was acceptable. For every young person who considered our society to be sexually repressed, there were two older people who knew it was. And for every young person searching for meaning, there were two older people trying and failing to find happiness in the trappings of the American Dream, or in alcohol or prescription drugs.

Dad voted for Nixon twice around. If you asked him why we were in Vietnam—and I did—he would say, "Because the government's right. And who are you to ask questions?" Abbie, so much his father's son, fought against that war with every particle of his being. The difference wasn't so much in their opinions: It went deeper, to the core value system one accepts. Somehow the younger generation had come away with a radically different set of values from their parents.

"Don't trust anyone over thirty" were words Abbie spoke often, and which people on both sides of the generation gap remembered. The older generation—in some ways rightly—saw him as a modern-day Pied Piper of Hamelin, and feared him. But just as Abbie's public often seemed to miss the seriousness in his antics, so did they miss the playfulness in many of his headline-grabbing pronouncements: At the moment he told us to trust no one over thirty Abbie himself was already thirty-two.

Nineteen sixty-eight saw the height of the conflict in the U.S., a conflict that would stop just short of ending in a civil war. Police violence, and the threat of greater violence, had occurred throughout the year and in all parts of the country—not just in Chicago. In New York; in Madison, Wisconsin; in San Francisco . . . The assassinations of the early part of the year can be understood as expressions of the same deep-seated anguish, frustration, and hate, which I felt directed at me on October 9. Everywhere, America teetered on the brink of larger acts of extreme physical violence between fellow Americans. In a way, the country had gone mad. And at many of the crucial junctures, the grinning face that appeared in the newspaper, the one that symbolized the conflict for millions of Americans, was Abbie's.

More and more, the cruelty of the war in Southeast Asia was the context for Abbie's type of theater. His was the politics of confrontation. He wanted to draw fire from the jungles of Vietnam onto himself. He knew that our government could continue to prosecute the war only as long as it could uphold two standards of behavior: one, the kid-glove treatment for the protesters at home, the other, the brutality of the genocidal bombings in Vietnam. And, of course, Abbie was right about so many things during this period, but he alienated many of us.

Although I would not have been able to articulate it at the time, what began for me in the aftermath of Chicago, and dawned on me forcefully on October 9, 1968, was a recognition of the possibility of Abbie's utter seriousness. In our family we were already used to believing Abbie capable of anything. He had convinced us that he was able to do whatever he wanted and get away with it. We considered him blessed and beloved. And things he told us about himself—some of it wildly exaggerated—we willingly took at face value, whether it was his grades at school or what he called his eidetic memory. But one thing he never took pains to convince us of was his seriousness. We always assumed that whatever he did, he did for the fun of it. That had always been true of Abbie growing up. That this could have changed was the hardest thing for us to accept.

In early 1992, the interviewer David Frost asked the writer Norman Mailer, "How would you like to be remembered?" Mailer had to consider the question for only a split second before answering, "I would like to be taken seriously." The problem wasn't just Abbie's. I believe that many public figures from the '60s, if they are honest, would answer that question the same way. It goes with the territory. In the '60s, the distinction between what was serious and what was not was blurred, because all of a sudden a variety of people doing a variety of strange things were having an impact. But to take someone seriously—especially when they were fooling around all the time the way Abbie was—you had to see them sweat and worry; you had to see their ideas evolve. And only a few people ever knew Abbie that way.

The dazzling first live pictures of the surface of the moon were televised on December 29 from Apollo 8. But by then there were over half a million American troops stationed in Vietnam and more than thirty thousand had been killed. And while Nixon—who would truly desecrate the flag by breaking the law countless times while in office—prepared for his presidential inauguration, Abbie was convicted of desecration of the U.S. flag for the HUAC arrest and sentenced to thirty days.[14] After finding him guilty, the judge asked if Abbie had any last words. Striking a solemn pose, Abbie gleefully delivered a speech that ended, "Your honor, I only regret that I have but one shirt to give for my country."[15]

Like many of the battles Abbie fought, he would win this one eventually. On March 30, 1971, the U.S. Court of Appeals would reverse the flag desecration conviction, finding that Abbie Hoffman did not desecrate the American flag by wearing a shirt that looked like one, since his "flag-style shirt was intended to cast contempt on the [HUAC] Committee but not on the flag." The Appeals Court judge, George E. MacKinnon, agreed with Abbie's contention that he was convicted "because of his well known public image which is highly controversial" and not because he had been contemptuous of the flag. In the two years after Abbie's conviction, there were many other convictions for flag desecration in a number of states. Thus the 1971 reversal was seen, by the ACLU among other organizations, as a decisive victory for freedom of speech. But as happened so often, by the time it came, Abbie's victory had cost him heavily and paid him no reward.[16]

Chapter Seven

1969–1970

For the first time in my life I was afraid of my government.
—Spoken by a Juror at the Conclusion of the
Chicago Conspiracy Trial

NINETEEN SIXTY-NINE was the year when Abbie came closest to find-ing himself—when he was funniest, but also when he was most fright-ened; when he acted the most courageously and also when his childhood antics were most pronounced; when he espoused violence, and also when he experienced his own nonviolence most deeply. It was the year when he became a bona fide world-class celebrity, when his audience was largest, and also when he felt most urgently the need for the closeness of his family, only to find that the effect of his notori-ousness on Dad had finally put their relationship beyond repair.

The event that both consumed and defined Abbie in 1969 was the Chicago Conspiracy trial. It has been called the most important political trial of the century. And for Abbie personally it was to be the seminal event of his life, acting upon him with the force of destiny. The Chicago trial was where, for a short time, Abbie's fate and the fate of the nation seemed inextricably intertwined.

The decision of who was to be indicted in the Chicago trial had been made at the highest levels of the Nixon administration, the FBI, and the Chicago prosecutor's office. As early as October 23, 1968, J. Edgar Hoover had drafted a memo urging prosecution against the leaders of the Chicago demonstrations, writing that "a successful prosecution of this type would be a unique achievement for the Bureau and should seriously disrupt and curtail the activities of the New Left."[1]

Throughout the winter of 1968 and early 1969 there were minor skirmishes as the government poked and prodded the various co-defendants, testing for weaknesses, and straining the defendants' scant resources. Abbie and Anita had to fly to Chicago several times for court appearances on minor charges stemming from the 1968 Chicago Democratic convention that were separate from the central conspiracy indictments to come, and for new nuisance charges such as Abbie's arrest for carrying a small switchblade in his pocket during one such flight. Sometimes there were fines to pay, other times Abbie was sentenced to jail terms of up to two weeks.[2]

On March 20, 1969, came the main charges—indictments handed down against an array of anti-government leaders, not all of whom were planners of the Chicago demonstrations, and several of whom hardly knew each other. The eight co-conspirators were, in the order in which their names appeared in the indictment, David Dellinger, Rennie Davis, Tom Hayden, Abbie, Jerry Rubin, Lee Weiner, John Froines, and Bobby Seale. By casting the net as widely as possible—grouping together the Yippies! (Abbie and Jerry), the Mobe (Rennie was national coordinator for the National Mobilization to End the War in Vietnam), SDS (both Tom and Rennie were among the founders of Students for a Democratic Society), The Black Panthers (Bobby Seale was National Chairman of the Black Panther Party), the New Left (particularly Tom and Rennie), the Old Left (Dave Dellinger was a prominent pacifist), and the university-based Left (John Froines and Lee Weiner were both anti-war academics)—the government planned to portray all those fighting to end racism, injustice, and the war in Vietnam as part of a deeper, darker conspiracy. The government hoped for a Soviet-style show trial, one that would paint the entire Left as anti-American and show Americans that these leading activists were mere criminals.

The indictments made use of an anti-riot rider that had been attached by Senator Strom Thurmond and other Southern Democrats to an open housing bill passed by Congress a week after the assassination of Martin Luther King, Jr., in April 1968. The bill had originally been intended as a tribute to Reverend King. But the anti-riot rider made it a crime to cross state lines to incite or promote violence. Ironically, the Southern Democrats wanted it to help rid them of civil rights activists in general, and prevent SNCC leaders H. Rap Brown and Stokely Carmichael in particular from stirring up more trouble in the South.

When the law was first proposed, progressive Attorney General Ramsey Clark lobbied against it, voicing the view of many legal experts that its crude language was constitutionally dubious and could hinder legitimate political activity. After all, the law defined a riot as any public disturbance involving as few as three people and an act of violence endangering another person or property. By that definition, a jury might come down against the organizers of a peaceful protest after their peaceful actions were disrupted by violent counterdemonstrators. Even before the Chicago convention, some anti-war leaders, including Tom Hayden, expressed concerns that the rider would be used to clamp down on dissent across the country.[3]

Shortly after the Democratic Convention ended, Chicago Mayor Richard Daley requested that Attorney General Clark invoke the new anti-riot law against the protesters. The liberal Clark refused. And when the voluminous, blue-ribbon Walker Report, whose purpose was to unearth the origins of the violence, concluded that "the vast majority of the demonstrators were intent on expressing their dissent by peaceful means" and that the predominant cause of the violence had been a "police riot," Clark went even further and ordered a federal grand jury in Chicago to begin investigating policemen who might have been in violation of federal laws.[4] Eventually, painstaking research conducted by the writer John Schultz among others would reveal that the notion of a "police riot" was actually an understatement for what had been, in fact, a systematic and planned police assault.

With the election of Richard Nixon in November 1968, and his inauguration in January 1969, the point of view of the Department of Justice swung completely around. Leaders of the Left across the country found themselves under assault; still searching for a unified post-Chicago strategy, they came under increased levels of harassment from the police and government. Clark issued a warning in the early days after the election: "If the new Administration prosecutes the

[Chicago] demonstrators, it will be a clear sign of a hard-line crack-down [on dissent]." Soon afterward, Nixon's new Attorney General, John Mitchell, pressed the Chicago U.S. Attorney, Thomas Foran, to balance out the indictment with demonstrators. The eight co-conspirators were chosen to equal the eight already indicted policemen. But there ended any notion of equality: Seven of the officers were charged under an ancient law that forbids public officials from inflicting summary punishment, the eighth was accused of perjury; all were acquitted.[5]

As he began preparing for the trial, touring the country making speeches at campuses to raise money for the defense, and participating in demonstrations, Abbie was increasingly a recognized and popular national figure. His face appeared regularly on television. Reviews of *Revolution for the Hell of It* were beginning to appear, and it was selling well. The Chicago Conspiracy trial indictments served to enhance his national stature, identifying him as a defender of civil rights, a voice of conscience.

Nineteen sixty-nine happened to be the tenth anniversary of Abbie's "Class of 1959" college graduation. And on April 17, a questionnaire from Brandeis found its way to Abbie. "Please write below a short resume of your activities since graduation," it urged, in a pleasant, collegy voice, "including such things as: marriage date, names and ages of children, graduate schools attended, degrees received, honors received, travel, community activities, occupations, etc." A whole world of implication. The rest of the page was left open for the alumnus to sum up his achievements of the past decade. Abbie filled in his response without missing a beat:

> *40 arrests—facing 10 years for crossing state lines to commit riot, 7 years for felonious assault on a pig, 30 days for wearing a shirt flag, 15 days for resisting arrest in Chicago, one year for possession of loaded guns, $50.00 fine for not fastening my seat belt on an airplane, 1 year for tackling a policeman at Columbia. Sorry to have missed Lester Lanin at the Brandeis Reunion in New York. Send us some bread*

*to help us plant a tree in Chicago during our trial—make
checks payable to "The Conspiracy"/109 No. Dearborn St./
Chicago, Ill.*

It's all right there in a nutshell. There were these two worlds.
One held class reunions and marked its progress according to marriage dates, names and ages of children, degrees, and honors. The
other was by its nature revolutionary. Anybody else but Abbie would
have assumed that the two worlds were mutually exclusive. Abbie
understood that the two worlds were carrying on a conversation all
the time. He saw no contradiction in being a Jew, a patriot and an
outlaw, a college rah-rah and a revolutionary.

The tree he mentions is a reference to planting trees in Israel.
When we went to temple as kids, after Israeli independence in 1948,
Ma would give us a quarter each to give to the teacher, and eventually
we'd contributed enough to have a tree planted in our names in the
homeland. Millions of trees were planted that way in the late '40s and
'50s, living symbols of the solidarity American Jews felt with the Jewish state, with the power to turn desert into fertile gardens. Tree-
planting may have been Abbie's earliest lesson in political
propaganda. To suggest planting trees in Chicago twenty years later
was to imply that, because of the trial, the city had become a kind of
new holy land.

Abbie had been hearing rumors about an upcoming rock concert
on farmland a couple of hours north of New York City since late
spring. He saw the event as "an opportunity to reach masses of young
people in a setting where they felt part of something bigger,"[6] but he
feared that the promoters were going to use the counterculture to
make a fortune for themselves. If that were allowed to happen, then
no matter how good the music might be, the message would be one of
greed, not enlightenment, a rip-off that would be bad for the Movement.

Abbie reached the organizer of the event, Michael Lang, and demanded $10,000, two hundred free tickets, an area for tables offering
political literature, and the right to leaflet the crowd. In return, Abbie
offered to help deal with some of the problems that were going to

arise, things the promoters weren't prepared to handle, like large numbers of people on bad acid. At first, Lang refused. Then, to Abbie's amazement, Lang said yes. Abbie got the money and immediately spent half of it on a press to print political leaflets on-site, to make sure issues would remain an essential part of the concert.

Lang had pulled together an amazing roster of musicians that included Jimi Hendrix, Janis Joplin, Santana, Creedence Clearwater Revival, Richie Havens, Jefferson Airplane, The Grateful Dead, The Who, Crosby, Stills, Nash and Young, and many others.[7] The promoters were expecting about 75,000 fans. Abbie felt there was a good chance the crowd would be much larger.

As Woodstock began, so did the rain, but people just kept coming. On Friday afternoon, people with nine-to-five jobs joined the rush. Nearly half a million people had showed up by Saturday despite the rain that had turned the entire area into mud. Abbie couldn't have been happier. To him, the phenomenon of Woodstock held special meaning that no amount of adversity could alter: It meant the Yippie! myth of peace, love, and music bringing people together was becoming a reality. Abbie felt that his job was to keep the struggle—against injustice at home and war in Vietnam—a part of the celebration.

Near dawn on Saturday morning, Abbie, high on acid, decided, rightly, that the instant metropolis that had risen around the forty-acre field was ridiculously unprepared for medical emergencies. Although he had no authority to do so, he commandeered the press tent alongside the stage, threw out all the journalists there, and announced that it was now a hospital. By 7:00 A.M., Abbie was barking his orders through a bullhorn. He had even commandeered a helicopter and made arrangements for more doctors to be flown in. Abbie may have acted obnoxiously but showed nearly perfect judgment that morning, and without the field hospital Woodstock might have been remembered very differently than it is.

The music was scheduled to begin on Saturday afternoon and last through Sunday. The New York Port Authority had stopped selling bus tickets to the area. National Guard troops had been mobilized. There was a rumor that the concert had been declared a disaster area. But the music was incredible, and by Saturday night the concert organizers knew they had pulled it off. Between sets, as The Who was getting ready to go on, Abbie sat on the side of the stage talking with Lang about the possibility of devoting a percentage of any movie revenue to a bail fund—in his mind was the recent imprisonment in Michigan of activist John Sinclair for possession of one marijuana joint.

Suddenly, Abbie decided it was the right moment for him to make a speech; still high on the LSD, maybe mixed in with some speed, he walked up to the mike and started rapping—about Sinclair, about the war in Vietnam, and the war at home. He went on for twenty minutes or so, then someone turned off his microphone. Angry, Abbie kicked over the mike and walked off. Peter Townshend of The Who was walking on. He passed Abbie and whacked him with his guitar, pushing him off the stage.[8]

Abbie wasn't seen again that weekend. In the Woodstock movie you don't see Abbie and you don't see his hospital. He continued talking about Woodstock Nation, and he would continue to feel that this was the nation to which he belonged. But he was shattered by the rebuke he had suffered. It put the fear in him that maybe other people didn't share his aspirations, didn't always care about the same things he did. I think it was the first time he felt like the leader of a party of one.

Years later, Townshend would tell *Rolling Stone:* "I deeply regret [kicking Abbie offstage]. Abbie at Woodstock really was correctly despairing. He was fucking right. If I was given that opportunity again, I would stop the show [to let Abbie speak]. Because I don't think Rock & Roll is that important. Then I did. The show had to go on."[9]

Back in the city, Abbie camped out in the Random House office of editor Christopher Cerf, son of publishing legend and Random House founder Bennett Cerf, and started filling yellow legal pads, writing longhand in a burst of manic energy. Random House had wanted a sequel to *Revolution for the Hell of It.* In *Woodstock Nation,* Abbie was able to give them the book they wanted by, in effect, finishing off the speech he had begun on the Woodstock stage, redefining the rock concert as a political event and counterculture symbol, and affirming in print what he had been prevented from affirming at the concert.

Dedicated to Lenny Bruce, the book is a breathless and random collection of essays, vignettes, poster-like images, and photographs whose most striking characteristic is that it obliterates the distinctions between politics and culture. He called it a "talk-rock album," and the chapters are referred to as "song titles." Jimi Hendrix and Janis Joplin are there, and so are Elvis Presley, Che Guevara, John Sinclair, and Norman Mailer. The politics of the book are pervasive, but nowhere as clear or as striking as in his other writings. The central theme is Abbie's recent Woodstock experience, an understanding of which in many ways still eluded him. The passion of the book is intense and appears on every page. But the frenzied quality of the writing denies it the saving grace of Abbie's other books, where underneath the zaniness you can feel the presence of an utterly clear mind and an uncluttered heart. For all its virtues, *Woodstock Nation* is a tract written to even the score by the guy who was thrown off the stage.

Back in Worcester, Dad's friends were giving him hell about Abbie. They bombarded him: Who did Abbie think he was? What was he trying to prove with all his antics? Wasn't he just making it worse for the rest of us, making people think badly of the Jews? Did he really think the powers that be were going to let him get away with it? And Dad could only shake his head and agree with all these criticisms. Abbie was his son, but he didn't know him the way a father should know his own son, and that made him mad. Dad felt that the underlying sentiment seemed to be a criticism not of Abbie but of himself: You're his father, control your son; what's wrong with you that you can't?

Then there were more sinister forms of harassment. Starting shortly after the Chicago convention, a couple of local FBI agents had become regular visitors to the store when Dad was around. Their visits were only quasi-official. They were guys who'd always come by the store to buy their vitamins. Dad wasn't against talking with them, just like he did with all his customers. But after Chicago, they started to get heavy, pressuring Dad about Abbie. Two agents from the Department of the Treasury's Bureau of Alcohol, Tobacco, and Firearms also started coming around, questioning us about any guns we, or Abbie, possessed.

A few friends and neighbors told us that they had been visited by the FBI and questioned about the Hoffman family—disturbing news since it made us wonder about all the friends, neighbors, and perhaps even relatives who were interviewed by the FBI and never told us. The harassment may have been subtle, but the toll it took was real and constant. It was almost as if the FBI were building prison walls around you in the minds of your friends and neighbors.

When Abbie's FBI files were released to me recently for the research for this book, again and again there appeared three categories of informants: neighbors, friends, and business acquaintances; the names of the individuals are crossed out, and often whole paragraphs or whole pages are crossed out as well. Whatever it was that these people did, to date none has come to me to say, "Those days are gone now," or "I wish I hadn't done what I did," which tells me that in the minds of many the battle lines are still drawn.

You've got to remember that this was all happening pre-Watergate. There was much more trust in government and in what government stood for than there is today. When FBI agents and other U.S. government representatives started to suggest that subversives like Abbie, and by extension the Hoffman family, were a *criminal element,* most of our friends and neighbors must have felt that they had to side with the government. To some people we must have appeared as traitors of the same stripe as Julius and Ethel Rosenberg, whom people still thought of as archcriminals. Jewish acquaintances might say to me, "What is your fucking crazy brother up to now?! He's an embarrassment!" And—it still makes me mad today when I think of it—gentiles would look at me and say, "Your dirty Communist brother, why doesn't he go back to Israel where he belongs?" or they would accuse me of "tearing down the flag." And they weren't being funny or ironic. They were angry, as if personally offended. It was often scary. And we knew no way to respond other than by walking away.

Dad felt pushed and shoved. He found that he was in fundamental agreement with those among his friends and business associates who despised his son. He loved Abbie and would never disavow him. But he believed that Abbie was striking out at him personally, hurting his business, hurting his standing in the community, hurting him, and for no reason. His instinctive loyalty toward his son was strong, but so was his sense of what was right. Dad had already decided against attending the upcoming trial, and now he prohibited Ma from going as well.

One day in the middle of September 1969, at the height of the media feeding frenzy surrounding the start of the Chicago Conspiracy trial, Dad closed the door of his office, sat down at his desk, and began to write Abbie a letter—not so much in the hope that Abbie would listen to him but out of a feeling of resignation: there were times when certain things needed to be said. "I will try my very best to talk to him," Dad seemed to be saying, "and then, whatever happens, I will wash my hands." It was as close as Dad would ever come to turning his back on his eldest son.

The letter he wrote filled three or four pages in careful longhand, and he showed it to me before he sent it. Despite its condemnation of Abbie's actions, the letter had taken heartfelt effort on Dad's part, and in its heavy tone of resignation was the expression of a sad faith, almost as if Dad were transmitting his blessing by expressing what he took to be the wisdom of our people, the wisdom of survival.

The letter decried the shame Abbie had brought on the family, and even listed some of his more notorious stunts. It extolled the virtues of America as the land of true freedom and democracy, and drew a comparison to the hardships Jews had historically experienced elsewhere, including pogroms and the camps. But mostly the letter asserted, timidly, the importance of respect. I cannot remember the exact words, but I recall the thoughts and the emotions they expressed as if it were yesterday. You must learn, Dad wrote to his eldest son, to conduct yourself in a respectable manner in the courtroom during the upcoming trial. And there are other things you ought to respect as well.

Dad didn't say outright that one of the other things Abbie ought to respect was his father—he didn't dare. And maybe that was the saddest thing about the letter. But I think Dad was trying to express that somehow the idea of respect was bound up with the idea of self-preservation. Without respect, he wrote, what have we left? Without respect, Abbie could read between the lines, they will put you in jail for a thousand years and your father won't be able to stop them.

After he read Dad's letter, Abbie took his copy of *Revolution for the Hell of It,* opened it to pages eleven and twelve where he had recounted his version of the biblical history of Abraham and Isaac, and wrote in the margin, "Letter to Dad":

> *Placing his son upon the carefully constructed altar, he binds and gags him to let his son know that he loves him, and yet he does not need to do that because the boy too loves his father and needs no bindings. There would be no pain.*[10]

Linking his own troubled relationship with Dad to the biblical tale of mercy—where God asks that Abraham be willing to sacrifice that which he loves the most, his son, and then spares him that sacrifice—helped Abbie forgive Dad, even if Dad still wasn't ready to forgive Abbie. The margin note embodied his wish that he and Dad could be reconciled somehow some day.

Civil war occurred in most American families that year. Ours was far from the worst. During the research for this book, I spoke to a retired FBI special agent, who still has not spoken to his son after twenty-five years.

The pretrial proceedings, including the swearing in of the jury, took place on September 24 and 25, with the trial itself beginning on the 26th. The gist of the government's case was that the eight defendants had crossed state lines to incite people—who had planned to come to protest peacefully—to violent and illegal rioting. On the face of it, all the government had to do to win was to persuade the jury to accept its own reading of a naturally ambiguous series of events involving the defendants. For example, it had to convince the jury that when various defendants requested permits and sanitation facilities to allow half a million protesters to march through the streets and sleep in the park, the defendants were making unreasonable demands that they knew the city of Chicago could not grant, thus creating an ungovernable situation. And that this was the desired result on the part of the defendants.

But the government had two immense problems. The first was that in order to make its case it had to produce a seemingly endless parade of barely reputable witnesses: government agents, FBI informers, surveillance experts, and undercover police officers who had been paid to do the dirty work of the state. During the Democratic National Convention, leaders of the movement, including all of the defendants, were tailed around the clock, often by several local, state, and federal agencies simultaneously. Many of those doing the tailing and infiltrating were people with prison records or other unsavory marks of character. The government had paid them to lie and to deceive in order to infiltrate the demonstrators' ranks. And even though one could argue that they were doing so out of patriotism, the image they projected was nonetheless one of dishonesty and worthlessness. In many cases, it was the government agents themselves who had encouraged acts of violence, not the demonstrators. In order to make its case, the prosecution had to unmask itself, in effect admit that it used questionable methods and tarnished operators to deny citizens their basic constitutional rights of privacy and freedom of speech.

In the early weeks of the trial, as the prosecution brought to the stand its procession of witnesses who had worn disguises, grown their hair long, sprouted beards, pretended to be members of motorcycle gangs, and posed as bodyguards for Abbie, Jerry, and other leaders, it was the prosecutors, not the defendants, who were turning the courtroom into a freak show. With each passing hour, America seemed less like the land of the free and the brave. In that courtroom the American people were allowed to see our government in its most terrifying aspect.

The second problem the prosecution had was that the defendants and defense attorneys, particularly William Kunstler and Leonard Weinglass, were in fundamental ideological accord. Despite the wide range of political philosophies they represented, they were united in viewing the trial as a political one, with trumped-up criminal charges, and thus an opportunity to put the government on trial. Ironically, the prosecution shared this view. Each group saw itself as the guardian of democracy in the fight against totalitarianism.

One of the first things Abbie had done after arriving in Chicago before the trial began was to survey the tops of the buildings surrounding the courthouse to get an idea from where a sniper might be likely to shoot. He felt that there was a distinct risk of being shot while going to and from the trial. Death threats had been made in letters and on call-in radio programs. At the same time, he felt that the courthouse itself was, strangely, a place of refuge. He believed he was innocent, and that nothing he might say in criticism of the justice system would impinge on its ability to find him innocent. Thus it was his underlying optimism that would enable him to stand so proud throughout the trial—his courage was inseparable from his naïveté.

The three-ring-circus atmosphere that would evolve during the trial has always been blamed on the defendants. But it was a natural response to the constant and relentless scorn of the prosecution, a survival response to the pressure-cooker atmosphere, in which the bravado of the defendants was pitted against the combined power of the state, the FBI, and the federal government. And partly it was an expression of the defendants' belief that they were going to be acquitted regardless of what they did in court.

Abbie's mood as the trial opened on the morning of September 26—despite the fear—was playful, almost joyful. In front of the courthouse he did a full frontal somersault, like he used to do when we were kids. An hour later, as the proceedings began in the courtroom on the twenty-third floor, the court transcripts describe a fleeting exchange between one of the prosecuting attorneys and the judge that eloquently records Abbie's gentle exuberance:

MR. SCHULTZ [*Assistant U.S. Attorney Richard Schultz*]: *Thank you, Your Honor.*
  In promoting and encouraging this riot . . . two of these defendants, the defendant Abbie Hoffman who sits—who is just standing for you, ladies and gentlemen—
THE COURT [*Judge Julius Hoffman*]: *The jury is directed to*

disregard the kiss thrown by the defendant Hoffman and
the defendant is directed not to do that sort of thing again.

The early weeks of the trial were characterized by incessant jock-
eying for position on both sides—with most of the antics, although
unwitting, coming from the judge and prosecutors.

On October 17, 1969, Bill Kunstler and Abbie, free on bail, addressed the radical National Lawyers Guild at Northwestern Law
School in Chicago. That day Abbie cracked the jokes—"We sent
Judge Hoffman so far about seventeen gallons of Geritol" and
"Maybe America is the most violent country that ever was. I know
where I live, on the Lower East Side of Manhattan . . . we've got a
plant that's been mugged"—and left the heart of the matter to Kunstler's justly famous oratory. Kunstler began:

> *They [the defendants] are saying to that jury, we don't think*
> *the institutions [of America] are* beyond reproach . . . *we are*
> *not going to* bend *to them, we're not going to* genuflect *to*
> *them, and we're not going to genuflect to you. If you want*
> *to convict us, convicted then we are and* as we live and as
> our lifestyles exist, *but if you want to acquit us, don't acquit*
> *us because we bend a knee and bow a head to you and your*
> *institutions.*

The larger question posed by the Chicago trial, according to
Kunstler, was whether the American justice system could cope with
dissent and whether the courts were being used to crush dissent:

> *I am not one who believes that we have,* at this moment, *a*
> *fascist state in the United States. But I am one who believes*
> *that there is* handwriting on the wall . . . *the* faint outline *of*
> *the swastika. . . . If we fail here [in Chicago], I'm not saying*
> *this is the end of fairness and the sweet life of free expres-*
> *sion, but I say that if we fail here that the shadow on the*
> *wall will be* darker . . . *because this case was* deliberately

designed to put dissent on trial. . . . *The state is attempting to* silence hundreds and thousands *of others through* these eight.[11]

Both Abbie and Bill Kunstler seemed to believe that the Chicago trial was bringing us close to the brink of revolution in America, and that people were going to have to choose sides, for change or against it.

Outside of the courtroom Abbie would switch crash-pads almost every night, for security reasons and because he was sleeping with a variety of different women. Anita was flying in for key press conferences and the like, but most of the time she was back in New York living her life and participating in the early activities of the nascent women's movement.

Charles R. Garry, attorney for the Black Panther Party, was originally to have been chief trial counsel for all eight defendants. But Garry had had to undergo gall bladder surgery and was unable to appear in court. Seven of the defendants were comfortable being represented by the other defense attorneys. But before the jury was selected and sworn in, Bobby Seale informed the defense attorneys that, in Garry's absence, he wished to defend himself, as was his constitutional right. Judge Hoffman was notified of this request and simply denied it.

For the next six weeks, until Judge Hoffman severed Seale's connection with the trial, Seale attempted to represent himself at every appropriate instance, wishing the jury good morning as the proceedings began each day and standing to cross-examine any witnesses who testified against him. And every time he spoke, Judge Hoffman silenced him with the words, "You have a lawyer to speak for you." The exchanges between Seale and Hoffman were at first the most entertaining, and then the most horrifying of the trial, as reprimands and contempt citations gave way to regular beatings of Seale by marshals in full view of the packed courtroom.

One by one the polite conventions on which the U.S. court system prides itself were thrown out the window, until Seale's struggle to defend himself became the bitterest and most lasting image of the trial. Over and over, Seale was brutally wrestled back into his chair by the marshals thereby exposing a darker side of American justice.

In the third week of October Sheila, Andrew, and Amy joined Abbie in the courtroom. He seemed uncomfortable with their presence at first. But they were only there to show their support, and before long Abbie was bragging to reporters how already Andrew had gotten into two fights at school on account of who his father was.

On October 29, Judge Hoffman declared that there would be a short recess during which he instructed marshals to take Bobby Seale into a separate room and "deal with him as he should be dealt with." When the proceedings resumed, the defendants found Seale seated on a metal chair, each hand tightly handcuffed to the leg of the chair. A gag was tightly pressed into his mouth and tied at the rear, so that when he attempted to speak, a muffled sound came out. Seale still managed to be heard through the gag and could wrench his arms free, so for the next several days the courtroom watched the spectacle of marshals adding ever heavier and more elaborate bindings.

On the afternoon of November 5, unable to silence him, Judge Hoffman severed Seale from the case and found the Black Panther chairman guilty of sixteen separate counts of contempt, sentencing him to three months on each: a four year sentence. Ironically, it was never clear to any of the defendants why Seale had been included in the trial in the first place, since he had come to Chicago for only one day, had not been involved in organizing any of the demonstrations, and none of the defendants except Jerry Rubin had even met him before. But in the end it was Seale who set the standard for the rest of the defendants. He showed courage in the courtroom as if it were a battlefield and taught his co-defendants that you can't reason with the enemy. Abbie ended up feeling that Seale's refusal to waive his right to defend himself was in many ways the most significant act of the whole trial, since by it Seale had forced the court to show its ugly face. And it was Seale's performance most of all that would inspire Abbie's testimony later in the trial.

At around 5 A.M. on the morning of December 4, 1969, fifteen state's attorney's police in Chicago raided the home of Fred Hampton, chairman of the Illinois Chapter of the Black Panther Party, and shot him dead in his bed. Hampton had been a friend of the defense and had visited Seale in jail early on. The defendants felt that the police were making a point, showing what they had the power to do. Out of mourning for the dead leader, defense attorneys requested a half-day recess, which Judge Hoffman denied. It felt as if a monster had been awakened. At night each defendant found himself wondering if he would be the next one the Chicago police would murder in his sleep.

On December 5, the government presented its last witness, and on December 8 the defense began to tell its side. One thing was immediately evident: While the government had called mostly lower-level employees of the police department, the FBI, or the state, the defense produced presidents of colleges, Members of Parliament, ordained ministers including Jesse Jackson, then employed by the Southern Christian Leadership Conference, famous singers like Phil Ochs (who, when asked on the stand if he could identify Abbie and Jerry, said, "Yes, Jerry Rubin with the headband and Abbie Hoffman with the smile"), Arlo Guthrie, Country Joe McDonald, Pete Seeger, and Judy Collins, the poets Allen Ginsberg (whom the prosecution tried to ridicule by having him read his poems to the jury) and Ed Sanders, the authors Norman Mailer and William Styron, the historian Staughton Lynd, the comedian Dick Gregory, former Harvard professor Timothy Leary, Georgia state congressman and SNCC leader Julian Bond, former Attorney General of the United States Ramsey Clark, the president of the Public Law Education Institute Thomas Patterson Alder, and others. Again and again, these well-known public figures described unprovoked instances of police officers randomly assaulting protesters and clubbing them viciously during convention week in late August 1968.

The defense team decided not to put all the defendants on the witness stand. Only Rennie Davis and Abbie would testify: Rennie because he would appear to the jury as such a responsible kid, and Abbie because, although he'd appear to be a prankster and a troublemaker, he would strike the jury as harmless and nothing like the dangerous criminal the prosecution was portraying.

*　*　*

Abbie went first, in response to questions from defense attorney Leonard Weinglass. It was December 23, 1969. The trial had been going on for three months during which it had become increasingly bitter on both sides of the aisle. Miraculously, in that congealed and stultifying atmosphere, Abbie presented himself, more or less spontaneously, in a way that had power and poignancy and yet was utterly nonconfrontational, transcending the bitter armed-camp mood of the courtroom. It was to be one of his defining moments.

Abbie raised his fist in the power salute before lifting his arm for the swearing in, and repeated the gesture at the end of the oathtaking. When asked to give his name, his first words of testimony were, "My name is Abbie. I am an orphan of America." The words reverberated, and still reverberate today, with the power of his indignation.

As he continued, dwelling on questions of identity, not conflict, and describing himself with wit and humor as both an activist and an artist, Abbie spoke of Woodstock Nation, and though the name had been around since the rock concert four months earlier and had served as the title of his most recent book, it was in Chicago that Abbie gave it meaning:

> *I live in Woodstock Nation. . . . It is a nation of alienated young people. . . . It is a nation dedicated to cooperation versus competition, to the idea that people should have better means of exchange than property or money, that there should be some other basis for human interaction. . . . It is in my mind and in the minds of my brothers and sisters. It does not consist of property or material but, rather, of ideas and certain values. . . .*
>
> MR. WEINGLASS: *Between the date of your birth, November 30, 1936, and May 1, 1960, what if anything occurred in your life?*
>
> THE WITNESS [Abbie]: *Nothing. I believe it is called an American education.*
>
> MR. WEINGLASS: *Can you tell the Court and jury what is your present occupation?*
>
> THE WITNESS: *I am a cultural revolutionary. Well, I am really a defendant—full-time.*

MR. WEINGLASS: *What do you mean by the phrase "cultural revolutionary?"*
THE WITNESS: *Well, I suppose it is a person who tries to shape and participate in the values, and the mores, the customs and the style of living of new people who eventually become inhabitants of a new nation and a new society through art and poetry, theater, and music.*

During his testimony, Abbie asked several times for water, adding, "The trial is bad for my health." Then, beginning with a fit of coughing he couldn't stop, he had a bronchial episode while on the witness stand—a bad one—and had to be rushed to Michael Reese Hospital. That night, a call came from Chicago to my home in Framingham—I don't remember if it came from our sister Phyllis, who was working in the defense office, or from Jerry Lefcourt, Abbie's lawyer. The message was that Abbie wanted me there.

That was on a Friday. Sunday morning I took an early flight to Chicago and took a cab directly to the hospital. The driver talked constantly about the trial during the ride, cursing the Chicago 7 (now that Seale's case had been separated from the others) and Abbie in particular. My natural urge was to say, "I'm his brother." But something had changed, not in me but out there in the public's perception of Abbie, as if it were no longer a question of whether what Abbie was doing was right or wrong. What was new, and I felt it clearly in the back of that cab, was the perception that Abbie was dangerous, a public enemy. Phyllis had warned me that there were so many off-duty cops in Chicago that you just had to keep your mouth shut. And so I did.

At the hospital entrance stood two U.S. marshals, looking the part right up to their beige trenchcoats. When I asked for Abbie's room number at the front desk, I noticed a delayed response from the receptionist. I couldn't tell anymore if it was the criminal thing or the celebrity thing. She said I had to wait, and a few minutes later a federal marshal came down to escort me. As we walked, he machine-gunned me with questions to prove my identity, starting with Ma's maiden name. By order of Judge Hoffman, Abbie was still under oath and thus under federal protection, the marshal explained. I'd only planned to visit my sick brother, but here I felt I'd unexpectedly entered a brave new world.

Outside Abbie's door were two more marshals. When I got inside, the first thing I noticed were the tubes coming out of Abbie's nose and the oxygen mask connected to a large tank by the bed. Abbie himself looked badly beaten up. I was horrified. But right away Abbie pulled the cannulas from his nose and spoke to me: "Hey, brother," he said in his hardiest, most gravelly voice. And once he'd started talking he kept going a mile a minute: "So what do you think of Chicago? Are you hungry? You want steak, lobster? I can get you whatever you want."

I stayed right through the afternoon and evening. Strangely, there were no other visitors. My brother kept up the Abbie road show for me, trying to entertain me with constant small talk. But you could see he was at the end of his rope, exhausted to the point of physical breakdown. "You've got to understand," he said, "I'm the star of this show," meaning the Chicago trial. We played cards, gin, and we watched a football game on t.v. Then he sent me home to the lodgings he'd arranged for me, an apartment where Tom Hayden was also staying, with instructions that I meet him the next morning at the courthouse.

Abbie was waiting for me when I arrived, looking washed out but high spirited. I followed him through the most extensive security apparatus I'd ever seen, as he told each guard that I was his brother. A month or two earlier I had sent Abbie my driver's license, and he'd been using it to gain admittance for a stream of friends and celebrities, including the actor John Voight since family members were allowed in without special passes. Now one U.S. marshal asked, "How many brothers do you have, Abbie?" Abbie grinned and said, "This is the only one." And when the man hesitated, Abbie pushed me through ahead of him, saying, "If he doesn't get in, I don't go in."

No matter how worn out Abbie was by the onslaught of the trial and the strain of touring the country on speaking engagements to raise money for the defense when court wasn't in session, his image as depicted in the media was so robust and so clearly defined that no one seemed to see his physical frailty. Or rather, they saw it, but they didn't *see* it. Even as fine a reporter as J. Anthony Lucas, writing in *The New York Times* of December 29, 1969, fell for Abbie's presentation of the facts over the facts themselves: "Abbie Hoffman came off his sickbed today to give a colorful performance at the Chicago conspiracy trial." The accompanying photo shows him smiling and bright-eyed, sitting in his wheelchair outside the hospital, pushed by a pretty nurse, with several microphones pushed near his face by reporters:

> *He was released early this morning, still a bit groggy from the sedatives. ("It ain't my usual stuff," he said.) But when he resumed the witness stand he quickly showed he was fully recovered.*
>
> *Winking, sighing, gasping, stretching, waving, making eyes at the judge and jury and hugely enjoying the whole thing, the 33-year-old defendant dominated the proceedings for nearly five hours.*

Abbie worked hard for that kind of coverage. In his autobiography, Abbie has a photo of himself in the hospital in December 1969, with an oxygen tube going into his nose, looking terrible. In the photo's caption, he says he was only faking pneumonia. But I never believed that.[12]

I sat three or four rows back while Abbie's testimony continued. I found it difficult to concentrate on what he was saying, so overwhelmed was I by the tension in the small courtroom. Two or three marshals were pacing up and down the aisle that divided "their side" from "our side." They being the white-stocking-bowling-league supporters of the prosecution, ours the long-hair-slacker-drug-eating-free-love-making-Communist side. The marshals kept their eyes fixed on our side, tapping us on the shoulder if we so much as coughed. Judge Hoffman also kept his eyes on us, his head barely rising above the bench. Now and then, U.S. attorney Tom Foran or one of his assistants turned to glare at us too.

MR. WEINGLASS: *Abbie Hoffman, prior to coming to Chicago, from April 1968 on to the week of the convention, did you enter into an agreement with David Dellinger, John Froines, Tom Hayden, Jerry Rubin, Lee Weiner or Rennie Davis, to come to the city of Chicago for the purpose of encouraging and promoting violence during the convention week?*
THE WITNESS [Abbie]: *An agreement?*
MR. WEINGLASS: *Yes.*
THE WITNESS: *We couldn't agree on lunch.*

During the cross-examination, Abbie took a slightly different approach, taking the force out of the prosecution's absurd argument by agreeing with much of it and making light of what was too funny to agree with:

MR. SCHULTZ: *Mr. Hoffman, while you were in Chicago, you deliberately told your police tails that you had had a fight with Rubin—*
THE WITNESS [Abbie]: *Yes. Deliberately.*
MR. SCHULTZ: *—in order to destroy any charge of conspiracy, isn't that right? Isn't that right, Mr. Hoffman?*
THE WITNESS: *Yes. God, I was sneaky. Yes, I told that to the policemen. It didn't work obviously. . . .*
MR. SCHULTZ: *Mr. Hoffman, while you were negotiating with City officials, you were secretly attending meetings and planning for spontaneous acts of violence during the Democratic National Convention, isn't that right?*
THE WITNESS: *How do you plan for spontaneous acts of violence? I would have no idea how to do that.*

Again and again Schultz put forward his perception that what happened in Chicago during the Democratic National Convention of 1968 was the result of a carefully conceived and methodically executed plan to entrap the local government into actions that would lead to violence in the streets. Thus the Yippies!' repeated requests for permits to sleep in Lincoln Park were seen as a ploy, self-defense seminars in the park designed to teach how to avert violence were portrayed as violence-generating, and the attempts of the Yippies! to help people keep calm were seen by the prosecution as ingenious subterfuges. Again and again, Abbie countered by trying to explain that Schultz was confusing Yippie! mythmaking with reality, and again and again Schultz demonstrated that he actually did not understand the difference.

Schultz had carefully read *Revolution for the Hell of It* and carried his heavily marked-up personal copy with him into the courtroom. (Once again it was Abbie's enemies who proved to be among his most diligent students.) Repeatedly, Schultz took statements made by Abbie after the convention, and tried to present them as being revelatory of Abbie's conspiratorial intentions before the convention. Incredibly, Judge Hoffman seemed wilfully blind to the absurdity of Schultz's argument.

"Isn't it a fact that you said that a society of love must be brought about with violence?," asked Schultz, referring to a speech Abbie had made at the University of Maryland almost a year after the Chicago convention. "I said that in order to love we had to learn how to survive, and in order to survive we had to learn how to fight," Abbie responded. A little later Schultz flatly stated, "Mr. Hoffman, you wanted to wreck this society." Abbie answered, "I feel that in time the society will wreck itself, and our role is to survive."[13]

Attempts by the defense to introduce the notion of Yippie! mythmaking as a possible alternative to the prosecution's dangerous conspirators theory were systematically frustrated by Judge Hoffman and the prosecutors. The prosecution's case relied on its vision of a two-dimensional world without myth. Yet Abbie's personality, his wit and spontaneity, belied the prosecution's case better than any counterargument could have. It was almost impossible to imagine Abbie as a conspirator. Nonetheless, after two weeks, including the time in hospital, Abbie's testimony was abruptly cut short by a vote of the defendants, reasoning that for all his bravado and brilliance he wasn't advancing their case.[14]

The week I spent with Abbie in Chicago had a powerful effect on me. To get in and out of the courthouse, you often had to pass through a crowd jeering "Commie bastards" and other insults. One day a guy in the crowd pointed at me and yelled, "That's his brother. He's a Commie bastard too." But despite such moments of unpleasantness, there was an electricity emanating from the trial, the feeling that this was history in the making, and you felt a tremendous pull to be a part of it.

I headed back to Framingham, my head filled to bursting with new ideas. I had to get back to the business since Dad and Ma were in Florida again. And I had to get back to be with Joan and our son Justin, since Joan would never stand my being away on New Year's. But I had also decided to become more politically active. I felt that as a veteran medic who'd seen some of the first body bags return from Vietnam and as a businessman with a stake in America, I had something to say that people might want to hear.

For a few months I kept the momentum going. I would show up at speaking engagements in a suit and tie, making a very different impression than Abbie did. Then one day two FBI agents visited me at my office and asked me to walk with them outside. I'd been invited to speak at an American Legion dedication of a park in Auburn, Massachusetts. As we walked, they explained that they feared trouble at the dedication. They also mentioned that customers of mine were friends of theirs. They were concerned, they said, that I could be hurt, and that my business could be hurt, if I went to the park dedication. The veiled threat couldn't have been more obvious. I suddenly understood why Abbie liked to travel light. The more ties you have, the more ways there are to hurt you. Without even having to think twice about it, I called the American Legion and told them I wouldn't be able to participate in the dedication.

But I didn't really believe the dedication was what the FBI agents wanted me to back out of. They wanted me to know just how vulnerable I was, and they succeeded. The thought that they were paying visits to customers scared me much more than it angered me. In that sense, I was an easy target for them. I simply did not feel that I had the option to let the business fail. I never for a moment doubted that its success was my primary responsibility. I understood, with a sad resignation that reminded me of Dad, that Abbie and I weren't separated so much by our views on how to end the war as by what we each felt commanded our primary loyalties. Abbie's allegiance was to his beliefs, mine was to my wife, our parents, my employees, and others to whom we were connected by fragile threads that would be broken if the business failed. Today I know that Abbie's way was brutally hard. But at the time, it seemed that the hard way to go was mine. And it only partly raised my spirits to think of us as playing different positions on the same team, Abbie shaking the world while I kept the home fires burning. I began to miss Abbie again, to understand him more intensely, even as I saw that the road he was traveling was taking him from us.

On February 14 and 15, after having already sentenced Bobby Seale to four years' worth of contempt back in November, Judge Hoffman conducted contempt proceedings against the remaining seven defendants and both attorneys. Abbie got eight months. The harshest sentence went to attorney Bill Kunstler, who got four years and thirteen days. David Dellinger, Rennie Davis, and Jerry Rubin each got more than two years; Tom Hayden and attorney Len Weinglass each got more than a year; Lee Weiner and John Froines each got less than a year.

Despite the four years' worth of contempt sentences received earlier by Bobby Seale, no one had expected such harshness. Especially frustrating was the fact that Judge Hoffman had the power to impose the sentences unilaterally, without the defendants having any recourse to seek justice from a jury. Everyone was crushed. The only strange sidenote here was that, of all the defendants, Abbie, who had been the most contemptuous after Seale, got the mildest sentence. Abbie always felt that Judge Hoffman's lenience bespoke the judge's actual fondness for him. Pretty amazing considering that on one occasion, after David Dellinger's bail was revoked and the pacifist was carted off to jail, Abbie had stood up in the courtroom and shouted at the judge: "You're a disgrace to the Jews . . . a *shande fur de goyim.*"

Abbie sent me a letter. I know the exact date because I still keep it in its envelope, with its wavy lined postmark over the six-cent Franklin D. Roosevelt stamp. He addressed it to me "c/o Worcester Medical Supply" rather than at home, and in the upper left corner of the envelope he wrote, "A Hoffman/Cook County Jail/26th & California/Chicago, Ill." The envelope is torn where I must have ripped it open. The reason I have preserved the letter with such care is the same reason why Abbie wrote the name of the jail on the envelope (he could have written the address only). For both of us, it is difficult to understand that they would actually put him in jail for the Chicago case.

The jokester in Abbie flaunted the fact of his imprisonment; he always boasted of his jail time. But another part of him felt shocked and betrayed that the country he had loved, the nation he had tried to keep honest to itself, at great personal risk, would lock him up as a criminal. And jail was scary, filled with scary people. And for somebody like Abbie, confinement for an extended period and the sharing of a 10' × 7½' cell (Abbie would reduce the dimensions of the cell for dramatic effect during his closing argument) placed him in an environment that was intolerable from one moment to the next, never mind for weeks, months, or years.

The letter inside, which was not mailed until February 23, was dated six days earlier, on the 17th. Mostly, it contained instructions. He wanted me to contact the mayor of Worcester, who happened to be a family friend, and ask him to call for a congressional review of Judge Hoffman's contempt citation or impeachment of the judge. But the letter was also reassuring, funny, and unflinchingly stoic. Before signing off he added that everything was okay, although Cook County Jail was no Grossingers.

Grossinger's was the Catskills luxury hotel for Jews; interestingly, Abbie hadn't yet been there, but I had and had described it to him: "Israel has a few more Jews, Abbie, but Grossinger's got better food." Abbie may have had in mind both the terrible food and the paucity of Jews in the jail.

On February 18, the jury—which Judge Hoffman had sent out of the courtroom so many times that they had missed about a third of the proceedings—found all the defendants not guilty of the main count of conspiring to cross state lines to incite a riot in Chicago.[15] Abbie, Dave Dellinger, Rennie Davis, Tom Hayden, and Jerry Rubin were found guilty of crossing state lines to incite a riot individually.

Lee Weiner and John Froines were found not guilty of anything and would have been free to go had it not been for the contempt sentences.

Two days later, on February 20, Judge Hoffman reconvened the court and surprised those convicted by sentencing them without prior warning, after first allowing each an improvised statement on his own behalf. Jerry took the opportunity to say how happy he was about the entire trial, ending with, "This is the happiest moment of my life."

Abbie began by recommending that the seventy-four-year-old Judge Hoffman try LSD, and then even offering to fix him up with a good dealer. Then Abbie talked seriously about his feeling that what he'd done in Chicago and here at the trial brought him closer to founding fathers Thomas Jefferson and Abraham Lincoln. Regarding the horrors of the Cook County Jail, Abbie said: "It wasn't funny last night sitting in a prison cell, a 5' × 8' room, with no light in the room. I could have written a whole book last night. Nothing. No light in the room. Bedbugs all over. They bite. I haven't eaten in six days. I'm not on a hunger strike; you can't call it that. It's just that the food stinks and I can't take it." He made you feel his vulnerability, his hurt. Then he ended with, "I'll see you in Florida, Julie"—the proposed site of the 1972 Democratic and Republican National conventions. After each of the five remaining defendants had spoken, Judge Hoffman sentenced them equally. Ironically, it was the first democratic-seeming gesture of the trial: Five years, plus a $5,000 fine and court expenses.

Despite the five convictions, Judge Hoffman pointed the finger at himself alone on sentencing day. Abbie and his co-defendants had survived. They had put the justice system on trial. And they had been acquitted by a jury of the main accusation against them: that they had "conspired together," with its tacit implication that the entire Left was a conspiracy rather than a movement.

I gave a long interview to *The Hartford Times* during which I announced that I planned to write a book about my brother, to be called "Dear Abbie," so proud was I of him. During the interview, I tried out some of Abbie's more inflammatory rhetoric in my own slightly tremulous voice, perhaps understanding his ideas for the first time as I spoke his words. I claimed that the prison sentences handed down against five of the co-defendants represented the imprisonment of "every kid who has stood up for peace and civil rights." I bristled at the suggestion that Abbie leave the country: "What can you do in Canada?" I fired back at the reporter: "The fight is here." And a few minutes later I added, "I believe in our legal system . . . but it was distorted in Chicago. If this is what [it has become], maybe it is time for a revolution."[16]

Two weeks after Judge Hoffman had denied bail to the five convicted defendants and sent them to Cook County Jail, an appeals court reversed the decision and the five were released. Two years later, in May of 1972, the appeals court ruled that Judge Hoffman had also been wrong not to allow Seale to defend himself, and at the same time reversed all the contempt citations against the defendants pending a new hearing.

In November 1972, the court of appeals threw out all the convictions due to various errors committed by Judge Hoffman and the prosecuting attorneys. And one year later, the new appellate court judge assigned to the case, Judge Edward Gignoux from the state of Maine, ended the case by upholding a few of the contempt charges but limiting sentences to time already served.

More facts came to light only years later, toward the end of the decade, as Freedom of Information Act files began to be released. It was revealed that Judge Hoffman was directly and indirectly acting as an FBI operative at the Chicago Conspiracy trial. Examples are numerous. On April 14, 1969—months before the trial had begun and nearly a year before Judge Hoffman handed down his outrageous contempt citations against the defendants and their attorneys—the Special Agent in Charge of the FBI's Chicago office was able to report to FBI Director J. Edgar Hoover that Foran had assured him that Hoffman planned to hold the defendants and their lawyers in contempt. And several months later, in October 1969, just two weeks into the trial, the same Special Agent had received assurances of the upcoming contempt charges from the judge himself: "Judge Hoffman has indicated in strictest confidence that, following the trial, he definitely plans to consider various individuals for possible contempt of court." Remember that both of these reports came before the contempts had occurred! On several occasions during the trial, Judge Hoffman quashed defense motions immediately after the FBI had expressed its wish that they be quashed. The one juror the defense considered potentially sympathetic was coerced into getting herself excused through an FBI ruse with Judge Hoffman's full cooperation. And repeatedly, meetings of the defendants and of defense counsel, including ones that took place in New York City and Newark, New Jersey, were illegally wiretapped by the FBI or local police forces, and the information passed on to the assistant prosecutor in Chicago, who ignored his legal obligation to inform both the judge and defense counsel. Through this system of wiretapping, the prosecution often knew defense strategy even before all the defendants did.[17] So it turns out that there was a conspiracy behind the Chicago Conspiracy trial after all—one between FBI Director J. Edgar Hoover, Chief Assistant Prosecutor Richard G. Schultz, U.S. Attorney Thomas A. Foran, and Judge Julius J. Hoffman.

Abbie had bragged in a December 1967 letter to Father Gilgun that he planned to bring 250,000 people to the Democratic Convention, 100,000 of them to be committed to disruption or sabotage. So, in a sense, he had indeed conspired, eight months before the fact, to cross state lines in order to incite to riot. But what he, his co-defendants, and their attorneys were able to show, by their original action and throughout the lengthy trial, was that we have a constitutional right to protest in an organized way, and to cross state lines to do so, and to challenge unjust laws that seem to make such actions illegal, and that in the long run the justice system will uphold that right.

In subsequent years, Abbie would make it sound as if he had been the emcee of the Chicago trial, fully in control and having the time of his life, but while he did enjoy the constant attention the trial provided, the fact is that from the outset he was unprepared for the intensity and zeal of the government's attack in the federal courthouse. In his heart he believed in his innocence and was convinced that the justice system would acquit him and his co-defendants, and after enough time passed that belief was for the most part upheld.

You could say that the Chicago trial had been a personal triumph for Abbie, and Abbie did say so. The trial had given Abbie and the other defendants the opportunity to prove to the American people, in a court of law, the injustice of the justice system. The trial was the vehicle that catapulted him to stardom and gave him his largest audience. But his triumph came at great personal cost. The trial had taken him away from his work as a community organizer and cast him in a different role; it had estranged him from his family; it had placed Herculean demands on his energy; it had kept the Yippie! party from growing during the critical two-year-period after Chicago, which in fact had put an end to the Yippies! as a political force. Perhaps most important, the experience of the trial had taken much of the sweetness out of Abbie's vision and replaced it with a new militancy. After Chicago, Abbie no longer believed you could have a revolution for the hell of it—all fun and no one gets hurt. But that conversion left him in a quandary, since Abbie wasn't suited to be a bomb thrower. Once again Abbie had to redefine who he was.

On March 4, 1970, a townhouse on West Tenth Street just off Fifth Avenue in Manhattan suddenly exploded into tiny pieces, killing three members of the Weather Underground who had been making bombs inside it. The accident was important, because it derailed plans for increased acts of violence, in particular the bombing of Columbia University. Of the townhouse explosion Abbie would write a decade later that it was both a tragedy and a "blessing in disguise," since the bombs had been intended to take innocent life: "People are flesh and blood, not symbols. Not only is this kind of terrorism an unworkable strategy, it is one which could only replace one heartless system with another."[18] But at the time, Abbie and Anita maintained significant contact with members of the Weather Underground and felt great empathy with their search for ever more extreme means to end the escalating war in Vietnam. Even if Abbie stopped short of endorsing their particular form of revolutionary activism, he avoided criticizing it.

In speeches, Abbie's words often turned harsh. The FBI decided that his "philosophy and activities portray him as an individual who would constitute a threat to the national defense of the country in time of a national emergency." This identified him as "Priority I" and meant that they were following him at all times. Agents taped his speeches everywhere he went, studiously transcribed them, and each speech was then transported, in a burgeoning file, to key FBI metropolitan centers across the country.[19]

On March 15 at Columbia University, sharing a platform with French playwright Jean Genet and Afeni Shakur of the Panther 21 before a crowd of 2,500, Abbie roared: "Have you heard the weather report? Seattle—boom! San Francisco—boom! New York—boom! boom! boom!" The Yippies!, he said, "believe in violating every law, including the law of gravity!"[20]

In New York City on March 27, Abbie appeared for thirty-five manic and confrontational minutes on *The Merv Griffin Show*. In answer to a question from Griffin as to why he was not currently in jail, Abbie cried out, "I'm not in jail because five hundred thousand brothers and sisters of mine took to the streets and burned the Bank of America and other state institutions . . . the government found it more expeditious to let us out than to keep us in." And when Merv suggested that Abbie was provoking and instilling fear in people with his promises of violence in the streets, Abbie warned against complacency, saying of those who might feel that the Chicago trial had been unfair but didn't think they had to do anything about it, "That's just what the good German said." A bitter dispute developed between Abbie and another one of Merv's guests, Virginia Graham. After a while, Abbie stood up and said, "It's getting a little hot." Then he removed his suede leather jacket to reveal his red, white, and blue flag shirt underneath.

If you lived in parts of the country that aired the show live, you saw Abbie wearing Old Glory for a few seconds, after which the shirt appeared black on the television screen. And most parts of the country didn't even get those few seconds of red, white, and blue. The black-out was explained the next day in a statement by CBS president Bob Wood as having been necessary to avoid, "legal problems . . . because of the possibility of violation of the law as to disrespect and desecration of the flag and to avoid affronting many of our viewers."[21]

At an outdoor rally at New York University a few days later, Abbie spoke before a crowd of 250, taking the platform, according to *The Washington Square Journal,* while "blowing his nose with a small American flag," saying, "It's just Old Glory blowing in the wind." Then he got serious: "All trials in America are political trials. All prisoners are political prisoners. . . . Ninety percent of the people in jail are black. Ninety percent are young. Ninety percent haven't had a fucking trial. Everyone should go to a minimum security jail like NYU. . . . We're all niggers. We're all Vietcong."[22]

On the evening of April 7, Abbie was in Fort Collins, Colorado, addressing a crowd of fifteen hundred at Colorado State University. Again Abbie began by blowing his nose into a tiny American flag, saying,

> *I have to apologize for not being stoned or having a cold. . . . They let us out [of Cook County Jail] on one condition: we're not allowed to give any seditious speeches. I hope everything I say is seditious. I hope everything we do, live, breathe and eat, fuck and shoot is seditious because we find ourselves in a state of war.*
>
> *The Yippies believe in banks. We invested in the Bank of America, Santa Barbara. That paid off heavy.[23]*
>
> *We have to redefine the language and one of the words we got to reorient ourselves to is the word violence. We have to talk about institutional violence.*
>
> *And I'll tell you, revolution is about life, it's not about dying. You don't die for the revolution, you live for it.*
>
> *I said I want to confess because I felt the government was calling me an enemy of the state and I am an enemy of the state.*
>
> *Everybody knows Mayor Daley and his cohorts were responsible for what happened in the streets of Chicago. [But] there isn't a court in America where you could put that pig on trial. Only in the streets. And that's where we're going to have our jury of our peers, in the streets of this country. It's going to be a long hot summer if Bobby [Seale]*

doesn't get out; it's going to be a burning fucking summer, and all winter is going to burn. Because [Bobby Seale] isn't there because of some murder in New Haven, he's there because he's the chairman of the Black Panther Party.

We're reasonable, we want everything; we're rational, we want it now; we're responsible, we're going to take it.

The university is a base for launching guerrilla attacks, that's all it is. It ain't a fucking place to get an education. It ain't a place to get a degree. It's a place where there's a mass of people, a place to launch a guerrilla attack on an institution of America and use it as such and that's all it's there for.

Tell your kids we belong to another nation. We ain't in this nation. We don't understand it. We've got chromosome damage. We never take baths. We're spaced-out freaks, anything you want to call us—commies, pinkos, freaking assholes, fags, hippies, revolutionaries. We don't give a fuck. Then they say, 'Why don't you salute the flag?' It ain't my flag.[24]

On April 14 Abbie came home to Worcester to speak at Holy Cross College. He slipped into town around dusk, and I met him at Weintraub's delicatessen, where his first question as we sat down was did I have Dodo Cotton's number. I asked him what he was talking about. He seemed to see the Holy Cross speech as his best opportunity to finally impress the one girl from high school he couldn't get out of his head. She was married now, but it was very important to him that she hear his speech.

Then he turned to the subject of his recent speaking engagements. "Did you hear the fuckers threw me out at Rice? Did you see how I blew my nose in the flag at Colorado?" Etcetera. It was ironic—this did you hear, did you hear, did you see—because Abbie sometimes called to tell me what he was going to do before he did it, and always told me what he'd done afterward, and then again the next day. Did I hear? I felt I knew some of his exploits better than he did. It was as if Abbie himself couldn't quite believe his own exploits and needed to see them reflected in my eyes for them to be real to him.

When we arrived at the Holy Cross gymnasium we were met by

a mob of hostile jocks determined to block Abbie from entering. As we pulled up to the back entrance, some of them began to rock the car, banging on the doors and the roof. I said to Abbie that I didn't think we should go in under the circumstances. "I'll take care of it," Abbie said, and jumped out of the car before I had a chance to stop him. He pulled out a knife and went right up to the largest guy he could see. I reflexively turned my head the other way. But then the crowd began to move away, leaving our path clear. I bounded from the car, grabbed Abbie, and pulled him into the gymnasium.

Abbie hopped onto the stage and started right in talking about the trial, giving his usual stump speech. Then he got onto the subject of Worcester, about things that were wrong here, about the reasons why he wasn't proud to be from Worcester anymore, and no longer considered it his home. He mentioned how his friends Country Joe and the Fish had gotten busted in Worcester for lewd and lascivious behavior during a performance of "The Vietnam Rag" at the local auditorium (part of "The Vietnam Rag" is the "F-U-C-K" cheer: "It's one, two, three, what are we fighting for . . . Gimme an F, gimme a U," etc.). Abbie used that occasion as the springboard, saying something like, "I heard my friend Country Joe got busted here. Well, I only got this to say about that: Fuck the auditorium that put the show on and made money from the show, fuck the courthouse with its inscription, 'Obedience to the Law Is Liberty,' fuck the justice system, fuck the city council and the mayor, fuck Robert Stoddard and his *Worcester Telegram* and Wyman and Gordon, fuck the administration of Holy Cross College, fuck all the chickenshits that didn't want me to speak here, fuck the FBI that are here tonight transcribing every word I'm saying." He went on for about fifteen minutes like that, cursing every hallowed institution of the city that he could think of, offering a complete tour of Worcester on a four-letter word.

He got off the stage and I grabbed him and held on, just wanting to get him out of there as quickly as possible. The first words out of his mouth were, "Did you see Do?" He wanted to know if Dodo Cotton had been in the audience, and that was the only thing he wanted to know.

Abbie's speech at Holy Cross was said to have cost the university half a million dollars in alumni contributions, and that summer, when it came time for Dad to renew his subscription to the Holy Cross football season—he'd had the same seats for the past twenty-five years, and they comprised one of his greatest pleasures—he was told his seats had been taken. Dad, who had been the first Jew on the Holy Cross Homecoming Committee, was offered a pair of seats in the end zone instead. Out of pride, he declined, ending an era in his life. He never went to a Holy Cross game again. You couldn't even mention the name Holy Cross in our home ever again. Although he grieved for the loss of his season tickets, it was the first catastrophe Abbie had caused for which Dad didn't blame him, so angry was he at Holy Cross.

On April 29, 1970, Nixon invaded Cambodia. At the same time, the secret B-52 bombings of North Vietnam, Cambodia, and Laos were a horrible, daily, round-the-clock phenomenon. Demonstrations broke out all over the country as May Day approached. I remember driving into Harvard Square in Cambridge to find the campus an armed camp with police everywhere. Shortly afterward, Boston area schools, including Harvard and Boston University, closed their doors early and sent the students home.

Then on May 4, 1970, four students were killed, and another nine wounded, by a National Guard contingent that opened fire without warning or provocation at Kent State University in Ohio. That week, thirty ROTC buildings on campuses across the country were burned or bombed.

In New York, Abbie received death threats and arrived at speaking engagements surrounded by bodyguards. At the Pace College strike center, truckloads of longshoremen assaulted students with baseball bats. At a demonstration in Foley Square, right-wing vigilantes armed with meathooks destroyed equipment and beat up strike coordinators. And what was happening in New York was happening all over the country.

"Without doubt," wrote Abbie, "this was the period of greatest struggle and tension of the era, [with cries of] 'All for Vietnam,' and 'Avenge the Kent State Four.' "[25] It was a moment, perhaps *the* moment, when the floodgates might have opened. Suddenly everyone felt that revolution might be nearer than anyone could have guessed just weeks before. And people started thinking of the price in young lives that such a revolution would cost. Then the moment passed.

On May 9, the Mobe brought together 100,000 people in Washington, D.C., to protest the war and the Kent State killings. For Abbie, the protest promised to be the most explosive demonstration ever, with massive civil disobedience—a heightened response to the new level of government violence in Vietnam and at home. He urged people to drop everything and head for Washington.

But the demonstration turned out to be just another large protest. Once again, it was the same old speakers warning Nixon about what was going to happen *next* time. Abbie's frustration with the "new" Left was intense. He felt betrayed. He railed against "people [in the Movement] who lack imagination, who failed to modify their tactics one iota during six years of protest, and who for all I know are still carrying out the same rally, with the same list of speakers, on the same corner of Union Square today. Left wing moonies!"[26]

A week later, on May 14, two students were killed and nine wounded at Jackson State, an all-black college in Mississippi, after troops fired over three hundred rounds at a women's dormitory during protests there. This time there was no national outcry.

The reasons the revolution stopped before it began may have had less to do with a lack of leadership and more to do with the silent efficacy of government agencies such as the FBI, whose business it was to suppress dissent, and who had grown much better at their job since their clumsy efforts to derail the civil rights movement early in the decade. The general prosperity of the country also tended to dampen revolutionary ardor. And the essential elasticity of the U.S. Constitution and Bill of Rights further diluted the need for revolution by making other forms of change seem possible. Over the next two years, the level of student protest would decrease steadily from this high water mark.

In a way, Abbie—who saw better than anyone what was happening to the country—didn't see what was happening to Abbie. His long, tangled, curly hair had become a national icon, just like Bella Abzug's hats and Gloria Steinem's glasses. Abbie took great pleasure in his stardom. In 1970, as he remarks in his autobiography, "Who did your hair?" was the question asked of him most frequently by reporters, prompting this answer, "Oh, I just lay down on Second Avenue and let a truck run over it." This media fetishism wasn't yet something that he complained about, as he would come to, bitterly, starting a year later when *Steal This Book* was published. He handled it well on the surface. But it was eating away at him all the same.

In recognition of his celebrity status, all kinds of businessmen offered him deals that would have made him rich. There were six-figure offers to endorse laugh-gadgets and "Abbie Dolls." Publishers offered him tens of thousands of dollars for various book projects. Random House suggested that he head a counterculture division within the parent company. The business world wanted to get hip to the counterculture's hundred million potential customers, but the armies of the counterculture and those of the establishment culture were so sharply divided that America's business community had no inside track leading to America's youth. One group wanted Abbie to write a pricey industry newsletter on "things happening in the youth scene." The William Morris agency wanted to package him as a "multitalented property," and promised that they could put him into the "top tax bracket."

Abbie turned down the merchandising offers one and all. And when he did earn substantial royalties from *Revolution for the Hell of It*, $25,000 went to bail out one of the Panther 21, and was forfeited after the Panther, Richard Moore, jumped bail.[27] The profits from *Woodstock Nation* went to the Chicago trial, to the Movement Speakers Bureau, to the defense of John Sinclair, and to the East Village anarchist group, the Motherfuckers, and the IRS.[28] But he reveled in his fame. As clear-minded and incorruptible as he was when it came to money matters, the temptations of his fame were another story. And it was in yielding to the price of his fame, in letting others try to define who he was, that, piece by piece, in 1970 Abbie's world showed the first signs of unraveling.

On June 3, 1970, the *New York Post* published an article entitled "Solid Gold in Haywire Left." The article featured Abbie and Jerry as youth culture entrepreneurs, living in "two worlds," one the world of revolution in the streets, the other of "literary agents, royalty checks, sales percentages, lecture fees, book and movie contracts." Abbie hated the article and others like it that appeared around that time. He suspected FBI dirty tricks, and it may well be that COINTELPRO was behind the story. The Counter-Intelligence Program, or COINTELPRO, was the FBI's effort to "disrupt, misdirect, discredit or otherwise neutralize" leftist movements in the sixties. [29] At the same time, there were grains of truth in the story, and people quoted in it included Abbie's lawyer, his agent, and his editors. The problem for Abbie wasn't the idea that he would be familiar with the language of royalty checks, lecture fees, and movie contracts. He did, after all, earn his living from his public speaking and his writings; that he could do so was what permitted him to be a full-time political activist. The problem was that he was no longer in the driver's seat, publicly or privately, when it came to defining who he was.

Within the Movement, Abbie's reputation remained a question mark, even as his fame grew. Some saw him as the clown whose disruptions gave the Movement a bad name. Others saw him as the one leader who made revolutionary struggle fun, funny, and human, and thus the one leader with the power to affect masses of people. But few people within the Movement felt that they knew this man well enough to follow him.

Abbie was saying to the world that he was a visionary Jewish road warrior, a full-time political activist, a revolutionary. But the world, as represented by the media and the government, was no longer simply taking Abbie's word for it. They were coming to their own conclusions. The *New York Post* had decided that Abbie was an entrepreneur. J. Edgar Hoover believed Abbie was an ideologue and a potentially dangerous political assassin, who had shown "evidence of emotional instability" and "a propensity for violence and antipathy toward good order and government." [30] Every revolutionary dare, every taunt and every exaggeration found its way into the voluminous memoranda on Abbie that crisscrossed the country between FBI regional offices. And during this period, Abbie, perhaps somewhat flattered by the notion of himself as a successful entrepreneur, and savoring the irony of the FBI perception that he was dangerous, sensed a certain amount of respect in both portraits. In time, these misperceptions would become sources of deep bitterness to him. But that would come later. For now, lacking the kind of respect he sought within the Movement, he bounced back and forth among the various public misconceptions that were forming, a kind of itinerant freelancer, taking solace where he could find it. To his credit, Abbie never became either an entrepreneur, as Jerry Rubin eventually did, or the kind of public enemy the FBI wanted him to be. In the end, as much as he tried to transform his natural optimism and naïveté into the politics of the gun, something in him refused to make that leap.

In the media, Abbie was thriving, almost to the point of being predictable in his unpredictability. And Abbie was doing everything possible to live up to his media image. But there were cracks in the surface. The person was straining to keep up with the media personality, and was in fact failing to keep up.

Abbie seemed to me to be in trouble emotionally. The lines that distinguished who he was from who he wanted to be, and what he believed from what he said, had become dangerously blurred. He was exhausted physically. He spent most of his time on the road and didn't see much of Anita. By the spring of 1970, the constant activity that had become his lifestyle had gradually taken over his life. He no longer chose which engagements to do based on any reasonable justification. Instead, he showed up at as many dates as he could muster, did his act, and proceeded to the next city on his itinerary, like a passenger without a destination. Sometimes he would call me long distance to ask what city he was in. And he wasn't kidding. Most of the time, the truth was that he was too tired to stop moving.

I could understand at least a little of the temptation his fame represented to him. Even as I recognized his pain and confusion, I relished his celebrity. Losing control didn't seem an unreasonable price to pay. Wherever he went there seemed to be new fans and a new woman to sleep with; Abbie considered sexual prerogatives to be one of the perquisites of his job. The July *Mademoiselle* named him one of the sexiest men in America. Abbie loved it. "For Movement women who are not off men completely," wrote *Mademoiselle,* "Abbie is the going sex symbol. . . . It's partly because he's funny and bright and stuff, but that's not all of it. It's partly the vitality and the action and the guts, but that's not all of it, either. Here's the paradox—what makes Abbie so appealing to the women is that, in the midst of radicalism rampant, he has an almost old-fashioned reverence and respect for his wife. . . . Abbie Hoffman—are ya ready—is the Rhett Butler of the Revolution."[31]

A clean break seemed to have come between Abbie's cluttered and confused inner life and the flawless persona he showed to the world.

Chapter Eight

~~~~

1970–1971

Free speech is the right to shout "Theater" in a crowded fire.
—A Yippie! Proverb

OF COURSE, ABBIE wasn't giving up. He never would—not until the very end. But in subtle ways, by mid-1970, he was beginning to shift allegiances and beginning to recuperate from the high-wire act of Chicago. He was looking for something new, distrustful of much of the traditional Left, and willing to try to settle down in some small way. He was a survivor and he didn't like to show his vulnerability. But at the same time, he was vulnerable, bruised, banged up, and undeniably bitter: The '60s were over, the smoke had cleared, and his side had not won: The war in Vietnam was worse than before; the people in power in Washington were worse than before. There were greater numbers of demonstrations and greater numbers of arrests. But at the same time, the Left was disaffected and disjointed. The emotion with which one went to demonstrations was often disillusionment. Even as we marched, there was the feeling among us that it was pointless, that nothing was going to change, that our earnestness was wasted on the politicians and policy makers.

That summer Abbie and Anita saw the Grand Canyon and gambled in Vegas. Wherever he went, he met people in the counterculture and asked them for their best survival tips. On July 15, back in New York, Abbie pled guilty to two criminal charges in New York City Criminal Court, one on criminal trespass charges relating to his arrest at Columbia University two years earlier, the other for resisting arrest on April 11, 1969. And on July 22, 1970, he paid fines totaling $1,050. This was a tactical retreat, showing Abbie choosing his battles more selectively. In Chicago, he'd had a taste of his own mortality. And while Abbie never let himself be terrorized by his enemies, he had begun to respect the damage they could inflict. He was still determined to win, but he no longer considered winning a foregone conclusion.

On August 30, 1970—one week after an anti-war activist bombed the University of Wisconsin army mathematics research center and killed an innocent graduate student in the name of peace—Abbie and Jerry Rubin were in New Haven, Connecticut, among a group of thirty or so demonstrators participating in a solidarity vigil while awaiting a verdict in the murder trial of a Black Panther Party member. In memoranda circulated by FBI agents, Abbie and Jerry are described "sitting on a low brick wall across the street from the court house," declining to be interviewed by "newsmen 'except for members of the revolutionary press,' " and unwilling to " 'talk to a crowd of less than 1,000.' "

The image conjured up by the FBI documents speaks volumes in describing the grim cat-and-mouse game that had evolved. On one hand, scores of FBI agents, fully aware that Abbie's and Jerry's presence in Connecticut without having informed the U.S. marshal's office in Chicago constituted a breach of the terms of their recent bail bond, knowing they were free to arrest the two, yet choosing not. to. And on the other hand, Abbie and Jerry, knowing they could be arrested at any time, and not really caring; uninterested in speaking to the press, disappointed in the number of their followers, unwilling to make speeches. There was weariness and bitterness in the air. Nothing in the description of Abbie and Jerry recalls the excitement and sense of danger that had characterized the FBI's descriptions of them through the long months of the conspiracy trial. The trial, now that it was over, had left the former defendants weak and tired.[1]

Abbie always used grass and LSD socially with friends. Except for the kind you shoot into a vein, which he considered dangerous and counterrevolutionary, Abbie endorsed drugs of all kinds, considered them an integral part of the counterculture, and used them when he felt like it. He believed they opened up the mind. He liked to give them away, too. In his mind this was just one more way to spread freedom and revolution. But now the nature of his drug use shifted, without his necessarily even realizing it. He started to take uppers when he felt he needed to work long hours, and downers to keep himself on an even keel. These drugs weren't so much part of his counterculture lifestyle as practical aids to help raise his energy level to where he liked it to be, or to control and subdue his mania, and they were addictive, physically and emotionally. I couldn't help thinking he was using them to compensate for a sense of meaning and fulfillment that was suddenly missing from his life.

But out of the ashes of his exhaustion, and in the midst of his natural, and sometimes drug-induced, manic periods, there were new shoots pushing through, new life. As he began to recover from the trauma of the trial, the confrontational and violent rhetoric of his speeches diminished. And new ideas began to flow. Sometime in the late spring of 1970, he conceived the idea for his most ambitious book project. Fascinatingly, it originated in Abbie's mind as a challenge to his publishers, daring them to issue a book that advocated stealing it right on its cover. Random House had wanted him to write a sequel to *Woodstock Nation,* focusing on the Chicago trial. Instead, he offered them *Steal This Book.*

Here's Abbie describing a mid-1970 conversation with Random House editorial heavyweight Jason Epstein:

EPSTEIN: *What book are you going to do next?*
ABBIE: *Jason, I'm going to write a book no one will publish.*
EPSTEIN: *(roars with laughter)*
ABBIE: *I'm going to call it* Steal This Book, *and it'll be a handbook for living free, stealing, and making violent revolution. I'm going to turn on the entire publishing industry. I want to test the limits of free speech.*
EPSTEIN: *You'll lose, Abbie; everybody loses in the end.*
ABBIE: *We'll see.*[2]

Random House eventually gave him a contract, and he started pulling together his notes into a manuscript. The project became his passion. He loved the idea of it and loved the prospect of pushing the buttons of publishing industry executives, coming up with an idea that would press people to go further than they would have thought they could go. That was how you expressed the power of what it meant to be free.

After publishing two books successfully, the profession of writing was actually the only one Abbie could call his own, the one that paid the rent. Where five years earlier he had thought of himself as an activist and organizer, pure and simple, now he considered himself more a voice for the Movement, and book publishing was actually the realm in which Abbie held the most respect, the most power. Writing provided him with the natural freedom and stature in which to act.

Abbie continued crisscrossing the country, ferreting out alternative ways of getting along in America as a citizen of Woodstock Nation, watching his book grow. "I traveled cross-country interviewing doctors, fugitives, dope dealers, draft dodgers, private detectives, country communalists, veterans, organizers, and shoplifters. Every time I met someone living on the margin I asked about a good rip-off or survival scheme. People love to tell how they screw the establishment."[3] Some of the best and most exciting chapters of the book would describe strictly illegal activities—everything from shoplifting and marijuana growing to making bombs. As Marty Jezer notes in his recent book on Abbie, "*Steal This Book* deliberately obliterated the moral distinction between legal and illegal activity."[4] But most of the book would have to do with survival techniques that were necessary, sometimes life-saving, and perfectly legal, ranging from first aid and birth control to advice on how to start a newspaper, hitchhike safely, or run a farm. Notes for the underground chapter came from real-life fugitives Abbie talked to. The legal advice came from hip attorneys.

The beauty of the final manuscript of *Steal This Book* was that, since it was a handbook, it didn't explain or defend Woodstock Nation so much as simply presume its existence. Just like Abbie himself at this point in his life, *Steal This Book* envisioned, and in a sense helped create, a nation of individuals entirely free of '50s materialism, a society whose culture survived in America and lived off America precisely the way a new living organism lives off a carcass.

The enormous power of *Steal This Book* stemmed from the fact that not a word in its 330 pages was hypothetical or theoretical. Every page describes actions and techniques that were already in use in all fifty states. *Steal This Book* simply brought it all together and put it in the palm of your hand. And by doing so, it said, in effect, "Look around you, people, the revolution we've been talking about for so long is already in process, it's already here." That was the one thing Abbie most wanted to say to anyone who would listen, the one thing he most wished to be true. And he knew that no one else in America could say it as well as he could. No one else would have had the manic energy to talk to that many people in the counterculture, the access that made them want to talk back, and the vision and imagination to pull it all together into one seamless text. "Free Speech is the right to shout 'theater' in a crowded fire" goes a Yippie! proverb. That was *Steal This Book* in its essence—a provocation, but not just a provocation.

In September, Abbie and Anita requested permission from the Chicago U.S. Marshal's office to travel to Europe on vacation and to visit publishers there. Permission was granted. Abbie submitted what he'd written of *Steal This Book* to Chris Cerf, his editor at Random House. And on September 30, Abbie and Anita boarded a plane at Kennedy Airport bound for Italy. Their itinerary included Rome, Florence, Venice, Split, Zurich, Paris, Amsterdam, Stockholm, and London, and they wouldn't be back in New York until the end of the first week of November. In Abbie's absence, Cerf fought for *Steal This Book,* but Random House executives insisted that certain changes would have to be made, and one in particular: The author would have to change the title. Apprised of the situation on his return, Abbie refused.

He shopped the manuscript around. Thirty publishers rejected it, Abbie would later say (and on the back cover of the published book he would later list them). In at least one case, a publisher offered him a forty-thousand-dollar advance, if only he would change the title.

Again, he refused. In December 1970, just before leaving New York to spend thirteen days in a Chicago jail on a prior conviction for having written "Fuck" on his forehead during the Chicago "disturbances," Abbie put the manuscript into the hands of Thomas Forcade, a counterculture entrepreneur, who had come to New York to direct UPS, the underground press syndicate. Forcade had a mixed reputation. He was basically a hustler, not a politico. But since he had dealt successfully with Madison Avenue before, Abbie felt he might be just the right person to build bridges for the book between the counterculture and the mainstream establishment.

On Abbie's return, two weeks later, Forcade presented Abbie an "editing" bill for $5,000. Abbie ignored Forcade's editing and his bill, offering to pay $1,500 of it, which seemed to him a fair compromise. Then Abbie decided he would finish the book, and publish it himself. He met with Barney Rosset of Grove Press, who told him that if he could deliver one hundred thousand finished copies, Grove would distribute them.

Meanwhile, on December 4, 1970, this FBI memorandum circulated among its major metropolitan and regional headquarters:

> COINTELPRO Recommend the N.Y. office be authorized to anonymously mail a leaflet to selected new left activists designed to broaden the gap between Abbott Howard Hoffman and Jerry Clyde Rubin . . . to fragmentize the organization and hopefully lead to its complete disintegration.

Below this statement was attached the following letter, drafted by the FBI, handwritten with doodles attached to make it look like a bonafide Yippie! communication:

> Abbie Oink Hoffman
> Wanted
> Wanted
> For ripping off the street people, for pissing on the revolution, for shitting on the revolution, for fucking Jerry Rubin and Yip—looks like a comic book prince (fag) talks

*with forked tongue (snake) favorite words: bread, cash,
gold, me.*[5]

I cannot read this FBI file without feeling a cold chill down my
spine. Vintage COINTELPRO literature, it would have been sent to
dozens of Movement leaders and would have increased their uncertainty about Abbie, who was already such an enigmatic figure to
many. It was typical of the COINTELPRO attacks on Abbie, and
shows how intent the FBI was on lessening his effectiveness. It also
shows how much they had learned over the years about creating divisions, and their imitation of the Yippie! style was frighteningly real.
Six months later, these were things that were being said about Abbie
on the street and printed in the mainstream press. The people who
drafted and distributed this memo could have been the same people
who were calling Abbie at 3:00 A.M. wanting to crash at his place, the
same people who were doing countless other things to harass him, to
erode his effectiveness often from within the Movement.

On January 18, 1971, Abbie had attorney Gus Reichbach (now a
New York judge) file incorporation papers for Pirate Editions, Inc.,
"to conduct a publishing business in all its phases."[6] Its sole purpose
was to publish *Steal This Book*. The logo for Pirate Editions displayed the Random House cottage in the process of being demolished
by a bomb, and in the foreground a revolutionary who looked a lot
like Abbie setting off the explosion.

In a matter of weeks, Abbie raised $15,000 from friends and was
able to have the book designed, edited, illustrated with drawings, dia-
grams, and photographs, typeset, pasted up, and printed. One hundred thousand copies were delivered to Grove Press. Ads were
designed. Hundreds of copies were mailed to reviewers. Abbie immediately gave away thousands of copies to groups in the Movement,
and circulated a letter to underground newspapers saying they could
reprint as much as they wanted free.

On January 21, 1971, Abbie spoke from 12:45 P.M. to 2:10 P.M.
to a group of two hundred seniors at Mamaroneck High School in
Westchester. And on that day's FBI report on Abbie's activities a curi-

ous paragraph was appended to the three-page document: "In view of fact that adequate security could not be assured as to the utilization of agent personnel with recording devices in a metropolitan area high school without the possibility of resultant embarrassment to the bureau, no attempt was made to institute such coverage on this appearance of the subject." In other words, since the FBI didn't yet have sixteen- and seventeen-year-old agents on hand, sending in a couple of old farts in gray raincoats holding tape recorders to blend into the sea of high school students might just cause a riot—best to let it go. One reason the FBI might have been so sensitive about getting adverse publicity of its surveillance of Abbie was that they might have felt they already had him where they wanted him—in increasing isolation—and needed to avoid any Chicago-like opportunities for him to regain his support within the Movement.

On February 9 Abbie spoke to the "Dade County Young Lawyers" in Miami. As he went down the list of ironies and absurdities that made up his stock speech, each point was beginning to sound almost like poetry, so condensed had it become after the years of enduring, and speaking out about, the same iniquities. Speaking of Chicago, where the judge had issued the heavy contempt sentences prior to the conclusion of the trial, he claimed for himself and his co-defendants "the distinction of having been sentenced before a verdict was returned." Speaking of his arrest for desecration of the flag, noting that Dale Evans had not been arrested for the same offense, he stated, "It's not what you do, but who's doing the what." Questioning why the real culprits behind the violence in Chicago—Mayor Daley et al.—couldn't be put on trial in America, he said, "The law is there to protect the forces of order, not to guarantee the freedom of the people," then appending his own adaptation of the words of Lenny Bruce: "In the halls of justice in America, the only justice is in the halls . . . and out in the streets."

Back in New York on February 10, Abbie filed papers of incorporation for a nonprofit radio production company, WPAX (*Pax* for peace, of course.). The idea was to produce four hours of half-hour and hour segments a week of news, music, and features totally free from army censorship and make it available, free of charge, to any and all radio stations, from the Armed Forces Network and Radio Free Europe to Radio Hanoi, which was heard all over South Vietnam, but which was currently broadcasting nothing G.I.s much wanted to hear. The plan was to go light on ideology and heavy on music, including soul, folk, underground rock, and jazz. Abbie and the others behind the idea—John Giorno and John Gabree—wanted to steer clear of the Tokyo Rose approach, especially since Radio Hanoi had already expressed interest in carrying the programs. WPAX would be peace-oriented, and would include news the G.I.s didn't usually hear, as well as such things as rap sessions about the problems of Viet vets, but it would stop short of pleading with soldiers to lay down their arms. Legally, the existence of WPAX relied on a fine point of the war—it had never been declared by Congress. Otherwise, anyone associated with the effort could have been tried for treason.

Eventually, WPAX broke down due to internal squabbles. It might have become a rallying point. But its brand of internationalism went beyond the comfort level of many within the Movement in the same way that the tactics of the Weather Underground did, although without the violence.

Many bookstores and book distributors were refusing to carry *Steal This Book.* Libraries across the country banned it. Stores that were willing to carry it were stocking just one copy and keeping that in the manager's office. Canada banned it—the first time in its history that the importation of a book was banned for a reason other than its being considered pornography. In Oklahoma, a class-action suit was filed against Abbie for "corrupting the youth." Meanwhile, corporations, and especially the phone company, scrambled to redesign their systems to prevent theft according to the scams detailed in the book. Many states passed laws making it a crime to publish information on how to cheat Ma Bell. In the whole country, only the *San Francisco Chronicle* would run the advertisements Abbie had prepared to promote the book. Every other mainstream newspaper and magazine rejected the ads.

At the outset, at least half of Grove's distribution outlets nationwide refused to carry *Steal This Book.* In his own informal canvassing, Abbie found that not one bookstore carried the book in Pittsburgh, Boston, or San Francisco, and in Philadelphia the only store he could find that carried the book was charging a dollar over the cover price. The Doubleday bookstore chain was boycotting the book, with the odd apology that, "We object only to the title. If it was called 'How to Live for Free,' we'd sell it." Presumably, that way, by the time people read the section on shoplifting, they'd already have paid for the book. Seeking clarification on that reasoning, Abbie stationed himself outside the flagship store on Fifth Avenue for an entire week, selling copies of *Steal This Book* out of a shopping bag.

Quietly at first, *Steal This Book* did gain a following. In many communities it became a lightning rod for debate in schools and libraries. And while the country seemed to unanimously condemn it, the book's supporters were not always shouted down, and, somehow or other, large numbers of people were going out and buying the book, despite the invocation of the title. Once again, Abbie's ability to garner publicity, even bad publicity, was attracting attention and selling books.

Abbie enjoyed the book's notoriety and had fun promoting it in the face of such overwhelming opposition. He thrived on the conflict and loved the action. But what was a little surprising, even to him, was the way in which the bad publicity surrounding *Steal This Book*, which wasn't necessarily hurting sales, was being used to impugn Abbie's character and reputation. The lies about him, which had shifted from a trickle to a cascade with the publication of *Steal This Book* in the spring of 1971, began to take their toll. The attacks in the media, to some degree prompted by misinformation aggressively disseminated by the FBI, fueled attacks coming both from the establishment press and from within the Movement. Abbie could understand being hated by his enemies. But what he couldn't stand was being scorned from within the Movement.

In the March/April issue of *Liberation* magazine there appeared a long analytical piece by Norman Fruchter, attributing the crisis of the Left, in part, to the disavowal of solid organizing practices in favor of media grandstanding by certain Movement leaders. Abbie was furious at what he perceived to be a personal attack on him.

Fruchter's analysis was at least partly justified. Abbie had metamorphosed from a grassroots organizer to a full-time revolutionary celebrity. Abbie's reasoning was that there was no difference between the two. As a media celebrity, he was simply reaching more people, getting the word out to tens of millions of America's youth instead of pockets of true believers on university campuses and at meeting houses here and there. But how much had Abbie come to tailor his message in 1969, 1970, and 1971 to the needs of the network programmers rather than to the needs of the Movement? What was the effect of his again and again promising a revolution that was not forthcoming? These were not questions that Abbie wanted to face. And the problem was, Abbie loved the attention he got. One could argue, as Fruchter did, that leaders like Abbie were a dangerously distracting influence. But with equal force, one could argue that had the New Left been less mistrustful of Abbie, had people like Fruchter had the imagination to share Abbie's vision and to follow his lead, the Movement might have been infinitely stronger, strong enough, perhaps, to have ended the war years sooner. Indeed, the deep concern and fear that Abbie inspired in members of Nixon's closest circle at the time would suggest the feasibility of precisely such a scenario.

On April 17, Abbie and Anita appeared together on "The Arnold Zenker Show" in Baltimore. Abbie was in a serious frame of mind, and, in response to a call-in question, he gave what may be his most meaningful interpretation of the meaning of his most famous battle cry, "revolution for the hell of it": "There is a revolution going on in this country," he began. "I don't think we want to explain it. . . . I am saying perhaps there is no historical corollary for this particular kind of revolution, where young white children, from families who have a great deal, look around and realize that in order to keep the silver spoons in the mouths they are going to choke, the way their parents [are choking]. They run off from home and become involved in different lifestyles than their parents. There is no real revolution that comes because you are pressed against the wall in a physical sense. The Vietnamese have no choice but to fight. Black people in the ghettos have no choice but to fight. It is a matter of survival. To the young white kid, it seems to be a psychic need . . . a need to strike out." Toward the end of the show, a member of the studio audience asked Abbie what were the means to achieve a classless society. "They are violent," he responded. Intrigued, host Zenker asked Abbie if he considered himself a violent revolutionary. Abbie's earnest response: "We keep a Buddha in the kitchen to guard our cooking and a shotgun in the bedroom to preserve our sleep. People have the right to defend themselves and their culture."[7]

On April 19, Abbie was in Boston, where he arrived at 8:30 A.M. to do *The Paul Benzaquin Show*. The show was a live one-hour morning interview program that aired on the local ABC television affiliate between 9:00 and 10:00 A.M. Afterward, he was interviewed by *Boston Globe Sunday Magazine* staff writer Bruce McCabe for a lengthy and very positive article that would eventually appear in the November 14 issue, heavily illustrated with a mix of new and stock photos from Abbie's heyday, 1968–70 (which now seemed like the distant past). In the article, McCabe contrasted the ebullience of the file photos—what McCabe calls the "flamboyant and somewhat grotesque caricature the media has been pushing for the last three years or so"—with the journalist's own impression of Abbie as "low key," "alone," and "genuinely surprised" to find a small group of six kids on hand to meet him.

The tender irony of Abbie's "low key" mood is captured during the television interview when Abbie, there to promote *Steal This Book*, mischievously suggests that its "reviews are better than the book," quoting one disdainful review which he particularly enjoyed that had proposed that Abbie should stick to writing on his forehead. And later in the interview, Abbie quips, "I mellow with age. Like blue cheese."

Analyzing his own intentions in *Steal This Book*, Abbie said, "I wanted people to look at the title on the book and think. Rethink their attitudes toward property. Should they swipe it? If they did, what would happen? What happens to you when you steal a book?" During the call-in portion of the show, a caller asked Abbie what he would do if someone stole something important to him. "I'd get upset, naturally, but then again, I can't exactly call the local constable, can I?" Abbie answered.

Those words were later picked up and distorted by the media

nationwide. The Associated Press translation read, "I would call a cop, of course." It was a big hit and hundreds of newspapers ran stories saying, "Abbie Would Call a Cop."[8]

Exaggerating only slightly, Abbie liked to quote one newspaper story that began, "Six-foot two-inch, blond-haired Miss Abbie Hoffman, age forty-two, leader of the Communist Party, left her fashionable East Side Manhattan penthouse. . . ." But many finger-wagging stories really did portray him as a radical millionaire who wore $400 suits, played tennis with Mario Puzo (author of *The Godfather*) and had drinks with Eisenhower's press secretary.[9]

In 1971 Abbie and Anita still lived in a $150-a-month, three-room railroad flat on a bad block on New York's Lower East Side. They owned no property, not even a car, had no investments, and never had more than a few dollars in their pockets. The distortions in the press about his luxurious life were ludicrous. He was thick-skinned, but they wore away at him. He tried for a while to live up to the media image he had engendered. But the disparity between it and the life he really lived left him sometimes without hope.

During a commercial break in the Benzaquin interview, Abbie asked the host to question him about his position on hard drugs. Back on the air, the host complied, giving Abbie the opportunity to say: "I come down strong against hard drugs. I don't mind drugs that explore consciousness, LSD, marijuana, peyote, but I disdain body drugs. All needle drugs should be avoided." There was nothing new here in Abbie's positions. He'd always argued for responsibility and against using drugs to drop out. But what was new was the slow realization that people might not have any idea what he really stood for, and he was finally concerned about it. What was new was his wanting not to be misunderstood.

As he was leaving the studio, a young girl asked him for his autograph. He signed the autograph without saying a word to her. Then a newscaster invited him to be interviewed for the late news, and he declined. In the street outside the studio, another young girl stopped him, and the following exchange took place:

GIRL (*worshipfully*): Abbie, will you write on my forehead?
ABBIE (*wearily*): Aah, come on.

It was as if the dream of Woodstock Nation had turned into the nightmare of Woodstock Nation from which Abbie was trying to escape. He was disenchanted, with the world and with his own place in it.

Accompanied by *Globe* reporter McCabe, Abbie walked into a Lauriat's bookstore in downtown Boston and demanded to see a copy of *Steal This Book*. And when the bookstore manager confessed they didn't carry it, Abbie grabbed an expensive edition of Currier and Ives prints and ran out of the store with it. Abbie next visited the offices of Boston's alternative paper, *The Phoenix*, and then took a ride over to Cambridge to Sheila's house to see his kids. Then Abbie hitchhiked his way out of town, alone, heading south.

At 5:30 that afternoon, on his way to a television appearance in New Haven, two Connecticut State troopers arrested Abbie on charges of "reckless use of the highway by a pedestrian," and Abbie was able to post the ten dollars bail only by calling the New Haven television station awaiting his arrival and persuading the host to come over and lend him the money, since Abbie was flat broke. Once again, it was as if the difficulty of Abbie's life was something people just couldn't see. To his admirers, his existence was an endless stream of cartwheels and free flight; to his enemies he was a name on a criminal rap sheet. And between these two poles, he was an increasingly solitary figure.

On April 28, Abbie flew to Oklahoma City, where he held a news conference at the airport. That evening, he spoke at the Stillwater campus of Oklahoma State University, before a crowd of fifteen hundred. Much of his speech was directed against the government and the war machine, as usual. What was new and different was Abbie's insistence that now, with the majority of the people on his side—he quoted a recent statistic that 75 percent of the American public favored immediate, complete withdrawal from Vietnam—the "revolution" should be moving to a higher level. In response to questions about the upcoming anti-war march in Washington, he said, "We ain't gonna march. We're into stopping the government—unless they want to stop the war. They've got about forty-seven hours." He also stated that in "the next two-week period, you will begin to see a rebellion taking place among [the U.S. troops,) in Vietnam." But his

Abbie, age 8, and Jack, age 5,
in front of Kanef's drug store.
(Jack and Phyllis Hoffman)

Abbie and Jack, Thanksgiving
1987, in front of their
mother's house on Ruth
Street in Worcester.
(Jack and Joan Hoffman)

The Hoffman family at Jack's Bar Mitzvah, October 5, 1952. *(Sid Plotkin)*

Abbie (front row, second from right) on the wrestling team in his junior year at Brandeis University. *(Ralph Norman)*

The Hoffman family at Abbie and Sheila's wedding in Warwick, Rhode Island, July 10, 1960. Left to right: Jack, Phyllis, Ma, Sheila, Abbie, Dad, the Bubbe. *(Jack and Phyllis Hoffman)*

Abbie takes a break from the revolution on Michigan Avenue in Chicago, August 8, 1968. *(© Stef Leinwohl)*

At the beginning of the Chicago trial, September 1969. *(© Nacio Jon Brown)*

Anita and Abbie at Thanksgiving 1970. *(Jack Hoffman)*

Jack, Abbie, and Phyllis on the day he surfaces, September 4, 1980.
(Jack and Phyllis Hoffman)

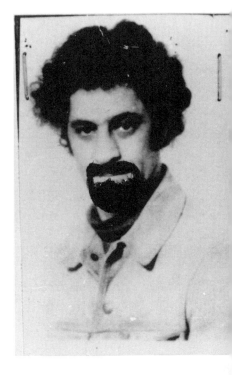

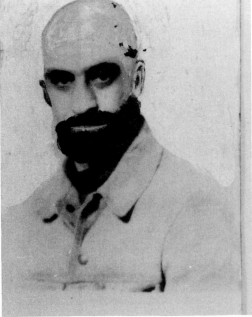

Photographs retouched by the FBI
showing Abbie as he might appear
with different hairstyles, circa 1973.
(FBI file #88–15696.
Jack Hoffman Archive #1733)

Abbie and Johanna, circa 1982. *(© William Coupon)*

Abbie and Ma on the streets of Northampton after the victory over the CIA in 1987.

Led by Pete Seeger, a crowd gathered outside Ma's Ruth Street house in April 1989 to begin a commemorative march to the synagogue for Abbie's memorial service. *(Reprinted with permission of the Worcester Telegram & Gazette)*

rhetoric was the expression of his frustration. Abbie knew that logically the Movement ought to be gaining strength now that it had won public support. At the same time, he looked around and knew that in fact the opposite was happening. At the very moment when it should be triumphing, the Movement was disintegrating. The next day, after a speech at the University of Oklahoma in Norman, Abbie took a flight directly to Washington, D.C., to prepare for the march.[10]

On the morning of May 3, the first day of the demonstrations, a conversation between President Nixon and White House chief of staff H. R. Haldeman was recorded for posterity by Nixon's White House tape recorder. They talked about setting an example for the rest of the country on how to deal with demonstrators. Here are excerpts, as published in *The New York Times* ten years later:

PRESIDENT: *. . . firm.*
HALDEMAN: *Stay firm.*
PRESIDENT: *Stay firm and get credit for it. That's my point. See, I don't want to make an accident out of it. I don't want to be doing on the basis, well, we're sort of sitting here embattled and doing the best we can. I think the idea here is to lead a noble—you see maybe, you, it may be that we're setting an example, Bob, for uh, for universities, for other cities, and so forth and so on, right? (tape noise) Let 'em look here. These people try something, bust 'em. . . .*
HALDEMAN: *What we've got is a, is a guy that nobody, none of us knows except Dwight—*
PRESIDENT: *Um-hum.*
HALDEMAN: *Who is a, uh, and, and, who is just completely removed. There's no contact at all. Who has a mobilized [sic] a crew of about—I don't what it is. He's, he's starting to build it now. We're gonna use it for the campaign next year.*
PRESIDENT: *(unintelligible)*
HALDEMAN: *Yeah.*
PRESIDENT: *Are they really any good?*
HALDEMAN: *In fact this guy's a real conspirator type who,*

who can sort of . . .

PRESIDENT: *Like Huston, then?*

HALDEMAN: *Thug-type guy, no, his, he's a stronger guy than Huston. Huston is a, is a—stay in back room.*

PRESIDENT: *Yeah.*

HALDEMAN: *This is the kinda guy can get out and tear things up . . . and then they're, they're, they're gonna stir up some of this Vietcong flag business as Colson's gonna do it through hard hats and Legionnaires. What Colson's gonna do on it, and what I suggested he do, and I think that they can get a, away with this, do it the teamsters. Just ask them to dig up those, their eight thugs.*

PRESIDENT: *Yeah.*

HALDEMAN: *Just call, call, uh, what's his name.*

PRESIDENT: *Fitzsimmons [president of the teamsters union].*

HALDEMAN: *Is trying to get—play our game anyway. Is just, just tell Fitzsimmons . . .*

PRESIDENT: *They, they've got guys who'll go in and knock their heads off.*

HALDEMAN: *Sure. Murderers. Guys that really, you know, that's what they really do . . . and they're gonna beat the [obscenity] out of some of these people. And, uh, and hope they really hurt 'em. You know, I mean go in with some real—and smash some noses. . . . I think getting Abbie Hoffman and, and this John—the other—they got.*

PRESIDENT: *(unintelligible)*

HALDEMAN: *. . . another of the Chicago Seven guys.*

PRESIDENT: *Aren't the Chicago Seven all Jews? Davis's a Jew, you know.*

HALDEMAN: *I don't think Davis is.*

PRESIDENT: *Hoffman, Hoffman's a Jew.*

HALDEMAN: *Abbie Hoffman is and that's so.*[11]

Seven thousand protesters were arrested that day in the Washington, D.C., demonstrations. And, true to Haldeman's word, Abbie was badly beaten up.

"For me," Abbie would later write, "it was the last roundup. . . . [They] chased me into an alleyway. I fought them with all I had. Swinging. Kicking. Clawing madly. . . . 'Fuck you, you bastards. You'll never take me alive. Fuck your father! Free your mother!' Like a cornered rat I crazily slugged it out with a bevy of big-bellied blues, each twice my size. Finally, two got the arms pinned back while another, snarling, administered the crushing blow—a billy club, full force, straight across my face. I could hear the bones crack under the blow, and I knew my street-fighting days were over. More Cyrano than Samson, my strength had always been in my nose and not in the fright-wig hair."12

Abbie's nose really was smashed and broken that day. After the march, he made a quick visit to the emergency ward and then returned to New York.

Two days later, on May 5 at around 11:30 P.M., Abbie—with four inches of white bandages covering the sixteen stitches over his broken nose—and Anita, who was now seven months pregnant, arrived at their apartment building on East Thirteenth Street, only for Abbie to be arrested for having crossed state lines to participate in a riot—a reference to his having urged people to join the Washington march at his Oklahoma State University speech—and for assaulting a policeman, presumably the one that had beaten Abbie up in Washington earlier in the day. He was taken to the New York FBI office, where he was stripped and searched, and then to the Federal House of Detention, and wasn't released on bail until late the next afternoon.

Although he'd hardly slept the night before, and in considerable pain from his broken nose and smashed upper lip, Abbie went straight to Newark Airport where, together with Chicago cohorts Rennie Davis, John Froines, and Leonard Weinglass, he participated in a press conference in which he stated that the indictments against participants in the Washington protests were Nixon's attempt to suppress protest, adding that he'd gotten his bandages by "assaulting a policeman's club with my nose."13 (Later in the month, doctors at Albert Einstein Hospital in New York would reconstruct Abbie's nose with the warning, "One more time and you'll be sneezing out your ear.")

* * *

With both *Steal This Book* and Anita's *Trashing* (a novelization of her life with Abbie in the '60s) in bookstores, Abbie and Anita were on an intermittent media tour as a husband and wife team to promote their books. On May 11, they were in Chicago for a local television show called *Howard Miller's Chicago.* Transcripts of the call-in program yield an interesting perspective both on the historical moment and Abbie and Anita's shared perspective. Several times, Anita answered questions addressed to Abbie, and often they answered in unison. When Howard Miller, the host, characterized Anita's novel as pornography, she answered, "Thank you." When Miller called Abbie the "clown prince" of the Movement, and asked him how seriously he took himself, Abbie turned the question on its head, responding, "It isn't enough to know the difference between put-on and reality. . . . Sometimes when I'm in Washington I kind of wonder about what's a put-on and what's reality."

Miller attempted to provoke Abbie by asking, "You advocate the destruction of our system of government. Is this what you profess to believe?" But Abbie answered simply, "Yes," without explanation or apology, making it sound perfectly normal. When Miller asked if Abbie was a member of the Communist Party, Abbie said, "I swear to God I am." To which Anita added, "And I'm a homosexual." Abbie then shot back, "I'm a drug addict." Anita responded with, "And I'm carrying [Mayor Daley's] baby." Abbie stared at her with mock surprise: "You are?"

In public appearances like *Howard Miller's Chicago,* Abbie and Anita, with almost one voice, managed to position themselves within the heart of Woodstock Nation, and could present their outlook, seamlessly, in such a way as to make it seem almost normal, and to make the status quo, un-Woodstock Nation suddenly look out of date—a throwback to the '50s, which in fact is just what it was. But as good as their act was, their battle was increasingly an uphill one. The problem was that the FBI's COINTELPRO activities against Abbie were also beginning to pay off, as false stories and rumors that had been composed on an FBI desk and distributed through the mail and in newspaper articles began to look like facts.

Several times during *Howard Miller's Chicago,* host Miller referred to all the money Abbie was supposedly making from royalties on *Steal This Book.* "You're also making a lot of money doing what you're doing," Miller stated, "are you not?" "We give it away," Abbie replied. "But you still make a lot of money and you live very, very well," Miller pressed on. "No," Abbie stated flatly. But Miller just kept on going: "But this is part of the image . . . and I assume that when you . . . fly back to New York tomorrow it will be in a classy airplane," Miller insisted. He didn't hear Abbie say that this was only because Miller's own television station was paying for the flight. The image he had in his mind of Abbie the hip entrepreneur was so firmly engraved that he was unable to consider the possibility that Abbie might be doing what he did for reasons other than self-interest and greed.

At one point during the call-in portion of the show, a caller asked if Abbie recognized the name of a Chicago law investigator and conspiracy researcher named Sherman Skolnick, who, claimed the caller, had been going around saying that Abbie and Anita were CIA agents: " 'cause, like, it's shaking up a lot of us here, man." Host Miller chirped in to say he'd heard it proposed that Rennie Davis was a member of the CIA, although not Abbie or Anita. At first Abbie and Anita were too perplexed by the line of questioning to do much more than laugh out loud at the suggestion. Finally, Abbie said, "I've had my doubts about Rennie. Yeah, I'll watch him carefully."[14] There isn't any record of Skolnick having made allegations of any kind about Abbie or Anita. The caller may very well have been on an FBI payroll, helping to turn the increasing visibility of *Steal This Book* into an opportunity to further isolate Abbie.

Back in New York the following week, Abbie joined three members of the Black Panther Party in suing the New York Police Department's Bureau of Special Services (BOSS) to force it to release its intelligence files to the court for inspection, and for its undercover activities to be placed under the control of the courts.

The ultimate irony was that at the same time that both *Steal This Book* and Abbie personally were being excoriated from all sides, you could pick up a copy of *Gentlemen's Quarterly* and find an advertise-

ment that featured a handsome male model with Abbie-like hair opposite the following text:

> Are you a fashion activist?
> *If . . . the only clothes rules you follow are ones you make
> yourself . . . then your fashion magazine is* Gentlemen's
> Quarterly. . . . *Read up on liberated hairstyles, macrobiotic
> foods, Black fashions and the music of Creedence Clearwa-
> ter Revival. Find out what fashion image the campus coun-
> terculture is adopting and check the meaning of words like
> "ecofreak," "scam" and many others in the glossary of The
> Liberated Language. Don't miss the magazine for the bold,
> new breed.*[15]

Even as he was being attacked, Abbie was being ripped off. Here
was *GQ* claiming not only that activism was nothing more than fashion but also that GQ was *Steal This Book*, the handbook of the counterculture.

By June 13, 1971—the same day on which *The New York Times*
published Daniel Ellsberg's Pentagon Papers—*Steal This Book* was
having enough of an impact to prompt Russell Baker to pen a wry
editorial in the *Times*, in which he chided Abbie for encouraging people to steal from the telephone company, since the phone company
was nice enough to let young hippies charge calls related to Movement activities to their parents. The book was gaining ground, and
the fact that the *Times* would devote an entire editorial to it, even a
scornful one, was a testament to its irrepressibility.

In early July, Abbie and Anita's son america was born at Mount
Sinai Hospital in Manhattan, weighing six pounds, nine and a half
ounces. He was the first of Abbie's children to be planned, and from
the first Abbie took up the cause of america, demonstratively shower-
ing him with attention. In the ensuing weeks and months Abbie actually became enthusiastic about diapering, and would call us to discuss
diapering techniques with Joan. He wanted to do right by america
and recognized—although he used to rationalize things by blaming
them for being ungrateful—that he had failed to do right by Andrew

and Amy. Before leaving the hospital that first day, Abbie let himself be photographed by the Associated Press cradling the infant america wrapped in an American flag.

On July 15 came an unexpected gift from the otherwise unforgiving *Times* in the form of a lengthy, favorable review of *Steal This Book* by Dotson Rader in *The New York Times Sunday Book Review*. Rader called it a "hip Boy Scout Handbook," and generously suggested that readers could use the book as a lens through which to obtain a true picture of its elusive author: "[*Steal This Book*] also tells you something remarkable about Abbie Hoffman, something about the gentleness and affection for his people that lies hidden under his public rage. It reads as if Hoffman decided it was time to sit down and advise his children on what to avoid and what was worth having in America. He says that if you want to be free, then America might kill you. You must know certain things if you are to survive."

Rader went on to portray the book as a powerful defense of the First Amendment. Pointing the finger of shame at every person, company, or group that joined in the suppression of *Steal This Book,* Rader articulates his own deep and righteous indignation: "Speaking as an American writer, I am frightened by the treatment accorded the Hoffman book by the publishing industry and the press. Everyone . . . who has aided and abetted the restriction of Abbie Hoffman's freedom to be heard ought to be deeply ashamed. . . . A kind of fearsome censorship by tacit understanding within allied industries has been established. And everyone's freedom has been lessened because of it."[16]

But with the approval of the mighty *Times* came more trouble. The public perception of the commercial success of *Steal This Book* brought forward two individuals who had helped Abbie research the book, whom Abbie hadn't heard from all year. Both came forward saying Abbie had ripped them off. First Tom Forcade claimed Abbie still owed him $5,000 and threatened to sue. Mutual acquaintances within the Movement persuaded him to accept the ruling of a "people's tribunal" instead, and Abbie also agreed to abide by the decision of his peers. The tribunal would consist of three arbiters, Mayer Vishner, writer Craig Karpel, and Howard Levy, an army doctor who had been tried and convicted for having refused to train marine medics to serve in Vietnam. The arbiters sided with Abbie, deciding he had to pay Forcade $1,000—less than the $1,500 Abbie had agreed to in the first place. But since they had agreed that some amount of money was owed, Forcade could claim at a press conference that he had won. And it was the story of Abbie's guilt that was carried in both the alternative and mainstream press.

Shortly afterward, a young man named Izak Haber, who had crashed with his girlfriend in Abbie and Anita's apartment for a few weeks and had helped Abbie with some research, charged in *Rolling Stone* that he was the true author of *Steal This Book*. Forcade's and Haber's attacks were being publicized together with the rumors of Abbie's penthouse apartment and limousine lifestyle. None of it was true, and today we still do not know how much this avalanche of bad press was fabricated by the FBI or how many of the individuals involved may have been FBI agents. But as Craig Karpel wrote of the Forcade fiasco, "Movement people generally assume the accused is innocent [when the government is doing the accusing], but perversely enough, when the accusation comes from *within* the Movement, you're guilty until proven otherwise."[17]

An August 1971 issue of *WIN*, a widely distributed magazine of the Left, carried a snide and dismissive review of *Steal This Book*. Angry, Abbie dashed off his response.

On the bottom left corner of the cover of the September 1, 1971, issue of *WIN* that carried Abbie's letter, there appeared this drunken configuration of words and question marks: "abbie hoffman? leaving the movement?" Maybe they doubted that Abbie himself really wrote the article. More likely, my brother's name itself presented something of an existential question to the editors at *WIN* at this particular historical crossroads. Who was Abbie Hoffman? What had he become? Could he really leave the Movement? Was he really a part of the Movement in the first place? Abbie Hoffman? Leaving the movement?

His smoldering letter filled two pages of the magazine. It was bitterly sarcastic, at times hilariously funny, and at heart filled with a profound sense of having been wronged. He called it his "retirement letter":

High!

    It was fun to see your review of Steal This Book. *I objected to the reference that the bomb diagrams and instructions do not work, and I defy anyone to prove that. If you like, I'll demonstrate each one in the WIN office sometime. . . .*

    Regarding your arguments about the badness of shoplifting. . . . Well, I never lay out the sort of irrelevant goody-goody martyrdom-go-to-jail-and-suffer morality that emanates from the purists who hang around WIN. In all these years, I really never made it clear whether I was a pacifist or violent. Revolution is like a poker game and, well, it just don't pay to show all your cards until the day the government [does]. . . .

    During the past ten years I've been in and out of jail over 50 times, with some 40 arrests. On Mayday, I was jumped on the street and beaten severely (about the 15th pig vamping I've sustained and the fifth requiring hospitalization). I have two permanent injuries, a broken nose, and a slipped disc. I've already had one operation and need another. I also received 16 stitches in my face. Later I was arrested by the FBI and face 10 years in prison and a lengthy trial, probably in November. I was in jail an extra eight hours because I didn't have $2,000 to bail myself out and it had to be raised by friends. Unlike the Chicago trial, this trial will be a lonely one. . . . In the last two years I gave away over $100,000 according to Jerry Lefcourt, my lawyer. I do not plan to give away a cent of Steal This Book. *I'm pissed at people in the Movement who help lay out the line that I'm a millionaire superstar or other shit. . . . I stay away from "Movement" people these days. . . . The Movement now represents to me the petty ugliness of Norman Fruchter's dribble in* Liberation *saying how we, Jerry Rubin, and I, "betrayed" the Movement. . . . The Movement to me now is a little group of vultures.*

    There was this terrific Mayday call from Washington

[after the demonstration at which there occurred 12,000 arrests], asking me to solicit money and objects of art from John Lennon and Yoko Ono for those busted in the demonstrations. I asked if I was included in the bail fund (again, I'm facing the heaviest charges of anyone, remember). They answered, "Oh, you're different, you're not in Mayday." Zowie!!!

I have a policy now of not answering the phone and return calls only from people whose names I recognize. . . . I don't use the phrase "brothers and sisters" much anymore, except among real close friends, and you'll never hear me use the word "Movement" except in a sarcastic sense. . . . I spent ten years in "the Movement."

This is a sort of retirement letter I suppose. Not that I'm going off to the country or anything. Let's just call it a parting of the ways. No more calls for me to do benefits or come to demonstrations or do bail fund hustles. Divorce is never an easy matter. After a few years perhaps we can again be friends. . . . Anything is possible, after all, you might not recognize me with my new nose.

There it was. For once, Abbie was saying the things he usually never said, because he knew the revelation of the part of his existence that was so hellish would shock, offend, and alienate. He felt aggrieved, wronged by those who took his support for granted while withholding their own. But he knew that saying so wouldn't heal his wounds or build bridges to those he was castigating, and so he voiced his disappointment and frustration as a letter of resignation.

A program devoted to counterculture issues called *Free Time* on New York's Public Television station had offered Abbie a segment scheduled for October 21, in which he was to interview some of the major commentators from the commercial networks, including John Chancellor, Morley Safer, and Howard K. Smith. Then on the day before taping, one after another, the networks reneged on their earlier agreements and declined to let their commentators appear. Abbie's response, after weeks of planning the public encounter, was: "They wouldn't have come off poorly in a pit of fire with radical me. There might have been a lot of healthy discussion. I wasn't going to tie them up and bite their noses. The subject was going to be to what extent the networks controlled the news we get on television. They've answered the question."[18]

The tide of popular perception against Abbie was now pretty much a tidal wave. Many in the young feminist and gay rights movements considered him to be more or less irrelevant to their goals. There was the sense that Abbie no longer represented anybody but himself. And there was not yet any awareness of how much the alienation people were feeling was the result of a systematic disinformation campaign on the part of the FBI and other government agencies.

Abbie himself did little to counter the public perception of his notoriousness. He took to wearing his blue yo-yo championship jacket in public, a relic of his pre-politics days, as if in ironic protest of—or silent acquiescence to—the accusation that political life for him was nothing more than public sport.

When you read the documents from Abbie's life between 1969 and 1971—his letters, speeches, the demonstrations, arrests, articles by or about him, interviews with him, the thousands upon thousands of pages of FBI files tracking his movements from day to day—you touch a life so exuberant, speeded-up, so electrically charged that this frenzy itself must have been a determining factor for many of the choices he made. He could not have had time to plan or reflect on what he did. So you respect the energy level but also recognize something underneath, a kind of pathos, as if he were a guy strapped to the front of a speeding train. A speech or a tactic might be based on nothing more than the feeling in his gut. Often those improvised speeches or spontaneous one-liners were the ones criticized for being calculated performances.

The main forces lined up against Abbie, of course, were not his critics within the Left but the security forces of various government bodies including the FBI, CIA, Army, Navy, IRS, the Bureau of Tobacco and Firearms, the New York Bureau of Special Services (BOSS), et cetera, et cetera. They followed him everywhere. They harassed his friends and family. They told lies about him and made sure those lies were widely disseminated. They tapped his phone. They made him afraid all the time. They, not infrequently, made sure that he got beaten up pretty bad. They didn't back off. They never backed off. They wore him out.

Perhaps even more telling, there was the power of the establishment media. Abbie had been the darling of the networks. The media hadn't changed. They had not made a policy decision to attack Abbie Hoffman or anyone else. It wasn't personal. There wasn't an anti-Abbie television conspiracy. Rather, television too was an institution with a natural tendency toward conservatism, whereas Abbie was just a man with a point of view. The networks' corporate headquarters were steel-and-concrete mile-high buildings joined by sophisticated communications system and commanded by executives with high six-figure salaries and million-dollar homes, while Abbie was working out of his Thirteenth Street tenement. Abbie's effect on the media could only be positive; they could take his punches and adapt; whereas the media's effect on Abbie could only hurt in the long run, since he was so exposed.

Around the same time Abbie tendered his "resignation" to WIN, he had put in a request to the U.S. Marshal's office in Chicago to change his residence to the Virgin Islands. Permission was granted on September 13. On October 22, Abbie, Anita and three-month-old america departed for the Virgin Islands under assumed names. For the next few months they relaxed in the sea and sand. Anita got into gardening, Abbie discovered scuba diving. They both could devote the kind of full-time attention to america that was impossible back in New York. Now and then, Abbie would take a paid engagement, like a November 4, 1971, appearance at Florida State University, returning right away to fantasy island. Abbie was testing himself, examining how good life could be outside the Movement. Occasionally, friends came down to visit and they would ask how Abbie could stand the quiet. Abbie was able to say he could stand it just fine. He had chosen one of the world's most gorgeous places for his self-imposed exile. And that was no coincidence. Instinctively, he wanted his friends to see that wherever he chose to be was happening.

Chapter Nine

1972

Once at the Miami conventions, during negotiations with the city council, I explained, "If your police force messes one lock of my curly hair, my father's never coming down here again." I was talking of generations, speaking figuratively. A councilman answered, "I know your father and he'll still come down. He loves the beach."

—ABBIE

IF 1968 HAD BEEN Abbie's year, the year when you could only reach Abbie on his terms, then 1972 was the year he sought to meet people halfway, the year he wasn't sure what to believe. Abbie's resignation from the Movement would turn out to be more than a gesture. Not only in the remaining months of 1971, but in all of 1972, 1973, and 1974, and until the North Vietnamese finally conquered Saigon on April 30, 1975, the anti-war movement struggled on without Abbie Hoffman. And it was a struggle of diminishing returns, with fewer protesters and an increasing sense of futility, against a president whose view of government was essentially totalitarian, a president who felt he must never give in to the anti-war demonstrators, and who never did. In its way Abbie's withdrawal proved, strangely, to have been a timely, almost a prescient, act. By "resigning," he put us all on notice that he felt we were entering, as he would put it, "a world more complex than that of the sixties."[1] He honestly didn't know what his role in this brave new world he saw dawning was going to be.

Part of the new complexity Abbie saw had to do with the war itself. Nixon had changed the stakes dramatically so as to pose a much greater challenge to the anti-war movement. American troop strength had been cut in half. By September 1971, only 220,000 American soldiers remained in Vietnam. Meanwhile, Nixon had vastly increased the far more life-threatening and indiscriminate air power. By November 1971, a Cornell University study concluded, Nixon had detonated more bomb tonnage in thirty months than the Johnson administration had in four years.[2] Squadrons of B-52 strategic bombers were killing massive numbers of civilians and causing even greater numbers to die indirectly by destroying their means to grow food. Over and over again, Nixon would increase the level of the bombing. By mid-July 1972, U.S. planes would be conducting three hundred strikes a day against North Vietnam alone.[3]

This was the underlying truth of Nixon's "Vietnamization" policy: At the very moment when he was making good on his commitment to reduce American troop presence, he was actually escalating the war. By shifting the war from one where, essentially, soldiers faced off and shot at one another to one where incalculable waves of destruction were unleashed from thousands of feet in the air, Nixon had progressed from war as it is commonly understood to genocide. Anti-war analyst Fred Branfman called Nixon's war the "Third Indochina War," since it was so different from everything that had preceded it. It was waged, he wrote, with "a completely ahuman kind of mentality."[4] With the keenest cynicism, Nixon had chosen to prosecute the war ever more ferociously, but at a lower cost in American lives.

Nixon's "Vietnamization" policy meant hugely increasing the rate of destruction in Southeast Asia even as he sanitized the perception of the war at home. He was betting that the peace movement would not be able to successfully convey to the American people the horror, brutality and immorality of this new war game.[5] Abbie saw the problem, but he didn't know what to do about it. By February 1972, he was ready to forgo his virgin island for a chance to get back into the fray, but he was still without a game plan. In February 1972, he reunited with old friends Jerry Rubin, Ed Sanders, and Stew Albert and called a press conference to announce that the Yippies! would be at that year's Miami Democratic National Convention in force. But there was no real planning being done by the group, and the ten thousand naked Yippies! they promised would join them were a pure fantasy. On April 23, early enough for it to be decisive, the Yippies! formally endorsed the presidential bid of South Dakota Senator George McGovern. They did so seriously and enthusiastically, since

McGovern's anti-war position was long-standing, but Senator McGovern's campaign apparatus wanted nothing to do with the Yippies! The Yippies! of 1972 noticeably lacked the electrifying sense of the moment that had made them irresistible in 1968. Then as extremists, Abbie and Jerry had wielded enormous power; in 1972, acting as reasonable men, they were shockingly impotent.

Abbie, Jerry Rubin, and Ed Sanders signed a contract with Warner to collaborate on a book consisting of their impressions of the upcoming Democratic and Republican conventions. Meaningfully, the book would be titled *Vote!* There was no irony intended. Here were three whiz kids of the counterculture who had always told us to do something different, usually something everyone else told us not to do. Now they were telling us to work within the system, telling us to vote. The first thing the co-authors agreed on was that the bulk of any profit would be used to organize new Yippie! demonstrations, as if they felt they needed that added justification to validate the project.

One of the many paradoxes of 1972 was that once he'd endorsed McGovern, one of Abbie's preoccupations became—after years of embarrassing candidates—how not to embarrass this one. Early on, Nixon's campaign manager, Attorney General John Mitchell, had shown himself to be adept at publicly linking McGovern with his anti-war supporters in such a way as to present the senator as a fringe candidate. At campus appearances Abbie urged support for McGovern and moderation. But the role of teetotaler suited him no better than the role of bomb thrower had.

In the first three months of 1972, President Nixon conducted as many bombing raids on North Vietnam as in all of 1971. On April 15, bombing began of the largely civilian North Vietnamese cities of Hanoi and Haiphong, for the first time since 1968. And on May 8, increasingly on the defensive, with his whole Southeast Asia policy on the line, Nixon escalated the war yet again, ordering increased bombing of North Vietnamese roads and rail lines and the mining of all North Vietnamese ports. Nonetheless, the North Vietnamese were gradually, but decisively, winning the war militarily. There was a new surge of anti-war protests in April. But then, in May, Nixon went to Moscow to sign the Strategic Arms Limitation Treaty, or SALT 1 arms limitation agreement, and his approval ratings shot up. In mid-May, approval of Nixon's Vietnam War policies rose to 59 percent and his handling of the presidency received its highest national approval rating since November 1969.[6] The new complexity which Abbie had foreseen continued to take the anti-war movement by surprise.

One month prior to the Democratic Convention, on June 17, 1972, five men were arrested for breaking into and attempting to bug the offices of the Democratic National Committee headquarters in the Watergate Hotel complex in Washington, D.C. The men would turn out to be employees of the Committee to Reelect the President (CREEP). But at the time, no one had any inkling that they might be the instrument of Nixon's downfall. And the President's tough claims of wanting "peace with honor" and "a lasting peace" were still succeeding in drowning out the calls of anti-war protesters, and increasing numbers of U.S. congressmen, for an end to the war.

In January 1972, I'd received a call from Mark Solomon, a Simmons College professor and Shirley Chisholm advisor. Mark wanted to know if I would consider running as a delegate in Framingham on the Chisholm ticket. I'd been involved since 1968 in anti-war activities, and routinely did volunteer work with retarded children. I'd been nominated as Employer of the Year by the Worcester Association for Retarded Children. That plus being Abbie's brother made me a good Chisholm prospect.

Congresswoman Shirley Chisholm was a former schoolteacher and the first black woman to make a presidential bid. She was running as a Democrat out of her home district in Brooklyn, New York. With her glasses and wig, she reminded you of a teacher you might have had in grade school, the one who really wanted you to make something of yourself. Very progressive politically, and a staunch admirer of Abbie, her platform was women's rights, civil rights, and an end to the war in Vietnam. My idea of a wonderful woman.

But Shirley wasn't about to sway conservative, parochial Framingham. I lost my race, but they invited me down to Miami anyway as a Chisholm campaign aide to work the floor. When I called Abbie to tell him I was going, I could hear the pride in his voice as he congratulated me. Kid brother makes good. He said he'd meet me there.

At three or four o'clock on a hot and humid Sunday afternoon preceding the start of the July convention, I walked off the plane at Miami International Airport wearing jeans, a tee shirt, and my prized Western boots. All the delegates I knew were going casual because this was gonna be the people's convention. Just in case the weather changed and a more conservative wind blew in, I had my other uniform—sport jacket, tie, and loafers—safely stowed away in my suitcase.

Abbie was there waiting at the terminal, waving like I was his long-lost uncle, his hair predictably long and wild. He not only had a rental car waiting, but there was some kid behind the wheel acting the chauffeur. As soon as we got in, Abbie started going on about me to the kid. "Jack's a delegate for Shirley Chisholm. He's going to tell us all about how the convention works, and he's going to get us in." Meanwhile, he was watching me expectantly. I was flabbergasted. Here was the brother I'd always wanted: solicitous, deferential, close, willing to share the spotlight—brotherly. I felt that Abbie was expressing the love I had always hoped he felt for me but had rarely seen expressed except indirectly or for fleeting moments. He was treating me as a trusted colleague and confidant.

"Are you hungry? Do you need anything?" Abbie asked.

As long as I'd been running the family business and raising a family, Abbie had seemed disappointed in me. But seeing me a Chisholm staffer made him feel that I was making something out of my life. And seeing him feel that family pride was enough to make me happy. It was that simple.

"We're on our way to the People's Hotel," Abbie said as we approached Miami. A few minutes later, we arrived in South Beach not far from the Convention Hall. Passing through the heart of the retirement community, passing old people beached here and there like flotsam, we arrived at the Albion Hotel. The Albion was hardly more than a concrete bunker with a nautical motif tacked on as an afterthought. There were portholes running up the side and something that resembled huge fins on the roof. But to us it represented the Miami of our dreams—white stucco, and with an interior pool and gardens. Abbie explained that closer to the Convention Hall the Yippies! also had an office in an upscale commercial building with real carpeting, where the name plate, "Youth International Party," looked just as serious as the names on the doors of the neighboring suite of doctors' offices.

Inside the Albion, the scene was pure chaos. The cost-conscious segment of the foreign media, including the entire Eastern European contingent led by several journalists from *Pravda,* were present in force, along with a variety of local newsmen. The low-budget crowd also included Southern Christian Leadership Conference leader Reverend Ralph Abernathy, and Yippies! Jerry Rubin and Ed Sanders. As we went up in one of the world's slowest, but hardest-working, elevators, Abbie confessed to me that the Albion's other distinction was that it had recently been targeted for bombing by the anti-Castro crowd.

"But don't worry," he added. He didn't say why I shouldn't worry.

Abbie had arranged for us to share a room with two twin beds. Like old times. With safety in mind, I dove for the bed furthest from the door.

Abbie stopped me: "Wait a minute, that's my bed." We flipped for it. I lost.

Abbie showed me a gun he had stashed under his pillow.

"Do you know how to use it?" I asked him.

"No," he replied, "Do you?"

We were sitting together on one of the beds in the room. It was around dusk. I felt the light changing and then looked out the window to see endless rows of the same hotels. When I turned back, Abbie was holding a small vial in his hand that he must have pulled from his pocket.

"You gotta get stoned," he said.

I didn't especially feel like getting stoned. I was already racing from the excitement of being in Miami with my brother for convention week—but I tended to do things when Abbie suggested them. I'd never developed resistance to his enthusiasms. He explained how to put a drop of the hash oil on my tongue—just like a decade earlier he had shown me how to smoke grass.

The hash oil hit me almost immediately. The next thing I knew we were in a packed car on our way to a party for Democratic Senator Wilbur Mills of Arkansas. "I'll show you how we get supper," Abbie was saying. We crashed the party in the senator's hotel suite, our whole group stoned out of our minds, all the backslapping pols drunk out of their minds. And we all got along pretty well. I remember schmoozing with Carl Albert, Speaker of the House. Women who didn't look like wives seemed to be everywhere. A sumptuous spread of food lay across a table that might have gone neglected were it not for the hash-oil kings. We were determined to eat and eat well.

There was no political tension whatsoever. Everyone seemed to be enjoying themselves. Eventually, I passed out. Later I remember being revived by Abbie, and I vaguely remember being loaded into a car, again by Abbie. Back at the Albion, before going to bed, Abbie somehow managed to get me to help him move the full-size refrigerator from the kitchenette to block the door, so that if anyone tried to break in during the night Abbie would have time to get to his gun and learn how to use it.

Early Monday morning I awoke with a gripping headache and this thought: I came to Miami with my briefcase and best attitude, only to find my brother Abbie, master of ceremonies, launching what is certainly going to be a five-day party. It seemed undeniably clear to me that Abbie's blissful and drug-induced insanity was going to subsume the entire convention in an irresistible whirlwind. For a split second I empathized with old Judge Julius Hoffman and wondered what he must have felt as Abbie set foot in his orderly and austere courtroom.

Before breakfast we headed off to the convention center to try and get passes for Abbie and some of the other Yippies!. I walked into the administration office in charge of verifying credentials and granting access to the floor of the convention with Abbie right behind me. I made the case that he was a special advisor to Chisholm, then I argued the case for press credentials for all the Yippies! Finally I requested special credentials for Abbie as the brother of a key Chisholm staffer. We left empty-handed, and in the end Abbie and I decided we would share my credentials.

It was too bad that Abbie wasn't really one of Shirley's special advisors. We could have used him. Our strategy, as worked out at meetings in Shirley's hot and airless trailer, was to try to sway delegates from other camps to get her on the ticket as the vice-presidential nominee since her presidential bid was pretty much symbolic. Each of us in the Chisholm camp had a list of delegates from other campaigns who might be sympathetic to our cause. We met with Gary Hart, who was managing McGovern's campaign. It wasn't a bad plan, but Abbie would have gotten us to crystallize our ideas more. He would have pushed us harder, and found ways to convince us that Shirley was the very best vice-presidential candidate imaginable, enabling us to then go out and convince others.

Outside the convention center, Abbie encountered a group of young cops who seemed hip and open-minded. Impressed, Abbie asked them, "How long are you guys going to keep your jobs?" Their response: "We don't know, things are changing . . . How long are you going to keep your job, Abbie?"[7]

The mood on the convention floor was exhilarating. The people in power included farmers wearing overalls and miners wearing the work clothes of the mines. One in five delegates were African-American. Forty percent of the delegates were women. Feminist leaders like Germaine Greer, Betty Friedan, Gloria Steinem, and Bella Abzug were the real stars, spokespersons for a power base that had never before considered itself as such. It really looked like representative democracy in action. This was the first time the young and progressive were on the inside. Celebrities seemed to be everywhere, not as stars but as citizens. Warren Beatty, Julie Christie, Robert Redford, Norman Mailer, Jack Nicholson, et al., came humbled before this new embodiment of the democratic process. Thousands of people filled the hall who were earnest and hopeful. In the Chisholm campaign we were all true believers. If the 1968 convention had been characterized by a kind of youthful savvy, a streetwise realism, the 1972 convention, by comparison, was delusional. We acted as if we believed the revolution had already been won. Abbie's old teacher from Brandeis, Max Lerner, who had once been a lover of Marilyn Monroe, appeared on the floor, amused and worried-looking.

Most of the people I talked to on the convention floor were politely interested in the Chisholm campaign, and desperately, urgently, intensely curious about what Abbie was going to do in Miami. He had somehow attained the stature of a living legend. Many of the delegates had been on the outside with Abbie at the last convention, unable to get seated inside. To them, Abbie played precisely the same role here that Che had in Cuba following New Year's Day 1959. Everyone wanted to know what Abbie and his crew were planning next. And everyone knew that what that question really meant was, Where will the spirit of revolution go next? As if Abbie were the personification of that spirit.

What people didn't know was that at that moment Abbie didn't have a clue. Many people still considered the Yippies! to be a political force. They didn't know that the Yippies! were no longer a force, and in a way never had been. They were a myth, just like Abbie had always said.

It looked to me like Abbie was attracting more media attention than some of the presidential candidates, and as much as the movie stars. Every couple of hours, we gathered underneath the bandstand to do a little more of the hash oil. I decided Abbie wanted to keep me continuously stoned, but I couldn't come up with the reason why. Newsmen were hounding us, wanting to know what Abbie was going to do. And Abbie was pulling me aside, asking me which interviews I thought he should accept. Meanwhile, the more stoned I got, the less I felt able to answer his questions reasonably.

On Tuesday morning, around 6:00 A.M., Abbie woke me up by dousing me with a champagne bucket full of ice. He was on his way to be interviewed by Barbara Walters for *The Today Show* and wanted me to accompany him. He'd kept the interview a secret until now so that it would have the fullest effect on me. I tried to roll over and go back to sleep, but he was insisting. Hung over, befuddled from lack of sleep, completely disoriented, his persistence horrified me.

He kept on saying, "Come on, Jack. This means free breakfast at the Fontainebleau." Wet and shivering from the ice, I crawled out of the bed. One hour later, on the terrace of the Fontainebleau Hotel, Abbie, in his tie-dyed shirt, was slouched low in an easy chair responding confidently to Walters's questions. A few minutes earlier, off-camera, Walters had said to Abbie, who was thirty-six years old, "But you're a nice Jewish boy from Worcester." She herself is a nice Jewish girl from nearby Brookline.

For the most part, the nationally televised seven-minute interview continued in the friendly bantering tone of the pre-interview. In response to a series of questions on his leadership role in any demonstrations planned for the upcoming Republican National Convention, for example, Abbie quipped, "You're trying to get me in another trial, Barbara." But when asked if his political ideology had changed, Abbie quietly said, "No, some of the tactics have changed, but not the goals."[8]

But the truth was that Abbie was bluffing Barbara Walters that morning. He didn't currently have any tactics.

Back on the convention floor things were just getting crazier and crazier. By now the hash oil was being referred to by a half-dozen different names by the dozens and dozens of delegates Abbie was turning on under the bandstand—"number one" and "honey" are the ones I remember. Abbie was dabbing the tongues of so many delegates so unabashedly, including Wallace supporters from Louisiana, that we heard that the Secret Service thought it was a throat remedy.

That afternoon Abbie introduced me to one of his "phone phreaks"—counterculture telephone systems experts who in 1972 were the rough equivalent of today's computer hackers. Abbie had gotten to know the best of them during his research for *Steal This Book*, and he'd stayed in touch. This particular guy had somehow gotten hold of the blueprints for the entire phone network of the city of Miami, and he had the notion that it might be fun to shut it down during next month's Republican Convention as an act of protest. We all headed back to the Fontainebleau where we descended on the hotel room of Jack Anderson, syndicated columnist and noted muckraker. Abbie made the introductions and, to elude any wiretaps, Mr. Phone Phreak and Jack Anderson went into the bathroom to talk, turning on the shower just to be doubly sure they couldn't be bugged.

While Abbie and I waited in Anderson's room, we discussed the chances of beating Nixon in the fall. Our optimism was unqualified; we were euphoric. We already felt like winners. We Democrats represented the people. We were going to thrash Nixon. We were going to make him choke on his ugly war in Southeast Asia, on his Plain of Jars (a beautiful region in Laos that had been secretly laid waste), on his Bach Mai Hospital (a hospital in Hanoi that had been bombed repeatedly), on his Thieu (the last puppet president of South Vietnam), and on his Phoenix Program (a secret U.S. plan to assassinate North Vietnamese sympathizers, which took thousands of lives). We couldn't even conceive of the possibility that we could lose, that the American people might not care about, or might not believe, what was happening in Vietnam. We were filled to overflowing with hope. How wrong we were.

Ironically, with the longhairs and the minorities dominating the convention, the old-timers were complaining that there wasn't as much horsing around as they were used to at a national convention. Maybe not for them. Allen Ginsberg could be seen seated in the lotus position not far from the podium chanting long Ahhhhs (having discovered that this worked better than Ommmmms). A Yippie!, all excited, ran up to Abbie to tell him that he had just cast a vote high on acid, the first-ever delegate to do so. As Abbie, Jerry, and Ed would write in *Vote,* "We lost in the courts, but we won in the Democratic Party."

Coming back to the room at the Albion that night I found Abbie in bed with a girl I recognized from earlier in the day: a wide-eyed, twenty-year-old Jesus Freak from Toronto, who had just filed her first story for her hometown newspaper. Abbie invited me in. But I demurred, walked around for an hour, then returned as quietly as I could and went to sleep.

Abbie's Wednesday morning power breakfast included Abbie, Jerry Rubin, me, Warren Beatty, and Julie Christie (Beatty's current co-star), and to my surprise the talk was about presidential politics! Not a word on the subject of movies. Beatty was asking questions. The two Yippies! were answering them with revolutionary zeal, and occasionally Abbie would toss the ball my way when the question called for something less outrageous.

On Wednesday, long after midnight, McGovern got the nomination. Like a bad omen for the whole upcoming race, the timing was all off. They missed the national news broadcasts. They even missed the late local news.

All I remember is that around 12:30 or 1:00 A.M. I found myself back inside the main hall of the convention, and suddenly—at first I thought it might have something to do with the hash oil, which had kept us powerfully stoned for most of the past three days—there was pandemonium all around me. People on all sides were jumping up and down, laughing and shouting. I felt once again with a sudden awareness how perfectly in tune with this convention madness Abbie was. Whereas I, as if naked in a dream, was again standing awkwardly in the middle of things, holding my damned briefcase, out of step.

It was now after 1:00 A.M. McGovern had gotten the nomination by beating out the conservative, pro-war candidate, Henry "Scoop" Jackson. Tom Eagleton was the vice-presidential nominee. Eagleton would later be replaced by Sargent Shriver. And for the next few months, the McGovern campaign would powerhouse its way toward election day, hugely optimistic yet doomed, beginning with this late-night nomination, too late for the evening news, even too late for the morning papers.

In August, after both the conventions were over, Abbie, Jerry, and Ed set about putting their notes together to produce *Vote!*, which was completed in August. The basic message of *Vote!* was: Vote, but don't give up the streets. Don't trust McGovern, trust yourselves, because if he loses, you'll need to continue on in the struggle. Consider your vote a vote for the Vietnamese people, who don't get to vote on what is being done to their country. "This is the first time since 1776 that America has been up for grabs. . . . *Vote* and it can be yours."[9] There isn't a sentence in *Vote!*'s 240 pages to rival either the wit or the ebullience that had characterized the Yippies! four years earlier. It isn't a bad book, just an honestly heartbroken one written during a heartbreaking time.

Abbie should have known that he wasn't any longer a player in 1972. But since he was still famous, he felt he was still an important leader. At the beginning of convention week, when I'd mentioned I was preparing to join a delegation to McGovern's handlers to lobby again for Shirley as vice president, Abbie advised me: "You've got to tell them how many votes I can deliver," just as, sixteen years later, he would ask me to meet with the Dukakis people on his behalf, sending me off with almost the same exact words: "Tell 'em I can deliver the votes."

Of course it was true that one of the reasons there was no sizable Yippie! presence at the 1972 convention was that this time the Yippie! "leadership" had asked people *not* to come down, in an effort to save McGovern from any potential embarrassment. But this too, the notion of a subdued, more reasonable and cooperative Yippie! party, was not, in fact, the sign of a newfound maturity but of a hollowness at the core, and a weariness. And yet, if the Yippies! didn't have clout in 1972, they still had respect. They were among the founding fathers of the new Democratic Party. The characterization of it in *Vote!* is eccentric but not inaccurate:

> *History works in strange ways. In 1968 the party bosses in their arrogant isolation controlled the Democratic Convention and had their cops physically assault the protesters in the streets.*
>
> *Guilt-ridden, the Democrats changed the rules to make this year's Convention more representative, and the outsiders of '68 fought for and won places under the new reforms.*
>
> *Then they expelled the party bosses. The Democratic Convention of 1972 was the closest we'll ever get to a Lincoln Park Alumni Reunion.*[10]

The Democratic Party had become more inclusive. But in giving up the streets, Abbie and his fellow activists had given up their power base and their hold on the national imagination including, particularly, the media. In 1968, Abbie had prided himself on being able to manipulate the television cameras to serve his purpose. In 1972, he saw the media as completely outside his control.

Here is Abbie, manic and euphoric, but also wise, writing about Chicago a few weeks after the 1968 convention ended, as published in *Revolution for the Hell of It*:

> *Our actions in Chicago established a brilliant figure-ground relationship. The rhetoric of the Convention was allotted fifty minutes of the hour, we were given the ten or less usually reserved for the commercials.* We were an advertisement for revolution. *We were a high degree of involvement played out against the dull field of establishment rhetoric. Watching the Convention play out its boring drama, one could not help but be conscious of the revolution being played out in the streets.*
>
> *Even if the media had decided on a total blackout of our activities, our message would have gotten through and perhaps with even more power. All people had to know was that America's children were getting slaughtered in the streets of Chicago and the networks were refusing to show it. We Can Never Be Shut Out. . . . We have often been accused of being media-oriented. . . . The impression that we are media freaks is created by our ability to make news.*[11]

And here is a very different characterization, from *Vote!*, written with Rubin and Sanders only four years later, that significantly appropriates a Native-American image of the fatal clashing of civilizations:

> *Photographers battled each other for the right angles. They kept reminding you of your other self, your media image. Each time a picture is taken of you, you die a little.*[12]

In a long, boldfaced passage in *Vote!*, vice-presidential candidate Tom Eagleton, after being hounded mercilessly by the media for weeks on the subject of his personal history of treatments for mental illness, describes his withdrawal from the race:

> *When I came out of the meeting with George on Monday night and made the announcement about withdrawing from the ticket, I had to be extra careful. The angle of my head was the most important thing. If I had dropped my head, that would have been the photo on the front page of every newspaper in the country. It was the way I was supposed to feel. My real feelings didn't matter much.*[13]

As described by the Yippie! authors in 1972, the awesome power of the media is no longer the power to communicate, but the power to humiliate. The Yippies!' arrogance, buffoonery and fearlessness are gone. Of course, it isn't just the Yippies! that have changed. Equally important, journalists and executives in media have become more savvy and more aware of their power. They have learned from the events of the last four years, and much of what they learned they learned from Abbie.

On the plane ride back to Boston on Friday afternoon I sat next to Dave Dellinger, and we talked. We discussed the future of the Democratic Party under McGovern. We were very up, very optimistic. The outside agitators of 1968, like Dave, were on the inside now. In the weeks that followed, as McGovern already began his precipitous dive in the polls—to where he was something like 26 percent below Nixon by mid-August—we in the Democratic Party continued putting our optimism into action. In Framingham, and all over the country, the Democratic party bosses continued to be shoved aside, replaced with new blood. Our enthusiasm knew no bounds.

In September on my thirty-third birthday, I happened to be in New York and visited Abbie. He always liked to give me a surprise if he saw me on my birthday. This time he waited until we were over at Joe LoGiudice's loft in Soho that evening. Out of the blue, Abbie pulled out a torn brown paper bag that must have weighed several pounds and gave it to me. "Don't open it until you get to Connecticut," he said. On my way home that night, I pulled off the highway at a rest stop and opened the bag. Inside was a cardboard box, and inside the box was a .22 caliber pistol, used but serviceable. It scared me. I didn't understand why he had given it to me. When I asked him over the phone the next day, he just said to forget it, that it was a birthday present.

In October, *Vote!*, was published in a mass market paperback edition priced to sell at $1.50, and dedicated to "The Vietnamese People," but it made hardly a ripple. On November 1, our daughter Jaime was born, a sign of hope in troubled times.

Our beautiful dream wasn't shattered until Election Day. On the afternoon of November 7, the first Tuesday in November, I called Sammie my bookmaker to see what odds he was offering on the election. He gave me 5 to 1 odds that McGovern was going to "get beat." I called Abbie in New York right away and tried to persuade him to go in with me on the bet. "We can still hope," I said, "All we need is a dozen good states," and I named them: "New York, New Jersey, Pennsylvania, Massachusetts, Ohio, Michigan, Illinois, Minnesota, Indiana, Iowa, Oregon, and Washington, and we can win." We were already somewhat disillusioned with McGovern, but, emotionally, we badly needed Nixon to lose. He was like Attila the Hun to us, an incarnation of utter evil. Abbie came in on the bet. Together we laid down a hundred to make five hundred.

At 7:35 in the evening, I was sitting in the family room of my home with hors d'oeuvres and Budweiser on the sideboard as evidence of our slim hope of having something to celebrate that night. Two friends from the Framingham Peace Committee were on their way over, and I feared I would really need their company.

Then all of a sudden it was over. With the first results in from Kentucky, where the polls had closed at 7:30 P.M., the t.v. networks were predicting a landslide for Nixon. At 7:45, my friends arrived with tears in their eyes. One of them said, "We're losing everywhere."[14] I understood that to mean that we were losing more than the election, more than the presidency—actually losing the whole fight to define America as some part of ourselves that was salvageable, renewable, and still filled with love and beauty. We, all of us, felt that what we were experiencing was the death of politics as we'd known it.

Abbie called a few minutes later.

"What happened?" he demanded, knowing I would have nothing to say in response, wanting to take out his anger on somebody, even me. We felt ashamed. We felt out of touch with the country and frightened. What majority was this that could stay unmoved by our Movement, that could reinstate a man like Nixon in the White House? To me, this was the day the '60s ended.

On January 8, 1973, even before the beginning of Nixon's second term, the five men arrested in the Watergate break-in would plead guilty. Seven weeks later, on March 19, James W. McCord, Jr., one of the five, would tell Judge John J. Sirica in a letter that their guilty plea had come under pressure and that others were involved in the conspiracy. McCord's letter would be made public, implicating members of Nixon's administration and making Watergate a bona fide Republican scandal. But by then it would be too late to turn our defeat into victory. Nobody seemed to notice that we'd been the good guys all along.

Throughout that fall and winter, Nixon—impervious to cries from within the political establishment that he was acting against the will of the people and exceeding his constitutional authority—relentlessly increased the level of saturation bombing of North Vietnam, including a "Christmas bombing" spree during the second half of December that reportedly killed 2,200 civilians in Hanoi and Haiphong alone. Then on January 23, 1973, Kissinger and Le Duc Tho for the North Vietnamese announced an agreement to effectively end American military engagement in Vietnam. The announcement had come so late in the war that leading activists responded with expressions more of pain than relief. And even with this agreement in place—essentially the same one that the North Vietnamese had proposed months earlier—the fighting in Vietnam would grind on horrifically for another two and a half years.

* * *

Abbie knew as well as anyone that the Movement, as he'd known it, was in its death throes. In conversations with me in later years he would use almost those exact words to describe the Movement of the early '70s. Isolating himself became the expression of his desire not to die with it, something he did out of necessity, by survival instinct. But he couldn't conceive of a life for himself apart from the Movement with which he identified so strongly, and which he loved. So he was caught, unable to do much else except wait for life—meaning political life, life within the Movement—to begin again.

On December 1, 1972, *The New York Times* News Service did a follow-up story on the activities of those who had been involved in the Chicago conspiracy trial. Abbie made himself unavailable for comment, and the only information on him included in the long article was that he had complained to friends that "the New York City police were paying too much attention to him," and that he had "now moved to Long Island."[15]

Chapter Ten

1973

PLAYBOY: *Were you guilty of dealing cocaine?*
HOFFMAN: *Well, not in the way that you and I'd use the term dealing. It wasn't my dope. . . . So the answer to your question is no, I was not guilty.*
—PLAYBOY INTERVIEW,
MAY 1976

THINGS WEREN'T GETTING any better for Abbie as the new year rolled around. Nineteen seventy-three was going to be a watershed year of a different kind. It would be the year when he ran out of breath, ran out of time waiting for the political reality to improve—the year when disparate elements of his life seemed to tear him apart. As I sit here more than twenty years later trying to make sense of what happened to him that year, I find myself thinking of him as a kind of stray.

Abbie's sense of place had once been so large a part of his survival instinct that he always seemed to know who he was by where he had come from. Now, feeling estranged from us, his Worcester cheering section, and estranged from the Movement as well, he seemed to lose that strong sense of himself. The choices he made about how to spend his time and where to put his energies started to have a weird tilt to them.

Stray dogs don't usually live long. Without homes, their survival instincts begin to unravel and they are prone to all sorts of accidents and catastrophes. You see them sometimes on the road, running easily from one side to the other, ignoring the rush of cars. And that is how I picture Abbie that year—with the sweet, sad, dereliction of a stray dog, pitifully vulnerable, weaving in and out of traffic. And yet he still had that boundless energy that enabled him to press forward, hoping for the idea or the break that would bring him out of his slump.

*   *   *

In January 1973, I got a call from Abbie:

"What do you know about soap?" he said.

"You wash your hands with it," I answered.

"Right," he said. "But listen to this."

Abbie's idea was to imprint bars of soap with the image of the American flag and market them with images of hippies finally practicing good hygiene. He even had the slogan worked out: "Cleanliness Is Next to Godliness." He wanted me to help him. I set to work, and within a couple of weeks I found a manufacturer in West Warwick, Rhode Island, a company owned by a Harvard graduate who'd inherited the business from his father. When I explained Abbie's idea to him, he loved it. For weeks he attempted to design a soap bar that had the American flag all the way through, so the image would last through to the last wash—Abbie insisted on this. But the soap manufacturer couldn't solve the technical problem, and since Abbie refused to go ahead with an American flag that would wash away, we ended up dropping the idea.

Abbie felt that his decision to back the Democratic Party presidential candidate in the last election had backfired. The realpolitik that had gotten us into Vietnam and overseen the troop build-up there had been nurtured within the Democratic Party. So as a Democratic Party supporter, how could one present oneself as an alternative to the system?

The only political activity that did capture Abbie's imagination during this period was the case of Tommy Trantino, a two-time convicted cop killer who had already spent twenty years in prison, the last ten on death row at New Jersey's Rahway Penitentiary. Abbie visited Trantino a number of times, making the trip to the bleak, fenced, and walled citylike facility in a barren part of New Jersey south of Newark Airport. He hardly seemed to notice the hellish landscape of the place.

He got involved helping to set up a defense committee for Trantino, and in his autobiography he pledges that "if New Jersey wants, they could parole him today in my custody."[1] Abbie felt at home with Trantino, in exactly the same way and to the same degree that he now felt at odds with his old colleagues in the Movement. If there was a distinction to be made between "us" and "them," he seemed to be saying, then he and Trantino would be on the same side of that line, lumping all the would-be do-gooders, the liberals, the New Leftists, and the bleeding hearts on the other side.

It seems almost too obvious to say that Abbie identified with Trantino, and perhaps saw himself as an outlaw of the same tribe. And to Abbie it was important to be an outlaw—more important than it was to be nice, more important than it was to be good. The corrupt system wasn't going to have much trouble co-opting most of the nice good people who came to demonstrations on weekends, Abbie knew. Maybe the outlaws stood the only chance of keeping the good fight going.

Quaaludes, a powerful sleeping pill, had recently come on the market, and the government was scrutinizing their distribution quite closely. Abbie liked Quaaludes at first and asked me to send him a dozen bottles from Worcester Medical. I did so without even thinking about it, filling out the necessary papers in such a way that the shipment wouldn't be easily traceable. A few weeks later, Abbie asked for the same quantity again. In the next few months he did so two or three times. I guess I might have gotten worried, but I just didn't think about it at the time. He said he was sharing them with friends.

Abbie liked to say, "There isn't a drug I haven't tried." They allowed him to replicate somewhat the natural high he experienced during his manic periods. And he never saw them as being in any way harmful. Bizarrely, drugs had also been Dad's business our whole lives growing up. Now they were the one area of common ground, the one concrete link, between Abbie's world and Dad's, between where Abbie came from and where he had landed.

With Abbie feeling hemmed in and harassed, even the success of *Steal This Book* rankled. No other Movement book had sold nearly as well. But instead of that success adding to his reputation, his credibility had mysteriously declined in an inverse ratio to the book's popularity. Even the distribution deal with Grove had soured and ended over a disagreement concerning the terms. He was still working hard on the distribution of *Steal This Book*. But with many of his colleagues in the Movement unsympathetic to what was perceived as an entrepreneurial thing, as opposed to a Movement thing, he wasn't able to call in the troops the way he might have in the past.

In the end, heartsick from all the troubles that had grown out of the book, he decided he no longer wanted to bear the responsibility of distributing it. He asked me if I would take on the task. The book had been hugely successful. Abbie used to say it had sold over two million copies. He exaggerated. But real sales had reached over a half million copies. By this time, sales had slowed, but they were still substantial. So between selling hospital beds and bedpans for Worcester Medical, I began calling on some local bookstores in Massachusetts, Rhode Island, and Connecticut, sending Abbie half the money. And Abbie was probably entreating a half-dozen friends all over the country to do the same.

The aftermath of the Chicago trial was still dragging on, but without the energy that had characterized the trial itself in 1969 and 1970. The life he lived in the public eye was in a tailspin. And as for his personal life with Anita, as he would confide to me in later years, there were problems there as well. He loved Anita, but with her increasing participation in the women's movement he felt she was distancing herself from him. She had his full support, and he loved being able to take a more active role with their son, america—something he had never done with his first two children. And he was wonderfully caring of "the kid," as he called him. But he missed the old closeness he and Anita used to have. And in his own mind, Abbie would date his earliest depressions to this period.

That winter, Abbie, Anita, and america were living in the resort town of East Hampton on Long Island about a two-hour drive from New York City, where Anita's mother, Leah, owned a house.

In East Hampton that spring he had his first serious encounter with cocaine, doing it regularly with people he'd met out there, looking for a way to bring himself out of his low moods. Meanwhile, Abbie would sometimes travel back to New York City, where he was researching what he hoped would be a sequel to *Steal This Book*, to be called *Book-of-the-Month Club Selection* and featuring the ways and means of the professional underworld. For the new book, he was interviewing hard-core outsiders of every stripe, from thieves and counterfeiters to dope dealers.

Meanwhile, and partly, once again, to combat his down moods, Abbie continued to push the boundaries of his life. He was preparing to have a vasectomy and arranged to have the artist Larry Rivers film the operation, planning on calling it *Vas*. He conceived of the vasectomy as "a statement of conscience: It says you're not going to let your sperm scatter through the world. . . ."[2] At the same time, he was spending more and more time looking after america while Anita pursued her work, which at this time included counseling women who had fallen outside society's survival net. And Abbie was involved in what he termed intense "sexual exploration," both with and without drugs, with Anita and with others, culminating in the experiencing of what he described as a female orgasm.[3] He may have been referring to orgasms growing out of a new kind of responsiveness he was feeling, since around the same time he would write in a letter to Anita, "Active-passive is probably the big Yin-Yang. . . . If you're active constantly in sex, you miss half the sensations, and never learn what the other knows."[4]

So here was Abbie, his trial finally over, the Vietnam War finally ending, his credibility within the Movement shattered, and the all-consuming project that had been *Steal This Book* grinding to a halt. It was something to behold, like the miracle of stop-action photography, like a ball hovering in mid-air: Abbie in repose. What I see now, and couldn't have known at the time, was how troubled a time this was for him emotionally.

On May 17, the televised Senate hearings into Watergate began, chaired by Senator Sam Irvin of North Carolina. I can remember sitting with Dad in the office of Worcester Medical watching on the small black and white set we kept there. Dad spent every free moment during the day watching. The President he had voted for twice was turning out to be a crook. Dad was learning that he had been wrong to place his faith in the authority of the U.S. government. The things he had believed in—our government leaders, and the American Way of Life—weren't worthy of his trust. Abbie had been right all along.

More important to Dad, who was always most concerned with

what other people thought, friends he respected were beginning to say to him, "Maybe your son was right after all." They would tell Dad this, perhaps thinking he'd be pleased to hear nice things about his son for once. And, of course, a part of him was glad to hear things that could stir up a father's pride. But more powerfully, his faith in his country, and the values on which he'd built his life, were now shaken by Watergate with particular intensity since he'd fought for them against his own son.

In the previous two years, Abbie had had little contact with his family, and almost none with our parents. They had seen their grandchild america only once or twice since his birth. For Jewish grandparents to hardly see their grandchild during his first two years of life is something that could only happen in times of war—not an unfair description of the mood in America during that period. But now Abbie was winding down his side of the war. The joys of fatherhood were now, perhaps, his main solace. And he began to return in his thoughts to our family. Pretty soon there were calls from Abbie inviting everybody to East Hampton for a family reunion.

In the end, there would be two outings, since there were too many of us now to all fit in the house at once. And so at the end of July, Ma, Dad, Phyllis, her two-year-old-son Hilario, twelve-year-old Andrew, and nine-year-old Ilya crowded into Dad's brown Lincoln Continental in Worcester and made the pilgrimage to visit Abbie and Anita on Long Island, and to meet their two-year-old son america. That weekend the lost time was pushed to the side and everyone tried to act as if things had never changed, as if the family had withstood all the craziness. They went clamming. They ate fresh duck which Abbie said he'd shot himself, which, of course, nobody believed. Abbie and Dad went deep sea fishing, just the two of them, as we once had done as children. Abbie had wanted to make peace with Dad. But you don't make peace in a day.

The following weekend, Joan and I gathered our children, Jaime and Justin, and went to join Abbie, Anita, and america for a long weekend. There was swimming, basketball in the backyard, and Abbie's fabulous fish barbecue. Our children played together. Even

Anita, before disappearing as she always did when we visited, was friendly at first.

Abbie seemed content, and happy to see us. As Joan noticed right away, he lavished attention on america and seemed to love playing the role of father. That came as something of a shock to us: In the past Abbie always insisted on being the center of attention, yet here he seemed to have no difficulty shining the spotlight on his son instead of himself. I wondered what could have changed to make things so different now.

He seemed to be really *there*, present, and available, as I'd rarely seen him before, and the weekend was one of the best times we'd spent together. But at the same time there were signs that might have worried me if I'd thought more about them, signs that he might be going through some kind of identity crisis.

He was subdued and seemed completely free, too free, of his usual egotism. He was growing a mustache, and it just didn't look right on him. He had recently had the vasectomy he'd been talking about, and had made good on his promise to have the operation filmed by Larry Rivers. "There"—he said shortly after we arrived, pointing to a glass jar with what looked like some tissue in it on the mantel—"my manhood." Proof positive that he was no sexist pig at heart, and a reminder to himself that he wanted no more children. Birth control from the dick-end. Very equality-minded to have had the operation, but a little twisted to want so suddenly to separate himself so completely from a part of himself he had once considered important, and to have had it filmed and made into a work of art, I thought. He had undergone the vasectomy with the same enthusiasm that he did everything else! Not exactly out of character, but as if his character itself were undergoing some kind of painful assault from within.

When Dad returned from his weekend with Abbie, I had asked him how it had gone, and he had said it had gone well but hadn't seemed interested in talking about it. Now Abbie told me how difficult the fishing trip with Dad had been. Abbie had wanted to talk a little about the last ten years, had hoped Dad would meet him half-way at least. But Dad had been too reluctant. He was still too stubborn to admit he'd ever been wrong. I told Abbie that if he'd been the one proven wrong, he'd probably be the last one to admit it too.

A few days after we got home Abbie called me at the office and asked me to send him some procaine.

"Sure," I told him, "How much do you want?"

"Five or six pounds," he said.

"For what?" I asked, surprised at the large quantity. He said people were starting to get high on procaine, that he had a buyer, that he'd be getting a few thousand for it, that I'd make a thousand for helping. Procaine wasn't a restricted drug, not one of the prescription drugs the regulatory agencies asked questions about. The six pounds cost me less than six dollars a pound wholesale. I didn't know that at that time procaine was the preferred substance used to dilute cocaine. So I ordered the procaine, and when it came in I scraped the labels off and sent the six amber glass one-pound jars down to Abbie by UPS.

About three weeks later, on the afternoon of Tuesday, August 28, Abbie called me at work from art collector and Chicago crony Joe LoGiudice's loft in Soho. He was manic, and he sounded high. The reason he was calling wasn't clear at first. Not for advice, or for anything else in particular, but because, for better or worse, he usually called me when something important was about to happen. He called for the record. Maybe he knew somewhere inside himself that twenty years later I would be here now trying to understand him.

"What the fuck are you doing?" I yelled into the phone, sensing catastrophe approaching. All he would say was that my thousand had increased to five thousand. In the background, at his end of the line, I could hear our friend Joe LoGiudice telling Abbie he was crazy.

Around 11:15 P.M. that night I got a call from my friend Richie Lenett, then living in New York.

"Did you see the news?" he asked. I'd gone to bed early, so I hadn't. "Your brother's been arrested with three pounds of cocaine," he said.

"Get out of here," I said, trying to sound relaxed, but I'd stopped breathing. Abbie was confined in the precinct jail awaiting arraignment the next morning by a special narcotics grand jury, after which he was to be confined in The Tombs, the Manhattan prison.

Ma and Dad simply didn't believe Abbie could have done it, and as I spoke to them over the phone on Wednesday, I told them, "Of course not," but inside I doubted my words even as I was saying them. I thought that he might have done it, and that if so he had purposefully made sure I would know. He had asked me to supply the procaine, and then called me just before leaving for the Diplomat Hotel, not to keep me in the dark but to make sure that afterward I would see the light.

The questions that nagged at me during those first hours after I learned of the bust didn't have to do with the arrest itself. My questions had to do with the surrounding circumstances. Who was his source? How had he been able to get that much coke? Had he been set up? Just as when a child shoots somebody, what we want to know isn't whether he did it or not, but "Where did he get hold of a gun?"

At the head of the sting that netted Abbie were two Queens Narcotics detectives, Robert Sasso and Arthur Nascarella, who posed as buyers dressed in silk shirts, patent leather high heels, gold rings and gold chains—going for the Mulberry Street look of Gambino family mobsters. By Monday afternoon, with New York City in the throes of a terrific August heat wave, Abbie had the cocaine, and had cut it with the procaine I had sent him. A meeting with Sasso and Nascarella was set up at the apartment of Abbie's assistant Carole Ramer, arranged by Ramer's boyfriend, a man named John Rinaldi, who owned a beauty salon in Far Rockaway, Queens, and drove a Mercedes.

Abbie swept into the meeting in tee shirt, jeans, and cowboy boots, calling himself Frankie, and carrying a bag he said contained the dope. "I got the best stoohff in New Yoohhkk," he said in his fakest New York accent. Under his worse-than-fake real mustache, Abbie appeared very high and totally manic. His friend Diane Peterson was with him, introducing herself to the group as Martha Mitchell. Abbie sold the undercover cops a "taste," and soon after they left to bring the cocaine sample to the police lab. Their impression of Abbie was that he wasn't much of a coke dealer.[5]

Tuesday morning, August 28, the lab results showed the cocaine to be around 17 percent pure—so diluted that a professional buyer, anybody but a cop—might have killed Abbie and his friends for having delivered three pounds of such low-grade product. But since they weren't really buyers, of course, the cops didn't care that they were being sold low-quality coke.

Plans were made to do the main deal late Tuesday afternoon at the Diplomat Hotel. As usually happens in the middle of a heat wave in New York, the elevators were out of order at the Diplomat. The room Abbie had rented for the deal was on the tenth floor. This time, Abbie arrived in the lobby carrying two large brown paper shopping bags, one under each arm, with three brown jugs visible in one and a large tri-beam scale sticking out of the other (Sasso had asked him for the scale to weigh the coke on the spot so that he could get Abbie's fingerprints on it).

During one of several climbs up the ten flights of stairs, the ridiculous became the sublime, as Abbie noticed a gun handle protruding from under the shirt of one of the cops and, still not suspecting anything, suggested to the detective that he had no need of that here. Finally the coke and the cash were exchanged in the hotel room, and Detective Sasso told him he was under arrest. At first Abbie tried to talk his way out of it: "All it is is a little powder. If you guys want it, you can have it and we can all go home." Sasso took aim at Abbie's legs and then Abbie carefully lowered the suitcase, raised up his hands, and back-up police entered the room on the run. Had they waited, hoping that Abbie would resist arrest and get himself killed? Maybe. In any case, the party was over. Within hours, it would be followed by a full-scale media circus.

Both cops would later insist that they had first heard of a possible drug deal involving Abbie Hoffman only the day before the bust. But on December 6, 1974, a year and a half after the bust, and nearly a year after Abbie had become a fugitive, at a hearing on a motion to have the drug charges dropped, two individuals gave sworn testimony that months before the coke bust the two arresting officers were on Abbie's tail. Carole Ramer's building superintendent, a Jehovah's Witness named Best Concepcion, testified that one Sunday during the spring of 1973 a man claiming to be a telephone repairman asked to be let into the basement to work on the phone box. Ms.

Concepcion remembered thinking that it was strange a phone man would come on a Sunday, and at the hearing she identified the man as Queens narcotics agent Arthur Nascarella. Nascarella would deny that he had tampered with any phones or been in the building on Twentieth Street until August 27, the day before arresting Abbie.[6]

Around the same time that Best Concepcion saw Nascarella, the building superintendent at 80 Park Avenue, a man named Janos Deszey, would testify under oath to having seen Nascarella's partner Sasso in his building—where Anita's mother had her apartment, the apartment from which Abbie had placed most of his calls while researching his new book, the apartment that had served as his Manhattan office for all of 1973 until the bust. And like Nascarella, Sasso would deny under oath that he had ever been there.[7]

Abbie had been under nearly constant surveillance for ten years, often by at least a half-dozen different government agencies simultaneously, and he was certainly under surveillance in 1973. Even as recently as August 14, just two weeks before the bust, as part of its surveillance of Abbie the Drug Enforcement Agency (DEA) requested information on him from the FBI.[8] In fact, so skeptical would the New York District Attorney's office prosecuting Abbie's case be that Abbie wasn't under surveillance at the time of the bust, that in March 1974, as the case proceeded toward trial and before Abbie went underground, Assistant District Attorney Dave Cunningham would inform both the FBI and the Justice Department that he "cannot proceed with prosecutive active action until [he] receives information . . . regarding any wire taps . . . which could 'taint' [Hoffman's] case."[9]

On an afternoon in the spring of 1992 while researching this book, we sat down in a Manhattan diner under the Queensborough Bridge with former Queens narcotics agent Arthur Nascarella, who had agreed to tell us "the truth" about the cocaine bust that had ruined my brother's life. He began by saying how sorry he was about what had happened and how much he'd liked and respected Abbie.

Nascarella was probably in his early fifties—Abbie's age—but tall, lean, and powerful-looking. He seemed to have no fat on his body whatsoever. He breathed rapidly, noisily, almost hyperventilating as he spoke, and it occurred to me he might be using speed. He said he'd read all Abbie's books—this from a guy who still carried his .38 Chief five-shot stuffed into his sock with a rubber band, a guy who had loved being a cop. You couldn't imagine someone more different from Abbie, and yet he had related to Abbie, identified with him, or so he said. For a second I couldn't help comparing them: little Abbie with the square jaw, the big talk, the mischief in his eyes; and this tall, muscular, angular, handsome detective with that hunger in his eyes.

"I guess Abbie got laid more than I did," Nascarella said to me, "but hey, he got fucked more than I did too." From Nascarella's standpoint, that was a fair characterization of the unofficial N.Y.P.D. position on my brother: Abbie had had a good time and messed with a lot of people, especially cops, over the years, so when they saw him ready to take a fall, they were going to make sure he fell hard. Nascarella then offered his condolences: "I was sorry to see your brother die the way he did." In my brain I kept hearing the echo of the sing-song refrain Nascarella used frequently to pepper his conversation: "Be-bop-bop, budda-bing, budda-bum." As if to say, "People come and go; some die; too bad."

I asked Nascarella if he'd mind if we taped the conversation. Taking up the challenge, he answered, "No, no, not at all." He said that he'd known Abbie at the Columbia demonstrations in 1968—his first assignment right out of the Police Academy—and that he had first heard Abbie's name in connection with the coke deal only the day before the bust. This confirmed the statement of his former partner Sasso, who had told us that Nascarella's first mention of the operation had been on that Monday, when he had walked into Sasso's office to tell him, "We're making a buy from Abbie Hoffman tonight," although it directly contradicted the testimony under oath of the two building superintendents.

He gave us his theory that Abbie's problem was that he felt that "he couldn't be touched." At one point in the conversation, after describing how poor the quality of the cocaine was, Nascarella smiled and said, "It's possible that us busting your brother saved his life that day." At another point, Nascarella looked us squarely in the eyes and described having watched Abbie leave the Columbia demonstrations in a chauffeured limousine, an utter falsehood. The strange admixture of sincerity and mythology in Nascarella's story left me feeling physically ill during the interview. I realized that after it was over I still wouldn't know the truth about the coke bust.

I had waited in Framingham until Thursday morning, two days after the bust, when I received the go-ahead from Abbie's lawyer and friend Jerry Lefcourt, and took an early flight to New York. Abbie's bail had been set at $200,000. Things looked horribly bleak. Once in Manhattan, I went first, at Jerry's request, to meet Anita so that she could give me a bag of essential articles for Abbie—some fresh underwear, deodorant, toothpaste, toothbrush, and soap—no frills. The meeting with Anita was a depressing prelude to seeing Abbie; we had never gotten to know each other, and Abbie's trouble didn't make us feel any closer. I couldn't help remarking to myself that at this moment when Abbie was going to need all the help he could get, I felt like an outsider, waiting for instructions from Jerry Lefcourt before I could even get on a plane, and then having to pick up Abbie's underwear from Anita. My impulse was to close ranks. I wanted this to be strictly a private family matter. I knew Abbie would lean on me in a way he wouldn't lean on anyone else. Yet I was being used as a go-between by people who, I had to admit, knew Abbie better right now than I did.

From Anita I went directly to the Tombs, where I waited outside in a line that stretched for half a block, all of us waiting for visiting hours to start. I was one of the only white persons on that line. Bizarrely, Geraldo Rivera and several other reporters were there, picked me out of the crowd, and started to grill me. But for once in my life I wasn't interested in talking about Abbie. I was too scared.

Abbie had involved me unknowingly in the drug deal by having me supply him with the procaine; for all I knew I could be indicted too. And here I was standing in a line of outcasts, and I was one of them, along with Abbie and the rest of our family. I felt this overwhelming sense of our powerlessness; we had gone too far, past the point of no return. There is no more terrible, hopeless feeling, and it doesn't go away. This arrest could not have been more different from the usual arrest after a civil disobedience, where you were on the side of right, where you were pointing a finger at injustice. Now the finger was going to be pointed at Abbie and at us. I waited in line for around forty-five minutes, listening to the sharp and tender melody of conversations around me in Spanish, feeling like I was in a foreign country.

Once inside the jail, still holding the paper bag of necessities for Abbie, I deposited money in his prison account. Then I waited for another hour or two in airless heat in a room downstairs, along with other visitors, sitting on hard wooden chairs. In the heat of that August hundred-degree day, the stench of perspiration and urine seemed to be everywhere. Finally, after being searched, I was led up a metal stairway with three or four other visitors to another waiting room, from where we could hear shouts and other noises from prisoners in the cell block. Seated under the greenish, graffiti-covered walls, I faced a glass partition several layers thick. Abbie was brought in and seated in a chair on the other side.

Sitting across from me, he put his hand to the glass. I began talking to him right away, while he kept pointing to the phone on the table. I didn't understand at first. Then I picked up the phone and heard his voice.

"How're you doing, Big Jack?" He was letting me feel that he was still there, still my big brother, having seen on my face how frightened I felt. Hearing that voice at first gave me a boost. But looking at him, unshaven, wearing the same clothes he'd worn for three days, his hair matted, dark circles under his eyes, and still with the comical mustache, I was filled with confusion. He looked out of place, horribly out of place. Then, all of a sudden, my apprehension of the whole experience increased, and he actually seemed to me not to be so out of place. For a second, I felt he belonged here. I turned my head aside, and then recovered enough to look at him again. Seeing my tears, he softened and turned to comfort me, saying that things would straighten themselves out.

"I'm doing okay, Abbs," I answered, embarrassed to be the one receiving kind words when he was the one in jail. "Everything's going to be okay," I added, a little feebly.

Then I mouthed silently, "What happened to the brown bottles?" Abbie gave me the thumbs-up sign in response and mouthed back that it was all okay and not to worry.

That morning, an article in *The New York Times* described Abbie's friends as being "either incredulous or downright suspicious"—a sign of faith in Abbie.[10] But the article also quoted the same friends describing Abbie's recent disillusionment. He was portrayed as "a man who had withdrawn into himself because of 'badmouthing' from other radicals, and money problems aggravated by legal fees, support payments to his former wife and two children, and financial problems with publishing companies." Bill Kunstler described how Abbie "had withdrawn a great deal," and had been "hurt, chastened, and upset" after the 1971 "people's tribunal" that ended the Tom Forcade debacle. The article also quoted Anita describing Abbie editing his movie of his vasectomy. It wasn't that Anita, or any of Abbie's friends, had said anything wrong or untrue about Abbie. Rather, the circumstances under which the article appeared made you read it with his assumed guilt in mind. You searched it for an answer to the question of why he might have done it, and not for any other reason. Abbie seemed vulnerable as never before because of the recent bust. I felt a powerful urge to protect him. It was almost like a sharp pain. And here he seemed suddenly so completely out of the reach of any help I or anyone could give him.

Immediately after the bust Jerry Lefcourt had requested letters of support on Abbie's behalf from a number of notable friends. Allen Ginsberg wrote six pages in praise of Abbie, including this interesting paragraph:

> *In time of communal Apathy synchronous with Abbie Hoffman's recent disillusioned withdrawal to private life (after crises of his public efforts to confound Government police bureaucracy and war led him to be attacked left and right), Mr. Hoffman is now to be congratulated on an arrest which by its very surprise, its simultaneous whimsicality and seriousness, re-unites many of his fellow workers once again to resist the steamroller of police state Power crushing another live citizen's body.*[11]

Other letters arrived from, among others: Kurt Vonnegut, Dwight McDonald, and Murray Kempton, whose letter began:

I have almost never heard from Abbie exept when he was asking me to help someone else in trouble. Now he is the one who needs us; and I notice that he hasn't thought to bother us by asking. But then I should have known he wouldn't.[12]

On the following Monday, Labor Day, Abbie sat down and wrote me a letter that filled several pages of his trademark lined yellow sheets in his usual ragged hand. He described how agonizing it had been for him to have to see me through the barrier of the visiting area's glass wall. He also implied that there were things that might vindicate him. And, after thanking me for visiting him, he told me not to cry for him. Most of the letter contained descriptions of life inside the jail—of how his view was of never-ending bars, and how, with the lights always on, he had no sense of time and little to fill it. He wrote about cop killers and other hardened criminals in the jail with him— and how killings inflicted by inmates on other inmates were routinely listed as suicides. He didn't think he could stand being incarcerated for any significant period of time. He asked me to reassure Dad and Ma that he still had time to accomplish something to make them proud. He ended with an outpouring of affection and encouragement toward me.

Here he was in the middle of his life and at the height of his powers, suddenly placed in a living hell, examining himself and his surroundings objectively, soberly, almost clinically, filled with love, finding in his own misfortune a kind of peaceful quietude almost as if he'd died a natural death. The letter moved me and, somehow, gave me hope: Abbie was going to roll with the punch, and that told me he'd live to fight another day.

Abbie's lawyers were able to get his bail reduced, first from $200,000 to $50,000, and eventually to $10,000. Anita had set to work with friends in the Movement raising money for Abbie's bail. Contributors would include Dr. Benjamin Spock and Daniel Ellsberg, as well as film artists Paul Newman, Jack Nicholson, and Woody

Allen.[13] The $10,000 was soon raised, and Abbie's release date was set for September 14. Jerry Lefcourt began planning a defense based on entrapment.

I visited Abbie again on my birthday, September 13, and that night, the eve of his release after eighteen days in the Tombs, he wrote to me again. His letter intermingled his relief at his imminent release with more of the remarkable humility and calm that had characterized his previous letter. He apologized for not having remembered my birthday the day before. Then, to my amazement, he wrote, "I feel awful bringing shame & scandal on the family." I think writing that sentence was a milestone for Abbie. If he could write that in a letter to me, I figured it was to show me that he had the strength to face things squarely.

A decade later Abbie would say that it was during those days in the Tombs that he made the decision to go underground. "I'd been prepared for fugitive life ever since 1970," he would write, and "I was sick of trials and jails. . . ."[14] But it was also true, as he said over and over in private, that he simply wasn't sure he would survive a long stretch inside.

Over the years I waited for my brother to describe again the shame he had felt after the coke bust as he had in that one letter written to me from the Tombs soon after the bust. But he never again expressed those painful emotions, at least not to me. Ironically for someone whose credo was all openness, Abbie was so often close-mouthed when it came to the things that affected him personally most deeply. He thought he had acted stupidly. He felt responsible for what had happened. The details of the bust seemed to matter a lot less to him than those two incontrovertible facts.

Abbie always said he'd been set up, but he never figured out exactly how it was done. He had all the same facts as I did, but he never put it all together. I think there were a few reasons for this. One was pride. Abbie would rather be thought of as an armed and dangerous archcriminal than a schmuck. And when you think about it, the truth might have made him innocent of the charges, but nothing could make Abbie's role in the drug deal look good. He felt tremendous guilt for having lost his way, and for having been willing to be persuaded to participate in a large dope deal; the fact that he may have been set up didn't change one bit the shame and disappointment he felt he'd brought on himself. It is also possible, as Johanna Lawrenson has suggested, that Abbie took the fall for others and kept his silence to protect them.

Another reason is a little less concrete, but equally important. Abbie, like most other leaders on the Left, never wanted to acknowledge the extent to which the Left had been infiltrated, for the simple reason that to do so would only make his life that much more difficult. The burden of constantly questioning who might be spying on you—the mailman, your kids' teachers at school, your neighbors?—and which conversations were being bugged—the phones, the house, the car?—was intolerable. So Abbie did what most of his colleagues did: He trusted rather than mistrusted the people around him, and hoped against hope that the enemy was on the other side of the barricades. He instinctively put out of his mind whatever clues he had that by 1973 the barricades had effectively been overrun.

Abbie may have been bored. And of course the main appeal to Abbie of the coke deal would have been the action, the excitement. His motivation would have been as simple as wanting to try something new. I don't think he would have been naive about the money. He would have liked the prospect of making that much money that fast. But more than the money, the attraction would have been the danger, the excitement. For someone who was beginning to experience bouts of profound depression, the need to keep himself up was not something he had the option to ignore. He liked the action, but in a way he also may have needed it.

In later years, Abbie didn't like to talk about the bust. He hoped that someday, somehow, either in a court case, or by a New York State Governor's commutation, he would be pardoned. But he did say repeatedly that there was at least one undercover cop among his co-defendants or their accomplices.[15] Just weeks prior to the bust, Abbie had been the only individual named publicly in a lawsuit against BOSS, the New York City Police Department's "red squad," that resulted in the destruction of intelligence files on thousands upon thousands of people.[16] That would have been only the most recent among a thousand reasons members of law enforcement had for wanting to put Abbie Hoffman away.

It may be that Abbie was entrapped. There is convincing circumstantial evidence to that effect. But so little of the record has been made public. Abbie's entire FBI file contains some 15,000 pages, many of which have been released to us with large areas blacked out by heavy black Magic Marker. Untold numbers of documents from the FBI and other government agencies have simply been destroyed. To date, the New York Police Department's Bureau of Special Services has released to me some 800 pages of files on Abbie. But since Abbie's FBI file describes communications between BOSS and the FBI that are not indicated in the BOSS files, we know that other BOSS files were either destroyed or are still being withheld.

The early '70s was a period when the FBI could destroy lives and, in some cases, whole movements with complete deniability. This was the period of their war against the American Indian Movement (AIM), the Puerto Rican Independence Movement, and the American Communist Party. As exhaustively documented by Peter Matthiessen in his book on the Leonard Peltier case, one of the more typical modus operandi of the FBI was to feed individual law enforcement officers exaggerated estimations of the dangerousness and maliciousness of activist leaders, thus tempting local police officers to exceed the letter of the law on account of the heinousness of their perceived enemy.[17]

The extent of the COINTELPRO activity against Abbie and other public figures on the Left is still open to question. The truth may well be that what is known represents only the smallest part of FBI dirty work.

If Abbie had really been dealing drugs, or was even suspected of dealing, wouldn't there have been some mention to that effect somewhere in the 15,000 pages of FBI files we reviewed? There is no mention of it anywhere in the FBI files. It is clear that Abbie's drug bust was an uncommon event filled with procedural irregularities and that today we still don't know the whole truth about it.

Chapter Eleven

1973–1976

I wouldn't say it's acting. I don't think I'm a good actor. But there's a dybbuk inside, you know, greased with chicken soup, that says, "Survive! Survive!"

—ABBIE

THE DRUG BUST was the worst thing that ever happened to the Hoffman family. We received it as you would a natural disaster. You don't try to fight off an earthquake or a hurricane; you wait until it's over and then try and clean up the mess. We didn't talk much about what had happened—not in those winter months of 1973 and not in the years afterward either. Even Dad was silent on the subject of the bust. We all were silenced by what had happened. What was there to say?

People in Worcester who had hated and scorned Abbie and our whole family for his politics seemed to get suddenly quiet too. Whereas before, Abbie had been holding up a mirror, making them look into the eye of *their* tragedy, now the only thing for them to see was our family's troubles, and so their sense of neighborly decorum returned and they stopped complaining about us. They understood the drug bust—proleptically, smartly, coldly, with the gossip's good intuition—as a kind of suicide: Abbie had taken himself out of play. Worcester's political conservatives breathed a communal sigh of wonderment, as if what had happened was so magical, so unexpected, so bizarre, that it was a kind of divine kindness, a right-wing epiphany.

Then the cosmic accident of the drug bust was followed, as by an equal and opposite reaction, by Abbie's cockeyed, if understandable, decision to flee, threatening to extend the period of our grief indefinitely, as if we were mourning a lost loved one whose body could not be found. Abbie simply didn't have the temperament that would have allowed him to bow his head and accept what had happened, regardless of the circumstances. His personality was unsuited to submission. So he had to flee the scene of such an overwhelming personal catastrophe. Had he stayed and gone to trial, Abbie would have done so unrepentant, and for that, even more than for his crime itself, he really might have been crushed.

Sometime in September or October 1973, our sister Phyllis received a letter at her home in Mexico City, where she lived with her husband Hilario, a cabinet-level agriculture minister, and their son, Hilario Jr. Inside the envelope, which was postmarked in Mexico, was the familiar lined yellow sheet. Abbie nearly always wrote his letters with a black pen on yellow legal pads. And the letter might have been from Abbie, since he was out on bail, awaiting trial. But the short note was signed "Howard" and was in a hand different from Abbie's. It began: "Dear Phyllis, would you be willing to help someone who might possibly be a fugitive and whose life is in danger?" More than a little frightened, Phyllis burned the letter and flushed the ashes down the toilet.

She was sure the letter was from Abbie, and it annoyed her that he hadn't signed it. She found something creepy about getting an anonymous letter from her own brother. Later, Abbie would tell Phyllis that the letter had indeed been from him and that he had written it with his left hand to disguise his handwriting. He had come south of the border for a few days on a sort of scouting expedition, and writing to her was his way of preparing her for the likelihood that he might return soon and more permanently.

Back in New York, Abbie requested a meeting with the Weather Underground. He wanted them to know he was planning to join those who had gone underground before him; in case he ever needed their help, he wanted to be able to call on them. The meeting took place in a darkened movie theater in Brooklyn, during a showing of *The Way We Were*. The Weather member asked questions, offered advice, and cautioned Abbie about the difficulty of the underground life in general and of the increased challenge of Abbie's particular case because of his being somewhat older and so well known. When Abbie mentioned that he didn't think Anita would be joining him, at least not at first, the conversation turned gloomy. "Alone is very tough. None of our people make it alone," the Weatherman offered.[1]

On December 4, 1973, Judge Gignoix, who eight months earlier had denied motions for dismissal by the Chicago defendants, now acquitted Abbie on three of the five contempt charges, but still found him guilty of the last two.[2] Two days later, on December 6, 1973, he threw out the entire case against all the defendants. This was a complete vindication of the Chicago 8 and a strong tacit condemnation of Judge Hoffman visited upon him by a colleague.

A few days later, Abbie, Anita, and america visited Phyllis in Mexico City. The first night he laid it all out for Phyllis and Hilario. He was facing fifteen or twenty-five years if he went to trial for the cocaine and got convicted and sentenced to hard time. If he was sent to Attica, Abbie was convinced that he would be killed. None of his lawyers were promising he would beat the rap, and Abbie wasn't willing to risk doing the time.

Overtures had been made to Albania, Algeria, Cuba, Israel, North Korea, North Vietnam, and Sweden to obtain asylum, Abbie explained. Only Israel had said no. The consensus was that Sweden would be the most livable country, but Abbie nixed that idea. He felt it was too far and would be too cold for too many months of year. A little surprisingly, Abbie decided against Cuba as well. He felt that going to a Communist country would close the door forever on his hopes of eventually returning and obtaining a pardon for the coke bust.

Hilario offered to make inquiries about obtaining political asylum in Mexico but said that any such process in Mexico would take six months to arrange. Abbie didn't feel he could wait that long. But he seemed to be inclined toward Mexico anyway. By the time Abbie left a few days later, Phyllis was convinced he'd made his decision. "I had no idea how or when, but I knew he was coming to Mexico." The thought frightened her. "I began to feel scared," she told me recently, "for me, for my son, for my husband."

*　*　*

During Abbie's earlier meeting with the Weather Underground in Brooklyn, he'd expressed his support for Anita's decision not to go underground with him. "It's too hard on the kid," he'd said. "[Anita's] tired of doing my thing. We'll try a year apart and see."[3] Initially, Abbie may even have liked the idea of making a clean break. But now as the day of his departure neared, the prospect of leaving without Anita and america, perhaps never seeing them again, became increasingly unbearable to him. Up until the very last moment, he wished that she would insist on going with him—"Inside I begged she would change her mind."[4] But he refused to say anything that might influence her. It was too large and terrible a decision to make jointly, one that had to be made by each of them for himself or herself.

Speaking of the months before going underground, he would later say, "I was miserable before I left; it was like falling off a cliff. For two months before I left, I was impotent, never happened before, just wouldn't get stiffo . . . it was *interesting*."[5] The gloom that had descended over the whole family had hit Abbie the worst. As he prepared to begin his life as a fugitive, he wasn't only running from the FBI but also from an urgent inner misery, part circumstantial nightmare, part biochemical depression.

In early January 1974, Abbie asked Phyllis to meet him and me in San Antonio, Texas, on January 17. When the time came, Abbie and I flew down together; Phyllis drove the 1,500 miles up from Mexico City. That evening, the three of us got drunk on tequila, smoked dope, and caroused through the town. Each time Abbie poured himself a shot, he torched the tequila with a cigarette lighter and then gulped it, flame and all. It snowed that night in San Antonio. Back in the hotel room, Abbie showed us $20,000 in cash that had been raised by donations from friends, and that he wanted Phyllis and me to stash away for him in Mexico. Drunk and stoned, we spilled the money all over the bed, throwing it at each other and laughing hysterically. Then we cried ourselves to sleep.

The next day we said our good-byes, wondering if we'd ever see each other again. I thought then that probably we never would; I looked toward the future with a hollow feeling, like a hangover that was going to last for the rest of my life with Abbie out of it. Strangely, that day, January 18, following Judge Gignoix's action a month earlier, the government dropped all remaining charges against the Chicago 8. Abbie told us the news, reciting it without interest, as if it were a bulletin from a past life. Phyllis and I looked at each other, uncomfortable that we should be happier about Abbie's news than he was, and feeling sad for him.

Phyllis and I took the $20,000 and drove to Mexico. As we waited in her new green Porsche in the line of cars at the border, Phyllis said she felt scared. I didn't know if it was fear of losing Abbie forever or terror of having him hanging around. The next day, after she had returned to Mexico City, Phyllis set up a mail drop and an emergency telephone contact, all according to Abbie's detailed instructions.

Her husband held a politically sensitive government post. I had a factory in Mexico vulnerable to confiscation by the government. And our parents sometimes vacationed in Mexico. By choosing this country for his new life, Phyllis thought Abbie was risking our safety for his own convenience. And yet it moved me to think that Abbie wanted to be in a country where, even if he couldn't be with us, he still saw nearness to us as a shield against the loneliness he anticipated ahead.

In February or early March 1974, Abbie had a speaking engagement in Richmond, Virginia. From there, he stopped briefly in Atlanta. Then, still not officially a fugitive since his court date was later in the month, he flew to California for a nose job. About ten days later, he was in Mexico City, where Dad and Ma were vacationing, although Abbie didn't know it. He called Phyllis and arranged to meet her at the Hotel Aristos, downtown.

Seated in the hotel lobby, Phyllis didn't recognize anyone. Then she found herself staring at a short, dandified man with a swollen nose trying very hard to look like a sophisticated Latin in a sophisticated Latin hotel and failing miserably. The dandy wore a cream-color summer suit, and his hair was very short. When he began to walk toward her, his gait was comical, almost a waddle. Not until he was very near and began to speak to her did Phyllis recognize his voice. Cosmetic surgery had changed Abbie's nose, but his voice was unmistakable. His first words to his sister were, "This is it," meaning this was the complete makeover, and how did she like it? She laughed. A few minutes later, she told him that Ma and Dad were only a few blocks away at that very moment.

"Under no circumstances," Abbie said darkly, "are they to be told that I'm here. It's going to come down heavy, but I'll be safe." He warned Phyllis to be careful, since "they"—the FBI et al.—would be looking for him. Phyllis wasn't used to seeing Abbie scared, but on that day, missing Anita and america and sensing the protracted isolation to come, Abbie was very scared. Their meeting lasted about half an hour. At the end, Abbie told her he was headed to a safe house in Yelapa, a tiny, beautiful resort town north of Puerto Vallarta. The house was owned by a Columbia Pictures executive and Abbie's stay there had been arranged by a trusted friend of Abbie's. He may have been inconsolable, but if he was going to have to suffer he was determined to do it in style. Abbie gave Phyllis the phone number there, to be used only in case of extreme emergency.

That Sunday, Phyllis went to dinner with Ma and Dad in Mexico City. At the end of the meal, Dad suddenly started crying, for no apparent reason. After a while he said to Phyllis, "I think Abbie's going to come to you for help and I want you to help him." Phyllis was struck by the similarity between the unusual anxiety she'd seen in Abbie and the equally uncharacteristic sadness our father had expressed to her in his tears and his words. This would be the last time she'd see Dad.

Around the same time, I met with Anita in New York and we agreed that, for security reasons, we shouldn't contact each other again for as long as Abbie was underground. Hell, Anita and I had never gotten along anyway. The communal life Abbie had shared with Anita and their friends had been completely disconnected from the one he shared with our family. So Anita may have seen me and our whole family as a kind of threat to the Abbie she knew and loved.

With Abbie gone, there was no glue, no reason for us to keep up appearances; the "security reasons" were just our excuse. Now there were no bridges left for me to my brother among his crowd.

Ma and Dad returned home to Worcester. A few days later, Ma called me at the office to say she wanted to talk to me in private, and that she was coming down so I should wait for her out in the parking lot. What Ma wanted to talk to me about was Abbie and Dad. She had gathered from Phyllis that Abbie might be in Mexico and didn't want me to mention anything about it to Dad. That was all she had to say. It was strange to me that once she broached the subject, she hadn't wanted to say more. Her concern was practical: she understood Dad's health to be fragile and didn't want it shattered by news of Abbie.

The next day, on Saturday, March 23, 1974, Dad took my four-year-old son Justin with him to the men's club at the YMCA—just like he used to take Abbie and me. I was to meet them afterward. Dad was overweight and had adult-onset diabetes. He had already had two heart attacks and was supposed to be on a strict diet. But when he suggested Weintraub's deli, I didn't think to object, since Weintraub's was our traditional Saturday meeting place. It would turn out to be the last time I would ever see him.

It was early afternoon and Dad and Justin were sitting across from one another at a large table. Dad was wolfing down what we call the Weintraub's antipasto: chopped liver, chopped herring, salami, a couple of pieces of corned beef and pastrami, egg salad, tuna salad—everything he wasn't supposed to eat loaded on one plate under a shower of vinegar, oil, and more salt. All designed to get you to Perlman's Funeral Parlor on the express train. On a side plate, there was *kishka,* a kind of meatless Jewish sausage made with grain and lots of grease, just to make sure the damage was done. Under the table he had his flask of schnapps. I was mad that day that Dad was drinking around my son and taking so little care of himself. And today, as I remember the sight of him, just days before he died, I am convinced that Abbie never showed more reckless abandon in any courtroom or at any demonstration than Dad did on that day, and on many Saturdays toward the end of his life.

On Monday, March 25, 1974, Abbie's fugitive years unofficially began when he failed to appear in court at a pretrial hearing. On Wednesday, in the early evening, Dad suffered a heart attack peacefully among his friends in the steam room at the YMCA. After a short ambulance ride, he died at 7:25 P.M. in the local hospital's emergency room.

Two days later, on Friday, March 29, everyone who was anyone in Worcester turned up at the funeral—the mayor, the chief of police, the chief of the fire department and leading members of the business community, as well as local loansharks and bookmakers, friends and family. Mourners numbered in the hundreds, perhaps as many as a thousand. It was the largest funeral ever held in Temple Emanuel. Of course the local FBI agents were there, standing in the corner, maintaining their standard surveillance of Abbie, without any indication that they might suspect him of being three thousand miles away in Mexico.

I confronted one of the agents, saying he could have left our family in peace for one day. He stood there like a statue, ignoring me. I thought Dad should be the center of attention at his own funeral. Yet everyone I spoke to asked the same question, "Is Abbie coming?"

"I don't know," I said to each.

More than one friend of Dad's approached me at the funeral to whisper a mixture of praise for Dad and put-downs of Abbie—as if it were likely to make me feel better to be reminded of the enduring conflict between them.

A few days after the funeral, Phyllis and her husband Hilario flew to San Francisco, where Abbie had asked her to be in touch with Michael Kennedy, an attorney and Movement figure whom Abbie trusted. Michael was distressed to hear that Abbie had jumped bail; he felt that Abbie could have gone to trial and won.

From San Francisco, Phyllis returned to Mexico and only then was she able to phone Abbie safely at the emergency number he'd given her.

"Daddy died," she told him. Abbie said nothing.

On April 15, Patty Hearst and eight other members of the Symbionese Liberation Army robbed a bank, purposefully not shooting out the bank cameras so that the world would see the newspaper heiress on the side of armed revolution. On April 16, Abbie was officially declared a fugitive, after he failed to appear in a New York court for the third time. His bail was forfeited and a bench warrant was issued for his immediate arrest. The front page of the *New York Post* for April 16 carried only two stories: the FBI "Steps Up Hunt For Hearst," and "Abbie Hoffman Jumps Bail." The only image on the page is a photo of Abbie, looking like hell, taken right after the bust, with the caption, "The search is on."[6]

Along with the FBI, Interpol was also alerted by the New York City Special Narcotics Prosecutor. Nine days later, on April 25, 1974, the FBI filed a separate complaint against Abbie, and a warrant for his arrest was issued in federal court for unlawful flight to avoid prosecution. Also on April 25, an urgent teletype memo was sent from the FBI's New York office to the regional directors of the FBI offices in Boston, Chicago, and Detroit, requesting that they try to trace Abbie through their New Left and narcotics contacts. The memo ends with the caution that Abbie should be considered a "dangerous-extremist" [*sic*]. And the next day a cablegram was sent from the FBI in Washington to its Foreign Liaison Unit in Mexico City informing them of the federal warrant issue.[7]

A car with one or two people in it was now parked at the end of our street at all times. The dark four-door Ford was a constant, and intimidating, reminder to us, and to our neighbors, that we were under surveillance—an eerie and frightening reminder of our vulnerability just when the two strongest forces in our lives—Abbie and Dad—had both been taken from us. We suddenly found our circle of friends was much smaller, and didn't include most of our neighbors. Our few remaining close friends learned not to ask any questions about Abbie.

*   *   *

In the last week of April 1974, I received a package without a return address. It contained Abbie's passport, his private address book, and an audiocassette. Immediately, Joan took the address book up to the attic of our house and hid it in the rafters, showing me where it was, so we both knew, "in case something happens to one of us," she said. That's how spooked we were. This was the first indication I'd received that he was okay and wanted me to know it.

Joan and I waited until 1:00 A.M. that night and then took turns listening to Abbie's audiotape on earphones—to avert any possible audio surveillance of the house. The cassette started off with a Cat Stevens song, "Oh Very Young," followed by Abbie's voice saying, "Oh what I'd give for a corned beef from Weintraub's and a sour pickle." I started crying. With all the anticipation and suspense, and with Dad's recent death weighing heavily on me, Abbie's opening line made me feel a rush of confused emotions, and yet his words seemed as good a thing to say as anything else. And funny, they were funny, thank God. I took a deep breath and let myself feel how much I missed him and Dad both.

Abbie went on to describe his life in Guadalajara—without naming the place. He said he had found work teaching English, was living in a nice apartment, and enjoying the weather. He had had cards printed, in English, giving his name as Howie Samuels, a writer with a business called Creative Image Agency—CIA—with the address of Abbie's real literary agent in New York, Elaine Markson. He still had money stashed away. He even sounded a little grateful, although he didn't say so, for the time away from everything associated with his old life. His talk was chatty and upbeat. Most of it was no more consequential than, "There's lots of señoritas here, Jack." His implicit message with every word was, "Everything's under control." And Abbie, being Abbie, took that idea a lot further than anyone else would have. He wanted me to know that the drug bust had forced him to change course but wasn't going to break his stride. If this were going to be his funeral, there would be fireworks, a party to remember.

Of course, I wasn't buying it. The more he bragged, the more worried I got. Probably the most reassuring part of the tape was the end, where he briefly touched on Dad's death, said how much he missed Anita and america, and how he wouldn't be able to stand this loneliness for long. Then, in his usual way, he loaded me down with instructions. The last thing he said was to be careful, since the government would be watching us, adding that we'd get together, but not any time soon. He also gave me a safe address. So now it was official, I was going to be part of Abbie's underground support team. I went out behind the house, poured Ronson lighter fluid on the cassette and burned it so that it would leave no trace.

One morning in Guadalajara, Abbie was reading a Mexican newspaper when he recognized a photograph of someone he had met in New York. She was Johanna Lawrenson, a fashion model Abbie had met through his friend Joe LoGiudice. Abbie looked up Johanna and they began spending time together. By the end of the first week of June 1974—around the time that the Democratic National Committee was awarded $775,000 in damages for the Watergate break-in—Abbie and Johanna moved together to San Miguel Allende, a small village that had become an international hot spot, in the mountains a few hours' drive north of Mexico City. In San Miguel, Abbie enrolled in Spanish classes, began writing his autobiography, and found himself falling in love with Johanna.

In letters to Anita, Abbie tried to suggest that she accept the distance between them and get on with her life: "Maybe what I'm saying is we probably should separate spiritually as well as physically. . . . Go your way, princess. You're too smart to cut the mustard with a macho maniac like me. . . . I think maybe my love for you is fading. I wish I could say what I feel. It's just changing."[8]

Anita and Abbie didn't keep things from one another if they could help it. In response to Abbie's letter, Anita wrote, "I've had an affair or two but nothing earthshaking. . . . Jealous? You should only have cause to be jealous. I could use a little excitement."[9] And finally, in mid-July, Abbie wrote, "I'm not sure how to write about [Angel/Johanna] to you because I'm not sure of all my feelings. . . . I should say that she's good for me and good for us. I'm just unsure about how to write you about another woman I obviously care about."[10] Anita began her next letter, "Dear man who may love another equally—It's okay. . . . I can't be jealous. I want you to be happy."[11]

Near the end of the summer, Phyllis called from her home in Mexico City to tell me—in our coded language that I was just getting used to—that "Howie" wanted me and Joan to come down for a little family reunion. One month later, toward the end of September, Joan and I flew down to Monterrey, Mexico, 120 miles south of Laredo, Texas. Then we drove to Saltillo, where I had my factory. I spent one day there partly doing business but mostly to shake any FBI tail. That evening we drove back to Monterrey and flew to Mexico City, where we stayed overnight with Phyllis and Hilario. Early the next morning we headed north in a rental car, and by late morning we were high up in the hills of Guanajuato on our way to San Miguel Allende.

Every detail of our itinerary had been written out by Abbie and sent to us by Phyllis on several sheets of the familiar yellow lined pages, covered in Abbie's recognizable hand, including which airline to fly, what travel agent to use, where to rent our Volkswagen, which roads to take, where to stop en route and where not to stop, ending with where and when we would all rendezvous in San Miguel. Our mood was up. Surrounded by that beautiful landscape, in Mexico's crisp, dry, late summer, confident that our various diversions had been enough to throw off any surveillance, Joan and I were happy to be together, happy to be outside the U.S., which in recent months had not felt much like the land of the free, and happy to be on our way to see my brother—who, like some exiled general, had called us to him.

For Joan, it was her first trip south of the border. And for both of us it was a great comfort to be on our way to see Abbie, after the long months during which we didn't know if a meeting like this would ever take place, or if we were ever going to see Abbie again. We were having our little taste of adventure, and it was just like Abbie to have set things up this way—to have turned the dreadful uncertainty of his being on the run into fun and games.

As we turned into San Miguel, we saw another Volkswagen Beetle parked by the side of the road with a man who could have been Abbie bent over the engine in the back. Joan thought it was Abbie; I didn't. In any case, our instructions were not to stop for anything. We continued into town, parked in front of the church in the main plaza and waited, following Abbie's orders. A few minutes later, the Volkswagen we had seen before drove up and Abbie jumped out to the sounds of Joan singing out, "I knew that was you."

For a minute I just stood and stared. Abbie looked better than I had ever seen him look before—relaxed, calm, at peace. His hair was short and he'd grown a close-cropped beard that seemed to make his eyes shine even brighter. He seemed slim and fit, with his rugged tan, his cowboy boots, and Western-cut slacks—every bit the prosperous young rancher. It's embarrassing to think of it now, but one year after reaching his all-time low, the image Abbie was cultivating down in Mexico was that of someone living a life of leisure, someone with money. Despite the new nose, Abbie looked like himself, only successful. I guess it made sense somehow, and he played the part well. In fact, we couldn't see any sign of disguise whatsoever. But it did occur to us, like a passing cloud during these happy moments, that his very familiarity itself might be a kind of disguise.

"Were the instructions okay?" Abbie asked.

"Perfect," I said.

Abbie hugged Joan, and he and I shook hands warmly. Then he got back into his car and we followed him about a half mile to a hacienda he was renting, complete with Saltillo tile floors, a gorgeous view of the valley, horses corralled out back, and a Viennese cook who doubled as a housekeeper.

Inside the house, Johanna was waiting for us. My first response on meeting her was embarrassment: She's gorgeous, I thought. And my next thought was that Abbie had it made; he'd really done it, managed to turn something bad into something good: this idyllic life in Mexico that lacked for nothing. I was impressed and jealous. It hadn't taken Abbie long to make over his life. It almost didn't seem right; where was his guilt, his sense of shame? But my disfavor didn't stay with me for more than a moment. I felt good that Abbie was well and happy.

Johanna really was beautiful. She was also very charming, and had that rare quality that made you feel in her presence that you shared with her some common pool of happiness. She made Joan and me feel welcome from the very first. In our minds we couldn't help comparing her to her predecessors. We felt that she brought into Abbie's life something that he needed and that neither of his two wives had been able to give him. Abbie and Johanna seemed close and caring of one another in a way I had never observed with either Sheila or Anita. I'm sure a lot of this closeness was sexual. In later years, Johanna would complain to Joan and me that Abbie needed to have sex with her three times a day in order to be satisfied. But I'm also sure that there were many other elements that contributed to their intense closeness. Johanna had taken him up when, despite appearances, he was down and out. She was someone from outside the Movement who had lived in Europe during most of the '60s and thus was aware of him only as a man, not a public figure. These were things that would have attracted Abbie. And her willingness to share with him the uncertainty of this outlaw time must have moved Abbie deeply. And, ironically, the circumstances of his exile presented him for the first time in his life with the opportunity to devote himself to one woman without the constant competing demands of his work life.

Johanna's mother, Helen Lawrenson, was a well-known writer, and her father, Jack Lawrenson, was an important progressive labor leader for the National Maritime Union. Being with Abbie, a writer and political leader, may have approximated a homecoming of sorts after the jet-set lifestyle she had known as a model. And she may have been someone who found what Abbie called the "tension and adventure" of the fugitive life exciting. She was his "shiksie," as Abbie used to call her, and she referred to him as "my Moses." They would remain together until death parted them.

That evening Abbie himself donned the apron, locked himself in the kitchen, and created a kind of thick soup with meat and vegetables that was unusual and delicious. At first he wouldn't say what was in it; then, as he served it to us, he turned to Joan, knowing that she was still a little uneasy with the foreignness of Mexico, and said, "Iguana stew, my dear; just the thing for what ails you." Joan shuddered and refused to eat the soup. But at the same time, Abbie had made her feel at home with his prank, and she appreciated it.

It was a great relief to be close to Abbie again. As the four of us sat around the dinner table, there were many subjects of conversation that were off limits—the drug bust, Dad's death, Ma, the future—things too sad or too uncertain to share just yet. But it wasn't that we were hiding these things, just holding off talking about them for a few hours. What was important first was accepting the fact of being together again, accepting it as a kind of blessing that had nearly been denied us, and being thankful for it.

The next day, we made the short drive to Guanajuato. After dinner the night before, Abbie had regaled us with stories of the mummy museum that is the city's most famous attraction. The story goes that years ago a poor family could not keep up the small annual rent on its plot in the cemetery and was forced to exhume its dead so that the plot could be rented to somebody else. When the day came to dig up the remains of the dead, the corpses came up fully mummified, right down to the family pets, on account of the composition of the soil here. A whole culture grew up around these mummified figures, centered on the Day of the Dead, the Mexican equivalent of our Halloween.

For Abbie, Johanna, Joan, and me, the macabre humor of the Day of the Dead seemed fitting enough. During the drive to Guanajuato from San Miguel, we smoked a joint in the car, listening to McCartney's "Band on the Run" on cassette. In Guanajuato, we consumed an abundance of wine with lunch. As we wandered around the city, suddenly quite proud of our broken Spanish, Abbie kept us laughing, telling us that the other people visiting Guanajuato were there to check up on their ancestors: "Well, they're all here checking on their Ma and Dad, the dog and the cat, digging them up, making sure they're fine." We snacked on mummy candy. And it seemed about as good a way of celebrating a world gone to hell as any other. Dad hadn't been dead five months, and Abbie and I hadn't talked about that yet. I guess that at that moment, we weren't looking for ways to make things less weird. It was enough to have this expression of just how weird things were. Like the little figurine skeletons on sale all over the town, we too felt like we were laughing at death.

That night, back in San Miguel, the four of us went out to the local American nightclub. Among the crowd of American tourists who had come to San Miguel to study Spanish, Abbie and Johanna—the mysterious, dashing writer "Howie Samuels" and his international fashion model companion—were anything but anonymous. To begin with, she was about three inches taller than he was. Dancing together, Johanna dominated the room vertically, while Abbie conquered it horizontally, cutting up the dance floor, needing a lot of space. They were both good dancers, and together they looked glamorous. You didn't have to be suspicious to wonder who they really were.

When they sat down, Abbie and Johanna told us how a week earlier, at the same nightclub, Abbie had gotten into an argument with a couple of law students on the subject of the Chicago Conspiracy trial. The students had been saying how the defendants had had no choice but to act the way they did, since the judge had systematically denied all their motions. Abbie had defended Judge Julius Hoffman and had even stood up to glare down at the two students to say, "There has to be decorum in the courtroom!" I would have given anything to see Abbie say that. I guess 1974 was just the year that everything got turned upside down.

Sunday morning, after coffee, Abbie and I took a walk around the plaza and talked. He told me that his defense attorneys were preparing motions to have the drug case dismissed, and he felt sure that something would be worked out legally. I took that to mean some way for him to return, to return as Abbie Hoffman, without doing time in prison.

I gave him my impressions of Dad's funeral, how so many people had come, more than I would have expected, and how I thought Dad himself would have felt proud of the turnout, would have taken it as a tribute to his life, a sign that he'd done good. And as best as I could remember, I told him who had come and who had been absent. And how the question on everybody's tongue was where was Abbie.

Abbie asked about Ma, and then after I told him she was holding up, he added, "You don't have to worry about her. She's a good soldier." I started to kid him about the soldier routine. I don't think he'd even realized that he'd started to organize his topsy-turvy world according to good and bad soldiers. After I called him on it, I felt he made a mental note, a reminder that people sometimes resent the "this is a war we're in" stuff.

Then I kidded him about something else. The day before, Abbie had given me an early draft of the first chapters of his autobiography. Mixed in with the basic story was a continuous stream of exaggerations, while many of the early experiences that I felt were most significant were left out. I told him this now. His response: "Jack, they've got to be able to read it in Peoria." And then, as if to mollify me, he added, "I got you in the book, Jack." He didn't mind my criticisms, but he wasn't looking for advice either.

In many ways, Abbie had achieved the impossible in the year since the drug bust: He had reinvented himself. And done so with his usual ebullience. It didn't seem right to drag him back down to earth. The sadness and the shame of the drug bust, of his derailed Movement work, of his two fatherless families—none of that needed to be talked about yet. For now, Abbie was making sure he survived. Even without knowing how long it would last, we felt grateful that things seemed to have gotten this much better so soon.

He was still taking risks, like the way he'd danced with Johanna at the nightclub—as if every time he pulled things together he had to wrestle with his own wrecker's impulse to tear them apart again. And the craziness of life underground had begun to take on its own logic: Here he was running from who he was, and then what does he do in his spare time but write an autobiography. You just had this feeling that his life was turning out marvelously and coming undone at the same time. And instead of struggling against the contradictions, Abbie was embracing them.

He made it look easy and fun. That was for the benefit of his "troops," to keep our morale high. He wanted us to feel that we were on the winning team—and it was working. After Joan and I left that day, on our way back to Mexico City and the flight back to Boston, I couldn't help feeling proud that my brother was beating the odds, thumbing his nose at the whole world.

But the abnormally extreme circumstances of his life as a fugitive were an almost constant test of his sanity and endurance. Already there were cracks in the surface. His moods had begun to swing back and forth, leaving him often in states of extreme despair and exhaustion. Sometimes he would call Phyllis to chastise her for not being a good soldier in his army. And then Phyllis, outraged, would give me a signal call in Framingham to head for a safe public phone, and when I got there she would vent her anger: "Who does he think he is, Napoleon?" she'd say. I'd laugh and tell Phyllis not to worry. I felt he was back in the driver's seat, back in charge of his life, at least for the moment, and that went a long way toward consoling me for the grief of the last year. But Phyllis wasn't wrong to be worried. Abbie could make his fugitive life look fun and easy, but looks were deceiving and despite the bravado of his new life, the things he was running from had a way of not letting him go.

On October 3, 1974, Anita published an article in the *Village Voice* entitled "Life without Abbie," describing the hardship of having to raise america alone, in semi-poverty, and in the face of frequent intrusions from large groups of FBI agents searching for Abbie in "our refrigerator" and "the trunk of the Volkswagen." "The police agencies may succeed in making me a little paranoid," she wrote, "but they will not succeed in making me afraid. To live in fear of one's enemies is to let them win. I'll be damned if I'll let nightmares of FBI flatfoots disturb my sleep."[12]

In a way, Anita fully shared Abbie's exile, with courage not unlike his, and suffering a comparable degree of isolation. You could even argue that hers was the harder road, largely because she was now left to raise america alone. She worked with a group of indigent young mothers on the Lower East Side. But just surviving economically was proving difficult. In addition, unlike Abbie, the FBI and other government agencies knew exactly where to find Anita. Shortly after Abbie became a fugitive, the IRS informed her that she owed $5,000 in back taxes on the $25,000 that Abbie had donated to the Panther bail fund, and then forfeited when the Panther whose bail he had helped raise skipped town. In the end, Anita would manage, proving that without Abbie she still had the perseverance to tough it out.

* * *

That winter, Abbie and Johanna were making frequent, short trips back into the States, to California mostly, and in large part their income came from bringing electronics equipment—stereos, radios, tape decks—back across the border into Mexico where they could sell them for substantially more than what they paid stateside.

In his calls, Abbie had gotten me used to following an elaborate protocol to throw off surveillance. I'd get a one-ring call at any hour that would send me bounding out of the house and into my car for a three-minute drive to a bank of pay phones in Framingham Center, where the phone would be ringing even before I could get out of the car. Abbie would tell me his and Johanna's latest activities, and then he'd spend most of the call giving me instructions for things he wanted done.

In a letter written to me sometime in 1974 and signed "Alan Ladd," Abbie wrote that he had no grasp of reality and couldn't care less."[13]

Abbie was, as usual, pushing the limits. But this time the playing field was his very identity. In another letter to me, he wrote that he was very excited about upcoming interviews and the prospect of big-money book deals that were going to allow him to set up hundred-thousand-dollar trusts for each of his three children. Hundred-thousand-dollar trust funds for each of his kids?! Who did he think he was? It was as if he really had lost all sense of reality, just like he'd said in the Alan Ladd letter.

As 1974 ended, Abbie was heading for a full-blown personality crisis. He'd proved to himself that he could outrun the FBI. He'd proved he could do just about anything except look at himself in the mirror. He now traveled with a trunk full of disguises. And he was beginning to question whether any one disguise was more real than the others. He was beginning to suspect that Abbie Hoffman was just another disguise, as artificial as the rest.

Until 1975, the FBI had been unable to apprehend any Leftist fugitives at all. An FBI informer by the name of Larry Grathwohl had managed to infiltrate the Weather Underground briefly in early 1970.

But immediately afterward the group tightened its ranks, and no government agent was able to get that close again. Jane Alpert had given herself up in the fall of 1974, but even she had done so out of exhaustion, not fear of imminent capture. Patty Hearst was still on the run. So were around thirty members of the Weather Underground, most of whom became fugitives after Grathwohl's testimony, facing massive assault and conspiracy charges and successfully evading intense FBI manhunts going on now for five years. Surviving underground itself was part of the Weather Underground strategy—to explode the myth of FBI effectiveness, and with more practical goals as well.

During this period, the Weather Underground had claimed responsibility for over twenty bombings—including that of New York City Police Headquarters, I.T.T., the State Department building, the Pentagon, and the Capitol. Usually the bombings had come directly after, and in response to, government violence such as the killing of George Jackson, the bombings of Hanoi and Haiphong, and the C.I.A.-supported coup that overthrew Allende's democratically elected government in Chile. The ability of the "Weather Bureau" to coordinate actions and refine a party line in the face of the massive commitment of man-hours and money that the Justice Department was devoting to it—including offers of immunity—was one of the few political developments during this period that interested Abbie. And I think it was partly due to these "successes" of the Weather Underground that in 1975 and 1976 Abbie would again begin talking a harder line (as he had for a time after the Chicago protests), saying he was a committed Communist, and that other celebrities should call themselves Communists too.[14]

Then the FBI started getting lucky. In early March 1975, they arrested Pat Swinton, a fugitive bombing suspect. On March 13, they arrested six-year fugitive Cameron Bishop. And a few weeks later, they captured Susan Saxe, who had been on the Bureau's Ten Most Wanted list for over four years. Rumors began circulating that they had cracked the Underground network. And it was during this period that Abbie had been most fearful of capture.

As it turned out, the FBI had not infiltrated the Weather Underground or its overground support system. The flurry of arrests had little to do with FBI effectiveness and much to do with the natural and self-imposed limits on how long an individual can stand the isolation of life underground—usually five years at most.[15]

Toward the end of 1974, Abbie had contacted people he knew at TVTV (Top Value Television), a counterculture video documentary collective, and struck a deal for a video interview. He asked for $5,000 and some television equipment. They agreed to $3,000. The interview would be taped under conditions to be tightly controlled by Abbie, including the choice of interviewer. Abbie chose Ron Rosenbaum, a journalist he'd known since 1968 in Chicago, and whom he trusted.[16]

On March 13, 1975, there was a 7:00 A.M. telephone assignation at a phone booth in Hollywood, where Rosenbaum received instructions from Abbie to pick up plane tickets in a nearby garbage Dumpster for himself and video documentary producer Michael Shamberg. Abbie gave the two the aliases Mr. Ray and Mr. Bremer, after Dr. King's alleged assassin. Under strict instructions to call or speak to no one, and with Abbie's warning that they were being watched at all times by female "professionals"—female to ensure against FBI infiltration, since there were as yet no female FBI agents—they were to fly to Sacramento, where more "professionals" would meet them upon deplaning, and pick up their luggage for them.

Rosenbaum and Shamberg accepted the cloak-and-dagger machinations in good fun at first. Arriving in Sacramento, they were hustled out of the terminal into a waiting van, stripped, forced to wear dark glasses with the insides taped over, driven around for hours in physical discomfort, and treated generally more as kidnapping victims than as journalists on their way to an interview. When they finally met Abbie later in the day in a nondescript hotel room—surrounded by props that included posters of Lenin and Patty Hearst, and a copy of *Prairie Fire,* the secretly published Weather Underground book on building a New Left—Rosenbaum suspected that maybe thus wasn't Abbie at all, but someone disguised as Abbie Hoffman. To resolve the matter, Abbie began the interview by writing his trademark signature on a chalk board. Then he informed Rosenbaum and Shamberg that in addition to the half-dozen disguised "professionals" they'd already encountered, there were two outside they hadn't seen yet who were armed, committed to protecting those within, and they weren't "gonna throw their hands up if the police entered our perimeters. Far from it."

General Abbie had gone to great lengths to make it very clear to anyone who eventually read Rosenbaum's articles or saw Shamberg's video that behind him there really was a secret army. He further implied that his army was prepared to respond violently to any acts of violence on the part of the police or the FBI. And he wanted to leave Rosenbaum with the impression that he was connected in some way with the Weather Underground, although when questioned directly on that point by Rosenbaum, Abbie would refuse to clarify the nature of the connection. Rosenbaum guessed, probably rightly, that Abbie's anarchist temperament made him incompatible with Weather discipline.

When the TVTV video interview eventually aired on public television and Rosenbaum's two-part article appeared in *New Times*, Abbie's strategy to create an impression of a secret society, armed, dangerous, and deadly serious, backfired. Instead of impressing Rosenbaum and Shamberg—both of whom began as extremely sympathetic to Abbie's cause—Abbie had alienated them and turned their initial good will into distrust. In both the articles and the video documentary, Abbie's subterfuges nearly replaced him as the main subject. Had he or had he not been wearing a disguise? Why all the cloak and dagger? Who were his associates? And even, was this really Abbie?

Yet in early April, fresh from what he felt had been the complete success of the TVTV interview, which was still a month away from airing, Abbie decided to repeat the experience. He contacted Ken Kelley, a former underground press editor of the Ann Arbor *Argus* and the *Berkeley Barb* who now wrote for *Playboy*, to see if he might be able to interest the magazine in an interview. The response from *Playboy* was positive. There followed several weeks of intrigue—instructions by prearranged pay phone connections, code names, addresses in various states—designed to give Kelley the impression of a sophisticated, nationwide, radical underground network, and culminating in a secret rendezvous with Kelley in Phoenix.

Arriving at the airport, Kelley was met by a car driven by

Johanna and asked to wear a blindfold for the drive to their destination. When he was finally allowed to take off the blindfold, he was in what looked like a hotel room facing Abbie in the uniform of a New York City police sergeant. When Kelley began to press for "three straight days of Q. and A." for *Playboy,* Abbie played hard to get, saying, according to Kelley, "We'll see. I have to consult my collective, you know, before I can give you a yes or no. I'm a full-fledged Commie now." Finally it was agreed that Abbie would keep Memorial Day weekend, about a month away, free for Kelley, and the journalist was sent back to the airport with assurances that he would be contacted.[17]

Meanwhile Abbie had hemorrhoid surgery that left him immobilized and screaming with pain for an entire week. Still not fully recovered, he suddenly decided to take Johanna to Vegas. Shortly after they arrived, Abbie broke down. For hour after hour during most of an entire day and night he yelled out his real name over and over. It was a bona fide nervous breakdown, as if the different parts of his personality were actually colliding head on.

In the middle of it, standing at a pay phone in the street in Vegas, he called me. I answered the phone to his voice shouting one sentence at me over and over: "Can you believe they don't believe I'm Abbie Hoffman?" Then Johanna got hold of the receiver, and said to me, simply: "What am I going to do?" I had no idea what was going on other than that Abbie sounded extremely manic. I couldn't know how bad it was.

Abbie himself would describe his Vegas collapse vividly a few years later:

> We have been racing madly for days, a step or two ahead of the body snatchers. Angel is trying to figure out what preparations are needed for what seems like inevitable capture. She's exhausted from watching the man she loves turn into a monster. My lips are cracked from hours of talk binge. I think that the doctors inserted a transmitting device during the operation. I'm trying to decode the beeps. I crawl rather than walk, avoiding the gaze of the people behind the two-

way mirror.... The TV set is talking to me. Everything is
code. Saigon is being liberated. Dominoes are falling in my
head. Soon Las Vegas will fall.... [18]

In the end, Johanna was able to get friends from California to
come to Vegas to help control him.[19] And from there Johanna found
a way to convince Abbie to come with her to San Francisco and see a
doctor there who prescribed some form of short-term medication.[20]
Was it here that Abbie was diagnosed as suffering from manic depressive illness? Or did that happen a few years later in 1979? My memory fails me. Somehow, the good times remain more fully
differentiated for me. I recall them without confusing either the
month or the year. But the outbreaks of mania and depression that
would overtake Abbie once or twice a year from 1975 onward blur
together for me, since they were largely repetitive, almost seeming to
exist outside of time altogether, like recurring nightmares.

By Memorial Day weekend, the date of the first long meeting
with Ken Kelley in San Diego, Abbie was still only partially recovered
from his breakdown. When Abbie and Johanna arrived, Kelley noticed "there was a choppiness to his gestures; a haunted look would
enshroud his eyes from time to time. I couldn't figure out why, but
Abbie scared me."[21] They decided to do the interview by the ocean in
Mexico, making the drive from San Diego and arriving in Guyamas
on Saturday evening.

While Abbie rested at the hotel, Kelley and Johanna had a drink
in town, where a freak accident occurred. A brawl broke out at the
far end of the bar. A full can of beer was hurled, missed its intended
destination and hit Johanna, opening a gash in her face. Kelley helped
get Johanna to a doctor and spent the rest of the evening trying to
make sure she was stitched up in a way that would prevent scar-
ring—a major problem for a model. Inside stitching was arranged,
with only a butterfly bandage on the outside. A few months later a
Miami plastic surgeon would be able to sand away all visible traces of
the scar.

Finally back at the hotel, they had to break the news to Abbie.
He jumped out of bed and said that they had to return to the U.S.

right away, Kelley and Johanna by plane, Abbie alone in the car. While they passed through the hotel lobby in the predawn hours, a very strange parade of familiar American faces filed through the lobby around them. There was Liza Minnelli, Burt Reynolds, Gene Hackman. This time, Abbie wasn't hallucinating. It turned out the actors were shooting the film *Lucky Lady* at the hotel. As soon as Abbie got wind of it, despite the hour, Johanna's condition, and his own sense of the urgency of their departure, he began acting up for the film crew, doing his best to persuade them that he was a big Hollywood producer. As Kelley tells it, the cast concluded instead that "he was an obnoxious creep." His manic intensity only increased with each passing hour into the night. By the time he drove them to the airport for their flight, both Kelley and Johanna just wanted to be free of him.

Abbie's manic phase gradually subsided, and with it his fear that he faced imminent capture. In Kelley's description, Thanksgiving Day 1975 found Abbie smiling behind dark glasses from the front seat of a white T-Bird tooling along a thin strip of road in the middle of a vast and sprawling ranch in Texas, Johanna next to him driving, Jerry Rubin in the backseat laughing, and Ken Kelley, there to put the finishing touches on the *Playboy* interview, sitting next to Rubin. Abbie even turned to apologize to Kelley for his behavior in the spring. Those days already seemed far in the past. In Kelley's description, Abbie is now much better off.[22]

By January 1976, fleeting visions of Thunderbird grandeur notwithstanding, Abbie and Johanna had in fact graduated from a Volkswagen bug to a Volkswagen minibus. Abbie told me he'd bought it from a guy who won it on *The Price Is Right*. Abbie and Johanna spent much of their time in the U.S. in the minibus, and made frequent trips to California, where he had friends and places to stay, where the underground network was strong, and where he felt more comfortable now than he did back East. For several months they lived communally with another couple in Santa Fe, and Abbie worked as a cook.

* * *

Early 1976 was a strange kind of high water mark for me, a time when positive things resurfaced, magically, after the long hopelessness we had all felt following Abbie's drug bust and Dad's death. I was spending more time with Joan and our two children and was preparing to sell Worcester Medical. I felt good in a way I haven't felt since.

My decision to sell the business was something I felt certain about. The market was right, the business was ripe. I could—and eventually did—get the price I wanted. And I planned to devote more time to my second business, manufacturing operating room disposables, which seemed to me to have more long-term potential. But Ma didn't want me to sell the company that Dad had built. It had been his whole life's achievement, and now it was a kind of living memorial to him and to our family that, in Ma's eyes, I was preparing to demolish.

On Sunday, February 10, 1976, I was in Mexico City on business. I had been awakened around dawn by a shaking. I opened my eyes to see the ceiling fixture swaying. I became fully awake with the certainty that I was going to die, there and then, as if in a dream. I'd never experienced that feeling before. I pulled my pants on with the thought that at least this way they'd find my wallet on me and I'd be identified. Then, barefoot and shirtless, I ran out of the room and down ten flights of stairs. The stairwell was separating from the wall as I descended.

In the lobby was a crowd of shocked European tourists milling about, wrapping themselves in wool blankets being handed out by hotel staff. I called Phyllis. She called Abbie, who happened to be in town. It turned out the earthquake had registered 7.2 on the Richter scale. And while I sat in the lobby with my hands trembling, waiting for somebody to come, I watched the people around me and slowly tried to fathom my own fear of dying as I had just experienced it.

As I began to come around, I found myself wanting to see Abbie very badly. And then, quite suddenly, there he was right next to me inside the Hotel Ángel lobby. Abbie and Johanna had gotten Phyllis's call and rushed right over. By coincidence, Johanna's mother was with them. Once they'd gotten me out of the hotel, it was decided that Johanna and her mom would take the van and Abbie and I would have the day to ourselves.

Abbie insisted we had to do something in honor of the earthquake, and decided we should take a cab ride to the shrine of Guadalupe to join the procession of devotees making the miles-long pilgrimage on their knees. When we arrived, Abbie told me to get on my knees, which I did, and after a little while he joined me. And he was right: Abbie knew something about what quieted the spirit after moments of terror like I'd experienced that morning. Moving down the street on my knees, I felt my strength come back to me.

In Guadalupe I told Abbie I was planning on selling Worcester Medical. He nodded. The company was my affair, not something he would have an opinion about, although I think he appreciated my telling him first. I told him the amount I expected to sell it for—around $350,000—and again he just nodded, as if the subject were one that didn't interest him. He told me that he and Johanna were living with friends outside Mexico City and traveling around in their Volkswagen van. He didn't tell me who the friends were, or the places they were visiting, and I didn't ask.

I would have liked to ask him what he felt about my having taken over the family business, built it into a successful company, and now selling it (the deal would go through the following July). But I knew it was a subject that was too loaded for us to talk about straight out. In his two years underground, much of it spent under duress, Abbie had assumed my loyalty, asked for and received my help, and gotten me to take risks on his behalf many times. But he'd never asked me for money, even when he knew I had it, even though he wasn't usually shy about asking other people for money when he needed it. I think that instinctively he saw the money I earned through Worcester Medical as Dad's money, since Dad had started the company. So he would always ask me for the things he knew were all mine—my ideas, my trust, even my anger, but almost never my money. He knew I'd take care of Ma. But if money were going from one to the other, he wanted it to be from him to me, from elder brother to younger brother. Throughout his career, whenever he signed a contract for a book or some other deal, he'd make sure there was some angle in it for me, usually the right to distribute at a good percentage. So now when I was talking about selling the business he just nodded as if he'd rather talk about something else.

Later that day over lunch, Abbie handed me a manila envelope with four or five handwritten sheets inside. It was something he intended as an Op Ed piece for *The Boston Globe* that he wanted me to carry back to the States for him, a remembrance of Dad he'd written that he was calling "I Remember Papa." I've always liked the things Abbie wrote when he turned his lights inward, and I wanted to read it right in front of him. But he asked me to wait until I was on the plane.

In "I Remember Papa," Abbie described how his views on our father kept changing as he worked on his autobiography, even though Dad was already two years dead. "I realize how much my father taught me and how much I miss him now," he wrote.

> *I know he tried his best, and I understand it wasn't his fault he died unhappy. His bitterness about life near the end was not any of his own doing. He adopted America's values without question, he supported its wars, its courts, its charities, its police, its government. He had great trust in America's leaders.*
>
> *Watergate killed my father. He had argued throughout 1972 in support of Nixon, and finally events proved Dad wrong even to himself. Unfortunately, he died before Nixon resigned. He passed away a loyal citizen, but with a lingering doubt that maybe his meshuggener (crazy) son had some good points to make after all.*

The *Globe* would print "I Remember Papa" on the Op Ed page on June 28, 1976. It was about Abbie needing to see Dad more clearly in order to see himself clearly. To me, reading it was like seeing Dad and Abbie walking side by side one last time.

I didn't hear from Abbie for a couple of months. Then suddenly in late April 1976, I got a call at home from Johanna, using her code name, "Jane," and directing me to one of our safe pay phones. The phone was already ringing as my car pulled up. I answered with the old fear in my gut, to hear Johanna's voice anxiously repeating my code name.

"Jason?"

"Yes," I answered.

"Meet me in San Antonio—tomorrow," she continued in the same breath. "Barry"—Abbie's code name—"has had an emergency and has had to leave the country. I'll meet you in San Antonio at . . ." and she named a hotel. Then she hung up, leaving me without a clue other than the fact that they were counting on me.

The next morning I was on a flight to San Antonio, trying not to think about what I was going to find out when I got there. At the hotel, Johanna told me that *Playboy* had betrayed them. She said they had had to leave all their belongings at my factory near Saltillo, and then Abbie had flown to Canada, while Johanna drove the van to San Antonio. She wanted me to help her sell it.

Johanna didn't show me the *Playboy* article. It was already on the stands, and I could have just bought it. But for the moment she needed my help, not my opinion, so I left it alone.

On the first day in San Antonio we couldn't find a buyer for the van. In the late afternoon, we returned to the motel to find the place overrun with reporters and police. We almost ran. Then I asked someone in the crowd what was going on. He told me they were having a reception for presidential candidate George Wallace. The next day we managed to sell the van and then I took Johanna to the airport. From there she flew east without telling me her exact destination.

In Canada, Abbie was in a manic phase again, convinced that the *Playboy* article had made him appear, "racist, sexist, and egotistical," and had revealed hiding places that would now allow the FBI to plug into his underground network. He was ranting against the perceived betrayal by Kelley and *Playboy* for hours on end, and without Johanna to ground him, he was out of control.

As soon as he'd arrived in Canada, he'd called the three Movement journalists he felt he could trust at that moment and got them to come immediately to help him launch a media counterattack, calling it an "underground press conference."[23] The three were Jeff Nightbyrd, former editor of *The Rat* (an alternative newspaper), who had already written about Abbie underground in the December 4, 1975, Austin *Sun;* Bob Fass of WBAI radio and an old friend; and Abe Peck, elder statesman of Movement journalists and once editor and publisher of the *Seed.* According to a long article published by Nightbyrd in the May 3 *Village Voice,* Abbie's friends were sympathetic but perplexed. Had Abbie been betrayed by Kelley and *Playboy,* or was he snapping under the pressure and isolation of life as a fugitive? Interestingly, the most powerful material in the Nightbyrd article doesn't concern the *Playboy* interview at all, but Abbie's descriptions of life on the run:

> *When a fugitive asks someone for help they're saying, "I trust you with my life." How many experiences in American society allow for that kind of human interaction? Certainly not jumping into bed with someone, certainly not going into business together. I'd say it makes for a deeper experience than even love. . . . The experience of going underground taught me to ask for help when I needed it.*[24]

Abbie also talked about his (temporary) conversion to Communism, about Johanna, and about Anita. He described Johanna—"Angel"—as equally comfortable hitchhiking across the Midwest or dancing at a debutante ball, and how "Anita and I have a sacred bond between us that's overcome the craziness of pop love." It was as if one part of his brain were condemning the betrayal by *Playboy* while another part was simultaneously constructing—fantasizing—a fugitive paradise out of the shattered pieces of his life.

Abbie's calls to my house became frequent and suddenly free of any security concerns. His anger at Kelley knew no bounds. And of course he was wrong as hell. He was paranoiacally accusing people who had been trying to help him. In *Soon to Be a Major Motion Picture,* Abbie describes himself as "terror stricken."[25] I believe it may have been the view in the mirror—his emotional honesty during the interview more than the blown underground cover—that had Abbie terrorized after *Playboy* hit the stands.

The May *Playboy* interview that had Abbie so upset all during the spring of 1976 was one of the more frank and unassuming public exhibitions of Abbie's career. In it, Abbie wasn't always an inspiration, but he talked straight—about the drug bust, about doing time, a lot about drugs, and a lot about sex. I think that there was something about the venue, something about the fact that it was *Playboy* that made him treat the interview with real respect. It made a difference to Abbie that *Playboy* wasn't a Movement publication, and yet, as Abbie saw it, the magazine was "clearly taking a risk . . . in effect saying that it won't cooperate with the Government in its attempt to capture and cage me. . . . I think it's very brave and courageous [of *Playboy*]."[26] In return for the favor, Abbie said a lot of things that were simple, true, and moving.

Describing his 1973 parting from Anita, for example, he said, "At first, we were so busy getting mobilized, in kind of a trance, nothing really hit us. When it did, we just cried. Nothing is as intimate as crying with someone—not loving, not balling." But something had happened in Abbie's mind between the time the interview process had begun, in the spring of 1975, and the time the published interview appeared a year later, so that the unusual candor with which he initially approached the interview was no longer tolerable to him.

Meanwhile, Abbie's jag in Canada continued unabated. After his "press conference," he left Montreal for a small off-season motel cabin in the Laurentians, about forty miles northwest of Montreal. Phoning anyone and everyone in the U.S. from his hotel room, he ran up a substantial bill that he couldn't pay. He was hauled off to jail and used his one call to contact Marty Carey in Woodstock, New York. Carey took $300 from his son's bar mitzvah fund and drove through the night to bail Abbie out.

Then Abbie tried to contact the Cuban Embassy in Ottawa, thinking he would at last take asylum in Cuba. But they froze him out, thinking, Abbie would later claim, that he was a CIA agent impersonating Abbie Hoffman. Carey was able to persuade Abbie to return with him to Woodstock, where, together with neighbors Stew Albert and Ed Sanders, he tried to calm Abbie down. But Abbie was completely paranoid—convinced on the one hand that he was about to be captured, and on the other hand drumming up fantastic new projects, including a plan to market Cuban cigars in the U.S. He claimed that Fidel Castro had granted him an exclusive concession and wanted to bring together some local folk musicians to record a promotional jingle he'd written. He refused to let anyone call him by his real name and walked around carrying a hunting knife.[27]

Abbie left Carey, returned to Canada to the same off-season resort area in the Laurentians, and rented an apartment. Still desperate, he placed frequent calls to Mayer Vishner, a trusted friend in New York, who became convinced that Abbie was in serious emotional trouble. Vishner consulted with Dave Dellinger, and the two of them made the drive to Abbie's hide-out, to try and help. But Abbie was inconsolable and nothing much had changed by the time Vishner and Dellinger left.

Abbie moved into a fleabag hotel in Montreal and found a job tarring the roof of an apartment building. He began confessing his identity to people he met. But they either didn't believe him, or didn't know who Abbie Hoffman was.

By his own description, his emotional state was "quite frayed." But that was an understatement. He and Johanna had agreed to live separately, fearing FBI detection if they surfaced as a couple. But without her, he had come completely undone. His life was hanging by a thread. As the Montreal Olympics began, he would write six years later, "I alternated between being manic, staying up all night, and being extremely depressed, not getting out of bed for long periods, not talking to anyone. For the first time in my life I contemplated suicide. . . . But what brought me to the edge of hysteria was an odd coincidence. One of Canada's Olympic athletes was a woman middle-distance runner. I'd turn on the TV and stare in bewilderment at an ad that said: 'Come to Montreal and see Abby run.' Totally bizarre. I was starting to flip out."[28] In an article he would write for the June 1977 issue of *Oui* magazine, he described this period even more forcefully:

> *I cried uncontrollably, realizing that I had chased away everyone I loved and had prepared myself for self-annihilation. I craved death but lacked the energy or initiative to do*

the deed. Instead I lay in bed and waited. Terror crept through my bones. . . . Every day began with thoughts of suicide and turning myself in; I was convinced that I had failed all those real and imaginary people cheering for me to go the distance.[29]

One day Abbie met a McGill medical student with an apartment to sublet. Inside the apartment, Abbie noticed a copy of *Steal This Book* on a shelf. He took it down, pointed to the picture on the back, and said, "I'm him. I'm in trouble. I'm very depressed. I need help," and collapsed.[30] The student settled Abbie into the apartment and put him in touch with a psychiatrist friend who began seeing Abbie on a daily basis and even became his regular tennis partner. Describing his state of mind, Abbie would write, "I'd already identified myself as manic-depressive, and knew it was related to my situation. Living underground is a form of functional schizophrenia. . . . I'd had six different identities. My head was splitting apart, and I had to do something."[31]

By late summer 1976, Johanna had destroyed all traces of her previous life with Abbie and moved into her family's summer cottage on Wellesley Island in the Thousand Island region of New York State, just south of the Canadian border. Her terror that she and Abbie were about to be captured by the FBI had abated. Abbie and Johanna were talking regularly on the phone. They decided that the "loneliness and hardship of being apart was worse than the risk of being together."[32] They agreed she would drive to Montreal, gather Abbie and his television set, and they would reconstruct their lives together. At the border, Abbie claimed for them the unique distinction of having smuggled a t.v. set *into* the United States.

That fall, Anita published *To america with Love: Letters from the Underground*. The book contained letters between Abbie and Anita during the period from April 1974 to March 1975, and it is a beautiful love story. Abbie had little to do with the compiling of *To america*. It was very much Anita's book. But Abbie completely endorsed the project. And in the end the book does reveal with great poignancy the tenderness that truly existed between them. By the time of its publication in 1976, whatever Abbie felt for Anita now coexisted with that other great love that he felt for Johanna, upon whom he was now increasingly dependent.

Chapter Twelve

〜〜

1976–1980

Now I know where the sixties have gone.
—U.S. SENATOR DANIEL PATRICK MOYNIHAN

ON WELLESLEY ISLAND, Abbie would at last plant roots and rid himself of the homelessness in his heart. Using the name Barry Freed and describing himself as a free-lance scriptwriter, Abbie settled in and healed. The Lawrensons' house had been built by Johanna's great-grandmother in the center of the town of Fineview (pop. 87). Since Johanna's family had been a part of the Fineview community for so long, she was easily accepted by it now, and her friend Barry with her. At first, he and Johanna would be there only during the short summer season, but over time the summers started earlier and lasted right through November. And anyway, it wasn't the number of months he stayed there each year that mattered so much as the feeling he had for the place and the healing effect it had on him. The great natural beauty of his new surroundings overwhelmed and soothed him, quieting the cacophony of voices in his head and helping him gain some perspective on the craziness he saw around him.

I know of only one piece on nature among Abbie's writings. It's the opening passage to a long essay he called "The Great St. Lawrence River War," and I think it's important. In it he uses a wholly different voice and a wholly different vocabulary from all his other articles and books. And yet it's very much him, very much Abbie, not a fake voice at all. It begins:

*I was introduced to the St. Lawrence River in the summer of
'76, approaching via the Thousand Island Bridge from the
Canadian mainland twenty miles north of Kingston, Ontario. It is the best approach, for rising to the crest of the
bridge a passenger's vision is completely filled by hundreds
of pine-covered islands. Scattered as nature's stepping
stones across the northward rush of the river's swirling waters. Here and there you can pick out a summer camp hidden among the trees. Its location betrayed by a jutting dock
and shiny boat. A few islands even boasted "Rhineland"
castles and mansions, rising in testimony to an opulence
that existed a century ago. But for the most part the islands
remain wild, inhabited only by rabbits, foxes, badgers,
skunks, and deer who had crossed the frozen river some
winter before. In the wetlands feed ducks, geese, loons, and
the great blue heron. While nesting on land are scores of
whippoorwills, woodpeckers, blue jays, martins, swallows,
robins, cardinals, orioles, hawks, and hummingbirds. . . .[1]*

The article goes on to describe in great detail the flora, fauna, geogra-
phy, and geology of the Thousand Island region, and counterpoises it
against the environmental destruction wreaked by the Army Corps of
Engineers' St. Lawrence Seaway, and then relates Abbie's own odyssey waging war against the corps while still a fugitive. What is extraordinary about "The Great St. Lawrence River War," written in
1981, is that, as never before in Abbie's writings, there is a sense of
balance displayed between the good and the evil in the world. As he
approached the end of his fugitive years, as he began to consider as a
real possibility a return to life as Abbie Hoffman, it was with a different outlook than he'd ever had before. It was as if, after all the terrifying crises, he'd passed on to a plateau where he was beginning to
experience a different perspective, one that embodied a newfound
wisdom.

"It's a strange thing about madness," Abbie would write a year
later. "It can be, as R. D. Laing suggests, breakthrough as well as
breakdown."[2]

* * *

Journalism was the only profession Abbie could practice while underground, and his writing improved steadily throughout the fugitive years. With its September 1976 issue, *Crawdaddy* magazine made Abbie a travel editor, under his own name, and using a complicated method of delivering his writing so that it couldn't be traced to him, thereby protecting both Abbie and the magazine. *Oui*, a men's magazine, also published his travel articles frequently. Subtly, his priorities began to change again. Before, his main purpose had been staying one step ahead of whoever might be trying to capture him, and any writing opportunities that might come along were secondary and incidental. But now this scheme of priorities was reversed. He was on the lookout for writing opportunities, and security considerations began to be an afterthought.

The beginning of the third week of January 1977 found Barry and Johanna en route to Washington, D.C., to attend Jimmy Carter's inauguration on assignment for *Oui*, and for a fleeting reunion arranged by old friends Sam and Walli Leff. It was a typical and foolhardy dare on Abbie's part, but now with his new occupation, it was primarily a good pretext for a story.

The morning of the inauguration, Abbie put special care into his disguise, reminding himself of the scene in *The Day of the Jackal* in which the political assassin disguises himself before making the hit. Then he hid the motel room key in the parking lot before driving with Johanna near the parade route. Strange to consider that, since the FBI considered Abbie capable of taking the life of a U.S. president, if Abbie had been caught that day, there might have been talk of a foiled Yippie! assassination plan. It just shows how little Abbie's enemies understood him after all.

During the ceremonies, Abbie found himself standing next to satirist and fellow Yippie! Paul Krassner. Afraid to embrace in public, they stood side by side, "trading stories as if they were passing atomic secrets." They then met up with Jerry Rubin and together again in this fleeting way the small group celebrated the changing of the guard as Jimmy Carter eschewed his limousine, choosing instead to walk back to the White House.

"For a moment," Abbie wrote, "the country looked the way [my] third-grade teacher had described it. . . . Carter seemed smaller than on t.v. Inevitably famous people [do]. And frailer. The frailty of the human experience made [me] shudder, and [I] felt nothing but good will toward the man." Actually Carter is quite tall and looks taller in person than he appears on television. Abbie's sudden recognition of the human frailty of those we lionize may have had more to do with himself—who, at five foot seven inches really did look smaller in person than he did on t.v.

As Carter passed in front of where he was standing, Abbie mouthed the words, "Good luck, Cracker!" He fantasized falling to his knees before Carter and kissing his shoe in the middle of the parade down Constitution Avenue as he begged for a presidential pardon: "Sets me free, massa Carter, sets me free," Abbie imagined himself pleading.[3]

After Carter passed, Jerry asked Abbie if he'd prayed for anything special, and Abbie shot back, "Yeah, I asked him not to flush the toilet while we were taking a shower." Two tough-skinned veterans reminding each other not to let their guard down.

The next morning, before leaving, Abbie and Johanna went through their established protocol of fugitive leave-taking, as they rubbed out their finger prints in the hotel room and flushed the contents of their traceable garbage down the toilet.

Before leaving Washington, Abbie claimed he took the guided tour of the spanking new J. Edgar Hoover Building, the national headquarters of the FBI. He even wrote a long and quite good article about visiting his enemy's lair. But years later he confessed to me that he'd made the whole thing up. Abbie was a hard worker and liked to take risks, but he also liked putting people on. "I got in line," he told me, "but after a few minutes I chickened out. But don't tell anybody."

In early 1977 I moved my factory from Mexico to St. Petersburg, Florida, and that year I was spending about half my time down there, living in an apartment in Clearwater. Business was booming. But Ma, still bitter over the sale of Worcester Medical, wasn't talking to me. I had offered her the Clearwater apartment for the winter, and not only had she refused but with her characteristic flair she had taken it upon herself to winter that year in Phoenix, just to goad me. Abbie and Johanna were living in the Miami area and I didn't understand why we weren't seeing more of each other. The fact was that Abbie's three years underground had left us feeling a little like we didn't know each other anymore, and my rift with Ma had just made the alienation between Abbie and me seem that much worse.

Abbie always had a sixth sense about these things. Just when I'd begun to worry about where we stood with each other, I got a call from him asking me to come and visit. Without leaving any room for me to play hard to get, he told me he was cooking and I'd be staying the night.

I arrived to find Abbie in fine form—in love with Johanna, happily planning an end-of-year European tour for the two of them. And he had a lot to tell me. Partly, he wanted to bring me up to date about Ma—knowing I'd be wanting to have news of her. And Abbie was at his most diplomatic: He didn't blame me, but at the same time he wanted me to know that I had to be some kind of jerk to have let my differences with Ma get so out of hand. And then there was something else he wanted to talk to me about: He was thinking, somewhere down the line, of surfacing, and he wanted to know my opinion. It was the beginning of what would become a three-year conversation, his way of welcoming me back into his inner circle. I felt glad, but at the same time I couldn't help feeling a chill for the period just past, during which I had been excluded.

As usual I tried to slip him a few hundred dollars the next day before I left, and as usual he didn't want to take my money. I almost felt insulted, especially now that I could afford it. I asked him how he was doing financially, and, as always, he said, "We're getting along." And the conversation didn't advance any further in that direction. I don't think he was trying to insult me, but I do think he was making a point: that I couldn't make my money in one world and spend it in the other, that the part of me that was a successful businessman wasn't his brother, and vice versa. It was his way of exerting pressure subtly to bring me over into his world and away from the status quo.

Then, just before I left, he asked me about his inheritance. It wasn't much money. I could have just loaned him the amount much more simply. But he wanted only what was due him: one-third of the residual sum left in Dad's estate after the taxes and the lawyers—around $3,000, not counting his share of a small commercial property Dad had also left us. For Abbie to withdraw even a small part of his share of the estate seemed like an unnecessary risk. But I told Abbie that "as a good soldier" I'd look into it, and then I headed back to Clearwater and a few days later was back in Framingham, feeling reconnected to Abbie and glad for it.

After three years underground, a new and strange suspicion had begun to haunt Abbie: maybe the FBI didn't want him. No thought was more unsettling to him. Even when Abbie had suffered false accusations and criticism within the Movement, he had always been able to count on the attention of his enemies. Among those who hated Abbie, many had misunderstood him, but they had never dismissed him. The FBI in particular had always been, in its own way, an ardent admirer. But now Abbie began to look over his shoulder with a new terror that maybe no one was following him.

I had a lawyer friend, Mort Glazer, see about Abbie's inheritance check. A clerk at the courthouse gave Mort a form for Abbie to fill out, stating that he was alive and well and ready to receive his share of the money. We forwarded it to Abbie, who signed it, had it notarized, and returned it to me. Mort presented the signed affidavit from Abbie at the Worcester County Courthouse. The clerks accepted the affidavit, and a check in Abbie's name was requested. That was all, no different from what would have been done for any other upstanding citizen. The only indication I had left that my brother really was a fugitive was the sophistication and intricacy of his own precautions.

Was the FBI just not really trying? Were they pretending they didn't want Abbie anymore? Was the FBI seeking to avoid a trial in which their wiretapping activities, which they had denied, might be revealed and along with them the fact that the drug bust was a setup? I find it hard to picture the FBI being so clever. It doesn't sound right. They were still looking for Abbie. A fugitive who doesn't get caught makes the FBI look bad, and the FBI hates to look bad. But at the same time, they were well aware that by pushing Abbie underground they had neutralized him completely, and without making a martyr out of him, which killing him would have done. In other words, their main aim had already been accomplished. Bringing him in was secondary. It didn't have the urgency it might have had otherwise.

Morty came over to the house in Framingham a few weeks after I'd returned from Florida. He had the certified check made out to Abbie in his hand. We both laughed about it. Morty credited the soulless bureaucracy: my opinion was that one or two of those people Abbie used to call his "35,000 close personal friends" worked in the Worcester courthouse. Before he left, I asked Mort something that hadn't occurred to me once in three years but had crossed my mind several times in the last week: "What could they do to me for helping my brother—just the way any brother would?"

"In some states you could get a ten- to twenty-year sentence," Morty shot right back at me, almost as if he'd been waiting a long time to say that but hadn't considered it right to do so until I asked. "But in other states they are very lenient on family members," he added.

"Is Massachusetts one of the good states?" I asked, a little squeamishly.

"I couldn't tell you," Mort answered. You could see he was still reading from some kind of script he'd worked out in his mind. He wanted to warn me but without getting more involved than he already was. He wasn't a criminal attorney. He probably guessed that I had been helping Abbie since the beginning and wasn't going to stop now.

"I'll bet you Massachusetts is one of the lenient ones," I said. Morty shrugged. Then I added that I'd been in touch with my brother all along, and that if anything happened I'd need a lawyer I could trust. Mort said I knew where to find him. And that was it. Nothing had changed. There was no way for me to figure in my own potential vulnerability under the law when Abbie's exposure seemed so much greater.

As spring warmed into summer, Abbie had Anita send their son america down to him for a visit, so he could show "the kid" Disney World. It was one of those rare instances of bizarre equilibrium for

Abbie, passing through the heart of establishment culture—Disney World—from the far reaches of fugitive fantasyland, just like any other normal parent.

Then Abbie and Johanna got ready to leave Florida and return north to the Thousand Islands, with a short stop in Framingham to pick up Abbie's inheritance money. They arrived a few days later, tanned and content—hardly fugitive-like at all—in a Plymouth station wagon, suburban impostors with large smiles. I'd somehow managed to get the check cashed. I felt like Monty Hall as I handed them the $3,000 in twenties.

Abbie and I went to a Red Sox-Yankees game at Fenway Park, sitting in my usual seats surrounded by acquaintances who could not have failed to know that the bearded fellow to my left might just be my brother. But the FBI didn't find us. And sitting there watching the game, I suddenly realized something about Abbie's relationship with the FBI. It may have been deadly serious, but it was also a game of chicken. Abbie wanted me to help him claim his three grand from Dad's estate because he needed the money, but it was also part of the game, a tip-off. He wanted to stay beyond their reach, but he wanted to keep it interesting. Abbie and the FBI were kind of like playmates, I thought. And the next day, when Abbie and Johanna were back in their station wagon and I stood waving good-bye in front of the house while they drove off, I tried to establish in my own mind the figure-ground relationship between what was serious and what was fun to Abbie—and couldn't.

In the fall of 1977, Abbie and Johanna started on a six-month tour of Europe. It was another case of doing something thoroughly enjoyable with a view to writing about it. His "passport" this time consisted of a forged letter on *Playboy* stationery introducing him and Johanna as "Mr. and Mrs. Mark Samuels, who have been assigned by our magazine to do a survey on the new French cuisine."

Letter in hand, Abbie and Johanna toured the great restaurants of France, Belgium, and Switzerland, including Le Duc and L'Olympe in Paris, Paul Bocuse's restaurant in Lyon, Comme Chez Soi in Brussels, and Girardet in Crissier, just outside of Lausanne. Abbie became a born-again gourmand, writing that some of the meals "produced such joy that . . . [we] were literally moved to tears." He came to appreciate the expertise of these master chefs as "the ultimate pop artists who carve and cook with total commitment, creating a work of exuberance only to [see it] instantly consumed by strangers." "So while I began the tour with my tongue-in-cheek," he claimed, "I soon developed an appreciation, which eventually grew to obsession. I could, for the first time, comprehend gluttony as a passion."[4]

On March 17, 1978, Abbie wrote to me from France, listing his recent accomplishments. He and Johanna were having a great time. By posing as *Playboy*'s gourmet editor they had consumed, without cost to them, almost $4,000 worth of haute cuisine. He added: "I'm going whacko over food!!"

He really did sound obsessed. I think that's what happens when a man used to being driven by the great issues of history turns his undivided attention to food. I wondered if he was getting fat too. A few weeks later a package came for Joan containing another letter from Abbie and an autographed copy of Paul Bocuse's cookbook.

By the summer of 1978, Wellesley Island had been home base for Abbie and Johanna for two years, ever since Johanna had first brought Abbie there from Canada. They had settled into a familiar routine in the cottage on the riverbank. Abbie was constantly rebuilding and repairing with a hammer and saw and was proud of how good a carpenter he'd become. The Fineview community was by and large conservative but also down to earth and friendly, and Abbie alias "Barry," got along with them just fine. They trusted him based on what they saw: his hard work in the garden, on the roof, and on the dock he'd helped build for Johanna (most travel in the area was conducted by boat); that was enough for him to begin to gain respect around Fineview.

Abbie and Johanna weren't year-round natives. But only about thirty of Fineview's residents were, given the extremities of rain, wind, waves, and snow that sometimes caused the community to be cut off from all forms of transportation other than airlifts in winter. So Abbie and Johanna weren't considered outsiders either. Johanna's family had roots in the region that extended back seven generations.

There was a framed DAR (Daughters of the American Revolution) certificate on the wall of the cottage. That helped, too.

One afternoon that summer of 1978, Abbie was putting some finishing touches on the dock he'd built, adjustments to compensate for the winter ice shift, when a neighbor boated by to tell him he needn't bother, since the Army Corps of Engineers, the same cool heads that had built the St. Lawrence Seaway over two decades earlier, were now planning to institute a program they called winter navigation—a combination ice-breaking and flooding operation that was going to finish the job of destroying the river's ecology that the Seaway had begun. A demonstration test had been proposed for that winter that would involve maintaining an ice-free, fifteen-mile long corridor. And local scientists from the New York Department of Environmental Conservation had drawn up an estimate of the environmental impact of the test. It was this study that the neighbor waved in my brother's face as proof that he needn't bother putting the finishing touches on the dock.

Abbie borrowed the report, stopped work, and locked himself in the cottage to read through the study that afternoon. As he read, he became convinced that the demonstration test alone would destroy the watering pools for the endangered bald eagle, ruin aquatic life chains and wetlands, and that waves from passing ships would rip apart shorelines, causing substantial erosion. The test also required that the river's fast current be deliberately slowed, and this, he believed, would cause flooding and the release of large quantities of chemical wastes into the river—which was the source of drinking water for most of the river communities. A fifteen percent loss of hydropower was predicted. Quoting from the Army Corps of Engineers' own figures, the plan called for ninety-four million cubic yards of river bed to be drained or dynamited from the U.S. side alone. The more Abbie read, the more clear it was to him that the basic idea was to change this rushing river into a "year round barge canal. A disaster."[5]

Abbie had stumbled on a cause he couldn't resist joining. But he needed to be sure that Johanna saw it that way too. Any political decision Abbie made now—he was living on Wellesley Island as

"Barry Freed" and would undoubtedly attract publicity—was going
to implicate Johanna, so it had to make sense to them both.

> *I called Johanna upstairs. "Unless we act, the river is
> doomed," I said. "The Army Corps of Engineers will bully
> their way in here. The people are not ready to fight the sys-
> tem. . . ." I was convinced joining this battle would mean I
> would be caught. Yet . . . how could I stand on the shore and
> watch corps engineers wire up the small islands across the
> way for demolition? I had listened to old-timers in the bars
> talk of how they had heard the explosions and watched
> whole islands float down river during the fifties. They had
> watched and cried; now they were alcoholics. "A six-thou-
> sand-year-old river," I thought, "and the last twenty-five
> years have been its worst." My fate was fixed. The rest of
> the night we spent shaping our identity.[6]*

Barry had found a cause that Abbie applauded. The two identities were moving perilously close to one another, yet it was happening
smoothly, inevitably, like a trembling tuning fork coming to rest.
Abbie's "six distinct personalities" were becoming one again. An
issue in need of leadership and direction had fallen in his lap, and the
various private issues that had dictated his life during the past five
years—questions of personal guilt, happiness, responsibility, pleasure, and survival—all dimmed and were forgotten. It was the beginning of what would become an amazing resurrection: Under a new
name and still a fugitive, with no outside help whatsoever, Abbie set
about launching a new political movement. And since it still meant
continuing their secret, fugitive life together—since in Abbie's mind it
seemed to serve as a substitute to surfacing—Johanna agreed to the
change with grace and enthusiasm.

As soon as Abbie was able to put his fugitive status at risk in this
way, then he could, for the first time in four years, completely forget
about that risk. Suddenly his priorities had become clear again, and
just like in the old days, survival *wasn't* at the top of the list; effective
political action was. Once he'd made the decision to jump in, saving
the river became his obsession. That summer, all his enormous energy

went into planning the strategy that would gradually involve his local community as fully as possible and end up beating the Army Corps of Engineers. And in the back of his mind, I think he also imagined this work as something that might, in the hands of a sympathetic judge, be considered in his favor at a future hearing—a public service to balance the public disservice of the drug bust. Suddenly Abbie's recent years out of service seemed like a kind of four-year-long spiritual retreat, so clearheaded and directed was he now that he was back in action.

That August the corps (as Abbie liked to call the Army Corps of Engineers, perhaps since it sounded like corpse, something dead, the exact opposite of river, a word so full of life) had scheduled a public hearing at nearby Alexandria Bay. Abbie's first decision was to use that hearing as an occasion to announce the creation of a new organization to protect the St. Lawrence River from the Army Corps of Engineers. But that gave him less than one month to make such an organization a reality. And Abbie knew that the people he wanted in, people from the community, couldn't be rushed.

First came small meetings on Abbie and Johanna's front lawn, with snacks and cold drinks. Discussion eventually moved to finding a name for the group, with Abbie, as Barry Freed, indisputably in charge:

> Names were very important. Best verb first. What you want people to do. "Shouldn't we have the word committee?" Committee is a bore. People want excitement, charisma. "What about St. Lawrence?" No, keep it simple. Everyone knows the river. Better for a name to raise a question than give an answer. Questions encourage involvement and involvement is what makes a citizens action group.[7]

They settled on Save the River, and it was the perfect name. During long phone calls throughout that summer of 1978, Abbie described to me the birth of this new environmental movement, and I couldn't help but be shocked by the boldness—I almost want to say the madness—of this new effort, just when things seemed to have calmed down a bit for both of us.

* * *

As he prepared for the August hearing, Abbie had to work on two fronts simultaneously: He had to counter the skepticism and apathy of those he hoped would eventually become his core group of fellow activists, and at the same time he had to create a public forum so that a large number of Thousand Island residents would begin to hear about Save the River and start to consider the issues it was fighting for. He placed an ad in the local newspaper, *The Thousand Island Sun*, a first step toward what would eventually develop into weekly articles he would write for the paper. Johanna designed a beautiful "Save the River" blue heron tee shirt. Soon, boats appeared on the river hoisting huge "No to Winter Navigation" sails. There were also signs that said "Ice Is Nice" and "Army Go Home." Telephone trees were formed in which each committed member of the group had to place calls to a certain number of prospective members or possible sympathizers.[8]

The August public hearing turned out to be a huge success. Instead of the usual thirty to forty curious onlookers, there were hundreds of concerned citizens. The corps had planned to use the occasion to softsell their plans. People listened quietly as the corps presented a comprehensive-sounding slide show that portrayed winter navigation as easy and constructive. Then it was the people's turn. Inhabitants of the small community of Grindstone Island asked how they were going to get their pickup trucks across the open river channel in winter. The answer made clear that winter navigation threatened their very existence. One citizen had found out that the corps' predictions of water level changes during the last hundred years had been wrong most of the time, and stood up now to inform the audience of that fact in the presence of the corps spokespersons.[9]

Then a man stood up who happened to have appeared in one of the corps' own slides standing near a channel in the ice as a ship passed. When presenting the slide, the corps spokesperson had noted how calm the man was. Now he told the crowd how terrified he had been, describing the ship's passing as feeling like an earthquake, hurling masses of vegetation, dead fish, and debris on the riverbank in its wake. The corps representatives couldn't have been more surprised by what the people were saying, and it just kept on coming.[10]

Probably the worst fear people had about winter navigation was oil spills, since no technology existed to clean up oil spillage locked under ice. Moreover, a major oil spill had already occurred in the area in 1976. People remembered clearly the dead fish and birds; much of the physical damage of that spill still had not been repaired, and it had happened during the summer. The corps representatives' assurances that this couldn't happen in winter only spurred people's distrust of the corps.[11]

The hearing had been a complete success for Abbie; he had routed the enemy forces. Save the River began to have the status of a local ball team on a winning streak. People all over the Thousand Islands region started saying "Save the River" as a greeting, instead of "Good morning" or "Nice day." More and more stores carried Johanna's tee shirts, which helped bring in money for the phone bills.

Now Abbie entered phase two: Without letting up on the public relations work, Save the River had to make sure that the enemy weren't the only ones who understood how it all worked. That meant doing a lot of reading about things like water-resource economics, cost-benefit analysis, water-level prediction, and aquatic life cycles so that they could hold work-study sessions in which they searched for corps errors in its own literature. It also meant finding sympathetic individuals within the scientific community. They found an economist at Syracuse University named Steve Long, who was able to explain to them how the corps misapplied its own figures in order to falsely demonstrate feasibility. Eventually, the group was able to print up an eight-page booklet translating material about winter navigation into lay person's terms. The booklet was discussed, as Abbie was proud to say, "in classrooms, at Bible study groups, in bars and pharmacies, everywhere."[12]

Abbie knew that he was winning, but he also knew that early on much of his advantage derived from the fact that Save the River did not look like a political group. Thus he fought against the environmentalist label, since people seemed to consider environmentalists political too. During these early months, it seemed like the greatest obstacle that had to be overcome was "convincing people it wasn't rude to protest."[13]

*　*　*

"Barry Freed" had built an organization from the ground up, and Abbie was loving it. More and more, his leadership of Save the River required him to go public. Where his leadership of the Yippies! had consisted almost entirely of creating an illusion for the television cameras, now his identity itself was the only illusion—everything else was real. He found himself giving speeches at local "fishermen's banquets, church suppers, high schools, universities,"[14] and he was interviewed on local television stations. It was a model political campaign. Soon the grassroots effort was succeeding to the point where local politicians began falling in line: Expressions of support started coming in from chamber of commerce members, town council members, and the St. Lawrence County Board. Save the River started sending delegations to parts of the country as far south as Baltimore.

Now Save the River launched a mini-campaign to get the attention of New York governor Hugh Carey, and succeeded, to everyone's surprise, within only a few days. Carey's office sent a supportive telegram, and during the next two years Carey himself would become a stalwart friend of Save the River. A Save the River delegation visited Albany and came away with a pledge of $25,000 to hire John Carroll, one of the few experts on water resource economics willing, in Abbie's words, to "bite the hand" of the powerful Army Corps. Eventually, Barry would receive a personal letter from Carey which stated in part, "I want to thank you for your leadership in this important issue, and for your sense of public spirit."[15] Incredibly, Save the River was outflanking and outgunning the corps on all sides.

Ironically, Barry Freed—an alias—became the vindication of both the democratic beliefs and the organizing skills of the identity Abbie had abandoned when he went underground. Barry was Abbie's appointment in Samara. Abbie had run for four years only to find not his own mortality but himself, as irrevocably as if four years earlier he'd made an appointment for the very place, date, and hour of the meeting. And Abbie drew strength from the phenomenon of Barry Freed, since he knew that Barry was just Abbie minus the drug bust. In the end, Abbie's identification with Barry helped him come to terms with the truth underneath his various "false" identities. It presented itself to Abbie as incontrovertible proof that he really existed.

And increasingly during the late summer of 1978 and after, it aggravated his deep longing to surface.

It was also during that summer of 1978 that some of Abbie's old '60s crew, including Bob Fass, Joe LoGiudice, William Kunstler, and others, decided to get together and organize a "Bring Abbie Home" night at Madison Square Garden's Felt Forum for the tenth anniversary of the Chicago Democratic Convention. Abbie thought it was a great idea. And as the August date approached, Abbie started hinting that he was planning on showing up. The truth was he was dying to be there. It was only through all our combined efforts that we were able to convince him that keeping his presence or absence a mystery would work just as well, and that if he came and got busted it would be a bummer for us all.

We rented three buses for the Worcester contingent, each with huge "Free Abbie" banners in pink lettering on the side. Ma came down on one of them, along with enough club sandwiches on Syrian bread, provided by Joe Aboody at the El Morocco, to feed an army. Phyllis also came, along with Worcester organizers Betty Price and Bob Solari, who could remember when they and Abbie had been among just a handful of civil rights activists in Worcester, walking down Main Street to catcalls from people standing in the doorways of local bars. These friends of Abbie were joined by more recent comrades, many of whom spoke that night to the large crowd—Jon Voight ("I consider Abbie a political artist"), Bobby Seale, Jerry Rubin, Rennie Davis, Paul Krassner, Bill Kunstler, actors Ossie Davis ("Abbie Hoffman is a treasured national resource") and Rip Torn, and writer William Burroughs.

The revue-style show at the Felt Forum had been written by Terry Southern (of *Candy* fame) and Joe LoGiudice, and staged by artist Larry Rivers. It was designed as a mock trial, with Rip Torn playing Richard Nixon as a court reporter, Kunstler as counsel for the defense, and Taylor Mead as Judge Julius Hoffman. The music was by Kinky Friedman, who opened with a subdued rendition of "Ride 'Em Jewboy." Later in the evening, Odetta sang a slow and beautiful version of "This Land Is Your Land," Paul Kantner of Jefferson Starship joined in a sing-along of "Jam for Abbie," and Eric Andersen performed an electric version of his classic "Thirsty Boots."[16]

Many of us wore plastic, Halloween-style masks with Abbie's face on them. The subject on everyone's tongue was where, when, and how—not if—Abbie would surface. Abbie sent a tape thanking everybody. And you could feel in the air that night how badly people missed him.

Ma came up to me at some point during the festivities, and I could tell from the look in her eyes that she had finally forgiven me. Somehow she had understood how hard I was working on my brother's behalf. She began to see that maybe she'd made too much of the sale of Worcester Medical, and she decided she could be my mother again, two years after our argument!

In the end, however hard all Abbie's friends and family tried, we just couldn't conjure forth his spirit without his presence. The evening at Madison Square Garden was a great success, but it had a hole in it where Abbie should have been.

In September 1978, Abbie and Johanna began traveling more frequently to New York City. I noticed that he was getting bolder. Instead of moving around between safe locations, they would just stay in her rent-stabilized apartment in midtown, an easily traceable location. We've learned recently from the FBI files that the FBI still hadn't identified Johanna. In fact, in all Abbie's years underground they never identified his running mate. But Abbie and Johanna had no way of knowing this at the time. From their point of view, staying in her apartment was risking capture, and showed an attitude far different from the one that had resulted in their months-long separation in 1976.

At the beginning of November, Abbie and I both happened to be in New York City, and Abbie took me to see *The Best Little Whorehouse in Texas* on Broadway, whose producer, Pete Masterson, had expressed interest in taking out a movie option on Abbie's life. That night Abbie wore no disguise of any kind. Out in the street, in the theater and at dinner afterwards, he could easily have been recognized and captured.

A few weeks later, Abbie came to Worcester to visit Ma, and

the two of us went to a Patriots football game at nearby Foxboro Stadium, where I had season tickets. Around us were mostly other season ticket holders who knew me and knew who my brother was. That day, with winks and nods coming at us from half the crowd around us, I was so terrified I had trouble concentrating on the game. Surrounded by more than 50,000 football fans, I figured we'd have no place to hide if they came after Abbie. Maybe Abbie, thinking seven moves ahead, realized that a football game or a Broadway play would be the last place the FBI would be looking, and being in the midst of a crowd of 50,000 sports fans was probably a pretty good place to hide. Maybe he was still playing chicken. But I began to sense that something else was going on. It was as if, having evaded the FBI for nearly five years now, the game was over. Abbie had won on time. By the winter of 1978–79 it just didn't matter anymore, as it had a few years earlier, when he came in. What still mattered, though, was how.

Back on the river, the first much-deserved triumph came when the corps postponed that winter's tests. But Abbie wasn't confusing the corps' tactical retreat for a Save the River victory, not yet anyway, since at the same time the corps' work on the upper Great Lakes had intensified. With Abbie at its helm as "publicity director," Save the River began planning for a flurry of new lobbying and consciousness-raising actions for the late winter and spring. And again, Barry's successes acted as both a spur and a temptation to Abbie's wanting to be Abbie again. After nearly five years, he felt he'd paid his dues and done his community service as well. His anonymity felt like an old skin. He wanted to come home.

That winter, Abbie and Johanna visited Chicago, where she took a snapshot of him mugging for the camera in front of the statue of General Logan, a rallying point during the 1968 Democratic Convention, and where he did an interview with Abe Peck for the 1978–79 New Year's Eve edition of the Sunday *Chicago Sun-Times*. "I'm not a genius or a media master," Abbie told Peck. "I am a good storyteller. I am an outlaw. And I'm a survivor."[17]

In early 1979—it may have been February—Abbie came to visit us in Framingham and he seemed to be in an intensely manic state.

Completely ignoring our kids, he talked at Joan and me nonstop; I might have fallen off my chair and he wouldn't even have noticed. Sitting in our kitchen he rattled off an increasingly loud and heartfelt litany of complaint after complaint, mostly about Johanna: "She's trying to run my fucking life. She and her old lady don't want me to surface because she doesn't want the people there to know who I am. She wants to put everything, including me, in a trunk up on the river." Then he turned his wrath on me: "You never help me," he said, glaring at me. "You didn't do shit for me as a fugitive. You haven't done enough for me. You and your sister." I thought that the next thing that was going to happen was that he was going to hit me. He seemed to be so agitated that it even occurred to me that it might be a good thing if he did, might help him to let off steam. I put my hand on his shoulder and only half jokingly told him to go rest before I hit him over the head with a frying pan. He let me steer him upstairs and into the bedroom. I returned to the kitchen, but Abbie must have turned around as soon as I'd left him, walked back down the stairs and out the front door, because when I checked on him a few minutes later he was gone.

For the next hour I panicked, fearing the worst. Then the phone rang. It was Ma.

"Abbie's cleaning out the attic," she said. Abbie had gone to Worcester, walked into the house, gone straight up to the attic and started discarding every cardboard box and every milk crate, the old clothes, the comic books, the school books, the uniforms, the base-balls, footballs, and tennis balls, all the evidence of his—and our—early life, except for the trophies, which were the only things he considered worth keeping. He'd even managed to have two trucks parked out front. And in an amazingly short time, he was loading them up.

"Well, what's he cleaning out?" I asked.

"Well . . . everything," she said. And then she added, a little tim-idly, "Do you think it's a good idea?"

Ma wasn't calling from her house. She'd left and gone to our aunt Ruth's a few blocks away.

"Well, I didn't want to agitate him," she said to me over the phone, to explain why she'd left the house. But there was another reason she didn't want to mention. Seeing Abbie in the middle of a manic phase was scary, and she didn't like to feel frightened of her own son.

"He thought it was time to clean up the attic," she added. Again, it was the things she wasn't saying that struck me. She'd seen her own sister lose her mind and she must have been afraid Abbie had lost his—so afraid she couldn't say the words.

It took him only two or three hours before every term paper, love letter, and photograph from the attic was in the Dumpster. Besides his trophies, he'd also spared Ma's college diploma. Then, as abruptly as he'd started, he left, carrying one last item under his arm: Ma's old violin.

Two months later Abbie signed a contract with Universal Pictures giving them the film rights to his life story, including, but not limited to, his autobiography, scheduled for publication the following year. The price paid was $250,000. Almost immediately, he got rid of the money, giving most of it, as he liked to say, to "three of the most important women in my life"—Sheila, Anita, and Johanna.[18] That was pretty much the truth too. Abbie gave $100,000 to Johanna, around $38,000 each to Anita and Sheila, and $5,000 to me. After taxes and various professional fees, that left him with around $25,000 or less. In other words, with his curious way of looking at things, he'd made sure to cut himself in for ten percent of his own deal—just as if it were someone else's deal and he'd only been the broker. It was as if, in order to sign that kind of big money contract, Abbie had to disassociate himself from his own actions.

In the spring of 1979, Save the River sent a delegation to Washington to testify before Congress, where Abbie was introduced as Barry Freed by Congressman Robert McEwen. Meanwhile, the water resource economics expert, John Carroll, who had been hired by Save the River with the help of state funding, completed his report. It was damning, showing that winter navigation would cost the State of New York upwards of $100 million annually in lost revenues. In April, the first River Day kept the home fires burning, with thousands of participants joining in marathons and hot-air balloon races during the day and a candlelight vigil that night. Now Abbie felt that Save the River was in a position to lobby Senator Daniel Patrick Moynihan, a member of the Senate Environment and Public Works Committee, to hold field hearings.

On the day of the field hearings, Save the River organized a flotilla of antique boats to give committee members a tour of the beautiful islands. Moynihan himself was outfitted with a turn-of-the-century paddle boat. The night before, Abbie spent hours putting the final touches on his speech, knowing that with each word he might be signing his arrest warrant. But it didn't matter. The next day "Barry" gave his speech and was met with a standing ovation.

After the speech, Abbie had this recollection:

Moynihan, sitting directly opposite, not more than twenty feet away, looked at me and said, "Now I know where the sixties have gone." Way, way inside, where Abbie lived, I fainted. Then he said, "Everyone in New York State owes Barry Freed a debt of gratitude for his organizing ability."[19]

On May 6, 1979, Abbie went to Washington for a huge antinuclear rally, wearing a suit and tie. Not even FBI agents wore suits and ties to Washington demonstrations. When he bumped into his old friend, television and radio producer Danny Schechter, and introduced himself, Schechter did a double take, and then invited Abbie to appear on a talk show he was producing. Abbie dismissed the idea—a breach of security. But by October, Abbie's security concerns had evaporated, and he was back in touch with Schechter to negotiate the conditions of the interview. Shortly before midnight on November 2, Abbie strode through the back door of the Boston studio, accompanied by a woman wearing a Kabuki mask, his children Andrew and Ilya (Amy), and a bodyguard carrying a metal detector. Schechter's impression was that Abbie was still his "old dazzling self"—but that he was "in trouble right now, head trouble," alternately "witty, even wise," and "near-hysterical."

Abbie had the completed manuscript of his autobiography with him in Boston, and he ended the televised interview by quoting its last lines:

I've had some good times, had some bad. Took some lumps. Scored some points. Halfway through life, at 43, I still say, "Go for broke." No government, no F.B.I., no judge, no jailer is ever gonna make me say "uncle." Now, as then, let the game continue. I bet my stake on freedom's call; I'll play these cards with no regrets.

But during the interview he had, by contrast, expressed several regrets. When asked if he'd rethought the '60s, he answered, "I used to think of [the '60s] as the second American revolution, but now I think of it as the second Civil War, because it turned brother against brother, and family against family." And when asked what he might have done differently, he unhesitatingly said, "I would have been a little neater, and had a few more manners, and more respect for the elders . . . things like that. And I would have known when to talk soft, and that it all doesn't have to happen in one day."[20]

Earlier in the day, in the Channel 56 parking lot, under ludicrously heavy, walkie-talkie orchestrated security precautions— "Breaker, breaker, this is Red Runner (Abbie) to Band-Aid (Jack)—Abbie had granted an interview to *Worcester Magazine* in which he'd insisted, "I'm getting out of politics, 'cause I don't want to lie anymore."[21]

A few nights after the Schechter interview, Abbie and Johanna came to spend the night with us in Framingham, and then sometime during the night, still in his manic state, Abbie disappeared on us. He had scheduled a birthday party for himself and all his close friends for the next evening in a chic New York City restaurant called David K's. So when the next day Abbie was still nowhere to be found, Joan, Johanna, and I drove down to New York anyway, hoping he'd show up there. We were the first to arrive, and there was Abbie in the private room he'd reserved, placing name cards in front of the place settings for the twenty-five or so guests he'd invited. As the room filled up, there were some familiar faces—publicist David Fenton, Sam and Walli Leff, the actors Carol Kane and Michael O'Donoghue of *Saturday Night Live,* Jerry Rubin, Jerry Lefcourt, Noah Kimmerling—and others we didn't know. The meal was a sumptuous feast of Peking duck washed down with a variety of good wines. After a couple of hours, Abbie stood up and thanked everyone for their support over the years, then added that he didn't want to break with tradition, so those with the credit cards could pick up the check. And then, followed by Johanna, he left. No one seemed to mind the $2,900 tab. People vied to be among those paying.

Sometime in December 1979 Abbie and Johanna were in Los Angeles and there was a war council of sorts at the home of Abbie's friend, the film producer Burt Schneider. Present in addition to Abbie, Johanna, and Burt, were Johanna's mother, attorney Michael Kennedy, and Dave Dellinger. The reason for the meeting was Abbie's ever stronger desire to surface. The goal was to help him make the right decision and then help him stick to it. In a sense, these were Abbie's most valued advisors, each with a different sphere of knowledge and all of them utterly trustworthy. Schneider, Kennedy, and Dellinger felt that the benefits of surfacing at that time outweighed the risks. Johanna was adamantly against surfacing and may have included her mother in the group partly so that together they would form a more substantial bloc defending her position.

Johanna's fear was that if he surfaced, Abbie would do substantial time in prison and that he would not be able to endure it. Abbie himself had said repeatedly over the years that he would not be able to endure doing hard time. Moreover, he felt sure that in prison he would be assassinated and had repeatedly stated that if he ended up in Attica he'd be killed just like Sam Melville, an outspoken Weather Underground member who'd been killed by guards during the suppression of the Attica uprising on September 13, 1971. But Johanna may have had more personal concerns as well. As long as Abbie was Barry he was all hers; once he became Abbie again, he would have to be shared with countless others, and she would lose him, or at the very least, she would become a smaller part of his life.

The meeting broke up somewhat inconclusively, with Abbie siding with Johanna against his will, to form a tie: three against three.

Abbie would try and wait a little longer, for Johanna's sake, but waiting was getting harder and harder.

While in L.A., Abbie had begun seeing a distinguished psychiatrist named Oscar Janiger, who confirmed the diagnosis of manic depression and put Abbie on lithium. Janiger was the psychiatrist of many creative and famous people, was himself a writer, and it was agreed that Abbie would see as much of him as possible while in L.A., and by phone afterward.

Abbie responded well to the lithium, and Janiger was optimistic about the prognosis. During the dozen or so office visits and an even larger number of phone sessions, Janiger came to see Abbie as plagued by feelings of inadequacy and self-condemnation on account of his uncontrolled behavior. At the same time, Abbie was exceptional in his insight, and it was this that made him overly aware of his own failings, according to Dr. Janiger. Abbie saw himself as a man of intelligence, good judgment, wisdom, and understanding—and thus he could neither rationalize nor forgive himself for his behavior during his manic episodes. Nor could he "correct" his behavior, since it was a manifestation of the illness. But in combination with other medications lithium seemed to ease his sense of hopelessness when he was depressed, and to moderate the mania as well.[22]

Joan and I had dinner with Abbie and Johanna in New York in early 1980, and when the subject of surfacing came up, Johanna broke in with "Abbie, you're gonna go to jail, you're going to jail," as if repeating words she'd spoken a hundred times already. And Abbie sat there uncharacteristically silent and docile. He was ready to leave Barry's life behind, but he hadn't created him alone. Johanna was integral to every part of his life as Barry Freed, and he still had to overcome her fear of his surfacing.

Joan and I knew all that, but we were still surprised by Abbie's willingness to accept his running mate as co-pilot. In the past we'd always seen Abbie do whatever the hell he wanted, regardless of who got hurt or how badly. Johanna had intimate knowledge of every facet of his new life. He was taking the lithium for his manic-depressive illness, and she would remind him whenever it was time to take his medication, almost as if she were his nurse. And the lithium itself, when he actually took it, had side effects: It brought on sudden diarrhea attacks, hair loss, and stomach bloat. His vulnerability only increased his dependency on Johanna. They had been through too much together. Abbie had shared all the contradictions of his soul with her, as he had with no other woman, not even Anita. The bond that had been forged between them was so strong that Abbie felt he could not surface, until they were both ready for him to do so.

In the spring of 1980 the Army Corps of Engineers, under pressure from Congress, withdrew all its requests for authorization and funds for work on the St. Lawrence River. Abbie told me that immediately afterward calls came in from elated environmental groups all over the country: This was the first time the corps had been beaten without a protracted court battle.

Meanwhile, Abbie started to come and visit us, without secrecy, at our home in Framingham. And on one visit he said to us, a little out of the blue, that we didn't have to hide the fact that we were in touch with him. He said something like, "That would be too hard, keeping it secret all this time."

Our bubbe Anna, Dad's mother, had always represented to us the gentlest part of the Hoffman family. Warm, loving, expressive, forgiving to the point where you knew you could do nothing wrong in her eyes. Now, with Dad dead, she had become the last living reminder of a part of our past. She was ninety-six years old. She could remember pogroms and Cossacks. We respected her for having survived. And we listened to what she said. It wasn't necessarily that she would tell you what to do, or even that her advice would be the right advice, but she made you want to tell her things. We all told her things. And we felt that what she said to us was the fruit of her experiences combined with the truths we had entrusted to her and others had entrusted to her during this long century of her life.

Bubbe's health had been poor for much of the last five or six years. But now, in April 1980, her doctors were of the opinion that she was days or at most weeks away from death. The whole extended family gathered together in Worcester for their last visits with her. Phyllis came up from Mexico, our cousin Joan came up from Putnam County in New York, cousin Cynthia flew up from Nashville, and as soon as I passed along the news to Abbie, he and Johanna said they would come. Bubbe asked that we come to see her one at a time.

I stood by her bedside, unsure what to ask or what to say. But I shouldn't have worried. She knew exactly what she wanted to tell me. It had to do with making pickles. She wanted to be sure I had her pickle recipe. I couldn't write it down, because she didn't want me to give away the secret, but she had to make sure I would continue to make them her way. She had me repeat it to her now, as I stood alone by her bedside.

First you have to carefully select the cucumbers, handpick them to make sure they're fresh and that none are bruised or scratched. They should all be roughly the same size because the larger the pickle the longer the pickling process. You need the right balance of kosher salt and water to produce the brine, and the salt water should sit for a day or two before adding the freshest available dill, garlic, red pepper, and pickling spices. Then there's the "little bit," as she would say, of vinegar. And finally there's a secret ingredient that I can't repeat to anyone besides Abbie and Phyllis, since that's what I promised Bubbe.

You stuff the jar or barrel with the cucumbers and add the brine and, depending on how you like your pickles, you leave it there for three to five days, or longer. Three days for a gentile pickle, seven days for something nice and sour. Bubbe would keep her pickles pickling for seven to ten days.

As I repeated her recipe back to her on her deathbed she nodded her head, the sign that it was good.

Six years earlier, just after Abbie had gone underground, Bubbe had been in hospital and, fearing she might not live, had decided to tell me a story of her youth in Russia that, perhaps because of a connection she saw in it to Abbie's troubles, seemed to weigh heavily on her now. It seemed that her brother had been a Bolshevik and village leader. She told me how before the Russian Revolution the Bolsheviks would meet in wells—the safest places in the village—and how they carried messages in their rings. She spoke to me in a combination of Yiddish and broken English, so I missed words and had to piece together the meaning of her story afterward. But the gist was that every time she saw Abbie's picture in the paper or on television, she became afraid because he reminded her of her brother the Bolshevik. One day a troop of Cossacks had come to the door and dragged him away, she told me. She was frightened that the same thing would happen to Abbie. She wanted me to tell him to be very careful.

Now, six years later, no longer as fearful as she had been that last time, since now she knew with certainty that death was near and she could face it quietly, Bubbe called for Abbie, whom she had not seen since before he went underground. He was there waiting and went to her bedside. The thing she had to say to him was like a weight on her chest. Of course, Bubbe hadn't understood the drug bust. She only knew that Abbie was a fugitive, wanted by the police as a rebel leader. She must have taken him to be the very spirit of her brother the Bolshevik. Her message to Abbie, as he related it to me later—after twenty minutes or so of hand holding and reminiscences—was: "Keep running. When they say 'Come back, everything is okay,' keep going, stay underground. Jews were meant to be underground. It's the history of our family."[23]

The way Abbie described it to me, her words were a kind of blessing, a funny, obtuse, and mysterious expression of approval. And the funny thing was that although she had advised him not to surface, Abbie left her room feeling that hers were the words that may have helped him, finally, to put the fugitive years behind him. He felt grateful to have been able to visit her, unlike his notable absence at the time of Dad's death. That absence had started Abbie's years of flight, and this last meeting on the brink of death helped bring him back into the light. Hearing the voice of his own fear issue from the mouth of his loving ninety-six-year-old Bubbe had the effect of breaking the spell. It made him feel that running away was somehow connected to the old way of doing things, to the way of our fathers, whereas he wanted to stand for a new freedom, the freedom not to run. Surfacing no longer seemed so fearful. That was the great gift that Bubbe was able to give Abbie before dying: letting him go against the grain of her instruction. After visiting Bubbe, Abbie left Worcester dead set on surfacing, and the only thing left for us to talk about was the time and the place. Bubbe died a few days later, on April 20, 1980.

* * *

The next call I got from Abbie began, "I'm doing it. Show time."
"Doing what, Abbie?" I asked.

"I'm coming in."

I think he'd convinced himself that he wouldn't have to do any time. He wanted to make his move soon, before that year's election might put Ronald Reagan in the White House. Also, reviews of his autobiography, *Soon to Be a Major Motion Picture,* were beginning to appear. And since that book effectively signaled Abbie's return, it increased the urgency of surfacing.

Then, just as Abbie was beginning to make preparations for his return, things started happening up on the river that put pressure on him to speed things up before they sped up on their own. More than once, after they'd overheard some chance remark suggesting that someone might know Barry's real identity, Johanna had driven Abbie to the nearest highway with a suitcase and plans to hitchhike to Syracuse and then fly to New York City. Each time he'd returned to Fineview, assured it had been a false alarm.

One afternoon, at the end of a town council meeting in Fineview at which Barry had given a speech, an off-duty border guard from the nearby Canadian line came up to him and said, "I agree with you, Barry, but what are we going to do when everyone finds out you're Abbie Hoffman?" And the guy didn't seem to be kidding. The way Abbie used to tell it, the guard happened to be a dead ringer for the English actor Michael Caine, so Abbie was able to shoot back, "Yeah, well, what are we going to do when everyone finds out you're Michael Caine?"[24] That night Abbie decided that the time had come and that it was far better to take the initiative than just wait until he was arrested. He knew that if he was apprehended, the judicial system was going to be much harder on him than if he surfaced voluntarily. And in the back of his mind, maybe Abbie had begun to fear that Johanna loved Clark Kent but not Superschmuck. Part of him wanted to test whether she could really love all of him.

So part of the problem he was trying to solve had to do with Johanna, but another part had to do just with himself. He was beginning to be so secure in his identity as Barry Freed that he needed to resolve what had now become the Abbie question. If he had waited any longer, he feared Abbie as Abbie would have ceased to exist in any real way. He said, "I feel as though the name Abbie refers to somebody else. It's like Carroll O'Connor and Jean Stapleton playing Archie Bunker and Edith. I have empathy for them when they walk down the street and somebody says, 'Hi, Archie,' or 'Hi, Edith.' " He had already begun to look on Abbie as another person. And even I could see that the life he had up on the river was the best life he'd ever had—with love, friendship, nature, and meaningful political work as well. "Barry. That's what the woman I love calls me and what my friends call me," he said. "Just my mother calls me the other name."[25]

That summer of 1980, Abbie and I were having detailed conversations about where and when he should surface. At the same time he would have been having similar conversations with other close confidants. He wanted to give himself up so as to get maximum publicity which—wrongly as it turned out—Abbie believed would help him in court. And he was determined to avoid negative publicity. He wanted to make sure we were allowed to put our spin on it, emphasizing Abbie's environmental work during the last several years. The primary goal was to keep him out of prison.

Abbie knew he would probably have to surface in Manhattan, since that was where his lawyer Jerry Lefcourt was trying to make arrangements with the prosecutor. But he also wanted people to see some part of the life he'd made for himself up in Fineview. As for when to surface, Abbie's approach was a little more casual than I would have expected: "Why should I give up my summer vacation?" he said to me. So we fixed a tentative date in the month of September, so Abbie could enjoy the best weather up on the river and still come in well before the election.

Once made, the decision to surface affected Abbie in an entirely positive way. And I was ecstatic too. Over the years, whenever he had asked me if I thought he should come in, I'd said, "Yeah, give it a shot," or something like that. I always had the feeling that as soon as he turned and faced the music, things would start going his way. I thought there was a strong possibility that Abbie had been set up, and it seemed worthwhile to try to prove it. The problem was this was just too big a decision on which to press him. In the end, it had to be his decision. After all, if my hunch were wrong, the person who would be doing time, and doing it alone, was Abbie, so how could you tell him to come in before he was ready?

But now that he *was* coming in, I felt excited. We all did. It was like seeing the soldiers come home after a war.

Jerry Lefcourt and others were working feverishly to finalize arrangements with the prosecutors. That's the way it usually is when a fugitive gives himself up. A judge was agreed upon whom both sides considered impartial. Bail amount recommendations were also part of the understanding.[26]

Abbie brought in former *Rolling Stone* publicity director and friend David Fenton to manage the media. *60 Minutes* had offered $10,000 for an interview—despite their claim to not pay for news, it's common knowledge that they do. But both Abbie and David preferred *20/20* and Barbara Walters's promise of thirty minutes, uninterrupted, to allow Abbie to tell his story without distortion. The plan was to bring Walters and her *20/20* crew up to Fineview and do the piece while Abbie was still underground.[27]

In the days before Walters was due to arrive, Abbie and Johanna sent america, who had been visiting, back to Anita, and called a meeting of their local friends to tell them who Barry Freed really was. Abbie was more than a little surprised by the responses of his friends. They weren't amused. Barry was really important to them, and they weren't going to accept that he had been little more than a prank. Abbie found himself feeling that he'd hurt them somehow, and in a way he had: "One guy cried. Karen, the office manager, just kept saying, 'Nope, nope, nope.' She had once quoted Abbie Hoffman to me."[28]

On Tuesday, September 2, the day of Barbara Walters's scheduled arrival in Fineview, Abbie had thirty-five people working security in New York City and upstate. There were lookouts posted at key locations communicating by walkie-talkie. Elaborate escape routes had been planned in case something went wrong. Timetables had been worked out; weather maps had been consulted. David Fenton escorted Barbara Walters and her two producers, Stan Gould and Katherine Harrington, to a chartered Lear jet first thing in the morning. They weren't informed where they were going until takeoff. Then Fenton told them the whole story of Barry Freed, illustrating his description with photographs and news clippings of him testifying before Congress, of his speech in front of Senator Moynihan, and the letter of praise from Governor Carey. Up to that point, Walters and *20/20* were taking a dangerous chance, and possibly breaking the law, trusting total strangers who had contacted them on Abbie's behalf for a story whose details they were not permitted to know. But now, as Fenton would later write, "They relaxed. They had a scoop."[29]

Meanwhile, in a second chartered plane, other security people working for Abbie were bringing in Walters's camera crew. Once both planes had landed, local escorts drove the *20/20* group in a caravan to a motel along back roads, communicating only by marine radio. There the ABC crew was kept under constant surveillance to prevent any of them from trying to get to a phone. Then they were loaded into waiting boats and piloted on the St. Lawrence River toward the Canadian border. Abbie and Johanna were waiting in their own boat on the Canadian side until they could be notified by their security people that it was safe. Then they took Walters alone into their boat, and let the current pull them back into U.S. waters, and on toward Fineview. Abbie was pleased when Walters told him his security was better than that of Yasir Arafat, whom she had also interviewed.

What Abbie and Dave Fenton didn't know was that when Walters arrived in the area she was recognized and word began to spread that she might be on her way to interview Abbie Hoffman. Around the same time, someone in the prosecutor's office had leaked to the *Daily News* that Abbie would be turning himself in on Thursday. So now Abbie was racing against the clock and didn't even know it. Moreover, the stakes were high: If he were caught, he could expect a much longer sentence than if he turned himself in, and there would be no half-hour interview on national television, something he considered crucial to his strategy of presenting himself to the American public in the best possible light.[30]

Not knowing that the story had leaked, Abbie had the camera crew film him giving a walking tour of Fineview. Then they returned to the house, where Walters began the interview that would last for the next three hours, with Johanna sitting next to Abbie, and Walters talking to them both.

Meanwhile, the FBI now knew that Walters was in Fineview interviewing Barry, and that Barry was in fact Abbie. A flurry of teletypes were sent between FBI offices in New York City and Albany, and then to the New York State Police and local police in the Thousand Island area, and in Canada. But before they could swoop in, they learned of the arrangements that had been made with the New York prosecutor's office for Abbie to turn himself in on Thursday. And they were fearful of the kind of publicity they might invite by breaking in on Walters and her camera crew in mid-interview.

After six and a half years of looking for him, instructions were now circulated by the FBI requesting that "No Investigation or Attempt Be Made to Locate and Apprehend Hoffman in View of [Abbie's plans to turn himself in, and] Particularly in View of News Media on Scene."[31]

The taping went off without a hitch, and shortly after it was over, Abbie and Johanna disappeared into a speedboat and then to a plane that would take them to Manhattan. There they would spend their last day together before Abbie's surfacing, and the 20/20 air date, both scheduled for September 4.

Walters and her crew were asked to wait until Abbie and Johanna were safe. The next morning, September 3, they were driven back to the airport. Only when media manager Fenton saw local reporters gathered at the airport waiting for Walters that morning did he realize that the story had leaked. Abbie was on page one of that morning's Daily News. In a panic, he called Abbie in Manhattan and got him to change hotels. Reporters were pouring into Fineview to interview Abbie and Johanna's neighbors. The New York Times was angry, since they had been promised the first exclusive for the Thursday morning edition.

Abbie had asked me to drive down to New York City on Wednesday, September 3, and to bring with me someone from The

Worcester Telegram and Gazette. Regardless of what David Fenton was promising *The New York Times,* Abbie told me I could promise the first exclusive interview to the Worcester paper. The reporter, Teresa Hanafin, and I arrived at the hotel Abbie had designated, the Gramercy Park, by late morning. Almost as soon as we arrived, Abbie called, asking me to come immediately over to the Ramada Inn on Eighth Avenue, and to pass the phone to Teresa so she could get her interview while I made my away across town.

When I entered their room at the Ramada, Johanna seemed pensive, while Abbie looked happy and excited, but even he seemed self-contained and momentarily at peace. Things were going extremely well. The media were responding on cue and more positively than he would have dared hope. ABC was promoting the Barbara Walters interview with Abbie almost hourly. Abbie was calling various reporters at different newspapers and offering each one "an exclusive on this," and saying pretty much the same thing to all of them. The New York papers were already beginning to print articles that referred to Abbie's rumored surfacing. Fenton was doing a masterful job. We were all convinced that Abbie would beat the coke charges and not have to do any time.

Physically, Abbie looked tan and slender. He had a closely trimmed full beard and his hair was beginning to thin. He looked like a middle-aged college professor, complete with plaid shirt open at the collar. But this time it was no disguise. He was feeling his age, wanting to be respectable without pretending to be any different than he really was. It occurred to me that this was the first time I'd ever seen him plan a major media event without some sort of prepared schtick or angle he was working. He wasn't looking over his shoulder, as he had for the last six and a half years. He was just looking forward. He wanted to surface without an act, just himself playing it straight. He suspected, rightly, that the media were going to play it very big, and he felt somehow that people were on his side. They hadn't forgotten him. They wanted to know where he'd been and how he was.

That night, the *20/20* interview with Barbara Walters aired nationally as scheduled—a full, uninterrupted, and extremely sympathetic half hour of Abbie at his best. When it was over we felt that in that half hour the infamy had been pretty much washed away from Abbie's name. The awesome power of television had acted like magical, purifying waters.

At 9:30 A.M. on September 4, 1980, Abbie surrendered, according to painstakingly prepared arrangements, to New York State Special Narcotics Prosecutor Sterling Johnson in New York City.[32] By the time he left the prosecutor's office in handcuffs, the media were waiting for him in force. There were over two hundred reporters and innumerable camera crews. When they caught sight of Abbie, they charged, at first ignoring Abbie's police escort. Then it was the cops' turn. They pulled out their nightsticks and pressed reporters against the walls. One fallen cameraman was injured badly enough to be sent to the hospital. Media manager David Fenton yelled out, "Take it easy, there'll be plenty of time to talk to Abbie later." But the crushing crowd ignored him. In the end, almost no one got a quote from Abbie or a photograph of him. And that night's evening news featured crowd shots of the media circus photographing one another. It had been the craziest scene since the arrival of the pope.[33]

Abbie was released later in the day without bail, since he'd turned himself in. He felt wonderful. The publicity strategy had worked brilliantly, and being released without bail seemed like the final triumph of a tremendously successful media campaign.

There followed a solid week of media distortions. The *New York Post* and *Daily News* seemed to vie with one another in the vilification of Abbie. "Laughing at the Law" read one *Post* headline. Abbie was the "first fugitive to turn himself in with a business agent," wrote the *News*. The *Post* complained that Abbie got released without bail, comparing him to a Puerto Rican grocer who had been denied bail after he'd been apprehended on cocaine charges. The *News* claimed that Abbie had never had a job, and had surfaced in order to counter bad reviews of his latest book.[34]

As in a fairy tale, when all the clocks in the village start working again to signify the return to normalcy, things suddenly reverted to the usual routine. Everything was different than it had been when Abbie walked the streets of New York seven years earlier. But his own role, now that he was back, carried on as if he'd never left. Abbie was vilified by some and lionized by others, as he always had been. It had taken no time at all for his emergence on the scene to be taken for granted.

On September 21, The Sunday *New York Times Book Review* printed an enthusiastic review of *Soon to Be a Major Motion Picture*: "[Hoffman always had] an infinite capacity to surprise us, and he does so again with this unexpectedly good book, easily one of the best autobiographies to come out of the '60s. . . . [The] life of an exile, hard on the man, did good things for his writing."[35] Nowhere in the review is there any mention of the incredible story of his resurrection, as if, for better or worse, the general opinion was that Abbie's presence was simply a part of life. You could say that this was the highest praise of all.

And in any case Abbie liked it that way. Free on bail, he was speaking again on college campuses and very much in demand. He and Johanna were living again in her Manhattan apartment. And, as so often in the past, he was preparing for his next court date. The trial was set for April 1981, and Abbie was concentrating most of his energies on developing a strategy with his lawyers to ensure that when he walked into court, he would be treated with respect and released.

Shortly after surfacing, Abbie met the psychiatrist Nathan S. Kline, who had been referred to him by Dr. Janiger, and became one of his patients. Kline, who coincidentally had once served as director of research at Worcester State, where Abbie had worked as a psychologist, was one of the true pioneers in the biochemical treatment of depression. As early as 1953, Kline had introduced psychotropic medications into the U.S. In 1956, he had been an early advocate of antidepressants, and he had co-authored the first paper on the management of alcoholism with lithium carbonate. Kline was a true optimist, who believed—long before this opinion became popular within the psychiatric community—that depression and manic depression were the result of a chemical imbalance and could be treated success-fully with drugs, particularly lithium.

Abbie's sessions with Kline were revelations akin to his discovery of Abraham Maslow's teachings a quarter of a century earlier. Kline was a powerhouse who had little patience with psychoanalysis in the treatment of depression. Under Kline's supervision, Abbie began to take his lithium medication with unprecedented discipline. Kline's faith in the drug helped Abbie overcome his distaste for its unpleasant side effects. He trusted Kline. He felt confident that with Kline's help he could keep his manic-depression under control. And according to Kline, patients like Abbie, who might have seriously considered attempting suicide in the absence of proper care, were precisely the patients who could be treated with the greatest chance of success.[36]

Chapter Thirteen

〜

1981–1986

QUESTION: What are you looking for?
ABBIE: Typical, average Americans who will just try to narrow the gap between what they profess and what's going on—between our vision of America and the reality of America.
—FROM AN INTERVIEW IN NEW AGE MAGAZINE, MARCH 1983

WE GATHERED IN the Manhattan courtroom at the end of the first week of April 1981, looking forward to good news. Abbie had previously been persuaded to accept a plea-bargain—a guilty plea on a reduced charge—hoping and expecting leniency in return. Instead, after a brief and impassioned speech by Abbie, the judge sentenced my brother to one to three years hard time. We sat in our seats, stunned and frightened.

In late April, Abbie made one last cross-country trip to do *The Phil Donahue Show,* then started serving his time at the Downstate Facility in Fishkill, at that time reputed to be the toughest prison in New York State—worse than Attica, where there had been some improvements after the famous uprising and Governor Rockefeller's murderous crackdown. Abbie told me he was the only prisoner doing time in Fishkill for a nonviolent crime.

Abbie allowed only three people to visit him at Fishkill— Johanna, his attorney Jerry Lefcourt, and me. But he discouraged even us. He wanted to spare us the humiliation of the strip search and the way they looked at you as you walked through the maze of corridors. "Don't come," he would say.

Johanna wasn't put off. It didn't matter what Abbie said. She came as often as she could—usually several times a week. One day

Abbie told her he had a craving for fresh cherries. On her next visit, Johanna had woven them into her hair as decoration and walked through the prison gates that way. And during the visit, Abbie was able to eat the cherries out of her hair.

I visited Abbie only once that summer. And when I got there I understood his warning. The guards somehow made you feel that you too were a prisoner. And I think the intimidation was purposeful.

In a large hall that reminded me of study hall at Worcester Academy, I waited for them to bring Abbie in. At a desk on a raised platform in front, the sergeant sat facing the rows of numbered tables. The nearest row was for the worst offenders and the fifteenth row in the back was for the least "offensive" prisoners. They had seated me in the second row. Johanna came in and sat next to me. There were guards everywhere. Neither of us said anything. We just waited for Abbie, lost in our own private thoughts.

We were told to keep our hands on the table at all times. After a while, it's hard to keep your hands resting on a table top. You start to feel an almost desperate need to scratch behind your ear or under your foot. What were they going to do, shoot me? So I scratched. Nobody seemed to notice.

Finally Abbie came walking toward us, smiling his old smile, but with something about the smile I didn't recognize. It took me a few seconds before I realized that his head was completely shaved, giving his smile a ghoulish effect. He looked ghastly. Under his prison uniform he wore heavy black boots, standard prison issue. He settled in as near to me and Johanna as he could get and then leaned forward and started talking.

Keeping his hands on the table close to his body, he pointed around the room by raising just his index finger, and told us what different prisoners were in for—"That one butchered his wife and put the pieces in garbage bags," he'd say with a twinkle in his eye, waiting for my reaction. Now he was pointing out to me the prisoners in the hall who were Jewish. "The good thing about doing time in New York is that there are a lot of the brethren in here with you," and then for the first time that day I heard him laugh out loud. Abbie knew his own survival in prison depended pretty much on himself. We couldn't really help him here. His humor was intended to ease our sense of helplessness rather than his own.

I stayed at Fishkill almost the whole day, leaving the room only for short trips to the men's room or the candy machine in the corridor. Much of the day, the three of us just sat there in silence, sharing the confinement and isolation that on most days he had to submit to alone. And when I left, some of Abbie's strength had seeped into me. "In just a few months when this is over," Abbie's easy laughter, storytelling, and relaxed manner told me, "the worst will be behind us. The image of his shaven head made me instinctively raise my hand to my own to make sure it wasn't shaved as well.

Abbie told me he got along all right at Fishkill largely on account of his being a strong softball player. He was able to win the respect of other inmates on the softball field right off. And he was smart enough to know who to stay away from, so he had no major problems with other inmates. The only trouble he had was with some of the guards, but he was able to stay away from the ones that would have liked to give him problems. Once prison time had become a certainty, I think Abbie took pride in getting through it with his head high. He thought of himself as a political prisoner, and that with pride. Although the original alleged offense may not have been political, the sentence he had received certainly was.

On August 4, 1981, after a little more than three months of hard time, Abbie was transferred to Edgecombe, a minimum security facility in New York City. He worked days as a counselor at Veritas, a drug rehabilitation center in Manhattan, returning to the prison to sleep. Sometimes I'd come down from Framingham and meet Abbie for lunch. His mood was down. He'd weathered the worst of the storm, but he was left with nothing. His "troops"—Johanna, me, his friends—were still loyal, but at the group's center he didn't feel like a general anymore. He said he didn't feel like he had anything left to give.

* * *

One day I got a call from Abbie, perplexed by something that had happened. Hilario, Phyllis's husband, had visited him at Veritas and said, "I want you to take your sister back."

"What was he talking about?" Abbie asked me.

"Don't you understand," I said. "It's the old way. He doesn't want her anymore. You're the patriarch of the family now. He wants you to take her back."

"But I'm in prison," Abbie yelled. "What was I supposed to say to him?"

"What did you say?" I asked.

"I said, call my brother." But Hilario never called me. Within a few weeks, the Mexican government seized my newly opened factory, without ever giving me a receipt or a reason. Hilario filed for divorce in Mexico and obtained it within a year. And for the rest of his life, I used to rib Abbie for having cost me my livelihood by not having the right answer to Hilario's request.

They say you always know you're going to get out of jail; in prison, you never know. That leaves a mark, and it left a mark on my brother. The prison experience had taken something away from Abbie.

That fall of 1981, with my Mexican factory seized, I visited New York frequently, overseeing the demise of my old business and trying to set up a new one, buying and reselling close-out merchandise. I saw Abbie a lot. We talked about what he would do after he got out the following April. Requests for speaking engagements were coming in. He said he wanted me to manage him. He was beginning to feel connected to politics again. He felt that Reagan was dangerous because he too saw himself as a kind of revolutionary, from the radical Right. He feared that Ronald Reagan could destroy a lot of what had been accomplished culturally and politically, and that gave him a new sense of purpose. With his experience in Save the River, Abbie also saw all the battles to be fought for environmental causes. You could feel Abbie preparing himself, like a pitcher warming up in the bullpen. He felt that he'd paid his debt to society—and more—and that too helped him refocus. The guilt he felt may not have disappeared, but it receded, and was no longer the debilitating curse he'd once had to run from.

In November 1981, Abbie began planning a massive fund-raiser for Veritas, to take place in January. He secured the ideal venue, Studio 54, then the hottest nightclub in the city, and got them to donate its use free of charge. On the night of January 18, 1982, celebrities turned out in force, from Carly Simon and Cher, to actors Jack Nicholson and Robert De Niro. Abbie made sure he got to be master of ceremonies and assigned me to deal with New Line. New Line had expressed interest in being Abbie's booking agent, and we'd been negotiating for several weeks. You'd think Abbie's popularity would have declined while he was in prison. But, inexplicably, the opposite seemed to have happened. He now commanded up to $5,000 per speaking engagement. At the same time, copies of *Steal This Book,* when you could find them, sold for $25.00—twelve times the cover price![1] The enormous media attention he'd received when he surfaced, especially the Barbara Walters half-hour interview on *20/20,* had had a dramatic effect. Having been through so much and survived, outsmarted the FBI, transformed himself clandestinely from a Yippie! into a leader of the environmental movement in the '70s, Abbie was now seen as our preeminent outlaw hero.

By 2:00 A.M. that night, I had an agreement written on a cocktail napkin, signed and countersigned by New Line, and their check for $10,000 as an advance for the right to represent Abbie on tour, made out to "Jack Hoffman Presents," our company, which we later renamed "Abbie Yo-Yo." I gave Abbs the thumbs-up sign, he came over with another bottle of champagne, and we popped the cork. He was back. With only three months left to serve, we both saw better times ahead.

Oui magazine asked him for an interview, but he rejected the idea with the argument that the press never asks him the right questions. When they said he could interview himself and they would print it unedited, he accepted. In the interview, Abbie asks himself what the underground years taught him. "Well, I think that life is basically a contradiction. . . . At the core, humans are good and decent. That's one [thing] I've always felt. The other is that life's absurd. The tension between goodness and absurdity allows for progress. . . . You have only the first and you take yourself too seriously, only the second, and you don't take anything seriously. Balance."[2]

He started wearing his olive green prison jacket with a "Save the River" button sewn onto it as a memento of recent hardships and past glories. That he would wear the prison coat in public in itself showed new strength. He wasn't hiding anything, had nothing to be ashamed of, and was moving forward. On March 26, 1982, Abbie was paroled from Edgecombe. His eight-and-a-half-year trip through the looking glass was over.

A new collection of his underground and prison writings, *Square Dancing in the Ice Age,* had just come out from Putnam. It was arguably his best book to date, filled with self-assured, careful, analytical, and inspired writing from 1975 through 1981. Included were his intimate eulogy to Dad, "I Remember Papa"; a long essay written while Abbie was in prison, about fellow prisoner/writer Jack Abbott called "The Crime of Punishment"; and tales of his underground experiences all over the world that show how he proudly defied the frequent hardship and mania of his fugitive life and his prison life. The book has little of the frenzy and confusion that characterized his autobiography, published only two years earlier. It stood as convincing proof that, in 1982, Abbie was able yet again to begin life afresh, with his old beliefs, without cynicism, with fresh enthusiasm and energy.

Don Epstein at Greater Talent, one of the agencies representing Abbie at the time, arranged a speaking engagement in which Abbie would debate Watergate mastermind G. Gordon Liddy. And on the last day of April 1982, the two heavyweight '60s celebrities went into the ring at the University of New Mexico in Albuquerque before a crowd of 1,600. Abbie was witty, energetic, and gracious—to the point of telling Liddy he had admired his unwillingness to cooperate with the prosecution in the Watergate trial, which had resulted in

Liddy's receiving the heaviest sentence. Liddy, in return, was moody, taciturn, and hostile.

At one point, Abbie asked Liddy why he hadn't put Abbie on his kill list. Liddy's response, with a slight smile, was that Abbie hadn't risen high enough.

The next day's *Albuquerque Journal* referred to Abbie as an "aging activist" but nonetheless acknowledged that he had trounced Liddy.[3] Abbie felt the debate had been such a success that he decided debates were going to be the future of his lecture circuit business. A few days later we discussed the following ad he wanted me to place:

JACK HOFFMAN PRESENTS

ABBIE HOFFMAN

My brother has the biggest mouth in America. Recently, at the University of New Mexico, he demolished G. Gordon Liddy in debate, scoring 75% on the applause meter to Liddy's 25%. Even conservative newspapers declared "Liddy Fizzles," "Abbie Wins Hands Down." He's through with Liddy and interested in bigger game. Therefore we make the following challenge: Abbie will debate the following people, winner take all.

Purse $10,000:* John Phillips on drugs, Phyllis Schlafly on nuclear disarmament, Tom Hayden and/or Jane Fonda on grassroots democracy, Jerry Falwell on morality, Jesse Helms on abortion, George Will on E.T.
Purse $20,000:* James Watt on the new Federalism, James Edwards on nuclear power, Alexander Haig on deterrence, David Stockman on Reaganomics.
Purse $50,000:* Menachem Begin on Zionism, Henry Kissinger on Vietnam.
Purse $100,000:* Richard Nixon on anything.

*Rules, place, and other particulars to be arranged by seconds. All is negotiable. Interested parties call me immediately at . . .
Purses could go higher with ancillary rights. By the way, Abbie has out-

*drawn Liddy at every campus two or three to one. He has drawn crowds
of 5,000 on three occasions.*

Abbie also had me issue written challenges to likely opponents by
letter, including General Westmoreland, Robert McNamara, and
Phyllis Schlafly. But there weren't any takers.

On September 27, 1982, *The New York Times* printed an Op Ed
piece by Abbie on the subject of interstate trucking of nuclear waste.
Shipments originating in Ontario, Canada, and destined for reproc-
essing in South Carolina were passing through New York State after
being banned in Vermont and Michigan. The environmental risks in
the event of a vehicular accident were enormous. Abbie's article was
hard-driving, factual, and intent on the specific problem at hand—
without a breath of identifiably left-wing ideology. Even the accompanying four-line biography of Abbie makes no mention of his long
history as an activist. He is identified only as "founder of Save the
River, a citizens' environmental group based in Clayton, N.Y." who
"lives two miles up river from the Thousand Islands Bridge."

Abbie was back in politics, but his politics were clearer now than
they had ever been. Some of the ideas and methods that he'd adopted
as Barry Freed out of necessity now became part of his program by
choice. He no longer felt an obligation to toe a party line or fit into
anyone else's agenda as he once had—particularly in 1972—and the
new freedom was exhilarating and strengthening. Around this time,
activist/historian Harvey Wasserman began interviewing Abbie for
an article that would eventually appear in *New Age* magazine. Wasserman, author of the popular *Harvey Wasserman's History of the
United States* among other books, was the perfect sounding board for
Abbie's new thinking.

"I think 'left wing' and 'right wing' are meaningless terms,"
Abbie told Wasserman early in the interview, "and so I don't use
them." Later when Wasserman asked, "What can we do to further
the cause of justice in this country?" Abbie's response was a brilliant
deconstruction of the question from a grassroots organizing perspective:

First of all, [justice] is not a cause. If you say "cause" to the average American, the first word they'll say is "lost." All causes are lost. I don't believe in causes. So I'm not bummed out by nuclear war happening tomorrow; I'm not bummed out by the poisoning of the planet; I don't want to combat world hunger—those are too big! . . . If you stop to contemplate them, [they will] immobilize you.

Instead, you have to break it down in terms of issues. . . . What is the issue in my community that is going to mobilize people—move them from inertia to action, and get them participating in the whole process of decision-making? Are they going to win? This is very important: you want people to win. Is this going to broaden their consciousness about the way the whole process is put together? Is this going to make our community a better community? There are a thousand issues, wherever you live. You could walk down the street and find a hundred issues.[4]

For the first time since the early '60s, the full force of Abbie's intellect and experience was going into hands-on organizing, rather than myth-making and media manipulation.

In the Save the River office Abbie had initiated a problem-solving policy whereby the prerequisite for bringing a new problem before the board was that you'd taken the first step to solve it. As Abbie explained it to Wasserman, "You can't come in and say, 'We don't have money to do anything,' unless you've come in with a hundred dollars. You can't come in and say, 'Memberships are falling,' unless you've gone out and got some new members. . . . The idea is to switch people from being problem-presenters to problem-solvers." And when Wasserman asked Abbie, "What are you looking for?" Abbie's immediate response was: "Typical, average Americans who will just try to narrow the gap between what they profess and what's going on—to close the gap between our vision of America and the reality of America."[5]

Abbie even reversed his most famous piece of advice. When Abbie had first said, "Never trust anyone over thirty" in 1968, he was thirty-two! Now, at the ripe age of forty-six, Abbie grew fond of saying, with a little lightning flash of mischief in his eyes: "I tend not to trust anyone under thirty, actually," in recognition of his newfound maturity.[6]

In the fall of 1982, Abbie and Johanna were back living in her cramped apartment. Since I was now in the closeout business, I'd go down to New York about once a week to buy merchandise and I saw them pretty regularly. At the end of the day, my van filled with assorted items that I would resell, I'd ring their bell and usually end up staying the night. The three of us were quite close, serving almost as bridges to one another. Abbie was in a subdued, low-key mood during this period and seemed to take comfort in my visits. We would often talk into the night, and in the morning he'd make me a huge plate of *huevos rancheros*.

Johanna liked having me around too. Since I was less political than Abbie, I was someone she could talk to about other things. As for me, maybe with my business in the underground economy going so well, I didn't feel as hopelessly middle class as I had sometimes in the past. I was in my own groove, and that made it easier for me to be around them.

But it still wasn't easy. They were arguing a lot, about marriage among other things. Abbie and Anita had been divorced for some time, and he wanted to get married. Johanna didn't. Abbie was trying to take his lithium regularly, but Johanna felt it wasn't working, or that he wasn't taking it as often as he should. In her opinion, he was on his way to becoming dangerously unstable again, and she wanted him to get on medication that would control the manic depression. I felt torn. I loved them both, and each of them wanted me to take sides against the other, which I wouldn't do.

In mid-November, Abbie entered another manic phase. He started sleeping less, working harder, and getting more intense, more crazy. On November 17, he had a speaking date at the Morgantown campus of the University of West Virginia. He was very sick with an upper respiratory infection, was running a 103 degree temperature, and mildly delirious. But he insisted that the show must go on. I called the organizers and arranged for them to have a van with a cot and a nurse or doctor in it meet him at the airport—a kind of people's ambulance. And that's how he got to the date. The funny thing was several people told me he gave one of his best speeches that night. Physically, it would seem almost impossible. But that's the way Abbie was: He loved to let his work take him away from his physical and emotional pain; he slipped easily into the work; he was a reverse-escapist.

One day in December 1982, about a month into Abbie's manic period, I was in New York when I got an urgent message from Johanna on my answering machine asking me to meet her at a coffee shop near her apartment. When I got there, she was already waiting for me. She had obviously been crying, seemed more mad and bewildered than hurt. But her face was swollen and the thought crossed my mind that Abbie might have hit her. In her eyes was a look that told me she was trusting me not to ask. So I didn't, and she didn't tell me. We let it be something unspoken between us. And I think that as much as she wouldn't have let me talk about it, she wanted me to see what my brother had done to her.[7]

When I went back upstairs, Abbie was in the midst of packing his things in a manic frenzy. When he saw me, his eyes opened wider and he seemed to get another surge of rage. I thought he was going to hit me too, but then he seemed to just turn off the switch, ignoring me completely instead. I looked over his shoulder as he thumbed through the yellow pages for the name of a mover until he came across one called "A Nice Jewish Boy," and called them. Then, surrounded by boxes and crates stuffed with his belongings, we sat and waited.

His psychiatrist, Nate Kline, whom Abbie had grown to like and depend on, was incapacitated with a heart condition. Without Kline's supervision, Abbie had begun to ignore his medication needs completely. I was scared. I saw Abbie in front of me, but I didn't recognize him. There was a wildness in his eyes, a furious and unappeasable rage. His speech was rapid and slurred. I couldn't see any recognition of me in his look. I felt I wouldn't have been able to stop him from hurting himself or me if he'd wanted to. And it seemed like he wanted to. So I just helped him move out; there was nothing else I felt I could do. I was so frightened and confused, it did not even occur to me to seek psychiatric care for Abbie. I just wanted to help him. Abbie had somehow found a studio apartment about a block away. There his manic state lasted, almost continually, for another three months.

The months Abbie spent working out of his studio apartment in what was largely a manic rush were extremely productive. He started spending time in Bucks County, Pennsylvania, where he'd been invited by some environmental activists. Sometimes he'd be accompanied by his young activist friend Al Giordano. A new pump had been proposed by the Philadelphia Electric Company (PECO) to divert water from the Delaware River to the Limerick nuclear power reactor. The grassroots effort against PECO's plans was named "Dump the Pump." Abbie signed on with the group "Del-AWARE" as a dollar-a-year paid consultant, and began organizing demonstrations at Point Pleasant to block the construction of the pump. In January 1983, two days of demonstrations brought out nearly 2,000 protesters, hundreds of whom were arrested in acts of civil disobedience. A frustrated PECO spokesman complained, "No one had ever heard of the damn place before Abbie Hoffman arrived."

Despite the grassroots opposition, conservative Bucks County commissioners granted PECO the right to pump 95 million gallons of Delaware River water to cool the nuclear power plant. Construction began on the pump. Del-AWARE demanded a referendum. The Bucks County commissioners denied its request. Del-AWARE occupied the courthouse until the early spring, and in May 1983 got its referendum and won it with an overwhelming majority. In the fall of 1983, Del-AWARE was able to help elect new anti-Pump commissioners and an anti-Pump congressman named Peter Kostmayer. Del-AWARE had won, for the moment, and Abbie was elated.

Meanwhile, on February 11, 1983, Nate Kline died during heart surgery. It was a tremendous blow to Abbie. But at first he seemed to stride right through it. February saw the National Association of College Activities (NACA) convention in Baltimore. Abbie had been invited to be the showcase speaker, and had prepared a speech on student activism in the '80s that was filled with optimism.

I drove down in advance to set up the booth we'd rented to capitalize on his position as showcase speaker. Stacked inside the booth were copies of *Steal This Book,* and since Abbie's speech was booked in advance to standing room only capacity, I had a large banner hanging overhead proclaiming: "ABBIE SOLD OUT." Abbie flew down the morning the convention began, loved the banner, and began signing copies of *Steal This Book.* Student Activities organizers lined up to meet him. By the end of the third day, we had booked fifty or so college speaking engagements, and would later confirm as many as half of them, mostly for the high season, which ran from mid-September until just before Thanksgiving. At $3,000 a pop, this assured Abbie of a decent income that year and gave him a much-needed ego boost. He wanted to feel that after everything that had happened he was as popular as ever. He told himself that his star was rising.[8]

But with Kline's death, Abbie's confidence in being able to control his moods through medication lagged. He had become utterly careless about his lithium regimen, and after three months of frenzied activity he suddenly crashed hard. In March 1983, in the middle of the night, Johanna called me at home in Framingham. Abbie had been found in his apartment, having turned on the gas and then swallowed approximately 40 tablets of Ativan, a powerful tranquilizer. Johanna said she didn't know what to do.

I urged her to get him to the nearest hospital. We agreed, at Johanna's suggestion, that we'd register Abbie as Barry Freed. I got on the early morning shuttle out of Boston and met her at Bellevue Hospital a few hours later. Abbie was still in the emergency ward, laid out on a stretcher vomiting into a bag which hospital staff periodically removed for analysis, so that the doctors could reconstruct what he'd ingested. He was weeping, and looking up at me as soon as he saw me he said, "Don't let me ever do it again." I think it may have been the only time I've seen my brother cry, among all the discarded, the gunshot-wounded, and cut-up people, in that hellish place.

That day Johanna and I took turns so that one of us was always by Abbie's side. New cases kept coming into the ward. I don't think there was a moment where there wasn't at least one other suicide attempt a few yards away, each a different version of the same pain, dreadful reminders of what my brother had done to himself. It was a god-awful day. Before nightfall, they moved him to the mental ward, where they kept him under observation for several weeks. By the end, he was calling me on Fridays and Saturdays from the pay phone in the hall to analyze the performance of the Celtics. And then he'd call his bookmaker to place his bets.

Abbie gradually seemed to recover. And his life began to take on its natural shape again. Six months after his suicide attempt, his calendar of speaking engagements was so busy that it constituted the backbone of his existence, as well as his only steady source of income. He liked the mania of life on the road and used to compare it to being on a rock concert tour.

With me as his exclusive manager, working on a nonexclusive basis through several different speakers' bureaus, we had drafted standard contracts. Both we and each host university or college had to sign these contracts. One clause specified that Abbie required a thirty-minute interval of complete privacy before the lecture so that he could listen to his favorite Creedence Clearwater Revival cassette before going onstage. Another asked that Abbie be given copies of local newspapers so he could incorporate the local political climate and any news-breaking local issues into his speech. For transportation we specified, "Please, no fancy limos!" Abbie abhorred them.

Abbie's March breakdown seemed to have given him, at least temporarily, a healthy fear of death. He was taking his lithium regularly again. His relationship with Johanna was going well. And the star of his celebrity did seem to be rising. There were even repeated requests to appear on television shows like *Miami Vice* in fictional roles, usually as villains, which were fun to get even though Abbie turned them all down. Life seemed better than it had been in quite some time.

Joan and I had by this time gotten to know Johanna quite well, and since we were among the few people who had had to put up with Abbie as she had through the years, she could talk to us about him openly. Sometimes Johanna and Joan would get into serious conversations, and, when the subject turned to sex, Johanna would remark that Abbie was sexually prolific. And once, when Joan asked her if Abbie was a good lover, Johanna answered: "Did you ever see him eat?"

In June 1984, Abbie's old friend attorney Leonard Weinglass talked to him about traveling to Nicaragua. Abbie and Johanna ended up organizing a citizen's tour of the country for the fifth anniversary of the 1979 revolution, taking sixty-nine people with them. And during the next few years they would keep returning, until, by 1987, he had been there five times. Central America became the subject of one of his stock speeches. Abbie saw the relationship of the U.S. to Nicaragua and El Salvador in the '80s as having striking similarities to the relationship between the U.S. and North and South Vietnam in the '60s:

> *The notion that somehow a country of three million people, suffering from dire poverty and astronomical inflation, having just survived a devastating earthquake, and not ten years young after its own revolution, is a threat to the national security of the United States, well, it's absurd, but it's also awfully similar to what they were saying about Vietnam once upon a time. . . . We've invaded Nicaragua at least 11 times already, before the Sandinistas were even around. But we aren't given the history here in America. In Nicaragua they say, "You are taught to forget the history between our two countries, we are forced to remember it. . . ."*[9]

During one of Abbie's trips, I got an angry call from one of our bookmakers in Worcester. Abbie had just called him from Nicaragua saying he was in Daniel Ortega's home and that Danny and a bunch of other people wanted to place bets on the upcoming game. "What is he trying to do to me?" the bookie complained, fearing, not unreasonably, that Abbie's call could bring down the full force of the FBI on his illegal operation.

And the FBI was coming down hard on people visiting Nicaragua during this period, as we know from its later-publicized illegal campaign of surveillance and harassment against the Committee in

Solidarity with the People of El Salvador (CISPES). On Abbie's return from one visit to Managua, his briefcase, with his address book in it, was stolen in the airport in Miami, and he suspected government dirty tricks.

In late summer 1984, Abbie began a long series of debates with Jerry Rubin. In recent years, Jerry had done an about-face and become a Wall Street entrepreneur. Abbie agreed to the tour initially because he saw it as an opportunity to show how far superior his point of view was to Jerry's newfound conformism. He imagined himself saving untold thousands of college students across the country from becoming yuppies—"Young Urban Professionals"—a term coined by Jerry. But I don't think he fully considered how disturbing it might be for him personally to debate Jerry as an opponent in much the same way he had debated G. Gordon Liddy two years earlier. After all, Jerry had once been a friend. However disdainful Abbie might feel toward what Jerry had become, he tried to show respect for Jerry's having put himself on the line over and over again in the '60s. No matter how many sarcastic remarks he might be willing to make about it onstage, Jerry's conversion caused him spiritual pain. He felt it mocked Jerry's prior political commitments and those they had shared. For Abbie, Jerry's switch from the side of justice to the side of greed was the worst betrayal of Abbie's life.

The first booking was a two-night stand at a San Francisco nightclub called the Stone. The event was publicized as "The Yippies! versus the Yuppies" and was sold out. Abbie wore his well-worn tweed jacket over rolled-up sleeves, Jerry sported a dark suit and tie. Both had plenty of prepared gimmicks. Jerry began with a parody of the American Express television ads: "You may remember me from the sixties. I led thousands of youths into the streets, and presidents fighting wars quivered at the sound of my name. . . . Now . . . no one recognizes me anymore, so I carry my American Express card wherever I go. You can have one. But first you've got to become a yuppie." Abbie countered by filling a Cuisinart food processor with yuppie ingredients: vitamins, stock certificates, tofu, credit cards, brie cheese, keys to a Porsche, etc.[10]

At first, Abbie considered the debates a success because they were popular, and he was convinced that he was winning hands down. But as the tour continued, he became increasingly defensive. One problem for Abbie was that it looked to a lot of people like the only reason he was doing the debates was for the money—$5,000 per show—to be divided among the two performers after subtracting expenses and brokers' fees, with Abbie getting slightly more than Jerry.[11] That didn't present any problem for Jerry with his new come-and-take-it philosophy of greed, but it made Abbie look like a hypocrite. "I'm doing these debates in order to attack the mythology that those who were politically active and idealistic inevitably become disillusioned, cynical, and self-centered, insulated from the social problems around us and isolated by the blinding drive for money and power," he said during one debate.[12] What he said was true, but it was hard to believe, and he knew it. He began to feel used. His was the name drawing in the crowds, he rightly felt, but the game he'd consented to play was Jerry's game, the money game.

In all, Abbie and Jerry did fifty or sixty debates in an eighteen-month period. Onstage, it was Abbie's show, with Jerry playing the straight man. And very often the same local reporters who clamored for time with Abbie after the show only gave Jerry an obligatory minute or two. Free-market ideas might sound convincing when expressed by someone who truly believed them, but when a recent convert like Jerry Rubin got up there and told you to get into the system, make money, and then change it from within, it had a hollow ring to it.

Abbie began to realize just how much he didn't like Jerry. He was careful not to put Jerry down in public, out of respect for the past. But offstage, Abbie wanted nothing to do with him. I remember one night during the tour when we were watching the world series at a bar. Jerry walked in and made his way to our table. Without a word, Abbie got up and walked to the far end of the bar by himself, so as not to have to be anywhere near Jerry. Sometimes, Abbie would joke that Jerry was the cause of his depression. It was only a joke, but after all they had been through together, Abbie just couldn't accept that Jerry had gone over to the other side.

And after Abbie's death I remember being interviewed by a reporter who refused to believe that Abbie and Jerry weren't still best friends. As proof, I let her look through Abbie's address book, which contained all the names of people Abbie considered to be in his universe—people he might pick up the phone and call. Jerry wasn't there.

Chapter Fourteen

1986–1987

You don't spend twenty-five years trying to change it unless you love it.
—ABBIE

IN THE EARLY or mid-'80s, when Abbie tried to talk to me about his manic-depressive illness, I wouldn't listen. I might have been scared, or I simply didn't know enough about the illness to make sense of what he was telling me. It was as if he were talking about a sport they played in a foreign country, with new rules and an inscrutable score-keeping method. The game might be as exciting as basketball, but that wouldn't stop my eyes from glazing over. In the same way, I just couldn't connect to Abbie's own awareness of his manic-depressive condition.

Then, some years later, I began to understand. Through my experiences with Abbie and with another member of my family, through talking to friends, physicians, and acquaintances, my definition of life expanded to include mental illness as part of it.

As I became more familiar with manic-depressive illness, I gradually came to piece together the nature of Abbie's personal struggle in the last years of his life. As I did so, two very extraordinary things happened. First, I discovered that Abbie was a classic, textbook-perfect manic-depressive. When I came across checklists of the typical signs or symptoms of manic-depressive illness, I found that Abbie had them all. Second, I began to be able to separate in my own mind the symptoms of his disease from elements of his personality. The symptoms can usually be managed biochemically, with drug treatments. But I had gone to school too late, of course. By now Abbie was gone.

* * *

Psychiatrists consider manic depression to be a mood disorder, as distinguished from schizophrenia, which is a thought disorder. Manic depression is also essentially different from unipolar major depression, and generally the treatments that can successfully treat manic depression, such as lithium, are different from the antidepressant medication used to treat major depression, which affects roughly ten times as many people as does manic depression. In fact, response to lithium is one of the indicators that a person is suffering from manic depression.[1]

The seven symptoms that characterize a manic episode, according to the American Psychiatric Association's revised *Diagnostic and Statistical Manual of Mental Disorders* (DSM-III-R), are inflated self-esteem or grandiosity, decreased need for sleep, excessive talkativeness, racing thoughts or ideas, distractibility, increased goal-oriented activity, intense involvement in pleasurable activities which may have a high risk of painful consequences. At least three of the symptoms need to be present for a diagnosis. When Abbie was manic, I think he scored seven out of seven every time.[2]

But that was only the beginning. Abbie's was a classic case, but in some ways was also unique. It is typical of a manic-depressive to make boastful, wildly ambitious work plans. But in Abbie's case, repeatedly, I'd seen him accomplish those plans. It is typical for a manic-depressive to talk for hours on end. But Abbie could do so brilliantly, and he was doing so before crowds numbering in the thousands, and they expected him to do so—and they listened! Calling old friends at any hour of the day or night, regardless of the cost and regardless as well of the inconvenience to the person receiving the call, as Abbie had done repeatedly during the fugitive years, was typical manic behavior, but it was also pure Abbie. Delusions are classic manic-depressive symptoms—the sincere belief that a person has special gifts or skills, or is famous. The problem was that Abbie really had all these qualities. Reading a book on the subject, I came across this sentence: "A [manic-depressive during a manic phase] might believe that [he] is the object of attention and whispers by friends and strangers, or that Dan Rather is sending [him] special messages during his newscast."[3] It reminded me of the time in 1971 when Walter

Cronkite had telephoned Abbie out of the blue right in the middle of the evening newscast (which at the time was on delayed broadcast in much of the country).[4]

When he was depressed, Abbie was also a classic case. Typical symptoms include a loss of interest in people and activities one cares about, and feelings of great sadness and emptiness. When on occasion Abbie expressed such feelings to me, I'd been stumped. Now I began to see them as the signs of a biochemical disturbance that he shared with between one and ten percent of the U.S. population, and which frequently led to suicide attempts.[5]

So the more I learned about manic-depressive illness after Abbie's death, the more I felt I was getting to know Abbie all over again—both as a manic-depressive and as someone I began to be able to recognise apart from his disease. But by far the most striking connection I found between Abbie and his illness had to do with self-medication.

Drugs of various types have long been known to trigger manic depression—steroids, for example, can prompt manic depression in athletes who "stack" the drugs. More recently, researchers have hypothesized that cocaine can trigger manic depression. Biologically, cocaine and other drugs can also mimic the mania—bringing about states of euphoria and intense thoughts and feelings that resemble the incredible high that manic-depressives feel during their manic episodes.

It turns out that "dual-diagnosis" patients—those suffering from both mental illness and drug or alcohol abuse—comprise the majority of mental illness patients! But the nature of the connection isn't necessarily what you might expect. Many of these people are using chemical substances, both consciously and unknowingly, to tame their mental illness. It is in fact true that certain narcotic painkillers, like morphine and heroin, will help calm erratic and violent behavior, and can clear the mind of disorganized and chaotic thought processes. It is also true that stimulants such as cocaine and speed will overcome the fatigue and apathy of depression, and can enhance concentration. Even alcohol can help relieve anxiety and hyperactivity. For a manic depressive, these effects can be more dramatic and more welcome than for the rest of us. They aren't using the chemical substances to get high, but rather to be relieved of abnormally low, anxious, or nervous states.[6]

You could say Abbie had been self-medicating since the early '60s when he first started experimenting with grass and LSD, and I don't think Abbie would have contradicted you. Increasingly, I even believe he saw the drug culture as a defense against the widespread, low-grade depression brought on by the meaninglessness and inhumanity of the status quo in contemporary society.

But after he went off lithium in late 1985—he felt he could control his manic symptoms without it, and hated the side effects—and without a psychiatrist he felt he could trust as he had Kline, Abbie began self-medicating more wildly to control his moods. Antidepressants were frequently prescribed for him by various doctors, as were a variety of strong antihistamines, antibiotics and anti-wheezing drugs. He regularly took Ativan, a highly addictive antianxiety medication.

One curious footnote to Abbie's interaction with Kline had to do with Abbie's interest in Kline's earlier experimental work of treating alcoholics with lithium. Abbie felt that Kline had been moving toward a theory of addiction as a symptom of depression. Throughout the '80s, first with Kline leading the way, and then on his own, Abbie increasingly saw a connection between his own drug use and his mental illness. On the one hand, he had become interested in using drugs as a means of self-medication. And on the other hand, he was willing to consider the possibility that his attraction to drugs was a symptom of his manic depression. And as he pursued both paths of inquiry, these two sides—his increasing dependency and his expanding knowledge—progressively seemed to merge in a kind of macabre dance on the brink of the unknown.[7]

Nineteen eighty-six was the year Abbie would turn fifty, and confronting his aging reflection in the mirror had become somewhat difficult for him. His hunger for life was as voracious as it had ever been. Yet he needed to slow down and felt a profound need to redefine his public image.

He experienced the usual age-related disturbances, sudden reminders of one's own mortality in the form of health complaints and worries about the future. But there was little of the stability and comfort one usually expects at his age to help offset the worry. And this brought an unyielding intensity to his complaints.

"What do I do about health insurance, Jack? Who's going to pay for it?" he would say to me, outraged at the indignity of it all.

He still called me out of the blue and at all hours to start right in about last night's game: "Ten points! Ten fucking points!" No opener. No etiquette. Just the point spread. And timing. Because there was no time to waste. He still wanted me to believe he'd always be there, a few steps ahead, making sure everything was safe, and so I did. But other things were no longer the same at all.

I'd always felt that Abbie had been self-created: The critic, iconoclast, bad boy, shit-kicker, road warrior he'd been most of his life had sprung full-grown out of his own head. But here that person was changing before my eyes. A humbler, quieter man was emerging, as if to acknowledge that while part of him was indeed self-created, another part was not.

Between the antic performer and the hermit, the street tough and the intellectual, the political scientist and the flower child, the middle-class child and the revolutionary, Abbie, in all his brilliant contradictions, was attempting to face himself. In this way, 1986 was both a high point and a breaking point.

I suggested that he open an IRA account. He surprised me by not being completely against the idea. Then he wavered. In order to convince him, I suggested he think of it as the Irish Republican Army. That worked. Of course he knew it was only a joke, but the imaginary association made the reality go down a little easier.

He saw himself as a middle-aged man facing an unknown future. That's what he was, but it was never all he was. The danger now, as he focused on that image, was that he might lose sight of the rest—of his enormous and ongoing contribution. The pain of sight now became as great as the joy of sight had been at other times. My brother's great gift—his vision—was turning mercilessly inward.

The brave and optimistic words he still spoke on the campus lecture circuit and in interviews were for other people now. As a Jew, Abbie had always said you either go for the gelt (the money) or you go for broke. He'd gone for broke. Now, like most of us as we grow older, he found living to be a more complicated proposition than he had ever imagined.

In late March 1986, Abbie and I attended the funeral of Dad's brother, our uncle Al, in Worcester. Since our uncle was to be buried in the Hoffman family plot, this would mean visiting Dad's grave too. Abbie and I walked into the Pearlman Funeral Parlor, and then into the private room, where ten or fifteen of our relatives were gathered. The last surviving brother, our uncle Sam, came over to us after a moment and, without even saying hello, asked Abbie, "Wasn't it bad enough that you killed one of my brothers? What are you doing here?"

Abbie didn't answer, and didn't move at first either. I took his hand and led him back into the main sanctuary. All that day at the funeral service and burial afterward, Abbie made no mention of Uncle Sam's outburst, which led me to believe that it had hurt him beyond words.

People like Uncle Sam, in thinking Abbie to be irresponsible or worse, misread him completely. Abbie's problem was that he felt too great a sense of responsibility for his own actions, even though at times—and particularly during his manic episodes—he could not control them. There was a part of Abbie that judged himself more harshly than his harshest critics. Had Uncle Sam known how, during his depressions, Abbie sat in judgment against his own arrogance and egotism, then Sam probably would not have said those words.

My brother no longer had many friends, not really. He knew so many people, but when you picture him sitting in a phone booth somewhere—he used to call them his private offices, which was very funny considering his thirty-year war with Ma Bell—having to make that one call to a friend, to somebody he could count on, who would know how to interpret the silences at the other end of the line. . . . Well, there just weren't many numbers. In his moments of greatest need, Abbie had to rely on himself. He had Johanna at his side. He knew he could call me and a few others at all hours and pretty often he did, but as you listened to him ramble on—from sex, to Celtics, to Iran-Contra, then back to basketball—you couldn't help feeling he was a drowning man, talking to save himself, and all you could do was listen, knowing that wasn't enough, but he wouldn't let you do more.

There was in my brother a kind of meta-hunger, a gaping need. Inseparable from his need to see justice in the world, or his need to be famous, to be recognized in his individuality the world over, there was his gargantuan appetite for life. But Abbie was too afraid of letting people down to really lean on them. Once I suggested to him that he had no true friends. The answer he shot back, although posed as a question, sounded final: "Aren't you my friend?" he asked.

A deeply ingrained sense of respectability in Abbie often made him turn away from confidences. His inner life was so out there, his public life revolved so powerfully around the things that mattered most to him, that in a way Abbie's most private life *was* the one he led publicly, and he had no time for another.

His loneliness was one aspect of his life that always has and always will deeply disturb me. He loved and was loved in return. Thousands upon thousands, maybe millions of people felt an important personal connection to him. You could even say that the measure of my brother's greatness was his ability to befriend so many. He used to say he successfully eluded the FBI for six-and-a-half years only because of the help he received from 35,000 "close friends," any one of whom could have betrayed him, none of whom did. He inspired loyalty. And more than that, he inspired in those loyal to him a strange and glorious sense of fun and mischief.

Consider Jerry Lefcourt, who acted as Abbie's attorney through the years and never charged him a penny; or Noah Kimmerling, the accountant who kept the IRS at bay year after year (Abbie always paid his taxes, and paid them on time, even while he was a fugitive!); or Johanna Lawrenson, who shared life on the run with few comforts and substantial hardship and danger; or family members who put up with his exhibitionism, egotism, and notoriety. In sharing parts of his life we were brought inside the ecstasy of it somehow. He took you where you didn't want to be taken. Then he'd make you pay the cab fare. And in the end, you still felt in your heart that it was where you wanted to be.

*   *   *

On November 24, 1986, Abbie participated in a sit-in at the University of Massachusetts in Amherst to protest CIA recruitment on campus. During the demonstration, some of the protesters, including Abbie, occupied a campus building and were arrested. Abbie was six days shy of his fiftieth birthday. Also arrested that day was Amy Carter, who had come up from Brown University in Providence, and crawled in through a window. No one knew in advance that she was coming.

It pleased Abbie to have a president's daughter on board. And he just plain liked Amy Carter. She had courage, a good sense of humor, and didn't waste words. She wasn't shy and she had the same attitude as Abbie, the one that says, "I don't care if you like me or not, but let's face it, you like me a lot." And then too, in his gravitation to Amy's side, I felt once again, but in a different way, his weariness. He wanted desperately to retire but would never do so unless he felt there were sufficient numbers and, more important, the right people, to carry the Movement forward. And they had to be young. A little more than two years later, and only two months before his death, on February 9, 1989, Abbie would say he could name "10, 15, 20 people from [the '60s] who are still very active, just in the same way that I am. I don't feel like I'm the last Japanese warrior in the caves of the Philippines fighting the war. . . . [But] it's kind of strange not to see yourself replaced."[8] He was on the lookout for members of the next generation who might be able to bring the Movement forward into the twenty-first century.

Abbie in the 1980s had become a little like a country doctor or itinerant rabbi of the Movement, arriving to perform the rituals of democracy as requested of him, in the form of sit-ins and civil disobedience actions. In a decade when the media, especially t.v., were notorious for ignoring the real issues affecting people in their everyday lives, Abbie got local issues covered again and again. He didn't do it with theatrics, but through solid organizing skills and grueling work. But by 1986 he was also beginning to fight for a new sense of himself in the world, something a little more in keeping with his age.

So when he arrived in Amherst on November 24, 1986, to be arrested, it was in some ways just another stop on the road. But in other ways the Amherst action was uncanny. They brought out the dogs that day, and helmets and gas. And for a day it seemed that all that had happened in America since the '60s was that the scary sophistication of Mayor Daley's Chicago police force had reached the small town of Amherst.

And then in the buses used by the police to transport the arrested protesters into town for booking, there was another odd note. As the protesters were pressed into the buses, Abbie strode up and down the aisles to make sure morale held. He wanted to come up with some songs of struggle they could sing together. The response was deeply disturbing to him—enough so for him to incorporate it henceforth into his campus speeches as a kind of minor mode, a despairing strain:

"You need music," he would say by way of introduction, and then:

> *When we were all arrested at the University of Massachusetts, it was the first time they had brought the police on in seventeen years, with attack dogs, helmets and everything, because civil disobedience has become a very polite sport in the last four or five years. But here they were very seriously beating up people, breaking legs and everything. People were being carted off to jail, handcuffed for hours. I went on the darkened buses and I said, "You folks know any freedom songs or anything?" And they said, "Oh yeah." They knew every song from "Hair." They start singing all these songs from "Hair." And I'm saying, "What the hell are you singing? "Hair" was a Broadway show. It was a rip-off, a fake; they were wearing wigs." They're saying, "What're you talking about, Abbie, it's a movie, it's a good movie." I thought it was kind of sad, because you do have to have your own songs and this was something they didn't have.*[9]

All Abbie was really discovering was that he had lived long enough to meet yet another generation of college students. The civil disobedience action at the University of Massachusetts represented, for the most part, an overwhelmingly upbeat and promising trend:

young people ready to take on some old enemies while welcoming some old friends.

Abbie didn't stay in Massachusetts for his birthday on November 30. Returning to New Hope with Johanna right after Thanksgiving, he concentrated his energies increasingly on the upcoming trial for the Amherst civil disobedience. He decided that his presentation at this trial would be different. He went out and bought a new Harris tweed jacket, and decided to conduct his defense *pro se,* acting as his own attorney. He was determined not to be dismissed this time as just a clown.

Abbie had always been willing to take his chances in the courtroom. With the exception of his flight after the drug bust, the law was the democratic institution he trusted most. Not always, or even most of the time—but sometimes—in a courtroom you could buck the odds and get a fair shake. It was a place where justice could triumph.

And he relished the opportunity to go up against the CIA on neutral turf. He believed this was a battle that could be won, using the little known necessity defense, which argued that the trespass against the CIA was required to prevent another, greater crime from being committed against the American people—in this case, that of the CIA's illegal wars in the Third World.

The trial lasted ten days and was held in Northampton, Massachusetts. As witnesses, the defense called a number of distinguished Leftist luminaries, including Howard Zinn, Daniel Ellsberg and Ramsey Clark, as well as a number of reformed government men, like ex-CIA agent Ralph McGehee, and former contra leader Edgar Chamorro. These witness gave example after example of documented CIA deceptions and crimes. Somehow the CIA seemed outnumbered in that courtroom. The enemy was in disarray, while friends seemed to be everywhere. The D.A. had prepared his case badly and the defendants seemed to have the CIA on the run. Media coverage was pretty heavy throughout the trial. For Abbie and me, the difference between the atmosphere in Northampton and the atmosphere in Chicago nineteen years earlier was actually disturbing, since we didn't know what accounted for it or what it meant. There Abbie had been treated by local working people for the most part as a criminal and traitor. Here, we were local heroes. No lunch spot in town would let us pay for a meal. They each wanted to think of us as their guests. What exactly had changed? we wondered. Had we entered history?

Sitting in the Northhampton courtroom on April 15, 1987, waiting for the jury to return from its deliberations, with Johanna seated on my left and Ma on my right, I felt my old pride in Abbie. For Ma, this moment was reparation for the old injury she had suffered by deferring to Dad's wish that she not attend the Chicago Conspiracy trial. She thought that her place was in the courtroom, that it was only proper for a mother to share in her son's fate, be it misfortune or triumph, and she had suffered Dad's order with deep resentment. Now she held her head high—but I could see how nervous she was— as Abbie began his summation, speaking in a strong and righteous voice about the case, and then, quietly and to my surprise, about Dad:

> *When I was growing up in Worcester, Massachusetts, my father was very proud of democracy. He often took me to town hall meetings in Clinton, Athol and Hudson. He would say, "See how the people participate, see how they participate in decisions that affect their lives—that's democracy." I grew up with the idea that democracy is not something you believe in, or a place you hang your hat, but it's something you do. You participate. If you stop doing it, democracy crumbles and falls apart. It was very sad to read last month that the New England town hall meetings are dying off, and in a large sense, the spirit of this trial is that grassroots participation in democracy must not die. If matters such as we have been discussing here are left only to be discussed behind closed-door hearings in Washington, then we would cease to have a government of the people.*

There was an honesty and decency to my brother at this moment, pacing back and forth in front of the jury in the Harris Tweed jacket and the tie, looking serious as hell:

This trial is about many things, from trespassing to questioning acts by the most powerful agency in the government. And here we are in Hampshire District Court. You have seen the defendants act with dignity and decorum. You have seen our lawyers try hard to defend our position. Witnesses, many of whom occupied high positions of power, have come before you and have told you the CIA often breaks the law, often lies. The prosecutor has worked hard but has not challenged their sincerity. The judge is here, the public, the press. I ask you, Is it we, the defendants, who are operating outside the system? Or does what you have heard about CIA activities in Nicaragua and elsewhere mean it is they that have strayed outside the limits of democracy and law?

I watched my brother and thought how he could have had his pick of lives, but chose this peculiar kind of public service that to him is the most important work in the world. Abbie had plenty of reason to be cynical and suspicious standing in that courtroom. But he chose not to be. He'd decided that he could win this way, playing it very straight. And in his whole life, he may not ever have fully considered that possibility before. It was still revolution for the hell of it. Abbie hadn't changed his goals one iota, but he'd figured out that you can take the fight to places the enemy thought they owned.

As the members of the jury filed back in—all were over the age of thirty—none looked at the defendants. They had deliberated for less than two hours. In response to the judge's question, the forelady answered unhesitatingly, "Yes, we have," and then, "Not guilty."

All twelve defendants being tried for trespassing, including Abbie, were acquitted of all charges, as were the three defendants, including Amy Carter, who were being tried on charges of disorderly conduct. Abbie was jubilant. Raising his arms in the victory sign, he embraced one of his co-defendants and then came over to where we were sitting. He hugged Ma first, then each of us.

There had been no compromise, no meeting halfway. The case had been won within the judicial system, by the rules. Ma was here.

And Northampton was just forty miles from Worcester, where Abbie and I were born. We were on home ground.

Dad really had brought us along to those town hall meetings in Clinton and Athol when we were kids, as Abbie had said in his summation. He really had instilled in us his passion for democracy—for going freely to temple, for tolerance, and voting, which to Dad was sufficient proof, because he'd seen it work at a local level, and because in the old country, as Dad would remind us, Jews had no rights.

At the close of his summation, Abbie quoted Thomas Paine on the subject of freedom, saying, "Every age and generation must be as free to act for itself . . . as the ages and generations which preceded it. Man has no property in man. . . ." I think Dad would have understood that, would have sensed Abbie's victory at hand and felt an immigrant's pride in an American son after his own heart, who cherished the very freedoms he himself cherished—and then he would have groaned with pain for all the years they hadn't seen eye to eye.

Riding home with Ma after the trial, it was thrilling to think about what I had just seen. Instead of Abbie's lonely isolation, here he was in all his glory. A man who risks his life for things, for his vision of social justice for example, does so out of necessity, because these are things he needs in order to live—in order to create an environment that will be habitable for him. When, rarely, his conditions are met, as they were for Abbie on April 15 in Northampton, there can be joy enough to go around. It wasn't just Abbie that day, it was all of us. And winning was, as Abbie used to say, "the greatest high of all."

A few weeks later, in May, Abbie returned to Worcester to receive the key to the city for his work with a community center called Prospect House in the 1960s, and for a gala twenty-fifth anniversary celebration for the center. Dad would never have believed it possible that the key to the city would go to his *meshuggener* son. Ma came to both ceremonies.

Del-AWARE's 1983 victory for "Dump the Pump" hadn't held. PECO had sued, and now, four years later, in the spring of 1987, a judge ruled in favor of the PECO pump. Abbie had by now been arrested three times defending the river, once with america, and he took the defeat very personally. In July 1987 he resigned from Del-AWARE.

That summer Abbie started working with National Student Action (NSA), an attempt to galvanize students nationally through a network of young campus organizers. I was promoting concerts, including one starring our childhood hero Fats Domino. Backstage, I asked Fats to sign one of his promotional photos for my brother. Fats said, "Yeah, I know about Abbie." Fats had been a fan of the Black Panthers at the time of the Chicago trial and knew my brother as Bobby Seale's co-defendant.

And whenever something good happened to Abbie—like winning the Amherst case, or receiving the key to the city of Worcester—it would get him thinking again about being pardoned. Abbie didn't like to talk to me directly about it. Since it was something he invested with ultimate meaning, he didn't like to talk to anyone about it—in the same way that sometimes people of faith don't like to talk about their God, even to others of the same faith, out of the superstition that speaking of something dilutes it. But he would drop hints. With Dukakis already an unofficial candidate for president, Abbie would turn to me at the mention of Dukakis and ask me if I thought Dukakis and Cuomo were close. He wouldn't say why he was asking, but I knew why. Since we knew people with access to Dukakis, Abbie was wondering if we could get Dukakis to speak to the New York governor about pardoning him on the drug charges. He was proud to be an outlaw, proud of his more than fifty arrests for political actions, ashamed only of this one criminal offense. Naively, he still expected that those in power could be made to acknowledge that his banishing the CIA from the U. Mass campus, just like attacking the judicial system in Chicago and beating back the Army Corps of Engineers, were acts of community service. And, uncharacteristically humble when it came to this one issue, Abbie was perfectly ready to let a Governor Cuomo or a President Dukakis, voices of mainstream democracy, absolve him of his sins.

After the triumph of the CIA trial, Abbie had returned to New Hope feeling like a weary world-class champion. Four days later, on

April 19, 1987, he had finished his introduction to *Steal This Urine Test*. In the introduction, you can still hear something of the strength and plainspeaking pride of the Northampton summation—Abbie as orator, as leader, Abbie all grown up, finally. Now the subject was the politics of drug testing, but there was a newfound maturity in the arguments he used and the manner in which he expressed them:

> *Drugs are being scapegoated in an attempt to avoid making badly needed social and economic changes in a disintegrating society. . . . I believe society would be best served by abandoning the reigning turbulence and moving to a calmer plateau from which we could engage in drug education, research, and treatment programs with a decent chance of success. It's easier to work on solutions without people shouting in your ear.*
>
> *Without minimizing the problem of drug abuse, our attention should focus on equally serious problems, such as poverty, homelessness, unemployment, and inadequate medical care. I don't believe we can cope with drug abuse on a meaningful scale until we are willing to tackle these more general and pressing issues.*

The central issue of *Steal This Urine Test,* of course, isn't drug use but the invasion of privacy represented by corporate and governmental urine testing. Abbie's argument is that it is wrong to see urine testing as a situation where the goal is a drug-free America with invasion of privacy as a small, necessary accompanying evil. The way Abbie saw it, the goal was the ability to monitor, control, and punish people for what they do on and off the job; getting rid of drugs was just the excuse. *Steal This Urine Test* may be Abbie's most credible book. And perhaps partly because it was co-authored by Jonathan Silvers, it is the first book by Abbie Hoffman that isn't primarily also about Abbie Hoffman, or even exclusively about the counterculture. It holds up a mirror for all Americans—not just fellow citizens of Woodstock Nation.

Chapter Fifteen

1988

You have to laugh with us, at us, and take us seriously all at the same time or you're going to miss the point.

—ABBIE

ABBIE'S AUTOBIOGRAPHY, *Soon to Be a Major Motion Picture,* which he wrote on the run, ends on November 8, 1979. And in a way it is true that the ten years he lived after that date were a sort of afterlife. He was productive, he was effective politically, and at the same time he was fighting a losing battle with himself. His life was a shipwreck, with many beautiful things in it, but with the sea running through it, battering it from all sides. His dependencies were a huge handicap, especially his deepening dependency on a wide variety of drugs for a ghastly configuration of physical and emotional pain. In 1988, every-thing from broken bones that wouldn't heal to respiratory prob-lems—heightened to a monstrous degree by his manic-depressive illness—led him, at his worst moments, to believe that there was no hope for him.

Although he had long since identified his illness, he didn't always connect it as he should have to the specific complaints that haunted him. He felt frustration in his relationship with Johanna, and feared that she might be planning to leave since she didn't want to marry him. He felt anger toward his children and his first wife Sheila, whom he sometimes felt were concerned only with what they could get from him and not with his well-being. And when he tried to look into his own future, he saw darkness. These perceptions acted as heavy weights on him. He thought he saw them more or less objectively, when in fact these depressing thoughts were, at least in part, the expression of the emotional lows of his mood swings.

I mention these things in part because it is only by understanding that the monkey on his back—as he himself experienced it—was an animal as big as a house that you can begin to recognize what strength he had to muster every morning just to get out of bed. And yet, not only did he get out of bed, he was writing, he was speaking on dozens of college campuses, organizing people around environmental issues, showing up at demonstrations in response to a continuous flow of requests, and doing it all with great enthusiasm.

I used to wonder how he could stand on the podium at campuses across the country, look out at the expectant faces, and say things like "the future is yours"—with energy and conviction—when I knew there was so little hope in his heart. But the truth is that the improbability of some of his enthusiasms—that, for example, a new student movement was dawning in America—was no greater than the improbability of Abbie's whole life up until now, of his still struggling for what he believed, fighting battles to replace the status quo with a new age of enlightenment, *twenty years after he'd lost the war.*

What enabled him to keep blasting away, defying everyone and everything, was his incredible energy, a kind of blessed madness deeply ingrained in his personality that existed according to its own laws and that, by now, was also inseparable from the symptoms of his mental illness. His mania was something Abbie was born with, and it was something he didn't want to lose, couldn't imagine living without, and was unable and perhaps unwilling to control.

I do not know whether objectively Johanna was or was not planning to leave him. I do not know whether in fact his kids were ungrateful, although I suspect most kids are, just as we were when we were kids. But Abbie's future still held much promise, and many of his physical ailments might have been transient. I think it is entirely possible that both Johanna and his kids loved him more than they had words to express, and that the narrowing and darkening he felt were the result of his growing disease, too little controlled medication, and too much uncontrolled self-medication.

* * *

In January 1988, Abbie was shopping around a book on the coming presidential election that he hoped to write with Jonathan Silvers, the same young writer with whom he'd written *Steal This Urine Test*. He was spending most of his time "on the farm," as he called his converted turkey coop apartment in New Hope. He was feeling his age. He was barely able to make enough money for basic necessities, and unable to send money regularly to either Sheila or Anita for his kids.

On February 6, 1988, Abbie addressed the first ever National Student Convention, organized by National Student Action at Rutgers University in New Brunswick, New Jersey. Taking the long view back on the last quarter century of student activism and imagining its continuation and expansion in the years to come, he found himself able to disregard his own deteriorating health and finances for that hour. The opportunity to address a national gathering of activist students under the aegis of an entirely new umbrella organization brought out his energy reserve. He found he had something new and important that he needed to say.

The speech itself was relatively brief, ironic in places, and heart-wrenching in others. "My vision of America is not as cheery and optimistic as it might be," he joked. "I agree with Charles Dickens, 'These are the worst of times, these are the worst of times.' " But then, in deadly earnest, he called on any true believers who might be out there:

> *Look at the institutions around us. Financial institutions, bankrupt; religious institutions, immoral; communications institutions don't communicate; educational institutions don't educate. . . . There are people that say to a gathering such as this—students taking their proper role in the front lines of social change in America, fighting for peace and justice—that this is not the time. This is not the time? You could never have had a better time in history than right now. . . .*
>
> *In the late sixties we were so fed up we wanted to de-*

stroy it all. That's when we changed the name of America and stuck in the "k." The mood today is different, and the language that will respond to today's mood will be different. Things are so deteriorated in this society, that it's not up to you to destroy America, it's up to you to go out and save America.[1]

It was the same thing he'd been saying for a quarter century, and yet the words and the emotion were different from before. They had a special urgency to them. There was a note of sadness along with the power in his urging and admonishment, a note of finality.

Abbie and Jonathan Silvers signed a deal with Penguin Books for the election book to be titled *The Faking of the Presidency: Politics in the Age of Illusion*. With the upcoming February New Hampshire primary only weeks away, they began work immediately. As they dug in, questions kept pointing back to serious improprieties allegedly committed during the 1980 contest between Carter and Reagan, when the Republican stranglehold on the White House had begun. They decided to write a personal letter to Jimmy Carter, asking his opinion on whether Reagan had stolen the 1980 election. To Abbie and Jonathan's surprise, Carter, who would have heard about Abbie from his activist daughter Amy, responded immediately with a detailed and thoughtful response.

We have had reports since late summer 1980 about Reagan campaign officials dealing with Iranians concerning delayed release of the American hostages. I chose to ignore the reports. Later, as you know, former Iranian president Bani-Sadr [gave] several interviews stating that such an agreement was made involving Bud McFarlane, George Bush and perhaps Bill Casey. By this time, the elections were over and the results could not be changed. I have never tried to obtain any evidence about these allegations but have trusted that investigations and historical records would someday let the truth be known.[2]

Carter's suggestion that there was a story there to be unearthed stoked the fire of Abbie and Jonathan's curiosity. The care with which Carter responded spurred their enthusiasm. They pitched it to *Playboy,* and got a go-ahead for a feature article to appear in the October issue—an October surprise pay-back on the eighth anniversary of the first October surprise. They got right on the trail of Iran-Contra, and while they weren't the first writers to follow this story, they would be the first to present its full dimensions in a widely read national magazine—and during the month prior to the national election.

Abbie had committed his support to Dukakis, but he was unenthusiastic about the Massachusetts governor. And in any case, his main battle was with his own apathy. More than once Jonathan called me from New Hampshire to complain that Abbie was distracted and unable to work on the book. With Dukakis the favorite at that time and Bush way behind in the polls, Abbie seemed incredibly pessimistic, and what was worse, unconcerned, almost as if he were unaware of what was at stake, unaware of how much a Bush victory in November would hurt all the causes he believed in, from the fight to save the Nicaraguan revolution to the environmental war being waged at home.

We argued and argued; the combination of his apathy and his willful ignorance surprised and shocked me. I would try and convince him why Dukakis had a good shot at winning. Abbie thought Dukakis was just another establishment liberal who was going to lose, just like McCarthy in 1968, McGovern in 1972, and Mondale in 1984. I countered that with Reagan gone, the economy troubled, and Bush unpopular, things might go differently. Dukakis could pull it off.

"He's Greek, his wife is Jewish, and he's going to win?" Abbie countered. "He won't even get out of the primaries a winner."

"He's going to win the primaries in Texas, and Florida," I replied.

Abbie had to think hard about that one. A candidate that could take those two key states in the primaries did have a shot at coming into the general elections with the wind at his back. After a minute's reflection he said, "Maybe Florida"—the only state where having a Jewish wife could play in Dukakis's favor.

"He's going to win Texas," I insisted.

"He doesn't have a rat's ass's chance in the Texas primary," Abbie assured me.

I offered to bet on it, and even gave Abbie two to one odds.

"Oh, is this going to be another one of your winning bets? Your record isn't so good there, Jack"—Abbie's reminder of our losing bet with Sammie, our bookmaker, on McGovern in 1972.

But Abbie took the bet anyway. I hadn't told him that Dukakis spoke Spanish, a key factor in my thinking on Texas. And when Dukakis won Texas handily, and after Abbie had seen Dukakis campaigning in Texas speaking in Spanish, he called me.

"You didn't tell me he could speak Spanish," Abbie said accusingly.

"You didn't ask."

"You cheated," he argued.

"A bet's a bet," I countered.

In the end, Abbie had to admit I'd played the angle pretty well and didn't mind that he'd lost.

In March or April Abbie flew to Paris to interview former Iranian President Bani-Sadr for the *Playboy* article, and came back almost euphoric about how the story was developing. He felt there was a smoking gun and that he was the guy to find it. He would call me up and the first words out of his mouth would be, "We got Bush, we got Bush. And we can determine who the next president of the United States will be."

Most of the time I would counter with, "No, you don't have Bush, and no, you won't make the next president." But then I started to believe him. And considering that he had seemed apathetic so much of the time recently, I was glad to see him enthusiastic again.

While Jonathan was doing most of the actual writing of the article, Abbie was trying to put together a plan to get the story quietly to Dukakis and Cuomo so that they would know that they owed any Democratic Party victory to Abbie Hoffman. I contacted people I knew I could trust within the Dukakis campaign and floated the idea of an early release of the information in the story, or the story itself, before the July Democratic convention.

I met in a Worcester diner with a Dukakis representative, and the seriousness of what Abbie and I were proposing came home to me when I realized that the guy sitting across from me was scared. A week later I heard back. In the meantime, Dukakis's people had contacted Carter and others for confirmation of the story. They were concerned, my contact, informed me, about Israel's involvement.

I took that to mean that if the story were released and it led to revelations that reflected badly on Israel, then there would be the risk of losing the Jewish vote. As it turned out, of course, Israel was heavily involved in Iran-Contra. My contact requested another meeting that would include others from the Dukakis campaign. I agreed, and was told they would contact me, but they never called. I guess the decision was made within the campaign not to pursue the revelations further.

Throughout the month of April, Abbie stayed in close touch with me—to the point where he might call two or three times a day. He wanted me involved in any and all bookings he took on, and he had his assistant, Kathy Devlin, refer calls to my office in Worcester. Abbie and I would talk over each offer, and then he would make his decision. Abbie said I was the only one he trusted. He wanted me to manage him again. This came at a time when my close-out business was erratic and I didn't always earn enough to meet my mortgage payments, so Abbie was helping me at a critical time. I couldn't tell whether he was doing it for my sake or his. Maybe he suddenly realized how much we both needed each other.

With increasing frequency, Abbie ended our conversations by complaining about Johanna. In many ways she remained the loyal, practical, and devoted partner who always packed condoms for him in his luggage when he traveled to make sure he didn't bring any diseases home. But he was afraid that their love might not last. It made him feel aged and hopeless to have to consider even the possibility of facing the future alone. He wondered aloud whether the divorce from Anita had been the right thing. He began to wonder if she had been his true soulmate after all, since she had been his companion during the most exciting years of his life, and someone whose thoughts and feelings resonated most powerfully with his own. In his mind, Anita came to represent what might have been, the life he could have had, the life he had glimpsed briefly in the early years after america was born.

At times he would threaten that if Johanna wouldn't come and live with him on "the farm," he would find someone else who would. Then he would say how much he still loved Johanna, how he still wanted to marry her despite any problems they might have. He seemed to be in an emotional tug of war with himself over Johanna, unable to stand being in doubt of her affections. And she seemed willing to keep him in suspense, refusing steadfastly to marry or move in with him, and yet, with equal steadfastness, remaining committed to their relationship.

When he wasn't going on about Johanna, he complained to me about his kids: "Money, money, money," he would begin, "That's all they want. Ilya wants money, Andrew wants the boat, and if he can't have the boat he wants money. And they don't give a fuck about me, and I'm dying." Abbie was moaning and coughing from a bout of the flu as he spoke. He sounded bad.

On April 29, Abbie arrived in Boston for a speaking engagement at Holy Cross the following evening. Earlier that morning, Joan had called her physician, Dr. Epstein, and he had agreed to see Abbie right away. (This was the same Dr. Epstein whose leukemia patient Abbie had helped out in 1968.) Joan now drove into Boston to pick up Abbie at the airport and bring him straight to the doctor's office in Framingham. From the minute he got in the car, looking tired and ragged, his eyes red and swollen, wheezing with each breath, Abbie talked nonstop: He'd had a fight with Sheila on the phone the night before; he and Johanna had gone to a marriage counselor; he was so perplexed, so unhappy, he didn't know what the hell to do, he didn't know what the hell Johanna wanted. Although Joan was usually Abbie's most patient listener, the details of Abbie's misery were unbearable even to her after a while. She asked him to stop. He apologized, but within a few minutes he had started up again as if nothing had happened.

Dr. Epstein diagnosed severe bronchial pneumonia and wanted

Abbie hospitalized. Abbie refused because of the Holy Cross booking. And he didn't want to stay at our home either out of consideration for the children, since he thought he might be contagious.

He asked me to get him into a hotel in Worcester. What he desired most in the world, he said, was two days of rest and solitude. On the phone, Dr. Epstein told me he didn't see how Abbie could give a speech in this condition. I told him I'd seen him give some of his best speeches when he was in worse condition than this. I promised I would ply him with chicken soup and make sure he rested.

I checked him into the Marriott in downtown Worcester, got him a quart of chicken soup from Weintraub's, and tried to leave. But he wasn't able to rest and wouldn't let me go. As sick as he was physically, he seemed worse off emotionally.

"What are we going to do, Jack?" he kept asking me. "I don't see myself doing this five years from now. . . ." I didn't know what to tell him.

Finally, he calmed down and we began to run through our usual routine. Abbie always used to like to go over his speeches the day before he gave them. And Holy Cross had a special importance for him, since it was his first return engagement there since the April 1970 speech that had caused Holy Cross to so humiliate Dad. So I stayed and we talked for a couple hours more.

The thing on his mind was how much of the forthcoming *Playboy* article, "An Election Held Hostage," to reveal in the speech. Abbie wanted to reveal most of the Iran-Contra story. I felt that he shouldn't mention it at all. I knew that his co-author Jonathan was against his making any mention of it this soon. In the end, we agreed to a compromise: He would plug the article, but not divulge its substance, telling the crowd only that the October issue of *Playboy* would contain an article that could change the course of the presidential election. And then I left.

The next morning I arrived at the Marriott expecting to have breakfast with Abbie quietly in his room while he recuperated, and perhaps to put the finishing touches on his speech. Instead, I found him in the lobby doing an interview with the local radio station, WTAG. Abbie was full of energy, but he looked frightening, with his hair matted and his eyes red and swollen. Of course, he didn't care, since it was a radio interview. Even so, I asked them to cut it short and hustled him back up to his room and into bed.

I stayed with him all day. His manic state was so pronounced that he seemed not even to notice his physical symptoms—the high fever, cough, breathing difficulty, and ear infection were like balloons tied to a high-speed train. He talked in a rapid stream, and I knew he wouldn't slow down until after the speech, when he was likely to simply collapse in the arms of whoever happened to be nearest the stage exit.

Abbie began the speech with his usual challenge to journalists in the audience. Holding up a $100 bill, he told them that it would go to any reporter whose article the next day contained fewer than three errors. Abbie used to love to say that nobody had ever won the bet. Then came another favorite joke: mentioning that one of the half-dozen subjects he spoke on most frequently was student activism, he added that these days that speech took only about three minutes.

With the audience warmed up, he spoke seriously about the '60s and jumped to contemporary politics generally and presidential politics in particular, attacking Bush without giving his support to Dukakis. He also talked about Nicaragua, environmental issues, and local issues—things we'd gleaned from the local papers that morning and the day before. The funny thing was that the only indication of his illness was the mug of tea with honey he kept beside him on the podium. No one in the audience could have guessed that he wasn't feeling great. His voice carried, his enthusiasm and commitment carried. As he swept back and forth between asserting the grandeur of his cause in a loud, brash voice and intimately ribbing his listeners for their ignorance about current affairs, the packed audience loved it, and when he finished there were cheers and strong applause. As soon as he came down from the stage, we got him into a car, brought him back to Framingham and kept him in bed. The next day, still extremely sick, he insisted on returning home to New Hope.

A day or two later, Abbie sat down in a mood of self pity and heartrending loneliness and wrote a three-page letter to Sheila, with whom he still corresponded irregularly, mostly about money for the kids. Abbie listed his flu symptoms as well as the details of what he called "the weird world I live in," as if these too were symptoms of an illness, including large numbers of crank calls and letters and the pain of being separated from Johanna. He said that some people's claims to know the real Abbie only heightened his sense of isolation. He regretted his failure to secure the creature comforts that others had, but insisted that he was going to continue to make his mark even though others continued to exploit his name. He referred to himself as someone who "cut off a certain part of their pain centers in order to function." The letter requested that they not meet that year, and was signed "X." The letter wasn't just bitter, it was filled to overflowing with despair and loathing.

Throughout the spring and early summer, when Abbie got to thinking about his life he often seemed to fall off a cliff into a black hole of hopelessness and bitterness. On the other hand, as the *Playboy* article progressed, with Jonathan doing the lion's share of the work, Abbie's enthusiasm for it reached new heights. He thought he had a shot at being the shining knight on the white horse who was going to dishonor Bush, end the Republican reign, restore hope and decency to the American people, and install a progressive Democrat in the White House. He felt that he could go down in history as the most important politically active Jew since Jesus Christ.

For my part, I understood his bitterness and despair, and I even understood that he had a shot at bringing down Bush and with him the dominance of the Republican Party—after all, *Playboy* was not *The New Hope Intelligencer*. But what disturbed me, other than the fact that we still didn't have a smoking gun on Iran-Contra, was having to watch Abbie bounce back and forth between such extremes of euphoria and despair.

It is interesting to me that in the letter to Sheila he bitterly describes his having to "cut off . . . pain centers in order to function." It was a clear and piercingly accurate reference to his self-medication, and perhaps indicated his own increasing awareness that its meager comfort might eventually entail a very high cost.

The public perception of manic depression concentrates its awareness on the depression. But it isn't by the depression that you will understand Abbie, or any other manic-depressive. According to what Abbie described to me over and over again, it is the mania, a natural high of incredible intensity, that affects them most powerfully. The world seen through the lens of his mania was a playground in which he could do anything. Abbie used to say, "There's no drug in the world that could take you to that level." When he was manic, he didn't want to come down.

In June, Abbie and Jonathan sent *Playboy* a rough draft of the article and a few days later *Playboy* requested a meeting with the authors to see the evidence they had to back up their claims. Abbie was thrilled to have the opportunity to present their case in person. On the morning of June 16, he left New Hope in his relatively new Ford Escort with a large case full of papers on the passenger seat next to him. He was to meet Jonathan at Newark Airport, then fly to Chicago for the afternoon meeting. Originally they were to fly separately and meet up in Chicago, but Abbie was intent on their flying together, "just like Woodward and Bernstein," the *Washington Post* reporters who broke the Watergate scandal. He was in a manic state, euphoric, wired, admitting no obstacles.

Not far from the airport, driving with one hand on the wheel and the other holding an ice cream cone, Abbie ran the Escort into the back of a trailer truck, totalling the car and sustaining very serious injuries to his ribs, feet, and hands, as well as multiple contusions. Without a thought to his injuries and impervious to the pain, Abbie grabbed his papers, walked away from the wrecked car, and hailed a taxi for the last mile to the airport.

Arriving just a few minutes before his flight, he called me and started talking in a stream as soon as I picked up the phone: "This fucking truck, this fucking truck swerved; fucking truck." I didn't get a chance to ask him what truck. Then, just as suddenly as he'd began, his tone changed, grew quieter and conspiratorial: "Jack, don't believe anything you might hear on the radio or see in the newspapers tonight. Whatever it is, it's not true." He didn't want me to worry if it was reported that he'd had a serious car accident. "Don't worry about it," he continued, "I'm fine. Gotta catch my plane." And he was gone.

Still reeling from the accident, Abbie walked into the *Playboy* meeting in a manic frenzy. His mood prevented him from making the impression he had so wanted to convey. That night he left his hotel in the middle of the night and went to Northwestern Hospital for some tests but still seemed hardly to acknowledge that he might be walking around with serious injuries. After boarding the flight home, he smoked a joint in the restroom before the plane left the runway, setting off the smoke detector. He was removed from the plane and placed on another flight. Instead of quietly conceding he'd had a bad trip, Abbie decided to sue Continental Airways for what he now called the false arrest, and threatened a boycott of the airline as well. When he got home, he dashed off detailed letters on the proposed boycott to Leonard Weinglass and Jerry Lefcourt, with carbon copies to Burt Schneider and me. Abbie seemed determined to turn a small personal matter into a major political campaign. And still he had done almost nothing to look after his injuries.

Back in New Hope, Abbie's manic phase continued unabated. On June 25, he did a marathon twelve-hour interview with writer Mark Hertsgaard, who'd been working for months on an article about him. Throughout the day, Abbie had been increasingly rude and belligerent to the journalist. And still he managed to overlook his injuries by means of the intense activity, which distracted him. Then, in the early morning of June 26, 1988, he awoke in terrific pain in his broken foot. He'd run out of painkillers and felt desperate. At 6:15 A.M., he called Hertsgaard and told him to come right away to drive him from New Hope to a hospital in Manhattan.

Hertsgaard arrived at Abbie's apartment to find him crawling around awkwardly on all fours gathering items for the trip. He immediately began ordering Hertsgaard around, and once they got into the car, despite—or perhaps because of—his pain, Abbie talked in an almost nonstop flow all the way into Manhattan, as if the ride were just the continuation of yesterday's interview. Getting into what he liked to call his performance mode seemed to help Abbie drown out the pain.

When they arrived at the hospital, Abbie got the attention of an orderly and commanded, "I'm Abbie Hoffman. You gotta let me in." It worked. And as they carted him off in a wheelchair, Abbie was "laughing and wisecracking all the way." It didn't occur to Hertsgaard that day that Abbie might be manic-depressive, but by the time he'd finished writing his article after Abbie's death, as he came to understand the nature of Abbie's internal struggle, Hertsgaard became convinced that the out-of-control behavior he'd seen was darkly symptomatic of Abbie's disease.[3]

Only now, ten days after his car accident, did Abbie learn in the hospital that his foot had been badly broken in several places, among other injuries. Casts were put on both his hand and his foot. But otherwise nothing he learned from his examination changed the course of treatment he'd already started. With the accident, his self-medication routine had shifted significantly in favor of painkillers, especially Percocet, a powerful narcotic. He found they killed the pain in his foot and seemed to help calm his mood. They also accounted for the slurred speech that would soon become a prominent and alarming new symptom.

In July, Abbie and Jonathan attended the Democratic National Convention to research their book on the election, and afterward Abbie tried to get back into a working routine. But the pain from his injuries was a near-constant irritant and kept him at a low ebb.

On August 22, Abbie sent a handwritten letter to Brandeis, offering the university his collected papers: "This November I will be 52, and I think it's time I started remembering where I hid early letters, manuscripts, tapes, etc. . . . and since there's no room in my small apartment they should be collected in Brandeis University's library. . . ." The Brandeis Library responded with enthusiasm to Abbie's offer. But the negotiations bogged down, and the process came to a halt without Abbie having donated his papers.

Still wearing the cast on his foot, Abbie traveled to Chicago in late August for the " '68+20" reunion of the 1968 Chicago protests. In a spirited interview with a *Chicago Sun-Times* reporter, Abbie reminded people that college kids today weren't as different from students in the '60s as the mythology might suggest. "You know who were the two most admired men on college campuses in 1968?" Abbie asked. "Richard Nixon and John Wayne." Abbie was one of the most sought-after participants of the highly publicized affair. His spirits lifted, but on his return to New Hope he fell right back into his exhausted and apathetic state.

Bookings for fall speaking engagements usually started coming in in August, but this year there were very few dates. Abbie felt the blame lay with his lecture bureau, Greater Talent. Checks from the agency had been coming weeks late, and objections were being raised to Abbie's expenses on the road. Abbie no longer trusted Greater Talent, decided he wanted to leave the agency, and asked me to intervene. I contacted APB in Boston, the agency Bob Walker had started in the '60s and which still represented many celebrities on the Left. We decided to switch, even though it meant probably losing or at least delaying pending payments from Greater Talent that were due us.

Earlier in the summer, completely out of the blue, Abbie had started talking about launching a new career for himself as a stand-up comedian.

"It's what I've always really wanted to do, Jack," he'd say.

"Abbs, you're getting a little too old for this," was my response. But I don't think he even heard me. We talked about it again and again. I had spent almost my whole life supporting Abbie in his decisions. This time, I felt he would be making a mistake and told him so. His plan was to take the funny parts of his speeches and present them on stage by themselves. It seemed all wrong to me, a debasement of who he was and of his message that needed to be heard.

Abbie listened intently, didn't argue with me, never said I was wrong, and only questioned me as to the particulars of my objections. But in the end, nothing I said deterred him. His debut stand-up appearance was set for Monday, August 29 in New York City. He called me the day before to ask me to be there with him.

* * *

Early Monday evening, after driving down from Massachusetts with my dog Lois in the passenger seat, I picked up Abbie and took him out to my favorite Manhattan dive, where we had hot dogs and papaya juice. Then we headed for the club, called Stand Up, on the Upper West Side. As we walked in we could hear the packed audience responding warmly to the set before Abbie's. Among small, dimly lit tables, a hundred people—mostly Abbie fans from the '60s—were already crowded into a space meant for half that number. In the street, there was a line, mostly thirty- to fifty-year-olds, mostly white. We went downstairs to a storeroom reserved for the artists and waited.

The stage was very small, the only props were a hand-held microphone and a barstool. As Abbie climbed onto the stage, still wearing the cast on his foot, I gave him the thumbs-up from where I stood on the sidelines. What struck me first was the feeling that Abbie didn't belong here. He looked old, almost feeble, to me. The laughter echoed in my ears: I could not tell if they were laughing at his jokes or at him.

For his whole life Abbie had been moving toward a kind of respectability, and here he was being laughed at. Lenny Bruce had gotten his laughs by risking, on stage, everything he thought and felt. But Abbie was going more for humor that was low-brow, Borscht-Belt stuff, not making use of his true brilliance at all. I decided they were laughing at him.

It took about a half hour before I realized that I had started crying. It was as if Abbie were finally conceding that he wasn't serious after all. So many years of trying to get people to see things his way, only to end suited up the way his enemies liked to think of him, as a buffoon. Of course there were many friends in the audience, but that didn't matter to me. What they were witnessing, I thought, was someone making a fool of himself.

I left the club, returned to my van, and sat with Lois and cried freely, remembering the talent show Abbie, Phyllis, and I put together in our basement as kids. I remembered our innocence then and realized how little we had grown up. And maybe what I felt was nothing more than the horror of growing old.

* * *

The October issue of *Playboy* featuring "An Election Held Hostage" hit the stands right on schedule in late September. The article was well-written, hard-hitting, and deserves credit for being the first attempt to pin the tail on the ass for all to see—to connect George Bush to Iran-Contra in a national setting as prominent as *Playboy*. But there was no public outcry. The article was largely ignored. It was as if even Abbie's strong achievements of this period, like the *Playboy* article, had begun to have a kind of disembodied air about them. Abbie wasn't Lenny Bruce and he wasn't Woodward or Bernstein, either. Missing from the *Playboy* article is the strength of the voice that wrote it. Indeed the bulk of the actual writing had been done by Abbie's co-author, Jonathan Silvers.

Abbie used to turn down most film or television offers, but that September he had chosen to appear at Toronto's Festival of Festivals for the world premier of Morley Markson's *Growing Up in America*, a powerful documentary on the '60s that featured Abbie. And now in December he was in Dallas filming Oliver Stone's *Born on the Fourth of July,* in which Abbie plays himself, and which Stone later dedicated to him.

Meanwhile, for most of the past year Abbie had been working on reissuing his three '60s classics, *Revolution for the Hell of It, Woodstock Nation,* and *Steal This Book* in a new edition. It was a project that Abbie believed in passionately. They were a part of himself he was determined to see live on. "I love my books as much as I do my kids," he'd written just a year earlier in *Steal This Urine Test*.[4] The books had sold almost a million copies in the late '60s and early '70s, and currently there was a '60s revival going on. Abbie still felt strongly that the books represented a solid and lasting contribution to the Movement and to history—that they belonged to the future. He stood by what he had written, every word. He wanted to add new introductions but not to change or revise any statement or opinion. He felt very much at peace with that period of his life. "No apologies or regrets for the sixties," as he so often said.[5] But after he'd made the rounds of all the major publishing houses, he was turned down everywhere.

In December 1988 he placed a classified advertisement in *The Nation:* "Serious publishers interested in reprinting 3 60s classics as 1 quality paperback immediately contact: Abbie Hoffman" with his post office box address in New Hope. A letter of interest came back from Four Walls Eight Windows, an independent publisher based in Manhattan. Abbie called them right away. Within a few weeks, Abbie had a new publisher.

But the pendulum was swinging wildly now, from extreme to extreme, from stand-up comedy to the high seriousness of "An Election Held Hostage." His attempt to go after Bush with Iran-Contra was as bold and incisive as his new career in comedy was pitiful and desperate. Like a kid, he was still testing to see how far and how high he could go before the ropes snapped.

In conversations with Joan that fall, Abbie described his relying heavily on Ativan. In part because of her experience as a women's health counselor, Abbie had grown used to discussing his mental illness with her. He said that he needed to monitor himself every day to see where he was, to make sure he wasn't getting too manic, and that he controlled the mania by titrating the Ativan—taking a little more or less as the mania rose or subsided.

Looking at them now, with the benefit of hindsight, conversations like these cut both ways, and painfully. Abbie was trying hard, almost heroically, to subdue his illness. At the same time, he was attempting to do so on his own, and this in itself was a typical and powerful manifestation of the very illness he was trying to control.

Chapter Sixteen

1989, The Final Days

There's always going to be someone who is the naughty judge, someone who's going to be the governor who double-crosses the people, and there has to be a me. If there isn't a me, we're in big trouble.

—ABBIE

THE LAST MONTHS OF Abbie's life saw him lose his grip, one by one, on the things that mattered most to him. The married idyll he'd wanted with Johanna, complete with their little house up on the river, gave way to his sense that their relationship was on the rocks. He became convinced that Ma, who had been diagnosed with cancer, was dying. Still frequently suffering from the injuries sustained in the car accident, and dependent on drugs to control the pain, he decided that he was no longer politically effective, and even wondered if he was still famous. He felt his life might be all over. He didn't want it to be. But he thought it might be.

He had found ways to sustain his optimism for the longest time in the face of overwhelming adversity. His optimism had always been a part of him—intuitive, spontaneous, practical, and inseparable from the rest of who he was and what inspired him. Now, feeling hopeless, Abbie was finding that living without his optimism was not something he knew how to do.

In late 1979, when lithium had been prescribed for him to help control his manic episodes, it had also been associated with myriad physical problems. Abbie hadn't liked lithium. It affected his speech, and he feared it also affected his thought processes. He felt it aged him. He took it somewhat regularly for a few years, especially while under Nathan Kline's care. Then Nate Kline died, and things had been more or less out of control ever since. Abbie had tried to work with other psychiatrists in the New York area, but none could inspire his trust the way Kline had.

Ironically, after Abbie's March 1983 suicide attempt, he had regained his balance for a while, having acquired for perhaps the first time a healthy fear of the abyss. He joined a manic-depressive support group in the New York area. He started to read up on the medical literature on manic depression, and throughout the '80s Abbie's knowledge on the subject increased steadily. One entire bookshelf in his New Hope apartment was filled with books on manic-depressive illness. Abbie had decided to write his own book on the subject. He was going to call it *The Hell of It.* In the mid and late '80s, on more than one occasion, Abbie said to me, "There isn't a day that goes by that I don't think about my manic depression."

But as early as 1983, he was self-medicating. When he traveled on the college speaking tour circuit, he was never without a zippered black leather pill case, like an old country doctor. As I remember it, there were at least six bottles of pills in that case. All the medications were legally prescribed, not least the powerful antihistamines he'd taken all his life, but the doctor who was carefully monitoring how all the different medications interacted with one another was Doctor Abbie. The more his illness seemed to resist prescribed management, the more he felt that he had nothing to lose by trying to do better on his own. And after the car accident in June 1988, when the powerful narcotic painkiller Percocet was added to the mix, Abbie was laying out and dipping into his drug armamentarium according to his moods in a typical, and very dangerous, display of manic-depressive behavior.

In January 1989, Abbie dipped lower. Not wanting to be alone, he started to spend more time at Johanna's apartment—most of it lying on the couch. When in New Hope he sometimes didn't get out of bed at all. He wasn't interested in the Super Bowl—for the first time ever. He had no desire to go out. We still spoke, as usual, nearly every day, sometimes more. But he didn't show his usual dynamism. Neither sports nor current events could break the hold of his lethargy. When I asked him if he was taking his medication, he would answer,

"Yeah, yeah, yeah," which made me think that he wasn't. And now at the end of our conversations, if he was at Johanna's, he would pass the phone to her and she would take over, filling me in on how Abbie had spent the day and how concerned she was about him.

In the January 18 issue of *The Guardian*, one of the few surviving Movement newsweeklies,[1] there appeared an apologetic-sounding strategy paper by Mark Rudd, one of the '60s leaders Abbie respected most. Rudd's heartfelt article was clearly the expression of a deep-seated bitterness that Abbie understood only too well. Speaking as a former SDS leader, he zeroed in on the 1969–1971 period, when SDS came apart at the seams, giving way to the more violent Weathermen faction: "The destruction of SDS and the rise of Weathermen . . . were historical crimes," Rudd wrote. "Not only did we wind up killing three of our own people, but even worse we helped murder the organized anti-war movement at the height of the war. Vast numbers of campus militants became paralyzed and demoralized by our guilt-based, idealistic arguments. . . . Our vanguard militancy led only to isolation and defeat."[2]

Abbie was enraged enough by what Rudd had written to rise out of his torpor. Even in the despair that was now darkening most of his waking hours, Abbie's mind was acute. His vision may have changed with the times, but it remained undiluted. His political beliefs were as firm now as they had ever been. And one thing Abbie could not stand was revisionism. Within minutes of reading Rudd's article, Abbie began drafting his response, which appeared in *The Guardian* a month later. It was vintage Abbie: impassioned, witty, chiding, eloquent, urgent.

It's good to see Mark Rudd thinking aloud in public again, but as much as I respect his historic and continuing contribution . . . I don't agree with his one-dimensional caricature of "60s" politics. . . . He chooses to create [a] false dichotomy between those who believe in nonviolence as a way of life and those who believe in "armed struggle. . . ." Successful social movements—revolutions, if you'll excuse an old-fashioned word—have always rested on a unity of

both philosophies. . . . Revolutionaries are born to love,
they are not born to kill.

If the choices in this world were between war and
peace, only the mentally deranged would choose war, but
life and global politics are not that easy. The choice has al-
ways been between justice and injustice, oppression and re-
sistance. . . . Good tacticians will be those who best respond
to the objective and potential conditions in which they find
themselves.

The name "Mark Rudd," just like the name "Jane
Fonda," means something. Having some regrets in life is a
human condition. [But it is] the architects of repression and
imperial wars [who] should be doing the apologizing, not
those who stood boldly in opposition.[3]

The thrust of Abbie's letter was that an apology sends the wrong message to "those who struggle on the side of justice today and tomorrow"—that it is in effect a shirking of the responsibility of leadership. And certainly the reason Rudd's confession got Abbie so riled was that the despair and bitterness expressed by Rudd were feelings shared, at least to a degree, by Abbie privately. Abbie's point, as he made very clear, was that Rudd shouldn't lose sight of the larger political debate in his sorrow. Abbie had not made that mistake himself. Personally, he was overwhelmed with regret; the marriages, children, wives, friends, and political battles won and lost were all piled up by the end of his fifty-two years like one of those mile-long, rush-hour California freeway car wrecks you see on the nightly news. Yet he stood stubbornly by every position, every book and article, every march, every civil disobedience, every cause that he had taken up in thirty years of activism. No regrets. He had never let his disappointments color his political analysis.

Abbie and Mark Rudd shared a common sense of loss, and both were still active in the fight for social justice. They were among those whose resistance to oppression had been lifelong. But their personal responses to a similar dilemma had lately diverged. Abbie, in 1989 no different than he was in 1969, was ready to die. What he was not ready to do was admit defeat. Sensing his own life drawing to a close, beginning to put his papers in order, arranging for the reprinting of his books so that they would be available after his death, contemplating suicide, perhaps even planning his suicide, he held ever more tightly the beliefs he had always held and stood ready like some aging knight of the Round Table to defend the Movement against attacks from any quarter.

When Abbie wrote that the names Mark Rudd and Jane Fonda "mean something," that they "have some responsibility [to those] who fought beside them," he was surely thinking that the name "Abbie Hoffman" meant as much or more and of his own comrades in arms. Abbie did not want to let people down in the way he felt Rudd had. And, rightly or wrongly, he may have thought, in his deep and seemingly endless weariness and apathy, that it would be better to die than to stop fighting. He may even have felt that it was necessary to die soon, before his own sense of loss and bitterness forced him publicly to recant as Rudd had, or in some other way to weaken politically. If Abbie was thinking about suicide, he would certainly have been analyzing it tactically, as something that might give added weight to his memory, or otherwise contribute to that for which he'd lived.

In the Hertsgaard interview from late 1988, Abbie spoke freely of death and claimed to have overcome his fear of it while he was a civil rights worker in the early '60s. Abbie also said he was "absolutely convinced I'll be fighting until I die." The converse of the statement would also have rung true for Abbie: that he would have to die the moment he became absolutely convinced he had stopped fighting. Hertsgaard asked him a follow-up question: "You're not planning to do that anytime soon, are you?"

"Well, I don't exactly get a choice in the matter," Abbie had replied, laughing hard.[4]

At the end of January a friendly and apologetic letter arrived from Anita requesting money to help with america's upkeep. "You know I hate to ask you," she offered, but she didn't ask how he was or what he was doing, and in Abbie's depressed state that made it the wrong communication at the wrong time. Several times in conversations in February and March, Abbie harked back to Anita's letter.

"That's all she wants," he'd say, "money I don't have." It was the first time I had heard him complain like that about Anita, almost as if he confused her in his mind with Sheila, as if he had entered into a delusional state in which he could no longer differentiate between his first two wives.

In mid-February, Abbie suggested to his psychiatrist that the various prescribed medications he was taking weren't working. Seeing himself slipping further and further into the black hole, as the depths of depression are called, he asked for something new. His psychiatrist prescribed the antidepressant Prozac, giving Abbie some free samples to start with and a prescription to fill for more.[5] According to Johanna, both she and his psychiatrist knew of his own concurrent efforts at self-medication with painkillers. But I wonder if either of them knew or understood the full extent of his self-medication. It is well documented in the *Complete Guide to Prescription and Nonprescription Drugs,* among other places, that using Prozac and Percocet in combination can increase the depressant effects of both drugs.

I found that where recently Abbie had been calling me twice as often as I called him, now I was having to place the calls. And he showed little interest in our conversations. Upcoming speaking engagements had usually been the subject of intense, animated discussions, but now he couldn't care less. Spring was usually the busiest time of the year. But there was only one speaking engagement in February, at Oklahoma State, none in March, and only three or four in April. It was the lightest his schedule had been in seven years.

And yet, at the same time, Abbie agreed to an unusually large number of interviews, some of which he had been turning down for years. He let independent radio producer Stuart Hutchinson come over and interview him for days on end, and was similarly generous with Chicago writer John Schultz, who was working on a new book on the 1968 Chicago convention, and with Howard Goodman, who was writing a long piece on Abbie for the Jewish-oriented, Philadelphia-based glossy magazine, *Inside.*

Abbie was tying up loose ends. He had the energy, somehow, to involve himself in a clear-minded way with the past. But for the first time in his life, the present almost seemed to bore him, as if time passing were itself now an enemy, signifying nothing more than that he was growing older, getting less famous, dying.

The one political battle that cut through his depressed state during this period was the Salman Rushdie affair. Abbie's view was that the policy of some bookstore chains not to carry Rushdie's book, *The Satanic Verses*, out of fear of reprisals from Islamic fundamentalists was an extraordinary act of censorship. Likening the situation to what he had faced with *Steal This Book*, Abbie saw himself as uniquely qualified to organize on Rushdie's behalf. The combination of censorship plus government complacency—given our government's reluctance to condemn the death sentence that had been passed against Rushdie by the Ayatollah—energized Abbie. He not only went to every demonstration and spoke at several key events but was a tireless behind-the-scenes organizer.

The following week, *The Phil Donahue Show* aired a special broadcast on the Rushdie affair with a number of famous authors—many of them the same ones who had first gotten involved after a wake-up call from Abbie. Abbie was not invited to be one of the participants, and the snub left him feeling doubly crushed, both as an organizer and as a writer. He kept up his organizing efforts in support of Rushdie, but in his mentally exhausted state he seemed especially sensitive to perceived attacks. As never before, his guard was down.

In the *Inside* interview, Abbie expressed his loneliness succinctly:

> *Being so heavily into politics is not the best way to make friends. I'm closest in a personal sense to the ideas I believe in, and in an abstract sense with a global movement. So there is a kind of emptiness around.*[6]

So there is a kind of emptiness around . . .

By late February I could feel Abbie withdrawing from me as if he were being pulled out to sea by a strong tide. I experienced the distance between us growing greater from moment to moment. Worst of all, my awareness of what was happening was not accompanied by any commensurate stirring to action; I felt completely helpless. In my own head, irrationally, we had come to the point where nothing I might do was going to make a difference, almost as if Abbie's depression was so strong as to weaken not only his resolve but also mine and anybody else's.

Then it was "March Madness," NCAA college basketball finals. Abbie and I always went full steam into our analysis of the games, trying to identify each individual player according to his strengths and weaknesses, betting beyond our limit. But this year Eli, our bookmaker, hadn't heard from Abbie at all. Abbie was $480 into his $500 limit from old bets, but that had never stopped him before. Eli called me to express his concern. He wanted me to let Abbie know that he would raise his limit, and to make sure everything was all right. Not knowing what else to say, I told him I would pass the message along.

Every year in Worcester, a group of us build a float to enter in the St. Patrick's Day parade in the name of our friends the Aboody family who own the El Morocco Restaurant. Abbie, when he was around, me, Jo Aboody and Richie—we'd all really get into it, arguing for almost the whole year leading up to it about how long, how high, what color, and anything else we could think of. Some years we modeled the float after a popular song or a Broadway play. That year, 1989, our float was the "Yellow Brick Road," after the Wizard of Oz, and we'd already spent hours discussing how yellow the yellow should be. By early March, we were hard at work weekends in the Worcester Bus Terminal, which had been loaned to us free of charge. But we still hadn't come to a decision about whether to go with a cadmium yellow or something more golden. Richie suggested we call Abbie to get him to settle it. So we called him.

I don't remember details of the conversation, but afterwards, Richie, our friend since we were six or eight years old, said, "Jesus, he sounds really down and out." And in response, before I could even think the words I was speaking, I said, "I'm afraid he's going to try it again"—meaning suicide. Until that moment, I hadn't let the thought into my mind, although it had been there, silently waiting. And now suddenly I felt the full force of all the fear I had been trying to protect myself from, coming over me like a blast of heat.

I called Johanna at her apartment in New York to tell her that I thought Abbie might be getting ready to attempt suicide again. She shared my feeling and seemed to be experiencing the same kind of helplessness I felt. Since she saw Abbie more regularly than I did, the pain of watching him slip away may have been even worse for her. And for Johanna, as for me, feelings of helplessness may have been compounded by anger at what we may have felt was his abandonment of us. But all she really said was that Abbie was trying a new medication, and that she was trying to visit him more.

According to Dr. Harry Markow, the psychiatrist Abbie was seeing at the time, Abbie had been showing signs of increased depression since early March. What he was depressed about, according to Dr. Markow, were the broken ribs and significant injuries to the hand and foot he'd received in the car accident. And this interpretation is largely accurate. Even after the casts had come off in the fall of 1988, Abbie had remained in excruciating pain.

Dr. Markow wanted to hospitalize Abbie for his depression. Abbie refused. The reasoning Abbie gave to the psychiatrist was remarkable. "Mr. Hoffman stated he had no desire to live," Dr. Markow told the Deputy Coroner, "yet claimed he would not commit suicide."[7] That this psychiatrist would accept such reasonings from a patient, and that he would seem unconcerned about the combination of the Prozac with the Percocet Abbie was taking, seems unbelievable to me now. But these were things that only came out afterward.

Abbie had a high threshold for pain. But in the winter of 1988 and then in the last months of his life, he would often raise the subject of the injuries from the accident with me in phone conversations. And each time we talked about it, the scenario seemed to have worsened: In the fall of 1988 there was the possibility that he might need bone surgery on his foot; the stairs up to Johanna's apartment were almost a torture; in January 1989, he was still talking about the possibility of surgery, this time on his hand: "Who knows?" he said, "I may never play tennis again." What he didn't tell me during these conversations was how he was killing his pain with Percocet. Others knew that he was taking the drug, which might have worsened his depression and conflicted with his other medications at the same time as it killed the pain. They knew, but they didn't know what they knew.

Johanna used to tell me how conscientious Abbie was about taking his Prozac. Once I asked her what the pills looked like.

"You know," she said, "little white tablets."

I did not know it at the time, but Prozac comes in very distinctive two-tone capsules. The little white tablets were the Percocet that Abbie was taking in addition to or instead of the Prozac, blunting the psychological and physical pain rather than treating it. But he wasn't about to tell that to Johanna.

On March 27, suffering from a bad flu and visibly exhausted, Abbie traveled to Jericho High School on Long Island to speak on the occasion of Human Awareness Day, an event organized by Students for Social Responsibility. And on April 4, in his last public appearance, Abbie appeared on stage at Vanderbilt University in Nashville, Tennessee, along with Bobby Seale and Timothy Leary. He somehow found the energy to perform but looked and sounded ragged as hell. When he got back to New Hope, he talked about killing himself to both his landlord Michael Waldron and Johanna. According to Waldron, Abbie asked him if he could hang himself from the rafters in the barn. Before the flabbergasted landlord could respond, Johanna stepped in, saying to Abbie, "Don't even kid around like that."[8]

Johanna and I were speaking frequently on the phone. We both had Abbie's last suicide attempt, in March of 1983, very much on our minds. I knew the risk, but I didn't see a way out. Johanna was placing her hope in the Prozac. She explained that it can take around six weeks to kick in. It had already been six weeks since he'd started taking it. "It should kick in any day," she said.

And it is possible that the Prozac was beginning to take effect. Some experts say that when a manic-depressive is in "the black hole" it is virtually impossible to make love. Yet Johanna would tell me later that four days before he died, on Saturday night, they were staying over in Abbie's apartment and enjoyed their best lovemaking in a long time. On Sunday she returned to the city and called me that evening. But there seemed to be very little to say.

On Monday, April 10, I called Abbie in the early afternoon to fill him in on a visit Phyllis and I had made that morning to Ma's doctor.

Ma had lymphoma and her doctor advised us to prepare for the worst: Our mother might die within thirty days. Abbie listened to me for about twenty minutes. The less he said, the more afraid for him I became. I pleaded with him not to do anything that would hurt him or us. I couldn't come out and say the word "suicide." The closest I could come was, "Don't get any ideas," and "You can't leave me now." But Abbie was so unresponsive that I wasn't sure he even understood me. "You're the patriarch," I tried. That got through to him, sort of. "Well, maybe it's time you took charge," he finally said.

I spent the rest of the afternoon attending to business matters in my office, trying to contain the pain and loneliness I was feeling. Around 5:00 P.M. my part-time secretary and friend Carole came in to type up the letters I'd written. She asked me what was the matter. Crying again, I said, "He's going to kill himself."

According to phone records, on Tuesday morning at around 11:30 A.M., Abbie put in a call to Loyola College in Baltimore, where he was supposed to speak that afternoon. He told them that he was cancelling the date because his mother was dying.[9] Given his depressed state of mind, the possibility that she might die became the certainty that she was about to die. And Abbie was taking the news very hard.

At around 1:30 P.M., Abbie left the apartment and drove to the post office to mail two letters: one contained a check for $1,500 to the IRS, his estimated quarterly federal tax payment, and the other a check for $4,000 to his accountant, the balance due on his state and federal income taxes.[10]

There is no indication that Abbie saw or talked to anyone else before he died. On Tuesday night I tried to call him to see how the Loyola speech went, but his answering machine was turned off. Sometime between Tuesday and Wednesday afternoon, Abbie emptied 150 or more 30-milligram phenobarbitals into a glass of Glenlivet single malt Scotch whiskey, gulped that down, and then filled and swallowed four or five more glasses of the Scotch as fast as he could. It only took a few minutes for the drug to take hold of him, and then he lay down to die.

Around 6:00 P.M. on Wednesday, April 12, Johanna called Michael Waldron to ask him to check on Abbie since he wasn't picking up his phone and she was getting worried. Waldron used his key to get into the apartment at around 6:30 P.M. and found him, with his boots on, lying fully clothed on his side in the bed. He'd pulled the covers over him, his hands were nestled under his cheek, like a sleeping child. The apartment was immaculately clean. There was no note.

Waldron called Johanna right away from Abbie's apartment, and Johanna reached Joan at our home in Framingham. When I got home and Joan told me, at first I only screamed and sobbed. Then the thought in my mind turned to the possiblity that maybe he was still alive, maybe he only seemed dead. I got on the phone and pleaded with Johanna and Michael to call the police right away so that they could get an ambulance there. Then I started to worry about Ma. If Abbie really was dead, it was important that Ma didn't hear it from some reporter. I drove to Ruth Street, making calls from the van during the half-hour ride, and by the time I got there, although the news hadn't yet been announced, I no longer had any hope that Abbie was still alive.

The Solebury township police department clocked Waldron's call at 7:57 P.M. and a police officer arrived at Abbie's home at 8:09 P.M. By the 10:00 P.M. news, Abbie was the lead story on local television and radio, and a major story nationally. On Thursday morning I was met at the Philadelphia airport by Kathy Devlin, Abbie's trusted secretary, accompanied by one of his Del-AWARE colleagues, who took me to Abbie's apartment.

It was the first time I'd visited him in New Hope, at the $400-a-month converted turkey coop, where he'd been living the last few years. It made sense to me somehow that this had been Abbie's last refuge. Cinderblocks and wood boards held CDs and books—works on a wide range of revolutionary struggles around the world, one shelf devoted to books on manic-depressive illness, and multiple copies of his own writings, especially *Revolution for the Hell of It, Woodstock Nation,* and *Steal This Book.* Between rows of books were the television and VCR, with a tape of *The Godfather* on video and ready to be played. To one side was his desk—immaculately clean—and next to it a computer station. I'd known his personal computer was linked electronically to several counterculture networks. But seeing it there in all its splendor was a little like seeing him sitting there.

About five feet from the desk, on the coffee table in front of the couch, the chess pieces were all arranged and ready to play. I could not take my eyes off them.

Over the kitchen counter hung a framed front page of the *New York Post* of September 4, 1980, when he surfaced after the years underground, with the headline: "Here's Abbie!" On the other walls of the apartment were posters or framed photos: the familiar silk-screened raised fist over the word "Strike!", a *National Lampoon* cover on Abbie, a Grateful Dead poster, a promotional poster of Abbie holding a test tube for his most recent book, *Steal This Urine Test*; Abbie with Jimmy Carter, with Daniel Ortega, with Jerry Rubin, with John Lennon and Yoko Ono. And there, above his computer, was the autographed photo I'd gotten for him of our childhood idol Fats Domino. Over Fats's signature it said, "To Abbie, Keep on Rockin'." Seeing the photo proudly displayed on Abbie's wall made me feel close to him: The part of him that loved Fats was the part I'd grown up with, and felt closest to. For all the changes Abbie had gone through, I thought, he hadn't changed much. I found myself shaking my head. It was hard to see all these signs of life with my brother dead.

Reporters and television camera crews were milling about Abbie's apartment the day I was there. I heard that one of the journalists was Andrea Fine from *People,* and I introduced myself. We started talking and I was impressed by her intelligence and sensitivity. But in the back of my mind I was thinking what Abbie would have been thinking: If I play this right, we can get the cover of *People.* I wanted that cover badly. I would have felt I'd disappointed Abbie if I didn't get it.

That's how he always liked to play it. For every battle won, Abbie liked to have a scar or two to show, indicating the price he'd paid for victory. And even when he lost, he liked to have some gain as proof that the fight hadn't been completely futile. For the next few hours I didn't let Andrea out of my sight, and I would follow up with calls to talk about my brother during the next few days. Abbie's *punim* took the whole front cover of *People* the following week, along with a six-page photo spread inside. It didn't bring my brother back, but it helped me feel that we were still a team even though we were one man short.

Abbie's death made the lead story on the local and national network evening news all over the country. And it was front page news in every newspaper. *The New York Times* printed not one but two different obituaries on successive days. There would be three large-scale memorial celebrations, one in Worcester which I organized, one that brought 6,000 partygoers to the Palladium in New York, and one in Los Angeles. Testimonials came in from all the far corners. Chicago columnist Mike Royko, who had covered him many times over the years, portrayed Abbie as a George Bailey for our times. "Now most of his 1968 pals have wised up," Royko wrote; "But Abbie? There he was, a graying 52, still protesting this or that injustice. . . . In the age of the bottom line, he had become the odd man out."

On the following Tuesday a toxicology report was released that listed the broad variety of drugs found in Abbie's apartment—grass, hash, psilocybin mushrooms, LSD, traces of MDMA and straws with traces of cocaine. None of these drugs were Abbie's, and none were found in his blood. Johanna has said that the pot, MDMA, and LSD were hers. The rest belonged to friends and visitors. Prescription drugs found included Ornade, a strong antihistamine; Temazepam; Xanax; Prozac; Inderal, a beta blocker; and Ativan. The prescriptions for all of the legal drugs had been filled recently, five of them in March, one in January, and one again in April. But none of these was found in Abbie's blood, and once the cause of death was established, repeated requests from the family to conduct further tests to ascertain whether Prozac was present in Abbie's body were denied. The only substance found in Abbie's blood, other than the booze and the phenobarbital that killed him, although it was notably absent from the above list, was the drug Abbie took most frequently, which would have augmented his depression and which may indirectly have been most responsible for his suicide—Percocet.

A few weeks after Abbie died, I would visit Johanna in her apartment in Manhattan and she would take me into the bathroom and show me two empty amber bottles labelled by Percocet's generic name, oxycodone.

"You know what these are?" I said.

She shook her head.

"Percocet." I told her. The bottles she was holding explained to me why the coroner's report had not listed the drug among those found in Abbie's apartment. Someone must have thought they'd held the phenobarbitals that had killed Abbie, and had removed what they considered to be incriminating evidence. She kept the bottles in a misguided effort to protect Abbie's memory.

Immediately after the release of the toxicology results, I called a press conference in Worcester to say I did not believe that Abbie could have committed suicide without leaving a note, and to announce the next day's memorial service at Worcester's Temple Emanuel. In those first hours and days I still couldn't accept—it was literally beyond the reach of my imagination—that it might have been suicide—that Abbie's pain and desperation could have been so great that he would have taken his own life. Although I'd been fearing Abbie's imminent suicide for weeks, facing the reality now, I couldn't come to terms with it. All the national networks and local media came. Even in my anguished state, as I stood in the middle of that room packed with journalists and electronic equipment, I felt some relief knowing that now Abbie's memorial service/celebration would probably be packed.

The next day we marched in a crowd large enough to block traffic from Ma's house to the temple, with our arms linked and Pete Seeger leading us in song. Once there, the service included a variety of friends who each said their *Kaddish* in their own way. Bernie Gilgun said, "To know Abbie was to know his family. . . . They filled his life and when he needed them they were there." Bill Walton, who'd met Abbie as a fugitive, described my brother as "a great man who gave everything he had, and more." Burt Schneider said, "It is my belief that Abbie died of an overdose of caring and love." And our cousin Sydney Schanberg, speaking for the family, told us, "He had the courage for the rest of us."

After Abbie died, Norman Mailer (whom Abbie liked and who liked Abbie, although they lived in different worlds) said something about Abbie and America that I think is true: that if this were a democracy, Abbie would have had a nationally syndicated column—in other words, his voice would have been recognized, respected, rewarded for what it was. Right after Abbie died, many people wanted to hear that he had been killed, that he had not killed himself. Those people weren't entirely wrong in the sense that Abbie's death was a human response to years of being denigrated, harassed, and shut out by the very same society he was serving, and by the very same institutions of government he was protecting.

On Christmas Day 1967, in a letter to Bernie Gilgun, Abbie had described his forthcoming book, *Revolution for the Hell of It:* "It's about Billy the Kid, Fidel Castro, & Abraham, which is to say the three stages of life." And I like to think of my brother this way, according to his own self-definition, passing through these three stages of life, from outlaw, to revolutionary, to. . . .

Of all biblical figures, Abraham is the most bumbling, the least well understood. He is also among the most blessed, because he obeyed his inner voice, what the Bible calls God's voice. I think of Abbie's suicide as a test, as was God's demand that Abraham sacrifice his son Isaac. Only in Abbie's case no angel stopped his hand.

Maybe I knew my brother better than anyone, although I'm not sure. Maybe I'd been preparing his Kaddish for quite some time. Out of compassion, a part of us is always relieved to see the pain of someone we have loved end. My tears aren't from guilt, they are tears of loneliness. And tears of anger. The world seems vast and empty as I watch the Monday night football game, as I read the election news in the morning paper, or eat a snack in the middle of the night with the kitchen t.v. tuned to C-Span. He ought to be here.

In the '60s, when Ma heard Abbie say that kids should kill their parents for the Revolution, she laughed. She thought that was funny. She understood.

Once Abbie was on a radio talk show in New York City and took a call from a listener, who said to him, "Wait till Jesus gets his hands on you, you little bastard." Abbie used to love to tell that story. He said it was his favorite audience response.

NOTES

CHAPTER ONE: 1936–1948
1. Abbie Hoffman, *Soon to Be a Major Motion Picture* (New York: Putnam, 1980), 7–8.
2. Ibid., 10.

CHAPTER TWO: 1945–1955
1. Worcester's ethnicity was still white-skinned in the '40s and '50s; in the '60s, '70s, and '80s a multiracial mix was added, including African-American, Latino, Vietnamese, and Cambodian communities.
2. Hoffman, *Soon to Be a Major Motion Picture* (New York: Putnam, 1980), 21.

CHAPTER THREE: 1955–1961
1. Richard Lowry, *A. H. Maslow: An Intellectual Portrait* (Monterey, California: Brooks/Cole, 1973), 81.
2. Abraham Maslow, "A Theory of Human Motivation," *Psychological Review,* 50 (1943), 382.
3. Hoffman, *Soon to Be a Major Motion Picture* (New York: Putnam, 1980), 26–27.
4. Ibid., 30.
5. Ibid., 34.
6. Abbie Hoffman, *The Best of Abbie Hoffman,* edited by Daniel Simon with the author (New York: Four Walls Eight Windows, 1989), 54.
7. From Ferlinghetti's "In Goya's Greatest Scenes We Seem to See."
8. Hoffman, *Soon to Be a Major Motion Picture,* 38.
9. Ibid., 40.
10. Ibid., 43.
11. Ibid., 43.
12. *Worcester Telegram,* October 30, 1961.
13. Hoffman, *Soon to Be a Major Motion Picture,* 57.

CHAPTER FOUR: 1962–1966
1. Hoffman, *Soon to Be a Major Motion Picture* (New York: Putnam, 1980), 61.

2. Ibid., 59.
3. Ibid., 61.
4. Ibid., 63.
5. Todd Gitlin, *The Sixties* (New York: Bantam, 1987), 196.
6. FBI file #100–3160–351; Jack Hoffman Archive #1559.
7. Hoffman, *Soon to Be a Major Motion Picture,* 68.
8. Ibid., 81.
9. *Nightfall* magazine, June 1987.

CHAPTER FIVE: 1966–1967
1. Hoffman, *Soon to Be a Major Motion Picture* (New York: Putnam, 1980), 95.
2. Marty Jezer, *Abbie Hoffman: American Rebel* (New Brunswick, New Jersey: Rutgers University Press, 1992), 84.
3. Hoffman, *Soon to Be a Major Motion Picture,* 86.
4. Ibid., 78.
5. Abbie Hoffman, *The Best of Abbie Hoffman,* edited by Daniel Simon with the author (New York: Four Walls Eight Windows, 1989), 85–86.
6. Ibid., 86.
7. Ibid., 16.
8. Hoffman, *Soon to Be a Major Motion Picture,* 101.
9. Hoffman, *The Best of Abbie Hoffman,* 53.
10. FBI files NY 161–445 and BU 100–44–9923; Jack Hoffman Archive #1732.
11. Hoffman, *The Best of Abbie Hoffman,* 51.; *Oui,* July 1977, 124.
12. Hoffman, *The Best of Abbie Hoffman,* 51–52.
13. Hoffman, *Soon to Be a Major Motion Picture,* 137.

CHAPTER SIX: 1968
1. Hoffman, *Soon to Be a Major Motion Picture* (New York: Putnam, 1980), 137.
2. FBI file 67C, Field Office File #100–161445; Jack Hoffman Archive #644.
3. Abbie Hoffman, *The Best of Abbie Hoffman,* edited by Daniel Simon with the author (New York: Four Walls Eight Windows, 1989), 63.
4. Hoffman, *Soon to Be a Major Motion Picture,* 144.
5. Hoffman, *The Best of Abbie Hoffman,* 59.
6. Ibid., 74.
7. Ibid.
8. John Schultz, "The Movie Isn't Over Yet." Unpublished article.
9. Ibid.
10. Not including "Fuck the System," a booklet on freebies, the precursor

to *Steal This Book,* that Abbie wrote in 1967 under the alias of George Metesky.
11. Simon with Hoffman, *The Best of Abbie Hoffman,* 55.
12. David E. Rosenbaum, "Yippie Leader Arrested on Flag Desecration," *The New York Times,* October 4, 1968, 30; Stanley Levey, "Murders Urged, HUAC Told," *Washington Daily News,* October 4, 1968, 9.
13. Telephone interview with Dr. Lawrence Epstein in Framingham, Massachusetts, April 15, 1992.
14. FBI file #100–161445; Jack Hoffman Archive #645.
15. Hoffman, *Soon to Be a Major Motion Picture,* 169.
16. Bert Barnes, "Court Overturns Conviction for Flag Desecration," *The Washington Post,* March 29, 1971, 48.

CHAPTER SEVEN: 1969–1970
1. Quoted in Hoffman, *Soon to Be a Major Motion Picture* (New York: Putnam, 1980), 179.
2. FBI file #176–34; FBI Field Office file #176–28; Jack Hoffman Archive #645.
3. Judy Clavir and John Spitzer, *The Conspiracy Trial* (Indianapolis/New York: Bobbs-Merrill Company, 1970); *Contempt,* foreword by Ramsey Clark, introduction by Harry Kalven (Chicago: The Swallow Press, Inc., 1970); Tom Hayden, *Trial* (New York: Holt, Rinehart and Winston, 1970); Mark L. Levine, George C. McNamee, and Daniel Greenberg, *The Tales of Hoffman* (New York: Bantam, 1970); "The Chicago Trial: A Loss for All," *Time,* February 23, 1970, 38–39.
4. "The Chicago Trial: A Loss for All," *Time,* February 23, 1970, 38–39.
5. Ibid.
6. Hoffman, *Soon to Be a Major Motion Picture,* 180.
7. Crosby, Stills, Nash and Young were then completely unknown. "This is only the second time we've played together in front of people and we're scared shitless," Stephen Stills would tell the crowd.
8. Anthony M. Casale and Philip Lerman, *Where Have All the Flowers Gone: The Fall and Rise of the Woodstock Generation* (Kansas City: Andrews and McMeel, 1989), 3–4, 7–8, 15–20.
9. *Rolling Stone,* December 23, 1993.
10. Abbie Hoffman, *The Best of Abbie Hoffman,* edited by Daniel Simon with the author (New York: Four Walls Eight Windows, 1989), 5–6.
11. FBI file 67C, p. 1339; Jack Hoffman Archive #644.
12. Hoffman, *Soon to Be a Major Motion Picture,* 211.
13. FBI file #176–22; FBI New York Office file # 100–161445; Jack Hoffman Archive # 647.
14. Ibid., 217–218.
15. "The Chicago Trial: A Loss for All," *Time,* February 23, 1970, 38.

16. Jewell Friedman, "Jack Hoffman to Write Book, 'Dear Abbie,' " *The Hartford Times,* February 23, 1970, B1.
17. William M. Kunstler with Stewart E. Alpert, "The Great Conspiracy Trial of '69," *The Nation,* September 29, 1979; Jack Hoffman Archive #036.
18. Hoffman, *Soon to Be a Major Motion Picture,* 249.
19. FBI file #100–449923; FBI New York Office file #100–161445; Jack Hoffman Archive #644.
20. Ibid.
21. Ibid.
22. Ibid.
23. On February 25, 1970, after a speech by William Kunstler, a crowd descended on the Isla Vista branch of the Bank of Santa Barbara and burned it to the ground; Jack Hoffman Archive #442.
24. FBI file #100–449923; FBI New York Office file #100–161445; Jack Hoffman Archive #644.
25. Hoffman, *Soon to Be a Major Motion Picture,* 251.
26. Ibid., 252.
27. Ibid., 222–223.
28. Abbie's letter in the September 1, 1971, issue of *WIN* details all these expenses.
29. Ward Churchill and Jim Vander Wall, *The Cointelpro Papers* (Boston: South End Press, 1990), x.
30. FBI New York Office file #100–161445; Jack Hoffman Archive #1607.
31. *Mademoiselle,* July 1970, 103.

CHAPTER EIGHT: 1970–1971

1. FBI file #176-34–124; FBI file #100–449923; Jack Hoffman Archive #660.
2. Abbie Hoffman, "Steal This Author," *Harper's,* May 1974.
3. Abbie Hoffman, *The Best of Abbie Hoffman,* edited by Daniel Simon with the author (New York: Four Walls Eight Windows, 1989), 190.
4. Jezer, *Abbie Hoffman: American Rebel* (New Brunswick, New Jersey: Rutgers University Press, 1992), 227.
5. FBI file #100–44698; Jack Hoffman Archive #1649.
6. FBI file #67–C, pp. 6–7; Jack Hoffman Archive #644.
7. FBI New York Office file #100–161445; Jack Hoffman Archive #647.
8. Hoffman, *The Best of Abbie Hoffman,* 195.
9. Hoffman, *Soon to Be a Major Motion Picture* (New York: Putnam, 1980), 235–236.
10. FBI file #176–34 and #176–282; Jack Hoffman Archive #647.
11. *The New York Times,* Thursday, September 24, 1981, D26; the *Times* erroneously lists the date as May 5, the third day of demonstrations, and

the fourth day of police actions, by which time the protests had fizzled and arrests had reduced the number of demonstrators to no more than a few thousand.

12. Hoffman, *Soon to Be a Major Motion Picture*, 260.
13. FBI file #176–22; FBI file #NY 100–161445, #176–282, and NY 176–505; Jack Hoffman Archive #647.
14. FBI file #176–34-187.
15. *Gentlemen's Quarterly*, May 1971, 17.
16. *The New York Times Book Review*, July 15, 1971.
17. Craig Karpel, "Steal This Court," *WIN*, November 11, 1971.
18. *New York Post*, Wednesday, October 20, 1971, 4.

CHAPTER NINE: 1972

1. Hoffman, *Soon to Be a Major Motion Picture* (New York: Putnam, 1980), 267.
2. *The New York Times*, November 8, 1971, 6.
3. Charles DeBenedetti, *An American Ordeal: The Anti-War Movement of the Vietnam Era* (Syracuse, New York: Syracuse University Press, 1990), 333.
4. "The Third Indochina War: An Interview with Fred Branfman," *Liberation* 17, April 1972, 20–22.
5. Ibid.
6. DeBenedetti, *An American Ordeal*, 324–332.
7. Abbie Hoffman, Jerry Rubin, and Ed Sanders, *VOTE!* (New York: Warner, 1972), 27.
8. FBI file #100–449923; Jack Hoffman Archive #639.
9. Hoffman, Rubin, and Sanders, *VOTE!*, 151.
10. Ibid., 42.
11. Abbie Hoffman, *The Best of Abbie Hoffman*, edited by Daniel Simon with the author (New York: Four Walls Eight Windows, 1989), 75, 82.
12. Hoffman, Rubin, and Sanders, *VOTE!*, 69.
13. Ibid., 83.
14. In the final tally, Massachusetts and Washington, D.C., would be the only votes won by McGovern in the electoral college.
15. John Kifner, "Freed 'Chicago Conspiracy' Men Still Active in Protest Roles," *New York Times News Service*, December 1, 1972.

CHAPTER TEN: 1973

1. Hoffman, *Soon to Be a Major Motion Picture* (New York: Putnam, 1980), 279.
2. Interview in *Playboy*, May 1976, 80.
3. Ibid.; Hoffman, *Soon to Be a Major Motion Picture*, 280–281.

4. Anita Hoffman and Abbie Hoffman, *To america with Love: Letters from the Underground* (New York: Stonehill, 1976), 45.
5. Conversations with former detectives Arthur Nascarella and Robert Saso, March 26, 1992.
6. FBI file #88–15696–1; Jack Hoffman Archive #541.
7. Ibid.
8. Jack Hoffman Archive #1733.
9. FBI file #100–449923-381-67C.
10. *The New York Times*, Thursday, August 30, 1973.
11. Letter from Allen Ginsberg to Gerald Lefcourt, August 29, 1973; Jack Hoffman Archive #A16.
12. Jack Hoffman Archive #A16.
13. Abbie Hoffman, "The Underground Odyssey of Abbie Hoffman," *Saturday Night*, April 1982, 40.
14. Ibid.
15. Hoffman, *Soon to Be a Major Motion Picture*, 283.
16. Ibid.
17. In 1976, FBI Director Clarence Kelley would claim that COINTELPRO had been discontinued in 1971. But Senator Frank Church's Select Committee on Intelligence would assert, also in 1976, that only the name COINTELPRO had been discontinued. Its policies had continued unabated. Peter Matthiessen, *In the Spirit of Crazy Horse* (New York: The Viking Press, 1983), 305–371.

CHAPTER ELEVEN: 1973–1976

1. Interview in *Playboy*, May 1976, 57; Jack Hoffman Archive #2765, 592; Hoffman, *Soon to Be a Major Motion Picture* (New York: Putnam, 1980), 286.
2. "Chicago Bid Denied," *The New York Times*, March 27, 1973.
3. Hoffman, *Soon to Be a Major Motion Picture*, 286.
4. Ibid., 287.
5. Ron Rosenbaum, "On Board the Underground Railroad," *New Times*, May 30, 1975, 27.
6. *New York Post*, April 16, 1974, 1.
7. *The New York Times*, April 17, 1974; FBI file #88-65062-A; Jack Hoffman Archive #508.
8. Hoffman and Hoffman, *To america with Love* (New York: Stonehill, 1976), 34–35.
9. Ibid., 39.
10. Ibid., 72.
11. Ibid., 82.
12. "A Sisterhood of Poverty: Life without Abbie," *Village Voice*, October 3, 1974, 10, 13, 16.

13. Original letter in Jack Hoffman Archive.
14. Ron Rosenbaum, "On Board the Underground Railroad," *New Times,* May 30, 1975, 14–29, and June 13, 1975, 32–42.
15. Ibid.
16. Ibid.
17. Ken Kelley, "Riding the Underground Range with Abbie," *Playboy,* May 1976, 67–69.
18. Hoffman, *Soon to Be a Major Motion Picture,* 292.
19. Based on conversations with Jonah Raskin in 1989, 1992, and 1993.
20. Conversations with Oscar Janiger, M.D., May 24, 1994.
21. Kelley, "Riding the Underground Range with Abbie," 67.
22. Ibid., 69.
23. Abbie Hoffman, "The Underground Odyssey of Abbie Hoffman," *Saturday Night,* April 1982, 42.
24. Jeff Nightbyrd, "Cover Blown, Blames Playboy: Abbie Talks Before Vanishing," *Village Voice,* May 3, 1976, 18.
25. Hoffman, *Soon to Be a Major Motion Picture,* 293.
26. Interview in *Playboy,* 58.
27. Jezer, *Abbie Hoffman: American Rebel* (New Brunswick, New Jersey: Rutgers University Press, 1992), 260–261; Hoffman, *Saturday Night,* 42.
28. Hoffman, *Saturday Night,* 43–44.
29. Abbie Hoffman, "My Life on the Lam," *Oui,* June 1977, 114.
30. Hoffman, *Saturday Night,* 44.
31. Ibid.
32. Ibid.

CHAPTER TWELVE: 1976–1980
1. Abbie Hoffman, *The Best of Abbie Hoffman,* edited by Daniel Simon with the author (New York: Four Walls Eight Windows, 1989), 343.
2. Hoffman, "My Life on the Lam," *Oui,* June 1977, 114.
3. Abbie Hoffman, "President Jimmy: The Outside Story," *Oui,* July 1977, 46–48 and 121–125.
4. Abbie Hoffman, "The Great Gourmet Rip-Off," in *Square Dancing in the Ice Age* (New York: Putnam, 1982), 116–117.
5. Hoffman, *The Best of Abbie Hoffman,* 350.
6. Ibid.
7. Ibid.
8. Ibid., 351.
9. Ibid.
10. Ibid., 351–352.
11. Ibid., 352.
12. Ibid.

13. Ibid., 353.
14. Ibid., 352.
15. Ibid., 353.
16. Charles S. Pierce, "Abbie! Calling a Native Son Home," *Worcester Magazine,* September 1978, 51–55.
17. Abe Peck, "Abbie in Chicago: 'Good to be Home,' " *Sunday Sun-Times,* December 31, 1978, 7.
18. Dan Kaplan, "Abbie!", *Worcester Magazine,* November 7, 1979, 12.
19. Hoffman, *The Best of Abbie Hoffman,* 355.
20. Danny Schechter, "Remember Abbie Hoffman?," *The Real Paper,* December 1, 1979; aired on WBCN and on *The Joe Oteri Show* on Channel 56 on November 25, 1979.
21. Dan Kaplan, "Abbie!", *Worcester Magazine,* November 7, 1979, 12.
22. Conversation with Oscar Janiger, M.D., May 24, 1994.
23. Howard Goodman, "The Last Yippie," *Inside: The Quarterly of Jewish Life and Style,* Summer 1989, 82.
24. Abbie Hoffman, "The Underground Odyssey of Abbie Hoffman," *Saturday Night,* April 1982, 46.
25. Teresa M. Hanafin in *The Evening Gazette,* Thursday, September 4, 1980, Worcester, Massachusetts, 1–2.
26. Abbie Hoffman, "The Underground Odyssey of Abbie Hoffman," *Saturday Night,* April 1982, 47.
27. David Fenton, "The Press Riots Over Abbie," *Village Voice,* September 17, 1980.
28. Hoffman, *The Best of Abbie Hoffman,* 356.
29. David Fenton, "The Press Riots Over Abbie," *Village Voice,* September 17, 1980, 17.
30. Barbara Walters, letter to Dan Simon, 5-26-94.
31. FBI file #88–65062; Jack Hoffman Archive #568.
32. Ibid.
33. David Fenton, "The Press Riots Over Abbie," *Village Voice,* September 17, 1980, 16.
34. Ibid., 77.
35. Review by Morris Dickstein in *The New York Times Book Review,* September 21, 1980, 7.
36. Nathan S. Kline, *From Sad to Glad* (New York: Ballantine, 20th printing, August 1991), 48.

CHAPTER THIRTEEN: 1981–1986

1. Peggy Constantine, "A Stolen Book That's Still Hot," *Chicago Sun-Times,* reprinted in *Newsday,* Sunday, August 16, 1981.
2. Mark Samuels, "Abbie Hoffman: Steal This Interview," *Oui,* March 1982, 112.

3. Joe Cassidy, "Liddy Fizzles in Great Debate," *The Albuquerque Journal*, May 1, 1982.
4. Harvey Wasserman, "Abbie Hoffman: Never Trust Anyone Under Thirty," *New Age*, March 1983, 33.
5. Ibid., 34–35.
6. Ibid., 32.
7. Conversations with Johanna Lawrenson and with Abbie in December 1982; conversations between Johanna and Joan Hoffman in December 1982.
8. Conversation with former Greater Talent agent Bill Stankey on March 9, 1993.
9. Abbie Hoffman, *The Best of Abbie Hoffman,* edited by Daniel Simon with the author (New York: Four Walls Eight Windows, 1989), 399–401.
10. Paul Krassner, *Confessions of a Raving Unconfined Nut* (New York: Simon & Schuster, 1993), 322–323.
11. David Corn, "The Abbie & Jerry Show," *Mother Jones,* February/March 1985, 16; Conversation with Bill Stankey, March 9, 1993.
12. David Corn, "The Abbie & Jerry Show," *Mother Jones,* February/March 1985, 16.

CHAPTER FOURTEEN: 1986–1987

1. Diane Berger and Lisa Berger, *We Heard the Angels of Madness: A Family Guide to Coping with Manic Depression* (New York: Quill/William Morrow, 1991), 55.
2. *Diagnostic and Statistical Manual of Mental Disorders, 3rd Edition-Revised* (Washington, D.C.: American Psychiatric Association, 1987).
3. Berger and Berger, *We Heard the Angels of Madness,* 47.
4. Hoffman, *Soon to Be a Major Motion Picture* (New York: Putnam, 1980), 266.
5. Georgotas Anastasios and Robert Cancro, *Depression and Mania* (New York: Elsevier Science Publishing, 1988), 198; Donald W. Black, M.D., et al., "Suicide in Subtypes of Major Affective Disorder," *Archives of General Psychiatry,* 44 (1987), 878–880.
6. Diane and Lisa Berger, *We Heard the Angels of Madness Sing: A Family Guide to Coping with Manic Depression,* 114–15; Edward J. Khantzian, M.D., "The Self-Medication Hypothesis of Addictive Disorders: Focus on Heroin and Cocaine Dependence," *American Journal of Psychiatry,* 142 (1985), 1259–64.
7. Abbie Hoffman with Jonathan Silvers, *Steal This Urine Test* (New York: Penguin, 1987), 76.
8. Howard Goodman, "The Last Yippie," *Inside: The Quarterly of Jewish Life and Style,* Summer 1989, 63.

9. Abbie Hoffman, *The Best of Abbie Hoffman,* edited by Daniel Simon with the author (New York, Four Walls Eight Windows, 1989), 407.

Chapter Fifteen: 1988
1. Abbie Hoffman, *The Best of Abbie Hoffman,* edited by Daniel Simon with the author (New York, Four Walls Eight Windows, 1989), 416.
2. *Playboy,* October 1988, 74.
3. Mark Hertsgaard, "Steal This Decade: The Last Interview," *Mother Jones,* June 1990, 34.
4. Hoffman with Silvers, *Steal This Urine Test* (New York: Penguin, 1987), 89.
5. Ibid.

Chapter Sixteen: 1989, The Final Days
1. *The Guardian* went out of business shortly thereafter.
2. *The Guardian,* January 18, 1989, 19.
3. *The Guardian,* February 22, 1989, 19.
4. Mark Hertsgaard, "Steal This Decade: The Last Interview," *Mother Jones,* June 1990, 34.
5. Ibid., 48.
6. Howard Goodman, "The Last Yippie," *Inside: The Quarterly of Jewish Life and Style,* Summer 1989, 63.
7. Coroner Report, Office of Thomas J. Rosko, M.D., coroner of Bucks County, Pennsylvania, 2.
8. Conversations with Michael Waldron, September through November 1989.
9. Conversation with Paula Scism, Abbie's agent at American Program Bureau, June 1989.
10. Conversations with Noah Kimmerling, Abbie's accountant, April 19, 1989, and July 1993; conversations with Michael Waldron, September through November 1989.

INDEX